XHTML: Moving Toward XML

XHTML: Moving Toward XML

Simon St. Laurent

B.K. DeLong

M&T Books
An imprint of IDG Books Worldwide, Inc.

Foster City, CA • Chicago, IL • Indianapolis, IN • New York, NY

XHTML: Moving Toward XML

Published by
M&T Books
An imprint of IDG Books Worldwide, Inc.
919 E. Hillsdale Blvd., Suite 400
Foster City, CA 94404
www.idgbooks.com (IDG Books Worldwide Web site)

ISBN: 0-7645-4709-7

Printed in the United States of America

10 9 8 7 6 5 4 3 2 1

1O/QY/QY/QQ/FC

Distributed in the United States by IDG Books Worldwide, Inc.

Distributed by CDG Books Canada Inc. for Canada; by Transworld Publishers Limited in the United Kingdom; by IDG Norge Books for Norway; by IDG Sweden Books for Sweden; by IDG Books Australia Publishing Corporation Pty. Ltd. for Australia and New Zealand; by TransQuest Publishers Pte Ltd. for Singapore, Malaysia, Thailand, Indonesia, and Hong Kong; by Gotop Information Inc. for Taiwan; by ICG Muse, Inc. for Japan; by Intersoft for South Africa; by Eyrolles for France; by International Thomson Publishing for Germany, Austria, and Switzerland; by Distribuidora Cuspide for Argentina; by LR International for Brazil; by Galileo Libros for Chile; by Ediciones ZETA S.C.R. Ltda. for Peru; by WS Computer Publishing Corporation, Inc., for the Philippines; by Contemporanea de Ediciones for Venezuela; by Express Computer Distributors for the Caribbean and West Indies; by Micronesia Media Distributor, Inc. for Micronesia; by Chips Computadoras S.A. de C.V. for Mexico; by Editorial Norma de Panama S.A. for Panama; by American Bookshops for Finland.

For general information on IDG Books Worldwide's books in the U.S., please call our Consumer Customer Service department at 800-762-2974. For reseller information, including discounts and premium sales, please call our Reseller Customer Service department at 800-434-3422.

For information on where to purchase IDG Books Worldwide's books outside the U.S., please contact our International Sales department at 317-596-5530 or fax 317-572-4002.

For consumer information on foreign language translations, please contact our Customer Service department at 800-434-3422, fax 317-572-4002, or e-mail rights@idgbooks.com.

For information on licensing foreign or domestic rights, please phone +1-650-653-7098.

For sales inquiries and special prices for bulk quantities, please contact our Order Services department at 800-434-3422 or write to the address above.

For information on using IDG Books Worldwide's books in the classroom or for ordering examination copies, please contact our Educational Sales department at 800-434-2086 or fax 317-572-4005.

For press review copies, author interviews, or other publicity information, please contact our Public Relations department at 650-653-7000 or fax 650-653-7500.

For authorization to photocopy items for corporate, personal, or educational use, please contact Copyright Clearance Center, 222 Rosewood Drive, Danvers, MA 01923, or fax 978-750-4470.

Library of Congress Cataloging-in-Publication Data
St. Laurent, Simon.
    XHTML : moving toward XML / Simon St. Laurent, B.K. DeLong.
        p.   cm.
    ISBN 0-7645-4709-7 (alk. paper)
    1. XHTML (Document markup language) 2. XML (Document markup language) I. DeLong, B. K. II. Title.
QA76.76.H94 S725   2000
005.7'2--dc21   00-055890
                                                       CIP

is a registered trademark or trademark under exclusive license to IDG Books Worldwide, Inc. from International Data Group, Inc. in the United States and/or other countries.

is a trademark of IDG Books Worldwide, Inc.

ABOUT IDG BOOKS WORLDWIDE

Welcome to the world of IDG Books Worldwide.

IDG Books Worldwide, Inc., is a subsidiary of International Data Group, the world's largest publisher of computer-related information and the leading global provider of information services on information technology. IDG was founded more than 30 years ago by Patrick J. McGovern and now employs more than 9,000 people worldwide. IDG publishes more than 290 computer publications in over 75 countries. More than 90 million people read one or more IDG publications each month.

Launched in 1990, IDG Books Worldwide is today the #1 publisher of best-selling computer books in the United States. We are proud to have received eight awards from the Computer Press Association in recognition of editorial excellence and three from Computer Currents' First Annual Readers' Choice Awards. Our best-selling ...For Dummies® series has more than 50 million copies in print with translations in 31 languages. IDG Books Worldwide, through a joint venture with IDG's Hi-Tech Beijing, became the first U.S. publisher to publish a computer book in the People's Republic of China. In record time, IDG Books Worldwide has become the first choice for millions of readers around the world who want to learn how to better manage their businesses.

Our mission is simple: Every one of our books is designed to bring extra value and skill-building instructions to the reader. Our books are written by experts who understand and care about our readers. The knowledge base of our editorial staff comes from years of experience in publishing, education, and journalism — experience we use to produce books to carry us into the new millennium. In short, we care about books, so we attract the best people. We devote special attention to details such as audience, interior design, use of icons, and illustrations. And because we use an efficient process of authoring, editing, and desktop publishing our books electronically, we can spend more time ensuring superior content and less time on the technicalities of making books.

You can count on our commitment to deliver high-quality books at competitive prices on topics you want to read about. At IDG Books Worldwide, we continue in the IDG tradition of delivering quality for more than 30 years. You'll find no better book on a subject than one from IDG Books Worldwide.

John Kilcullen
Chairman and CEO
IDG Books Worldwide, Inc.

Eighth Annual Computer Press Awards ≥1992

Ninth Annual Computer Press Awards ≥1993

Tenth Annual Computer Press Awards ≥1994

Eleventh Annual Computer Press Awards ≥1995

Credits

ACQUISITIONS EDITORS
Ann Lush
Judy Brief
Grace Buechlein

PROJECT EDITOR
Andy Marinkovich

TECHNICAL EDITOR
Steven Champeon

COPY EDITOR
Victoria Lee

PROOF EDITOR
Neil Romanosky

PROJECT COORDINATORS
Danette Nurse
Louigene A. Santos

DESIGN SPECIALISTS
Kurt Krames
Kippy Thomsen

COVER ILLUSTRATION
Noma/ © images.com

GRAPHICS AND PRODUCTION SPECIALISTS
Robert Bihlmayer
Jude Levinson
Victor Pérez-Varela
Ramses Ramirez

QUALITY CONTROL TECHNICIAN
Dina F Quan

BOOK DESIGNER
Jim Donohue

ILLUSTRATORS
Rashell Smith
Brian Drumm
Mary Jo Weis
Gabriele McCann

PROOFREADING AND INDEXING
York Production Services

About the Authors

Simon St. Laurent is a web developer, network administrator, computer book author, and XML troublemaker, and currently resides in Ithaca, NY. His books include *XML: A Primer; XML Elements of Style; Building XML Applications; Cookies;* and *Sharing Bandwidth.* He is a contributing editor to xmlhack.com, an occasional contributor to XML.com, and moderator of the XHTML-L mailing list.

B.K. DeLong is Research Lead for Web standards consultancy *ZOT Group,* staff member of computer security site *Attrition.org,* and general Web standards troublemaker (read: member of the Web Standards Project steering committee). He lives on the North Shore of Massachusetts with his wife and two cats.

For Tracey, who shines the brightest light.
— Simon St. Laurent

This book is dedicated to my wife, Kirky. Without her patience and support,
I would never have been able to be a part of this project.
— B.K. DeLong

Preface

HTML is on the move, headed to a new future as XHTML. This book will show you how to apply your HTML skills to the brave new worlds of XHTML, and help you figure if, when, why, and how to transition your sites to XHTML. Along the way, we'll explore what XML brings to HTML, and how XHTML may be a transition to a more XML-centric approach.

Who This Book Is For

There are still a lot more HTML people in the world than XML people, and this book is intended to help the HTML community move toward XHTML.

This book is written for those with a solid working knowledge of HTML, as well as some familiarity with the rest of the Web infrastructure, such as HTTP, scripting, and graphics formats. It doesn't, however, assume an understanding of XML, and doesn't go into depth about XML features that aren't used in XHTML. (For a more complete picture of XML, see *XML: A Primer*, by Simon St. Laurent, also from IDG Books.) Similarly, it covers the transition from HTML to XHTML, but not every element and attribute used in XHTML.

If you've come from the XML community and are looking for an explanation of the HTML vocabulary, or are a beginner getting started with HTML, you probably want to find a different kind of book.

Icons Used in This Book

The following icons are used throughout this book to point out special information that will help you to better learn the topics being discussed.

Notes provide extra details about the topic being discussed, which not everyone may find as exciting as I do. Notes provide extra information that is useful but not critical.

Tips are the kind of information that often doesn't make it into traditional documentation, but are learned through hard experience. Tips are appropriate to every situation, but can be real time-savers when they appear.

Caution icons are important. You may not think there's a problem, but seemingly ordinary actions can have dire consequences if you're not careful. Read all Cautions to avoid potential catastrophes.

 Every now and then I mention something that's discussed in more detail elsewhere. Cross-References tell you where to go and how to get there.

For More Information

XHTML is a rapidly moving target. XHTML 1.0 is finished, but XHTML 1.1 and even XHTML 2.0 are in the works. I've set up a mailing list (XHTML-L) where readers and others can discuss XHTML, and which hosts a variety of XHTML links and news at `http://www.egroups.com/group/XHTML-L`. There will also be an updates and errata site at `http://www.simonstl.com/xhtml/`.

Acknowledgments

I'd like to thank Ann Lush for believing in this book early on, Judy Brief for helping it through a transition, and Grace Buechlein for seeing it through to the end. Andy Marinkovich kept the production process humming, and Victoria Lee did a great job copy-editing. Steven Champeon kept the book sharply on topic and saved me from a few interesting but rather unsupportable claims.
— *Simon St. Laurent*

I'd like to thank my wife, Kirky, for tolerating the long hours I spent in front of my laptop (even though I knew she thought I was playing *EverQuest* the whole time), for letting me borrow bandwidth, and for being my own personal PHP, Perl, and C programmer. I'd like to thank my father, Edwin, for bringing an AppleIIe home from work one day; my mother, Barbara, for bringing me into this world and heavily encouraging my use of computers; my little ones, Nessa and Chelsie, who constantly came upstairs to see what Daddy was doing and to find out why he wasn't lavishing attention, canned cat food, and catnip toys on them; my brothers, Nate and Jon, for thinking what I do is "cool;" the entire staff at ZOT Group who were very patient in letting me work on my first book project; and Tara Calishain for introducing me to the world of computer book publishing. Thanks also to Art Clifford, Ethan Katsh, Rick Hudson, Rick Newton, Bruce MacDougall, Scott Conti, Duncan Chesley, "Uncle John" Nelson, Nico Spinelli, Marcie Williams, and Karen Strom for helping me create my first Web site, for answering my annoying barrages of questions, and for tolerating me in my role of "student representative" on various UMass Amherst Technology Committees. And, of course, UMass Director of Network Systems and Services, Dan Blanchard, and former Associate Vice Chancellor for the Office of Information Technology, Doug Abbott, for telling me the Web would be a fad that would come and go as fast as Gopher. Finally, I can't forget the staff of Attrition.org (Jericho, Punkis, Cancer Omega, Modify, McIntyre, and Munge) for lovingly and sarcastically berating me for not updating "The Mirror" while I was writing this book.
— *B.K. DeLong*

Contents at a Glance

Preface ix

Acknowledgments xi

Part I   The HTML Problem: The XML Solution

Chapter 1   A Fresh Start: Moving From HTML to XHTML 3
Chapter 2   HTML and XHTML Application Possibilities 13

Part II   The Ins and Outs of XHTML

Chapter 3   Coding Styles: HTML's Maximum Flexibility 27
Chapter 4   Coding Styles: XML and XHTML's Maximum
                Structure 37
Chapter 5   Anatomy of an XHTML Document 51
Chapter 6   Reading the XHTML DTDs: A Guide to XML
                Declarations 103
Chapter 7   Exploring the XHTML DTDs 123
Chapter 8   Style Sheets and XHTML 135

Part III   Making the Big Jump

Chapter 9   Using XHTML in Traditional HTML Applications . 167
Chapter 10   The Big Clean-Up: Fixing Static HTML
                (The Easy Part) 173
Chapter 11   The Big Clean-Up: Fixing HTML Generating Code
                (The Hard Part) 201

Part IV   Moving Forward into XML

Chapter 12   Using XSL to Generate (X)HTML 215
Chapter 13   Integrating the Document Object Model with
                XHTML Generation 227
Chapter 14   Moving to Modules: Creating Extensible Document
                Structures with XHTML 1.1 245
Chapter 15   Fragmenting XHTML 255
Chapter 16   Extending XHTML 277
Chapter 17   XHTML Inside XML: Using XHTML in an
                XML Context 291

Part V   XHTML and XML Futures

Chapter 18   A Case Study: WAP and the Wireless Markup
              Language 305
Chapter 19   Case Study: Mozquito Factory and FML 321
Chapter 20   XML and the Next Generation of the Web 369

              Appendix A: XHTML Elements, by DTD 377

              Appendix B: Commonly Used Encodings 405

              Appendix C: Language Identifiers 407

              Appendix D: Country Codes 411

              Index 417

Contents

Preface ix

Acknowledgments xi

Part 1   **The HTML Problem: The XML Solution**

Chapter 1   **A Fresh Start: Moving From HTML to XHTML** 3
     HTML: Describing Documents 4
     XML: A Structured Way to Describe Information 5
     HTML + XML = XHTML 5
     Using XHTML: Adapting and Growing Applications 7
Chapter 2   **HTML and XHTML Application Possibilities** 13
     From Presentation to Reprocessing and Interaction 13
     Flows and Trees: HTML and XML Parsing 15
     Application Layers for XML Document Processing 17
         Presenting documents 17
         Transforming documents 18
         Linking into and referencing documents 20
         Storing documents 20
         Searching and indexing documents 22
     XHTML User Agents: Preparing for the Next Generation . . . 23

Part II   **The Ins and Outs of XHTML**

Chapter 3   **Coding Styles: HTML's Maximum Flexibility** 27
     Errors: Don't Stop, Don't Report 27
     Case: As You Like It 28
     Understood Omissions: Leaving Out Endings 28
     Overlaps 32
     Abbreviated Attributes 32
     Multiple Names 33
     Tag Soup 33
     Extending the Browser 34
     Creative Comments 35
     Validate? Why? 36
Chapter 4   **Coding Styles: XML and XHTML's Maximum**
     Structure 37
     Cleaning up HTML 37
         Case matters 37
         Clean (and explicit) element structures 38

Empty elements 39
Quoting and expanding attribute values 39
Unique identifiers. 40
Validation and reliability 41
Rules for comments 42
New to XHTML 42
XML declarations. 42
Processing instructions. 44
CDATA sections 44
Namespaces 45
Internationalization: xml:lang and lang. 47
Rules for vocabulary extensions. 49

Chapter 5   Anatomy of an XHTML Document 51
An Initial HTML Document 51
Two Remedies 53
Remedy 1: The Transitional DTD and CDATA Sections 54
Remedy 2: The Strict DTD and Entity Replacement 60
Converting to strict HTML 60
Converting to strict XHTML. 64
Browser Testing. 69
Netscape Navigator 1.22/Windows NT 4.0 70
Netscape Navigator 2.02/Windows NT 4.0 73
Netscape Navigator 3.0/Windows NT 4.0 76
Netscape Communicator 4.7/Windows NT 4.0 79
Netscape Navigator 6 Preview Release 1/Windows NT 4.0 82
Internet Explorer 3.01/MacOS 8.1 84
Microsoft Internet Explorer 4.0/MacOS 8.1 87
Microsoft Internet Explorer 4.01/Windows 95 89
Microsoft Internet Explorer 5.01/Windows NT 4.0 91
Opera 3.62/Windows NT 94
Amaya 2.4/Windows NT 96
Lynx 2.8.2/Windows 95. 99
Lessons 102

Chapter 6   Reading the XHTML DTDs: A Guide to XML
Declarations. 103
Element Type Declarations 104
The EMPTY content model. 105
The ANY content model 105
Structured content models 105
Mixed content models 107
Attribute List Declarations. 108
Types of attributes 109
Defaulting attribute values 113
Parameter Entity Declarations. 115
General Entity Declarations. 119
Comments 121

Chapter 7   **Exploring the XHTML DTDs** 123
Choosing Your DTD 123
Starting Out 125
  Including character entities 125
  Imported names 126
  Generic attributes 127
  Text elements 128
  Block-level elements 128
  Content models for exclusions 129
Building Structure: Element and Attribute Declarations . . . 129
  Document structure 129
  Document head 129
  Frames (frameset and transitional only) 130
  Document body 130
  Paragraphs and headings 131
  Lists 131
  Other elements 131
  Anchor element 131
  In-line elements 131
  Objects and applets 132
  Images and image maps 132
  Forms 132
  Tables 132
Beyond the XHTML DTDs 132
Chapter 8   **Style Sheets and XHTML** 135
Separating Format from Content 135
The CSS Processing Model 137
Using Selectors 138
Formatting Content with Properties 145
Rules for Rules 163
Application Issues 163
Is XSL for XHTML? 164

Part III   **Making the Big Jump**

Chapter 9   **Using XHTML in Traditional HTML Applications** . . 167
Lessons from Previous Technology Shifts 167
Making Certain Nothing Looks Different (to the User) 168
Supporting the Widest Possible Base in XML 171
Balancing Needs and Retraining 172
Chapter 10   **The Big Clean-Up: Fixing Static HTML**
(The Easy Part) 173
Why Convert Existing XHTML? 173
Starting with Your HTML Document 174
  Step 1: All elements are lowercase 175

Step 2: All attribute values must have quotes 176
Step 3: All elements must end 176
Step 4: All elements must be in the right place 177
Step 5: Adding XHTML declarations
   and definitions 178
Using a Tool to Convert Your HTML
   Documents to XHTML. 180
   HTML Tidy 180
   HTML-Kit 199
   Java Tidy 199
   BBTidy 200
   Batch conversion 200
   Document Validation 200

Chapter 11   **The Big Clean-Up: Fixing HTML Generating Code**
              (The Hard Part). 201
   Y2K Revisited? 201
   Preliminaries 202
   Pitfalls: Case-Sensitivity 203
   Pitfalls: Well-Formedness 204
   Pitfalls: Valid XHTML 205
   Testing, Testing, Testing. 207
   Strategies for Managing XHTML Generation Code 208
   Text 208
   Templates. 208
   Modularization. 210

Part IV   **Moving Forward into XML**

Chapter 12   **Using XSL to Generate (X)HTML** 215
   Introduction to XSL 215
   Basic Transformation Principles. 217
   Preliminaries 217
   Creating the result document 219
   Applications for XHTML and Beyond 226
Chapter 13   **Integrating the Document Object Model with**
              XHTML Generation 227
   Building Trees, Not Streams 227
   DOM Implementations 228
   DOM Examples 229
   Making Logic and Structure Mobile 242
Chapter 14   **Moving to Modules: Creating Extensible Document**
              Structures with XHTML 1.1 245
   Different Needs, Different Tools 245
   The Master Plan: Fragmenting and Extending HTML. 247
   Didn't Namespaces Solve Everything? 248
   New Issues: Content Negotiation & Context Tangles 250

Chapter 15   Fragmenting XHTML..............................255
              XHTML as Framework...............................255
              Abstract Modules 256
              XML DTD Modules.................................263
                 .datatype 264
                 .attrib...265
                 .attlist..266
                 .content 268
                 .class (and .extra)..................................268
                 .mix 270
                 .mod..270
                 .module 271
              Schema Modules...................................272
              Putting XHTML 1.1 Together 272
Chapter 16   Extending XHTML 277
              Building Your Own Modules.........................277
              Building or Modifying Driver Files 283
              Namespaces, Validation, and Other Complexities 286
              Documenting Extensions.............................288
              Supporting Your Extensions on the Server...............288
              Supporting Your Extensions on the Client 289
Chapter 17   XHTML Inside XML: Using XHTML in an
              XML Context.....................................291
              Beyond the Browser and Within the Browser.............291
              What HTML Has to Offer XML........................292
              Applications for XHTML Islands 293
                 Images, scripts, and forms in browsers....................293
                 Documentation for Human Consumption...................296
                 Document containers 298
                 Inline and mixed-up markup 300
              Is Formal XHTML Module Inclusion Worth the Trouble?...300

Part V   XHTML and XML Futures

Chapter 18   A Case Study: WAP and the Wireless Markup
              Language 305
              Choosing Your Emulator 305
                 WAP emulators..306
                 Downloading the Nokia WAP Toolkit.....................307
                 Using the Nokia WAP Toolkit............................308
              Authoring a WML Document 310
                 A deck of cards..310
                 Hello World 310
                 Navigation 312
                 Time-based automation 313

User input and forms 315

Submitting a form 317

Images in WML 318

Creating WBMP images 319

Integrating WML and XHTML 320

Chapter 19   Case Study: Mozquito Factory and FML **321**

The Mozquito Factory Approach 321

Using Mozquito Factory 322

When to use Mozquito in your Web development 323

Downloading and installing Mozquito 323

Learning Forms Markup Language 1.0 (FML) 323

Error-checking your XHTML-FML 324

Pushing your FML through to a browser 326

The E-Commerce Order Form 327

A simple contact information form 329

Input validation 330

Submitting forms 333

Mandatory field requirements 334

Editable lists 338

Creating an open-ended pull-down menu 340

The finished form 342

The Shopping Cart Form 345

Start with a single product 345

Layers 357

Cleaning up 358

Adding in the Contact Information Form 360

Making your Mozquito HTML/JavaScript Accessible 366

Chapter 20   XML and the Next Generation of the Web **369**

Person to Person and Machine to Machine 369

Automating – and Fragmenting – the Web 370

Information Leaks 371

Reviving the Agent Dream 372

Will XHTML Survive? 373

Efficient, Friendly, Invisible 374

Appendix A: XHTML Elements, by DTD **377**

Appendix B: Commonly Used Encodings **405**

Appendix C: Language Identifiers **407**

Appendix D: Country Codes **411**

Index **417**

Part I

The HTML Problem:
The XML Solution

CHAPTER 1
A Fresh Start: Moving From HTML to XHTML

CHAPTER 2
HTML and XHTML Application Possibilities

Chapter 1

A Fresh Start: Moving From HTML to XHTML

HYPERTEXT MARKUP LANGUAGE (HTML) is getting an enormous and overdue cleanup. Much of HTML's early charm as browsers reached a wide audience was the ease of use created by browser tolerance for a wide variety of syntactical variations and unknown markup. Unfortunately, that charm has worn thin through years of "browser wars" and demands for new features that go beyond presenting documents.

The *World Wide Web Consortium (W3C)* is rebuilding HTML on a new foundation, preserving HTML's well-understood vocabulary while preparing the way for a very different style of processing. In some ways, the W3C is returning HTML to its roots—rebuilding it as an information format that can be processed and reused, and discarding some of the wreckage created during the browser wars between Microsoft, Netscape, and a host of smaller participants. The new framework is *Extensible Markup Language (XML)*—a generic syntax for documents that has much stricter rules than HTML. By combining the old HTML vocabulary with the stricter XML syntax, the W3C hopes both to reinvigorate HTML and open the door to major expansions of the Web's capabilities.

The benefits of XHTML won't all come for free, however. Developers will have to learn a few basic rules in order to take advantage of XHTML, and adoption probably will be fairly slow. While XHTML is mostly compatible with HTML, many older HTML documents decidedly are not compatible with XHTML. Some developers, notably those creating *dynamic HTML* documents, already have encountered the need for stricter and more consistent structures. It's very hard to create 'dynamic' documents if the scripting logic can't consistently reference points in a document. Still, others need to be convinced of the benefits before moving forward. Like almost all standards, using XHTML makes more sense and costs less when more people use it. While XHTML can fix a lot of problems in some areas, early adopters of XHTML likely will be application developers rather than Web site managers. XHTML brings application developers a new set of (largely free) tools from the XML world that can simplify development and information management more than enough to make up for the minor inconveniences that XHTML imposes on HTML developers.

HTML: Describing Documents

HTML began as a very simple tool that marked up documents for exchange over a network. Because the markup was so simple and the description for it open and available, it was easy to present the same information on different computing platforms. Because browsers were relatively easy to write at first, developers wrote simple browsers and an explosion of new browsers appeared — each with its own slightly different take on how to present the information described by HTML. These different takes were part of the original plan for HTML to describe document structures, such as headlines and paragraphs, rather than describe explicit formatting. By sticking to high-level descriptions, HTML avoided the snarl of formatting that had made many previous systems accessible only to advanced users. As a result, HTML spread far more quickly than Tim Berners-Lee, its inventor, had dared hope. People around the world began composing HTML directly — something that he never expected would happen. (Originally, HTML was expected to be a format hidden behind tool frameworks; one of the earliest pieces of HTML software was a WYSIWYG editor that Berners-Lee built himself.)

This mostly structural approach led to high hopes for a number of ventures, notably automated agents that would scour the Web for information and present it to users when they wanted it. These tools could interpret the basic structures of HTML documents along with their content to gather information in a more sophisticated way than was possible with simple text-based searches. Some HTML management software also used these structures as the foundation for more efficient handling of large sets of documents. These possibilities were foiled quickly, however, by several developments in the HTML world that made HTML very difficult to process.

The snarl of formatting quickly arrived as HTML spread to more demanding users. While the Web provided the first Internet medium that was used easily (and not especially controversially) as an advertising medium, the simple high-level approach that had spurred its early growth quickly became anachronistic. Users demanded more control over formatting; they objected especially to the variations in appearance that appeared when the same document was opened in different browsers. The tools that were available to generate HTML took wildly divergent approaches to how they built pages; some relied on tables for precise placement of images and text while others used more flexible approaches for different kinds of information. The early *hand-coders* of HTML, developers close to the markup, soon found their skills in significant demand because they understood how to intervene in a document directly to achieve certain effects across browsers that the automated tools weren't flexible enough to support. Even hand-coded HTML rapidly became more intricate and more commonly aimed at formatting consistency than document structures.

As the W3C began to take control of HTML, it tried repeatedly to stamp out these features. The W3C did this by marking key formatting tools such as the FONT tag as "deprecated" and creating more formal descriptions of HTML using *document type definitions (DTDs)* from HTML's original inspiration, the *Standard Generalized Markup Language (SGML)*. While W3C Recommendations for HTML provided a foundation that application developers could reference, these recommendations have had relatively little effect on the main body of HTML developers. These developers continue to create documents using tools and methods that work in browsers, with little concern for how they might fit the rules of a standard specified using an obscure formal language. While the chaos of the browser wars has settled down a little as Netscape and Microsoft have curbed their onslaught of new features, HTML itself is a snarled mess (even if it is one that people are accustomed to).

XML: A Structured Way to Describe Information

XML began with a different set of premises than did HTML. While HTML set out to describe documents, XML set out to create tools that developers could apply in describing any kind of structured information. While XML shares HTML's syntactical inheritance from SGML, such as the use of < and > as markup delimiters, XML provides no vocabulary, thus enabling developers to create their own tag sets, effectively new vocabularies. At the same time that it opens up the vocabulary possibilities, however, XML slams the door on a wide variety of structural variations that were common in HTML and even in SGML. XML simplifies and adds extra rigidity to SGML, while HTML was effectively an application of SGML. The simplifications and extra constraints of XML are designed to make XML documents exceptionally easy to process, providing a level of consistency that HTML didn't guarantee.

You can describe XML documents in terms of containment. A single *root* element may contain other elements, attributes, and textual content; *child* elements themselves may contain a similar mix. While HTML developers often talk about *tags* — the markup used to begin and end elements — they rarely focus on the element structures those tags create. (Significant exceptions exist among dynamic HTML developers and others with more need for structure, certainly.) XML developers use tags that look exactly like HTML tags, but XML developers are more concerned with creating clean structures in which all of those tags produce elements that are organized neatly. Every element has a *start tag* and an *end tag* (or something new, a tag representing an empty element), and those tags are arranged so that element boundaries never overlap. These stricter rules make it very easy for an application to figure out and combine the structure of the document with its understanding of the document content to perform further processing.

HTML + XML = XHTML

By combining the well-understood vocabulary of HTML with the clean structures of XML, the W3C is building something new: XHTML. *XHTML* at its simplest is just HTML cast into XML syntax, with a few tips for making sure that XML syntax doesn't interfere with older browsers. XHTML should work just fine in older software, although HTML has a harder time getting into XHTML software. Cleaning up HTML in this way has many useful effects. For example, it provides XHTML tool creators with additional development frameworks and document repositories (originally built for XML). It also establishes a firm set of rules for document structure that can simplify projects such as dynamic HTML in which scripts manipulate the document structure. For the average user, nothing is likely to change on the surface, but what happens below that surface will be more efficient.

The long-run implications of the move to XHTML dwarf these simple effects of XHTML 1.0, however. Applying XML's stricter rules to HTML document structures opens up a new range of possibilities, including some significant changes to the HTML vocabulary itself. While version 1.0 of XHTML simply recasts HTML 4.0 into XHTML, versions 1.1 and beyond start to move beyond tried-and-true HTML. XHTML enables developers both to shrink the HTML vocabulary (by declaring that they only use portions of it) and to expand the HTML vocabulary (enabling them to supplement HTML with MathML, SVG, and other markup vocabularies.) Instead of leaving HTML as a monolithic set of vocabulary, the W3C is breaking HTML into modules and providing tools for additional modules. Rather than try to shoehorn every piece of information into some HTML representation, developers will create their own vocabularies and integrate them with those of HTML. Then HTML documents could contain that information as XML, or XML documents could contain portions of HTML.

For example, while cellular telephones and *personal digital assistants (PDAs)* have become increasingly powerful tools, they still have limited processing power and graphic displays that typically are black and white instead of color. These lightweight devices may not support images, ActiveX objects, Java applets, or even (in some cases) forms. While users may enjoy surfing the Web from their cell phones — sometimes meetings do last forever — the phones aren't really up to the tasks demanded by a full Web browser. By implementing a subset of XHTML, however, these phones can tell servers that they can accept information only in that subset, thereby giving the server the chance to build Web pages designed specifically for cell phones with that particular profile. Informative (hopefully) but low-bandwidth text will replace full-color images, enabling cell phone users to retrieve information from the Web without having to throw most of it away.

Going the other direction, XHTML opens the door to the Web's original application of exchanging information among scientists. While HTML and the Web are important to this community, HTML's lack of math support has hindered a lot of work. (It appeared briefly in HTML 3.0, then disappeared with 3.2, without widespread implementation.) The W3C created another specification, *MathML*, which provides support for a wide variety of mathematical information from simple equations to integrals, square roots, and all kinds of symbols. By adding MathML as a module to XHTML, scientists can integrate these two vocabularies. They also need an application that supports both vocabularies, of course, and those are mostly still in development. The W3C's Amaya browser and the developing Mozilla browser both support XHTML and MathML, but building these modules is difficult.

 Microsoft already has pioneered the use of XML *data islands* in Office 2000 documents — a strategy somewhat like that just described. The HTML surrounding these data islands is not XHTML, however, and Microsoft's approach is not supported by any activity at the W3C. Hopefully, future versions will support XHTML rather than data islands. (Office 2000 documents aren't a total loss, however. As you see later, there are tools for converting them into XHTML just like any other HTML document.)

Finally, XHTML is easy to use within XML documents and it provides a well-known format for document-oriented information. Any time an XML developer needs to add a space for extra description of something, XHTML is available. XHTML enables these developers to use an HTML vocabulary, thereby taking advantage of the many tools available for processing, creating, and displaying HTML (including components that can be built into non-browser applications). XML developers don't need to reinvent the wheel every time they must include a few paragraphs or some images because they can build on what came before without fear of "contaminating" their XML with old-style HTML.

Using XHTML: Adapting and Growing Applications

XHTML has implications at many different levels of Web development. In its simplest usage, XHTML is treated just like HTML with a little more attention paid to syntax (and, as you see in the next chapter, all the tags move to lowercase). A typical *static* Web site can use XHTML exactly the way it uses HTML, as shown in Figure 1-1.

By changing over to XHTML, this Web site makes its content available to users with pickier XHTML software instead of the usual HTML browser; very little changes otherwise. Similarly, Web sites that generate content can make sure that their CGI programs, Active Server Pages, Java servlets, or other tools produce clean XHTML while remaining in the same application framework used for HTML (see Figure 1-2).

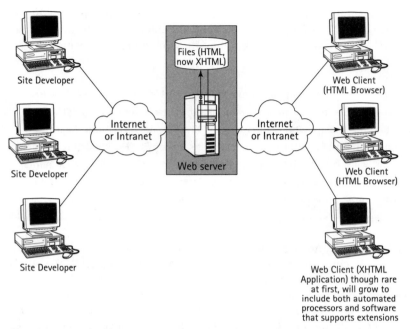

Figure 1-1: XHTML fits into the same static Web site framework that HTML uses.

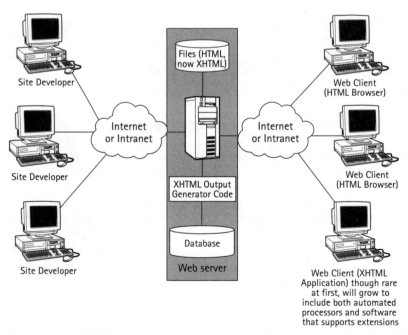

Figure 1-2: XHTML fits into the same dynamically generated framework that HTML uses for Web content.

Application developers now produce material that XHTML applications can use, but they may not have gained very much for the effort it often takes to clean up HTML-generating code to XHTML standards. Converting HTML generators to XHTML is often as much fun as Year 2000 remediation, although (usually) without the penalty of a crisis if you don't do it. Programmers often have to wade through code, testing all kinds of different circumstances to make sure that the application consistently produces XHTML and not plain old HTML. You can use the preceding frameworks, but the benefits of XHTML really grow when you start taking advantage of XHTML's XML nature. In Figure 1-3, the developers substitute an XML document repository for the file system used by most static Web sites, giving them additional management and versioning control for their XHTML development. Users still haven't seen any changes at their end, but developers start to gain a few more conveniences from the tools XML makes available.

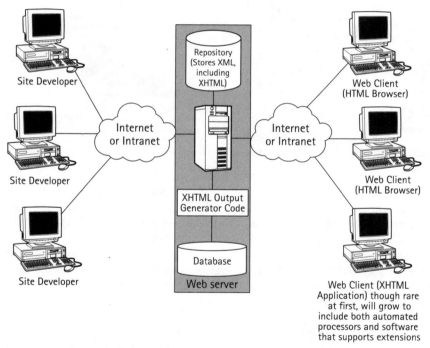

Figure 1-3: Replacing the file system with a repository

XML *document repositories* offer some conveniences that file systems can't provide, notably quick access to document fragments and the ability to reference portions of documents without needing to retrieve the entire document. (These repositories store documents as a set of fragments, making querying and retrieval easier.) In Figure 1-4, the developers add some processing between the Web server and the repository to provide filtering and possibly transformation capabilities to their Web application.

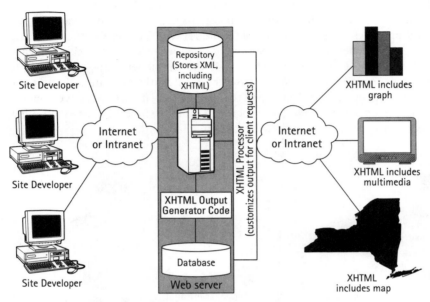

Figure 1-4: Processing XHTML before it gets sent to clients

When clients become XHTML-aware, this kind of processing can get even more sophisticated. The software providing the XHTML processing or generation can collect information about the clients and send each client a different view of the information that is appropriate to its capabilities (as shown in Figure 1-5).

At the same time – much like existing HTML search engines – new tools for searching through XHTML content may emerge, some with extra capacities for handling embedded XML. These machine-only clients may process the XHTML to meet their own needs, potentially making the agents that were broken by the vagaries of HTML viable again (see Figure 1-6).

While the first steps toward XHTML – shown in the first two figures – may seem like they require a lot of extra work without much payback, you have to view them as a beginning not an end unto themselves. XHTML is an enabling technology, something that lets developers build new technologies on old; it is not a technology that produces instant transformations of existing work.

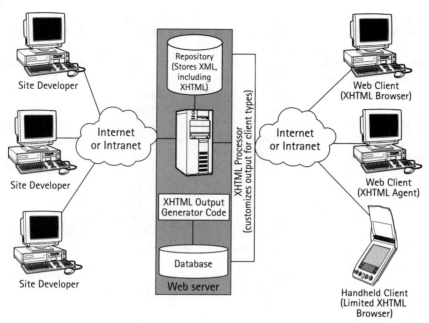

Figure 1-5: Processing XHTML to provide different views to different clients.

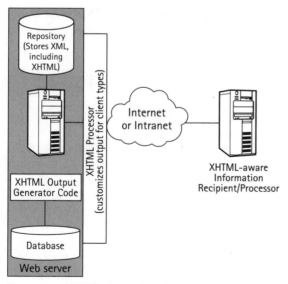

Figure 1-6: XHTML also makes machine-to-machine communications simpler and more flexible.

The rest of this book details the many steps involved in transitioning from HTML to XHTML and eventually XHTML+XML, giving you both the established HTML vocabulary and the potential to extend that vocabulary. The first few chapters show you HTML from an XML perspective, and provide you with the XML foundation you need to understand XHTML. (It's a remarkably small foundation, fortunately.) After the basic tour, you start applying XHTML to existing sites and exploring ways to clean up your coding processes for new documents, as well as converting your older documents to the new standard. The hardest part is cleaning up your applications, but we look at some tools that may help you avoid the painful process of reading and testing all of your code by hand. In some cases, you should be able to upgrade to XHTML by changing a line or two of code—it all depends on the application's architecture. In addition to cleaning up existing applications, you explore the newer tools XHTML makes available for building applications including the transformative power of Extensible Stylesheet Language (XSL) and the Document Object Model (DOM). By shifting your work to some of these tools, you may be able to move between HTML and XHTML by changing a single setting while simultaneously getting powerful tools that reduce the amount of code you need to write.

Along the way, you explore the costs and benefits of XHTML. Unfortunately, XHTML makes more demands than any previous upgrade of HTML. At the same time, however, it offers capabilities that Web application developers dreamed of for years but had to work without. XHTML promises these developers much more powerful tools for tasks such as exchanging information in client-server applications, as well as more sophisticated methods for providing appropriate content to many different kinds of clients. While not everyone will jump on the XHTML bandwagon initially, those who do will have access to a much larger set of possibilities than those who only see the costs.

Chapter 2

HTML and XHTML Application Possibilities

SHIFTING FROM HTML TO XHTML requires a significant change in mindset from the design-oriented free-for-all that characterized the early years of the Web. This change in style reflects movement in the underlying architecture toward a more powerful and more controllable approach to document creation, presentation, and management. Understanding the connections between the architectural and stylistic changes may help you find more immediate benefits from XHTML – even as the tools only start to catch up. Looking ahead to the possibilities that XHTML opens can assist you in planning a transition to more sophisticated Web applications.

From Presentation to Reprocessing and Interaction

HTML is designed to present users with reasonably attractive pages (although Web designers always can make them glorious or hideous) and to support a very simple level of interaction through forms and hyperlinks. The application logic that Web browsers support – at least on the level of HTML pages and scripts, not the extensions of Java applets, plug-ins, or ActiveX controls – is relatively simple. Applications designed for the Web tend to centralize their processing on the server, storing information in databases and using Web browsers as mere windows on the server's information. This makes it possible to use more sophisticated server-side facilities for security, processing, and connectivity. Figure 2-1 shows a typical division of labor in a Web-based application.

While dynamic HTML made Web browsers a more advanced interface capable of animated views of information, the forms interface remains the main way for users to manipulate information and enter new information. Some Web browsers enable users to edit HTML and send it back to a server; but the editor is more or less a separate application useful only for editing HTML, not general-purpose interaction with a server application.

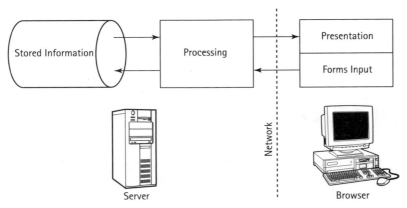

Figure 2-1: Most Web applications centralize the logic on the server and treat the browser as an interface.

XML isn't about interface, but it does open new possibilities for client development that go well beyond the browser. Custom XML vocabularies enable applications to exchange information over networks without the limitation of document-oriented formatting. XML vocabularies can represent spreadsheets, invoices, documents, program structures, and nearly any kind of information. XML enables clients and servers to ship almost any kind of information (though binary formats remain more convenient for some kinds of data) back and forth, although both sides need to understand what the information means on some level. While there are plenty of generic XML editors and processors, most XML vocabularies work hidden under an interface layer that conceals their immediate structure from users. Figure 2-2 shows how Web applications (and network applications in general) can take advantage of these facilities.

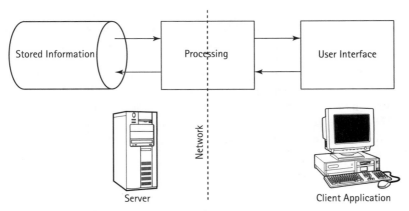

Figure 2-2: XML-based applications can give the client more work to do, distributing processing more evenly.

XHTML provides a transition from the HTML model for Web applications to the more powerful and more flexible XML model. While XHTML applications will start out much like HTML applications, XHTML will enable application developers to integrate XML tools with the HTML vocabulary. XHTML is not merely a foil for XML's eventual takeover – it promises to keep the well-known HTML vocabulary alive in this new world.

Flows and Trees: HTML and XML Parsing

HTML and XML processors tend to treat the text they receive very differently. While both kinds of processors read a document from start to finish, HTML processors read HTML documents using HTML-specific understandings. However, XML processors tend to parse documents more generically. Applications then apply their own logic to the results of the parse, without really participating in the parse itself. This separation requires that XML documents conform tightly to the XML specification because applications can't apply their own logic to provide loopholes or modify basic structures.

HTML parsers typically are built for one purpose: to read HTML. Whether the parser builds a browser view of the document, retrieves information for a search engine, or feeds a shopping agent information, HTML parsers need to know a lot about HTML's vocabulary. This crucial information includes a complex set of rules about which elements don't need end tags, how to properly end elements when end tags are omitted, and rules for dealing with some particularly tricky elements. The META element, for instance, defines its real purpose in an attribute and that purpose may influence the parsing process substantially for the rest of the document when things such as character encodings are declared. The INPUT element similarly uses an attribute to define its true purpose. It would require processors to keep track of a considerable amount of information to process a form correctly if INPUT elements are nested, so nesting INPUT elements is outlawed.

As a result, HTML parsers tend to be tightly bonded to their particular applications, applying processing rules that make sense for their particular application. Search engines, for instance, usually discard all markup and focus on text – except for META elements that provide keyword information. Browsers need to collect as much information as possible from the parser, but they apply their own rules as to how markup transforms into document structures. Instead of being a separate generic component, HTML parsers generally are built into applications (as shown in Figure 2-3).

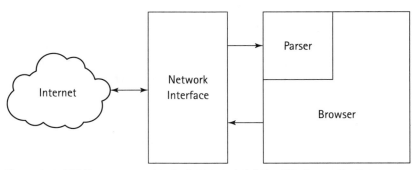

Figure 2-3: HTML parsers tend to be integrated tightly with the applications that use them.

While XML parsers have a similar job to do, they don't expect to see a particular vocabulary; hence they can't do the kind of interpretation that HTML parsers do. Instead of interpreting the flow of information with a sophisticated set of guidelines, XML parsers extract and report a tree structure that is described by the elements, attributes, text, and other information within the document markup. XML parsers rely on explicit markup structures in the document to determine what gets reported to the application, but they don't take orders from the application much beyond instructions for which file to parse.

XML parsers are typically quite separate from the rest of an application and usually are separately distributed components that developers can connect to their programs or even swap for a different component (see Figure 2-4).

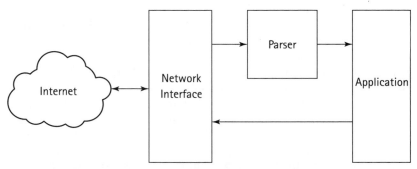

Figure 2-4: XML parsers tend to be only loosely integrated with applications.

This loose connectivity makes it easy to use the same XML parser to interpret XHTML, MathML, SVG, or any other possible vocabularies and structures. Applications have a new option of processing information generically and opening up a new set of architectures for handling information.

Application Layers for XML Document Processing

XML's generic approach to markup opens numerous new possibilities for document handling, all of which you can use with XHTML. While it might seem counterintuitive that 'dumber' processors can lead to more powerful applications, XML's approach leaves more room for applications to solve a much wider range of problems.

Presenting documents

XML parsers don't make any assumptions about how information should be presented — they really can't because they don't interpret the vocabularies used in documents. `P`, `B`, `EM`, `FONT`, `CITE`, and everything else used in HTML are just names to an XML parser — nothing else. On the other hand, XML does provide a very clean set of structures on which presentation information can be layered to build the information needed by a browser.

Cascading Style Sheets (CSS) provide one set of tools for annotating document structures with rules for presentation. CSS include a formal vocabulary for describing different types of presentation roles for elements (such as blocks, tables, or inline text) and details about how their content should be presented, from color to font family to font size. *Extensible Stylesheet Language (XSL)* is another possibility, as described in the following section, "Transforming documents."

You can use CSS with both HTML and XML, but it is more important and easier to use with XML. When used with HTML, CSS supplements — and to some extent overrides — the rules for presenting particular elements. On the other hand, XML provides a clean slate on which CSS can operate. In fact, the CSS2 specification provides a "sample style sheet" for HTML that outlines a nearly complete set of presentation rules an XML application can use to render HTML. (See `http://www.w3.org/TR/REC-CSS2/sample.html` for details.)

Developers who are not used to separating all the style information from the document content may have to adopt a different model, as shown in Figure 2-5. This model also makes it easier to store style information in separate documents, thereby simplifying management and updates.

XHTML offers the possibility of bridging these two approaches. When an HTML processor is used, it can understand the markup well enough to produce a rendering — with or without the assistance of the style sheet. When an XML processor is used, it can apply the rules in the style sheet to produce a rendering without having to understand the ins and outs of HTML. Developers who have relied on HTML's internal mechanisms for describing presentation (the `FONT`, `B`, `I` and other tags) may find it worthwhile to switch to the XML model. Separating the presentation description from the documents makes it much simpler to reuse formatting across a large number of documents (for example, building a consistent look without relying on templates).

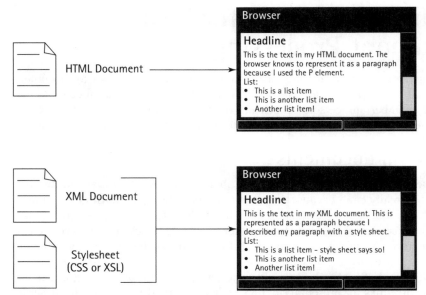

Figure 2-5: While HTML only requires an HTML document for presentation,
XML requires both a document and a set of presentation rules.

Chapter 8 discusses style sheets and their uses in much greater detail.

Transforming documents

Because the structure of XML documents is defined tightly within the document,
it's relatively easy to convert information from one vocabulary and structure to
another. HTML documents typically are treated as final containers for information
and used primarily for delivery to end users. You can use XML documents – and
XHTML documents – as waystations for information, holding information in a particular form until the user wants to work with it in a different form.

A simple example of this is a set of information, such as a table storing financial
results over a ten-year period. While reading a table is useful, being able to tell the
application to "show me this information as a bar graph" also is handy. Right now,
that process typically requires copying the information out of the HTML table, past-
ing it into an application that supports graphing, and then creating the graph. If the
table is stored in XML or XHTML, you easily can tell an application to apply a style
sheet to the table that presents the information as a graph – perhaps using the

W3C's *Scalable Vector Graphics (SVG)* XML vocabulary for displaying graphics. Different transformations of the same document can yield completely different presentations, as shown in Figure 2-6.

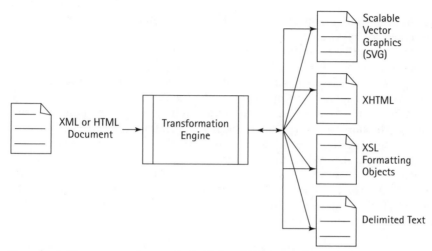

Figure 2-6: You can transform a single XML or XHTML document into many different document types.

The generic, but highly structured, nature of XML makes it easy to create scripts. You can use JavaScript, VBScript, Java, or whatever is convenient. You also can create style sheets, typically using the W3C's *Extensible Stylesheet Language Transformations (XSLT)* that automate conversions from one format to another. These conversions, once written, provide pathways among different formats that you can reuse on different instances of the same format. There are some limitations because a graphing vocabulary might not understand what to do with certain content – for instance, converting 'n/a' in a table to a bar graph – but a whole new range of possibilities emerges.

The W3C's *Extensible Style Language (XSL)* is probably the most developed use of this approach. XSL style sheets are written as transformations (in XSLT) from particular XML document structures to a vocabulary composed of formatting objects, elements, and attributes that describe presentation in a very detailed way. While CSS (described in the preceding section) merely annotate document structures to provide rules for presentation, XSL enables developers to transform any kind of XML documents into documents that purely describe presentation.

While XSL is probably overkill for most designers working with XHTML, XHTML is a popular target for XSLT transformations. Converting information stored in XML documents into XHTML makes it possible to read that information on a much wider range of browsers using a commonly understood vocabulary. Chapter 12 explores this process in greater detail.

Linking into and referencing documents

Because HTML documents have such flexible structures (enough so that different processors can interpret them differently), it's very difficult to create reliable and usable tools for describing locations within HTML documents. Even something as simple as "the third paragraph of the second section" is hard to pinpoint. Because XML is designed so that every parser sees the same structure in every document, it's much simpler to describe locations within XML documents.

This makes it much easier to build links to and from portions of documents without requiring the use of *anchor tags* (`<A NAME="location">`) throughout a document. Effectively, it enables developers to point to parts of documents they don't control. This, in turn, makes it possible to build much more detailed pointers from search engines, bibliography sites, or just general reference without coordination between the people creating the link and the owners of the target document.

The W3C has several working groups addressing these issues for XML, though it isn't clear yet how the work of these groups — XLink, XPath, and XPointer — will be integrated with XHTML. XHTML will make it much easier for XML documents to point into (X)HTML, as shown in Figure 2-7. Adding that functionality to XHTML itself may take a while longer, however.

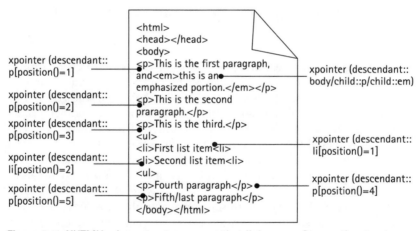

Figure 2-7: XHTML's clean structures mean that links can reference the structure of the document rather than explicit anchor locations.

Storing documents

XML's hierarchical nature opens new possibilities for document storage and management as well. While many HTML documents are generated from databases, it's very difficult to cram HTML into databases in any form more useful than an ordinary file system. HTML's chaotic flows of text work well when stored as linear files, but they're very hard to break down into smaller components for storing and indexing. You can store XML as a text flow, but it also is possible to decompose XML into a lot of smaller bits, store them in a database, and retrieve and recombine those bits as needed. This allows random access to the information stored in those documents without requiring applications to load an entire document, parse it, and pull out the desired information.

This approach is useful in two cases. In the first case, the information in the XML document is a data stream much like those traditionally stored in relational databases. Mapping XML information into and out of a relational database isn't very difficult, and tools for making this process look like an ordinary file system appear in databases from Oracle, IBM, and other vendors. Establishing the rules for such mappings takes a bit of effort; but those rules can ride on the XML document structures once established, making it easy to roundtrip XML documents to and from a database (see Figure 2-8).

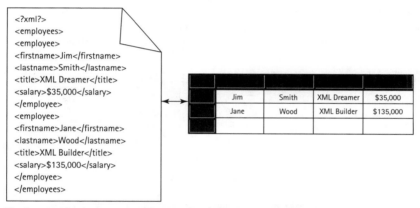

Figure 2-8: Sometimes you can store data-oriented XML documents in a relational database and reassemble them easily.

In the second case, fragmenting XML documents gives readers and writers access to smaller pieces of documents so they can avoid downloading and operating on potentially enormous documents merely to retrieve a tiny bit. In this case, the XML document's native hierarchical structure is preserved – not just a mapping to and from a set of tables. While it's possible to do this fragmentation in a relational database framework (several relational vendors are pushing this), other options such as hierarchical and object databases provide a different storage mechanism that more naturally reflects the structures inside the XML document. This tends to work better for XHTML documents in which the structures may contain wildly varying amounts of text and other content.

In both cases, the system can look much like an ordinary file system. However, searching is made easier using indexing inside the data store and programs can rely on the data store's facilities for fragment retrieval and storage rather than working with complete documents. Other possibilities, such as version tracking on an element-by-element basis, also open up in these frameworks. While they may be overkill for a small Web site or for simple document sets, these features make it much simpler for multiple people to work simultaneously on the same large document without constantly tripping over one other. Figure 2-9 shows one possibility for such a repository.

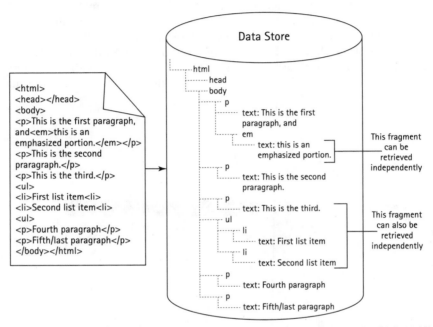

Figure 2-9: Hierarchically structured storage can keep XML as fragments, which makes retrieval and storage of particular pieces of a document easy.

Searching and indexing documents

The same structures that make referencing and storing XML documents easy make searching and indexing them simple as well. With the referencing tools, you easily can build tables of contents and indexes that address the parts of an XML document where a search result appears. In addition, the flexibility of XML's naming structures makes it possible to search for information in particular fields. Documents using XHTML lose some of the field-based potential because they employ HTML's vocabulary for presenting information. However, other possibilities within XHTML — such as using the class attribute to provide the "real" description of what a given element contains — can provide hooks similar to XML element names.

Most search engines today discard the markup in HTML documents, preferring to use full-text strategies. While META elements occasionally may receive some attention, no conventions for identifying content and content types ever emerged in the HTML world. XHTML may not provide the free-form labeling of content that XML offers, but its capability of reliably referencing fragments should make it easier to find information within documents.

XHTML User Agents: Preparing for the Next Generation

The XHTML 1.0 specification provides a set of rules for XHTML (*User Agent Conformance*) that includes a rough description of how XHTML software differs from HTML software, though these rules exist mostly to bring XHTML rendering practice in line with the rules for parsing XML 1.0. XHTML also is designed to remain compatible (mostly) with the previous generation of HTML applications, so it may take a while for the transition to occur. Pure XHTML user agents (also known as *XHTML processing software*) aren't likely to be useful for a while, at least without some kind of conversion process that allows the enormous amount of legacy HTML to enter in some form.

Developers who want to build XHTML processors can get started with the wide variety of tools available from XML sources. Parsers, various kinds of processors, integration with databases and object structures, transformation engines, and more are often available as open source. Building XHTML applications generally involves integrating tools and making them meet your needs — more so than starting from scratch to build a piece of software that understands everything about XHTML. While the legacy HTML problem remains daunting for now, the tools and techniques discussed in the chapters to follow help you get over those hurdles and enable you to start applying these kinds of techniques to your daily Web site work. As XHTML becomes more widespread, vendors hopefully will provide many of the tools just described to enable you to work more efficiently without having to build your own tools.

If you need to track down XML development tools and software, try http://www.xmlsoftware.com. For news on the latest emerging tools, go to http://www.xmlhack.com. For coverage of XML application design, read *Building XML Applications* by Simon St. Laurent and Ethan Cerami (McGraw-Hill, 1999) or *XML and Java*, by Hiroshi Maruyama, Kent Tamura, and Naohiko Uramoto (Addison-Wesley, 1999).

Part II

The Ins and Outs of XHTML

CHAPTER 3
Coding Styles: HTML's Maximum Flexibility

CHAPTER 4
Coding Styles: XML and XHTML's
Maximum Structure

CHAPTER 5
Anatomy of an XHTML Document

CHAPTER 6
Reading the XHTML DTDs: A Guide to
XML Declaration

CHAPTER 7
Exploring the XHTML DTDs

CHAPTER 8
Style Sheets and XHTML

Chapter 3

Coding Styles: HTML's Maximum Flexibility

WHEN HTML FIRST GOT STARTED, the relative ease with which beginners could create a page using a few simple tags inserted into text made it extremely attractive. The phrase, "Learn to build Web pages in half an hour" actually was a believable promise – though it only gave users a start. By avoiding the strict rules and many prerequisites of other hypertext systems, the Web leapfrogged past its competitors; along the way, a number of convenience techniques became quite common. While these techniques served their purpose, many of them created roadblocks for software developers that now stand in the way of making the Web an all-purpose application framework. In the following sections, we explore these techniques and their place in current Web development and highlight them for replacement in the new world of XHTML.

Errors: Don't Stop, Don't Report

HTML browsers have a long tradition of "best-effort" presentation. If browsers encounter markup that doesn't make sense to them, they do their best (as described next) to present the document's content; but they don't ask users questions about problems with documents. For Web designers, this means that a careful inspection process is necessary to make sure that pages are presented as expected. The HTML features described in the next few sections often vary among different browsers, making it hard to predict how a page looks in Internet Explorer or Lynx based on its appearance in Netscape. This convenience for users and beginner HTML coders means a lot of additional gruntwork for professional designers. It also gives designers with more experience an edge because they've seen the results of miscoded HTML more frequently and can use those results to their advantage.

 The addition of scripting languages — such as JavaScript and VBScript — has led to pop-up dialog boxes announcing problems and asking users if they want to continue, breaking this tradition to some extent. Pop-up dialog boxes cause a lot more interference with the browsing experience so most browsers reserve them for special cases.

Case: As You Like It

HTML was extremely forgiving about user preferences for uppercase or lowercase in element and attribute names, and in values for attributes as well. Browsers treat all the following examples identically:

```
<P ALIGN="CENTER">Hello!</P>
<p align="center">Hello!</p>
<P align="CENTER">Hello!</P>
<p ALIGN="CENTER">Hello!</p>
<P ALIGN="center">Hello!</p>
<p align="center">Hello!</P>
```

All of these produce a page that looks like that shown in Figure 3-1.

Figure 3-1: Any variety of case produces the same paragraph.

This is very handy if you're just getting started and don't want typos to cause problems. In addition, it enables users to choose how they want their markup to look. (For instance, I prefer my element and attribute names in uppercase, which separates them nicely from the content even if it looks a bit odd.) Ignoring case requires a bit more work from the browser, but that tradeoff is considered acceptable in HTML.

Understood Omissions: Leaving Out Endings

HTML picked up a convenient trick from SGML: enabling developers to leave out end tags in many cases. This trick works best when it's obvious that one element can't contain another and must end before the second element starts. For example, it doesn't make sense for one paragraph to contain another paragraph. This means that the beginning of a new paragraph is treated as the end of any previous paragraph mark. For example,

```
<p>As more and more people create vocabularies, a certain amount of
standardization will no doubt emerge, based on the convenience
factor it promises. While mapping information between schemas may
not be terribly difficult, common vocabularies promise to reduce the
need to do such work at all. Rather than starting with a complete
vocabulary, however, a distributed approach would let people build
their own vocabularies and gradually map their intersections into
'suggested' conventions.</p>
<p>While this approach might take longer than an expert community
developing standards, it might also better reflect the needs of all
involved. Experts might well have a role in exploring intersections
and developing solutions that will be optimal, for a time, but the
point is to leave final decision making with users rather than
strapping them into a straitjacket someone else built. </p>
<p>...
```

The italicized end tags for the paragraphs (*</p>*) are optional so the browser treats them as being there whether or not they actually appear. (Sometimes browsers present information slightly differently depending on the details of the markup.) The same thing happens within lists, as shown here:

```
<ul>
<li>bananas</li>
<li>apples</li>
<li>oranges</li>
<li>persimmons</li>
</ul>
```

Although paragraphs and lists are fairly simple cases, similar things happen through HTML in most browsers — despite subtle variations in the rules for interpreting them. The following code adds an open b element, which appears in the third line of code (but is never closed).

```
<html>
<body>
<p>Hello! <b>This is a stickup!
<p>Hand over all your money.
<h2>I mean it!</h2>
<p>Thank you for your time.
</body></html>
```

Does this open b element mean that all of the text after it should be in boldface? Netscape Navigator 4.x and Internet Explorer 5.0 seem to think so, as shown in Figure 3-2.

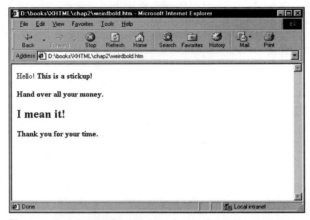

Figure 3-2: Internet Explorer 5.0 bolds the entire document following the <b> tag's appearance.

On the other hand, the W3C's own Amaya browser treats the b element – and therefore the bold effect – as ending with the paragraph. Only the words "This is a stickup" are in bold, as shown in Figure 3-3.

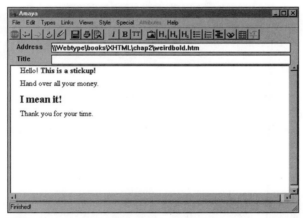

Figure 3-3: Amaya stops making text bold at the end of the paragraph that contains the open <b> tag.

Amaya even shows you how it interprets a particular document structure with a special view (available from the View menu) that displays the structure of the document rather than its content. Element names (some of which are filled in automatically, such as TITLE) are displayed in a tree structure with the containment hierarchies indicated by vertical bars and indentation, as shown in Figure 3-4.

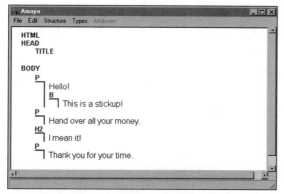

Figure 3-4: Amaya stops making text bold at the end of the paragraph that contains the open <b> tag.

Although it hasn't taken the world by storm, the Amaya browser is an incredibly useful tool for learning how the W3C sees the world. While Amaya hasn't implemented W3C specifications completely, it sticks much closer to the letter of the spec than any of its commercial competitors and is driven by the W3C's agenda. It also now supports XHTML — the first browser to do so. You can find out more about Amaya at http://www.w3.org/Amaya/.

Developers who rely on HTML browsers to fill in their end tags have encountered these kinds of issues for a while. Making dynamic HTML work (even in a single browser) sometimes requires cleaning up documents to clarify their structure; style sheets that rely on document structure to apply formatting often have similar problems. Still, letting the browser figure out where an element ends is a common (and successful) practice and it is built into HTML tools of all shapes and sizes.

Some HTML browsers took advantage of the loose structure of HTML to produce special effects. For instance, Netscape enabled developers to flash background colors using multiple BODY opening tags that specify different colors. Most of these effects aren't in common use any more, and some of them were declared bugs. Generally, scripting techniques that accomplish pretty much the same things in more structured ways replaced them.

Overlaps

Most HTML browsers do more than just close your tags automatically; they also support more complex markup such as overlapping tags. Structures like the following one are common in HTML documents, often produced by tools as well as hand-coding.

```
<b>This is bold. <i>This is bold italic.</b> This is italic.</i>
```

In many browsers, this code produces results like those shown in Figure 3-5.

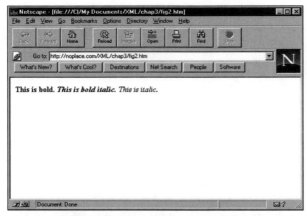

Figure 3-5: While it doesn't work in every case, many browsers support overlapping tags.

Overlapping tags also commonly appear with the font element, which you use for formatting that doesn't correspond to the structure of the document. In general this is a risky practice, one that the W3C has long considered troubling.

Abbreviated Attributes

HTML supports a feature from SGML that enables document creators to include the name of an attribute without any value. This feature exists even in the "strict" version of HTML 4.0. For example, the checked and disabled attributes of checkboxes (or any input component) allows:

```
<input type="checkbox" checked disabled>
```

HTML 4.0's transitional version (and most browsers) also supports a `compact` attribute for list items:

```
<li compact>Squeezed tight!</li>
```

Even though no value is provided for these attributes, browsers note their existence. (It actually doesn't matter which value you provide!) If a `compact` attribute appears at all, the browser displays the list item in a more compact form.

HTML also enables developers to omit quotes around attribute values. While the quotes are necessary for values that contain spaces, they aren't required for other values. You also can write the input element just shown like this:

```
<input type=checkbox checked disabled>
```

Multiple Names

There are two separate mechanisms within HTML for identifying particular elements. The first, which comes from HTML's hyperlinking within documents, uses the `A` element and a `NAME` attribute to identify a position in a document:

```
<A NAME="Section1_1"><H2>1.1 Conformance</H2></A>
```

The second flavor of identification, used most frequently in dynamic HTML implementations, uses ID attributes on elements to identify them to scripts:

```
<H2 ID="Section1_1">1.1 Conformance</H2>
```

While both of these attributes identify content within documents, they remain separate pieces in HTML. This enables hypertext link managers and script developers to stay out of each other's way.

Tag Soup

HTML browsers typically ignore any elements or attributes that they don't recognize. This makes the development of new versions of HTML much simpler because older browsers don't have problems digesting new code. At the same time, it enables browser vendors to modify the language. They can add new features such as `BLINK`, `MARQUEE`, and `LAYER` without fearing that they might set off catastrophic problems for users of other browsers. While these vendor-centric creations may cause Web designers heartburn, the general rule that browsers ignore mysterious tags makes it possible to create cross-browser solutions that work even for complex problems (like the wild variations between dynamic HTML as proposed by Netscape and Microsoft).

This feature also enables Microsoft to create *XML data islands* within HTML documents, storing information in a non-HTML vocabulary within an HTML document without fearing serious problems in browsers. This is probably the most extreme case of HTML extension, but fortunately its side effects in older legacy tools are fairly minimal. (Its effects on future browsers will likely be much more complicated.)

Extending the Browser

HTML presentation remains the core of Web browser functionality, although scripting has become an important component of that presentation. Developers who need more capabilities than what HTML+ scripting can provide have to extend the browser. Java applets are one solution, plug-ins another, ActiveX components one more, and helper applications still another. Integrating these tools with HTML can be difficult because there isn't really a way to express the information they need through HTML, except as a series of name-value parameters. The following examples show one style of parameter passing:

```
<APPLET CODE="StockGraph.class" WIDTH=100 HEIGHT=100>
<PARAM NAME="company" value="T">
<PARAM NAME="startDate" value="12221999">
<PARAM NAME="endDate" value="01302000">
<PARAM NAME="scale" value="60">
<PARAM NAME="style" value="tradLine">
</APPLET>
```

or:

```
<object classid="clsid:D27CDB6E-AE6D-11cf-96B8-444553540000"
codebase="http://active.macromedia.com/flash2/cabs/swflash.cab#versi
on=3,0,0,0" id="OpenFlash" width="200" height="200" name="Flash
Demo" align="left">
<param name="movie" value="FlashDemo.swf">
<param name="quality" value="high">
<param name="bgcolor" value="#000000">
</object>
```

The following excerpt illustrates the approach taken by many extensions: using HTML only to set up the presentation of the incoming content, but then referencing an external file that contains all the information the extension needs rather than providing it through the HTML.

```
<APPLET CODE="LinkMap.class" WIDTH=405 HEIGHT=257>
<PARAM NAME="src" value="maps/map1.xml">
</APPLET>
```

HTML itself provides just enough room to support these kinds of extensions, although developers find plenty of ways around its limitations.

Creative Comments

There are a few cases in which HTML's "ignore tags you don't understand" approach can't prevent conflicts with newer flavors of content. Browser developers have had to improvise to support these cases, and thus have found a few tricks to avoid the problems. The main issue surfaced when JavaScript appeared, using < to mean "less than" instead of "markup tag starts here." To keep browsers from displaying scripts on pages and tripping over < signs, developers use comments to hide scripts as shown here:

```
<SCRIPT LANGUAGE="JavaScript">
<!-- Hide This Code From Non-JS Browsers
document.writeln("<P>See? This was created today! </P>");
var today = new Date();  // Use today's date
var text= "Today is " + (today.getMonth() + 1) + "/" +
today.getDate() + "/" +today.getFullYear()+".";
document.writeln(text);
//-->
</SCRIPT>
```

JavaScript ignores lines that begin with an HTML comment opener, <!--; the closing of the comment is hidden from JavaScript with a JavaScript comment, //. Older browsers just interpret the contents of the SCRIPT element as one large comment and they don't display any of the material inside. Newer browsers understand that the comment is "just kidding" and they process the JavaScript properly.

Similar tactics are used often with STYLE elements when they contain style sheets directly:

```
<STYLE TYPE="text/css"><!--
H1 {font-family: Arial, Helvetica; font-weight: bold; font-size: x-
large; color: red}
H2 {font-family: Arial, Helvetica; font-weight: bold; font-size:
large; color: blue}
H3 {font-family: Arial, Helvetica; font-weight: bold; color: green}
A:link {color: red}
A:visited {color:lime}
A:active {color:yellow}
H1 B {color:purple}
H1.black {font-family: serif; color: black}
H3#freaky {font-family: serif; color: aqua}
/* End of stylesheet */--></STYLE>
```

Browsers that support cascading style sheets ignore the comments, while other browsers treat the style sheet as a comment and politely ignore it.

Validate? Why?

The W3C has spent a fair amount of time (with some success) trying to convince developers to check their pages against the standard. Many HTML documents are prefixed now with a DOCTYPE declaration similar to:

```
<!DOCTYPE HTML PUBLIC "-//W3C//DTD HTML 4.01//EN"
"http://www.w3.org/TR/html4/strict.dtd">
```

The DOCTYPE declaration points the browser (and other processors) to the formal SGML document type definition for HTML. HTML 4 actually has three different document types; the preceding declaration points to the "strict" version, which is probably the least used in practice. While most browsers don't use validation, the W3C does provide a service that checks your documents for conformance (go to http://validator.w3.org/). There's even an icon that you can put on your pages after you validate them to let the world know you're paying close attention to the spec.

Validation, if used consistently, can help developers ensure that their pages conform to the specification. However, it doesn't do much to solve the problems of clients who tend to see documents from the same point of view as users — as a particular rendering in a specific browser. If making it look right (or simply consistent across implementations) is a more important requirement than conforming to an abstract specification, then validation isn't going to receive high priority. Browsers aren't concerned about validation and so they support all kinds of possibilities that fall well outside the rules for validity. Thus, validation isn't a high priority for most Web developers. With XHTML, that will change.

Chapter 4

Coding Styles: XML and XHTML's Maximum Structure

XML PARSERS ARE FAR more brutal about rejecting documents they don't like than are HTML browsers. XML's clear focus on structure demands that the practices described in the previous chapter must change. However, most of those changes shouldn't cause more than minor inconveniences — at least for newly created documents.

 If reading this chapter makes you groan with pain about the amount of work this transition involves, don't panic. I devote much of the rest of this book to making these changes easy and (where possible) automated. Some of the choices the XHTML team made may not be to your liking, but you can adjust to most of them fairly easily. (I even learned to accept lowercase markup after years of protest.)

Cleaning up HTML

The issues described in this section are changes you can make in existing HTML without knowing about any of the new features introduced by XML. For the most part, the cleanup dominates the transition to XHTML 1.0. While some of these issues may require developers to rethink the way they create documents, they generally don't cause problems for older browsers.

Case matters

XML is case-sensitive and it treats IMG and img as two different element names entirely. In large part, this is because XML supports a much wider set of characters than most HTML implementations. Also, many languages either don't have case or they follow different sets of rules for how case works. As a result, the W3C settled on a single standard for XHTML markup. They chose lowercase for all element and attribute names, and anything that purports to be XHTML must use lowercase. The same applies to all attribute values in which choices are provided. For example, in regular HTML 4.0, you can include this code in a form:

```
<INPUT TYPE="TEXT" VALUE="Singing Fish"></INPUT>
```

To represent the same item in XHTML, you have to change the case of almost the entire element:

```
<input type="text" value="Singing Fish"></input>
```

The element name is now in lowercase, as are the attribute names. The `type` attribute value changes to lowercase as well because it represents an option chosen from a list of possibilities. The `value` attribute's content, however, can appear in whatever case is appropriate — it only represents the default value for the text, not a particular choice an XHTML browser needs to understand.

Clean (and explicit) element structures

HTML browsers have never been picky about element structures, but that will change with the advent of XHTML. HTML documents are supposed to have a structure like that shown here:

```
<html>
<head>...</head>
<body>...</body>
</html>
```

Most browsers don't enforce this structure, however. Browsers display fragments quite happily — with or without `html`, `head`, and `body` tags. In XHTML, you must provide this basic framework and put content in only the `body` element.

XML and XHTML don't permit the implied end tags and overlapping element structures described in Chapter 3. Instead of:

```
<b>This is bold. <i>This is bold italic.</b> This is italic.</i>
```

you now have to use:

```
<b>This is bold. <i>This is bold italic.</i></b> <i>This is
italic.</i>
```

or:

```
<b>This is bold.</b> <b><i>This is bold italic.</i></b> <i>This is
italic.</i>
```

Both of these alternatives produce a cleanly nested element structure. No element ends inside of a different element than the one in which it starts, and processors can tell which parts of this fragment are supposed to be bold and which are supposed to be italic.

Empty elements

XML has a slightly different syntax for *empty elements* – elements that don't contain other elements or text – than did HTML, and XHTML requires further change. In HTML, a normal start tag represents empty elements:

```
<img src="mypic.gif">
```

In XHTML, you need to add a slash to the end of the tag:

```
<img src="mypic.gif" />
```

The space before the slash isn't necessary, but it keeps some older browsers from displaying the slash on the page. The same guideline applies to horizontal rule and line break end tags, which you should enter as:

```
<br /> <hr />
```

You can also write empty elements as `<br></br>`, with no whitespace between the start and end tags, but this tends to confuse older browsers.

Quoting and expanding attribute values

XHTML makes more demands on attribute formatting than does HTML. The most obvious change is that *all* attribute values – whether or not they contain spaces, their content is text or numbers, or they reflect a choice from a list or a more free-form approach – must be surrounded by quotes. The programmer still has one option: you can use single quotes or double quotes as you like, provided that you start and end with the same kind of quote. This means that the following examples are both legal XHTML:

```
<img src="mypic.gif">
<img src='mypic.gif'>
```

Despite this leniency, XHTML does require that all attributes have values. The mere existence of an attribute name is no longer enough. This HTML:

```
<input type="checkbox" checked disabled>
```

must become this XHTML:

```
<input type="checkbox" checked="checked" disabled="disabled" />
```

and this HTML:

```
<li compact>Squeezed tight!</li>
```

must become this XHTML:

```
<li compact="compact">Squeezed tight!</li>
```

XHTML has one other important attribute "gotcha." While HTML allows the use of ampersands within attribute values — they're common in URI query strings, for instance — XHTML requires that you use an entity (&) in place of ampersands. The HTML form:

```
<a
href="http://www.simonstl.com/example/test.jsp?name=Simon&birthday=1
125&haircolor=brown">Birthday link</li>
```

must become this XHTML form:

```
<a
href="http://www.simonstl.com/example/test.jsp?name=Simon&amp;birthd
ay=1125&amp;haircolor=brown">Birthday link</li>
```

Unique identifiers

The conflict between NAME and ID described previously was resolved in favor of ID (although now it's id). The XHTML specification describes NAME as *deprecated* — a limbo that enables developers to use the attribute but suggests a short lifespan. Deprecated elements do survive in HTML browsers for the most part, but it's unclear if XHTML will treat deprecation and eventual removal from the spec more seriously.

In XHTML 1.0, you can create identifiers in two ways. The first way is simpler, but it loses backward compatibility:

```
<a id="Section1_1"><h2>1.1 Conformance</h2></a>
```

The second way looks like unnecessary duplication, but it works for both HTML and XHTML browsers:

```
<a id="Section1_1" name="Section1_1"><h2>1.1 Conformance</h2></a>
```

In the long term, shifting to ids will make it simpler to integrate XHTML with the new tools for hypertext linking that are emerging in the XML world. It also will encourage consistency in existing projects such as dynamic HTML by making it easier to apply Cascading Style Sheets and the Document Object Model.

The change to XHTML brings with it one additional shift for identifiers. They now have to start with a letter, underscore, or colon, and may consist of letters, digits, underscores, colons, hyphens, and periods. Spaces are no longer permitted, for example.

Validation and reliability

XHTML 1.0 makes validation an important part of processing. While it doesn't require validating XHTML 1.0 processors, it does require that strictly conforming XHTML documents must be valid XML documents and conform to one of the three document type definitions (DTD) the W3C created for XHTML. The DTDs are the core of the XHTML specification and the foundation for further development.

In some ways, this isn't a departure from its HTML predecessors, which also had validation discussions; but the move to XML may make it more likely that validation will matter. First, very few validation tools are available for HTML. While some HTML editors included validation as an option, and the W3C hosts its own Validation Service, validation checking wasn't likely to ever take place in a client — and if it did, it would be optional. As XHTML brings HTML into an XML environment, however, validation is likely to become much more important. Applications that use commodity XML parsers will be unable to read XHTML documents that don't meet the validation requirements if they expect all documents to be valid — a fairly common requirement in the XML world. As various XML applications and repositories link into, process, and store XHTML, the requirement for valid XHTML will increase.

Validation promises to simplify XHTML processing by reducing the number of possibilities that browsers need to accommodate. Structures meant to mark up text within a block of text (such as bold, strong, em) can be limited to existence inside appropriate block elements (such as p and li) to simplify the work browsers need to perform in order to render a page. Designers building style sheets don't have to support odd usages because validation makes structures very predictable. Using validation regularly, and breaking the habits ingrained by years of HTML, may be difficult; but cleaning things up can enable you to use new tools and avoid complicated situations.

Chapter 8 explains in more detail how you can take advantage of XHTML's clean structures to style your pages consistently.

The new emphasis on validation has another important side effect. While HTML 4.0 included three different descriptions of HTML — the *strict, transitional,* and *frameset* DTDs — it never was important to choose one set and stick with it. *Strictly conforming documents* are required to pick one of these DTDs and declare it at the very beginning of the document in a DOCTYPE declaration. As you start applying XML tools (some of which may be validating) to your XHTML, you see how making these choices becomes much more significant. Chapter 7 walks you through these DTDs, helping you choose ones that meet your needs.

Rules for comments

The tricks described in Chapter 3 that use comments to hide scripts and style information don't work reliably in XHTML. XML processors tell the scripting or style engine when it receives an empty element. As the XHTML 1.0 specification delicately puts it, "the historical practice of 'hiding' scripts and style sheets within comments to make the documents backward compatible is likely to not work as expected in XML-based implementations." If you want your scripts and style sheets to work, you need to learn about a new tool called *CDATA sections* (described later in this chapter). You also must reserve comments for comments that can disappear without affecting the content of the document.

New to XHTML

XHTML brings a few new tools to your Web development arsenal. In some cases, they replace older HTML tools; in other cases, they bring XML functionality to XHTML. You should get used to these fairly quickly, although some of them may cause problems in making XHTML work with older HTML browsers. As the shift from HTML to XHTML becomes more pronounced, you'll be able to use these more and more easily.

XML declarations

XML documents typically are prefixed with an *XML declaration* — an odd-looking bit of markup that indicates the XML version number and sometimes the encoding of the characters used. For example, a document might start with:

```
<?xml version="1.0" encoding="UTF-8"?>
```

This indicates that the document is an XML document (or should be, anyway!) written to conform to version 1.0. The character encoding used is an 8-bit transformation of Unicode. The values used for the encoding declaration are the same as those used by the HTML meta element's charset attribute, and the XHTML recommendation suggests using both. (In case of a conflict, the XML declaration wins, though.)

For example, an XHTML document might start out like this:

```
<?xml version="1.0" encoding="US-ASCII"?>
<html>
<head>
<title>My US-ASCII document</title>
<meta http-equiv="Content-type" content="text/html" charset="US-
ASCII" />
</head>
...
```

The XML declaration is optional, as are the version and encoding declarations it contains. For example, you can include this simple XML declaration at the start of an XHTML document:

```
<?xml?>
```

Or this one:

```
<?xml version="1.0"?>
```

Or this one:

```
<?xml encoding="UTF-8"?>
```

Some older HTML browsers display the XML declaration at the top of the page, so you can omit it if this bothers you. Without the XML declaration, however, you are limited to encoding your documents in UTF-8 or UTF-16 — at least if XML software processes your XHTML documents at any point.

For a list of common encodings, see Appendix B.

Processing instructions

XML also enables developers to pass information to the application through *processing instructions* (often called *PIs*). Processing instructions use a similar syntax to the XML declaration, although the rules for them are much less strict. Processing instructions begin with <? and end with ?>, but the developer generally dictates their contents. The first bit of text before a space appears in a PI is called the *target*. The target must start with a letter, underscore, or colon, and may consist of letters, digits, underscores, colons, hyphens, and periods. A target can't start with any case variation on XML. After that, any characters may appear. (Although if ?> appears inside of PI content, the PI ends abruptly and the document probably won't parse.)

The general syntax is:

```
<?target whatever?>
```

For example, you can use a processing instruction like this:

```
<?page 212-555-1212?>
```

in the middle of an XML document, or:

```
<?paint mix red and green and smear them around?>
```

Obviously, most XHTML applications don't know what to do with these and many older browsers treat the contents of the processing instruction — or part of the contents — as text and include them in the document. Using processing instructions is not a good idea unless you pass your XHTML through XML processors that understand particular processing instructions or the W3C creates some standard ones, which isn't very likely to happen for XHTML.

Processing instructions can appear anywhere in an XML document except inside of markup. They can appear before a document (but after the XML declaration, if there is one), any place text can appear within elements (though not within the tags), and after a document. They follow the same rules as comments, and you can think of them as comments meant for computer consumption.

CDATA sections

XML provides a new tool for protecting content, such as scripts and styles, which uses markup characters (<, &, and >) for purposes other than markup. CDATA (or character data) marked sections tell parsers to ignore any markup that appears within the section until its end is reached. By using fairly distinctive syntax, CDATA sections are hard to miss.

```
<![CDATA[protected content]]>
```

To protect this script, for example, you can use:

```
<SCRIPT LANGUAGE="JavaScript">
<![CDATA
document.writeln("<P>See? This was created today! </P>");
var today = new Date(); // Use today's date
var text= "Today is " + (today.getMonth() + 1) + "/" +
today.getDate() + "/" +today.getFullYear()+".";
document.writeln(text);
]]>
</SCRIPT>
```

This isn't a perfect solution because older browsers will choke on the strange new syntax and scripts may not behave. However, it does make it much easier to integrate XHTML with XML processing.

You can use CDATA sections any place you expect to have a run of markup characters, or you can use the built-in entities (< for <, & for &, and > for >).

Namespaces

Namespaces are one of the most controversial aspects of XML, and their usage in XHTML produced a significant obstacle in XHTML's passage toward becoming a W3C Recommendation. Fortunately, the scheme in question was dropped in favor of a much simpler scheme so you easily can work with the results.

Namespaces address the key problem of overlapping names that emerges when developers try to mix more than one markup language. A title in XHTML is a title for the Web page, while a title in a markup language describing books probably identifies the title of the book. As XHTML is expected to be used (eventually) both as a container for XML information and within XML documents, some mechanism needs to distinguish XHTML elements and attributes from those in other markup languages. (This mechanism makes it much easier to build applications that process XHTML as well.)

Namespaces enable document authors to assign *Uniform Resource Identifiers* (*URIs*), a superset of the familiar URLs used to identify documents and other components on the Web to element and attribute names. For example, the namespace for XHTML is:

```
http://www.w3.org/1999/xhtml
```

Effectively, namespaces can add this to every element name in an XHTML document to identify them clearly as XHTML. Typing this over and over is repetitive, and most URIs would result in prohibited element and attribute names anyway, so the namespaces tools provide an easier mechanism. Namespaces are declared in special attributes that begin with xmlns. These namespaces then are available to all the child elements of the element containing the attribute, unless those child elements override the declaration by making a new one of their own. It sounds a bit tricky, but it's actually easier than it sounds.

There are two ways to attach namespaces to elements and attributes. Both use the same declaration mechanism; but one allows the creation of a default namespace, while the other creates namespaces that correspond to particular prefixes. The default namespace is used by most XHTML. The prefix mechanism will probably be applied to other types of XML contained within XHTML, and occasionally to XHTML contained in other types of XML.

To declare a default namespace, create an attribute named xmlns and assign it a URI value. For example,

```
<html xmlns="http://www.w3.org/1999/xhtml">
```

The default namespace is applied to the html element in which the declaration is made and to all of the elements contained within that html element that don't have namespace prefixes or new declarations of the default namespace. In XHTML, it also applies to all of the attributes of those elements that don't have namespace prefixes of their own — although you can't count on this in other flavors of XML.

For example, in the following simple XHTML document, all of the elements and attributes (except the namespace declaration itself: the xmlns attribute) are in the XHTML namespace (http://www.w3.org/1999/xhtml). The namespace declaration is *required* for XHTML 1.0 documents.

```
<?xml version="1.0"?>
<html xmlns="http://www.w3.org/1999/xhtml">
<head>
<title>Namespace test</title>
</head>
<body>
<h1>Namespaces!</h1>
<p>All of the elements in this document are in the
http://www.w3.org/1999/xhtml namespace, even the picture.</p>
<img src="namespacesquare.gif" height="100" width="100" />
</body>
</html>
```

An XHTML parser reading this document receives two pieces of information about every element here: its name and the namespace attached to it.

You can represent the same document using a different namespace mechanism: *prefixes*. You declare prefixes using a similar attribute syntax, but the prefix follows the xmlns and a colon. Prefixes cannot begin with xml or any case variant of xml, such as XML or XmL. For example, to declare the namespace prefix xhtml, use the attribute name xmlns:xhtml. A version of the same document that uses this format looks like:

```
<?xml version="1.0"?>
<xhtml:html xmlns:xhtml="http://www.w3.org/1999/xhtml">
<xhtml:head>
<xhtml:title>Namespace test</xhtml:title>
</xhtml:head>
<xhtml:body>
<xhtml:h1>Namespaces!</xhtml:h1>
<xhtml:p>All of the elements in this document are in the
http://www.w3.org/1999/xhtml namespace, even the picture.</xhtml:p>
<xhtml:img src="namespacesquare.gif" height="100" width="100" />
</xhtml:body>
</xhtml:html>
```

There are a lot of issues with namespaces and XML 1.0, the worst of which is incompatibility between XML 1.0 validation and namespace prefix changes. As a result, this document – which technically represents the exact same information as the preceding version – won't make it through a validating XML parser although it may well work in non-validating environments. This form is available if you need to include XHTML content in other XML documents, but it's best to stick with the simpler default namespace form for XHTML documents.

I suggest you do *not* apply prefixes to XHTML attributes. While it may be appropriate if you want to apply XHTML attributes to non-XHTML element names in some combination with other vocabularies, no real rules exist for processing such documents.

Internationalization: xml:lang and lang

Internationalization (often abbreviated *i18n* because 18 characters appear between the i and the n) gets a significant boost with the shift to XML primarily because of XML's use of Unicode as the underlying character model. While not every document needs to encode Chinese, Cyrillic, Arabic, and Indian characters, Unicode makes it possible for all of these forms to exist within a single document. In addition, XML and XHTML allow for the possibility of other encodings. In order to make this support more useful to programs that may need to know what language they are processing, XML and XHTML provide a tool for identifying the language used for content in a particular element. While XML and HTML both use the same mech-anism for identifying languages, they have slightly differently names for the mechanism. Therefore, XHTML 1.0 recommends using both. If for some reason the values aren't the same, XHTML processors should use the value given by xml:lang.

The xml:lang and lang attributes accept one or two parts in their values, reflecting *ISO 639* and *Internet Assigned Numbers Authority (IANA)* two-letter language identifiers and (optionally) *ISO 3166* country codes or other identifiers. Appendices C and D of this book provide lists of language identifiers and country codes. Values of xml:lang and lang attributes begin with the language identifier and are followed by a hyphen and country code (if a country code is provided). Table 4-1 shows sample values and their meanings.

TABLE 4-1 EXAMPLES OF LANGUAGE IDENTIFIERS THAT WORK
         WITH HTML, XML, AND XHTML

xml:lang/lang Value (Case is Irrelevant)	Meaning
En	English
en-US	English as used in the United States
en-UK	English as used in the United Kingdom
La	Latin
la-VA	Latin as used in Vatican City
Qu	Quechua
Ja	Japanese
fr-CA	French as used in Canada
en-cockney	"Cockney" English. The subcode doesn't have to be a two-letter code, but most applications don't understand cockney even if they understand the other codes.

Like namespace declarations, xml:lang and lang attributes apply to the children of the elements that use them. This makes it easy to mark an entire document as being of a particular language, while still allowing pieces of documents in different languages to override the language choice. For example, this document is marked as appearing in U.S. English:

```
<?xml version="1.0"?>
<html xmlns="http://www.w3.org/1999/xhtml" xml:lang="en-US"
lang="en-US">
<head>
<title>Languages test</title>
</head>
```

```
<body>
<h1>Languages!</h1>
<p>All of the elements in this document are in U.S. English.</p>
</body>
</html>
```

To override a language identifier for a particular piece of text, just put new xml:lang and lang attributes on that portion:

```
<?xml version="1.0"?>
<html xmlns="http://www.w3.org/1999/xhtml" xml:lang="en-US"
lang="en-US">
<head>
<title>Languages test</title>
</head>
<body>
<h1>Languages!</h1>
<p>All of the elements in this document are in U.S. English except
the following bit from Cicero.</p>
<p xml:lang="la" lang="la">O tempora, o mores! Senatus haec
intellegit. consul videt; hic tamen vivit. Vivit? immo vero etiam in
senatum venit, fit publici consilii particeps, notat et designat
oculis ad caedem unum quemque nostrum. Nos autem fortes viri satis
facere rei publicae videmur, si istius furorem ac tela vitemus. </p>
<p>This is in English again, since it isn't contained by the
paragraph in Latin.</p>
</body>
</html>
```

XHTML doesn't require the use of language identifiers. However, it's excellent practice and it makes it easier for you to style your documents for different languages and for users to apply automated tools like machine translators.

Rules for vocabulary extensions

XHTML 1.0 describes a core vocabulary and set of structures, but it leaves room for future vocabularies. XHTML 1.0 is a foundation that gives the W3C a start for further development that can be fragmented and rebuilt as needed.

Chapters 14 and 16 explain how you can extend XHTML with your own markup or with standards such as MathML and Scalable Vector Graphics (SVG).

Chapter 5

Anatomy of an XHTML Document

THE TRANSITION FROM HTML to XHTML will come with a fair number of bumps. While later chapters introduce tools to help you get past those bumps — and figure out where they come from — this chapter examines what's going to change and demonstrates a few strategies for handling those changes. Along the way, we visit the ghosts of browsers past and explore problems that exist in current browsers. In turn, you discover how prepared and unprepared various tools are for XHTML.

 Some of the solutions covered in this chapter apply tools described in much more detail in later chapters — notably the XHTML DTDs and cascading style sheets. If you encounter issues you don't understand, keep them in mind and study the chapters describing those issues more closely when you get to them. The steps covered in this chapter are more important for establishing the context in which you use certain technologies than for explaining those technologies.

An Initial HTML Document

The following document, which I use as a test case, isn't an ordinary HTML document. It's designed to contain some of the serious "gotchas" that conversions to XHTML involve. It's more or less a worst-case scenario, although its contents aren't unusual. (It's a little more meaningless than usual, but fairly ordinary otherwise.) This single document produces five derivatives, representing different paths to XHTML conformance.

The following document is reasonably small, but it contains a lot of problems in a small space:

```
<HTML>
<HEAD>
<TITLE>Non-XHTML HTML</TITLE>
```

```
<SCRIPT LANGUAGE="JAVASCRIPT">
function presentCount() {
counter="";
for (i=0; i<10; i++) {
  counter=counter + " " + i;
}
alert (counter);
}
</SCRIPT>
</HEAD>
<BODY BGCOLOR=#FFFFFF>
<FONT FACE="Times" SIZE="24" COLOR="BLUE"><B>Non-XHTML
HTML</FONT></B>
<P><A NAME="description">This document opens in most HTML browsers,
but it is definitely not XHTML.</A>
<P>The cleanup shouldn't cause too many problems, we hope.
<LI><a href="javascript:presentCount()">Click me for a
count!</a><br>
<LI><a href="query.htm?val1=1&val2=2&val3=3">Click here for a
query!</a>
<li><a href="#description">Click here for a description of this
page</a>
<p>Copyright 2000 by the Wacki HTML Writer <br>
All rights reserved.
</BODY>
</HTML>
```

Figure 5-1 shows Netscape Navigator 4.7's rendition of this document.

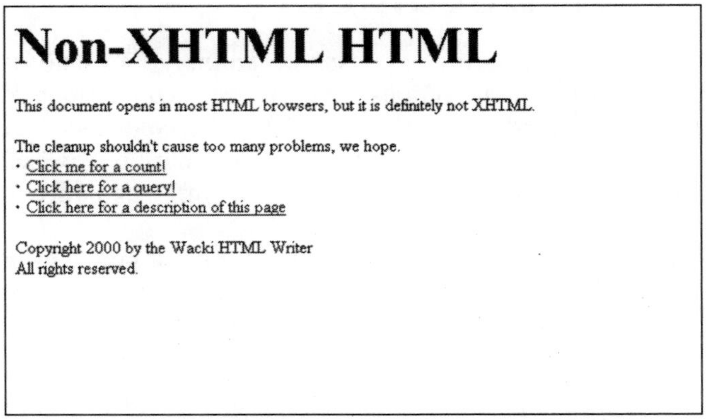

Non-XHTML HTML

This document opens in most HTML browsers, but it is definitely not XHTML.

The cleanup shouldn't cause too many problems, we hope.
· Click me for a count!
· Click here for a query!
· Click here for a description of this page

Copyright 2000 by the Wacki HTML Writer
All rights reserved.

Figure 5-1: Netscape Navigator puts a reasonably pretty face on some ugly code.

The document's flaws, from an XHTML perspective, include:

◆ No DOCTYPE declaration.

◆ Mixed case for element names – some are uppercase, some are lowercase.

◆ Structural problems – LI elements floating in the BODY, not enclosed by a list.

◆ Some attributes don't have quotes around them.

◆ The script is called using an obsolete mechanism and it contains a < character.

◆ Anchor elements have all kinds of problems, from a NAME with no ID to ampersands appearing in an href attribute.

◆ Overlapping tags – the FONT and B elements aren't nested properly.

◆ An empty tag (the br element) that needs to be marked as such.

◆ The SCRIPT element uses LANGUAGE instead of TYPE.

◆ The FONT SIZE attribute is expressed in points, not 1-7, as expected by the HTML specification.

Fixing these flaws and making the transition to a pure XHTML document takes some work.

Two Remedies

While the initial HTML isn't in incredibly bad shape, it uses the FONT element – a deprecated element that the W3C is trying to stamp out and replace with cascading style sheets (CSS). Web designers have two choices for dealing with this shift. The first approach uses XHTML 1.0's transitional DTD to avoid this complication entirely, while the second bites the bullet and makes some more structural changes to fit the document into the strict DTD. While the first approach is simpler in the short run, it may mean more work later. The second approach has more of an up-front cost – and may mean that you spend considerable time toiling over complex documents – but it should prove more stable and more manageable in the long run.

There are also a number of cases in which XHTML provides multiple approaches to solving the same problem. We'll take advantage of the fact that we're creating two different versions of the XHTML document. The two versions will test two strategies for keeping the < sign in the script from causing problems in browsers and XML parsers. (Neither works especially well in HTML browsers, as it turns out.) We'll also put each strategy through two different phases of development. The first phase keeps all the resources used by a document (such as scripts and style sheets) inside of the document, while the second phase moves those resources to separate files.

Remedy 1: The Transitional DTD and CDATA Sections

By using the transitional DTD, you can preserve the formatting used in the document — mostly the large, blue headline — without having to change the overall document structure in any significant way. While this document is simple enough that the changes aren't that difficult (as shown in the second approach), more complex documents require an enormous investment of time to convert them to the strict DTD.

For starters, you need to add the DOCTYPE declaration to the start of your document. (You can add the XML declaration, but leave that to the second approach. For the transitional DTD, that means:

```
<!DOCTYPE html
 PUBLIC "-//W3C//DTD XHTML 1.0 Transitional//EN"
 "http://www.w3.org/TR/1999/PR-xhtml1-19991210/DTD/xhtml1-
transitional.dtd">
```

This identifies the document as using the XHTML 1.0 transitional DTD from the W3C, allowing validating XML parsers to check the document using the formal declarations it contains. The opening HTML tag needs several changes. First, you must change it to lowercase; second, you must include an attribute declaring the XHTML namespace for its contents (as described in Chapter 4). The new version looks like this:

```
<html xmlns="http://www.w3.org/1999/xhtml">
```

You need to change the tags for the HEAD and TITLE elements to lowercase, as well as change the title to reflect the document's new identity:

```
<head>
<title>Transitional XHTML - Phase 1</title>
```

The SCRIPT element presents a larger problem. It contains the forbidden character <, which needs to be escaped to get past an XML parser. For this pass, use a CDATA section to mark off the contents of the (now lowercase) script element. This allows the characters <, >, and & to appear anywhere within a script. (If the sequence]]> appears, you need to break it up with whitespace like]] >.) The script element also needs to have a type attribute added to it. The W3C supports the language attribute, but insists on a type attribute with a MIME content type identifying the scripting language as well.

```
<script language="javascript" type="text/javascript">
<![CDATA[
function presentCount() {
```

```
counter="";
for (i=0; i<10; i++) {
  counter=counter + " " + i;
}
alert (counter);
}
]]>
</script>
</head>
```

The `script` element is inside the `head` element, so the `CDATA` section shouldn't cause problems with display – although it may make browser scripting engines malfunction.

 TIP Another trick that can help you avoid problems with < in scripts is to recast expressions like i<10 to 10>i. XML parsers may raise warnings when they encounter the > symbol, however.

The body of the document presents some more complicated problems. Because you're using the transitional DTD, you can keep the `bgcolor` attribute (put in lowercase, of course) on the `body` element. However, you have to add quotes:

```
<body bgcolor="#FFFFFF">
```

The headline is the next challenge. The transitional DTD supports the `font` and `b` elements, but you need to rearrange them so that they nest cleanly. You also need to store these elements in a higher-level element. The `p` element serves nicely, although you also can use the `div` element. We'll also change the `size` attribute's value to 6, as these are supposed to be expressed as a range from 1 to 7, not as a point size:

```
<p><font face="Times" size="6" color="blue"><b> Transitional XHTML -
Phase 1</b></font></p>
```

Once again, you change the title so that it more accurately describes the content of the page.

The next element, the first paragraph, includes an anchor with a `NAME` attribute. Lowercase this and then supplement it with an `id` attribute. The `p` element also needs a closing tag at the end of the paragraph.

```
<p><a name="description" id="description">This document is
transitional XHTML - we'll see how it does in the browsers.</a></p>
```

(Yes, the text changed again.)

The next paragraph just needs you to make its P element into a lowercase p and give it a closing tag:

```
<p>The cleanup shouldn't cause too many problems, we hope.</p>
```

You need to put the following list items in lowercase, give them end tags, and enclose them in some kind of list element—ul, for unordered list, seems most appropriate. The br element following the first list item is unnecessary so you can remove it.

```
<ul>
<li><a href="javascript:presentCount()">Click me for a
count!</a></li>
```

The use of javascript in href attributes isn't recommended, but you can leave it for now as it isn't expressly prohibited (although you change it in the second approach).

The next line also includes a URL, this time with ampersands. The cleanup process needs to replace them with &.

```
<li><a href="query.htm?val1=1&amp;val2=2&amp;val3=3">Click here for
a query!</a></li>
```

The last list element is mostly fine, although it needs an end tag. You must close the ul element as well:

```
<li><a href="#description">Click here for a description of this
page</a></li>
</ul>
```

At the end, you have a paragraph containing a line break. You need to add a closing tag for the p element and make the br element into an empty tag rather than just a start tag:

```
<p>Copyright 2000 by the Wacki HTML Writer <br />
All rights reserved.</p>
```

Finally, you must convert the closing tags of the BODY and HTML elements into lowercase to match the start tags:

```
</body>
</html>
```

This completes the cleaned-up version:

```
<!DOCTYPE html
 PUBLIC "-//W3C//DTD XHTML 1.0 Transitional//EN"
 "http://www.w3.org/TR/1999/PR-xhtml1-19991210/DTD/xhtml1-
transitional.dtd">
<html xmlns="http://www.w3.org/1999/xhtml">
<head>
<title>Transitional XHTML - Phase 1</title>
<script language="javascript" type="text/javascript">
<![CDATA[
function presentCount() {
counter="";
for (i=0; i<10; i++) {
  counter=counter + " " + i;
}
alert (counter);
}
]]>
</script>
</head>
<body bgcolor="#FFFFFF">
<p><font face="Times" size="6" color="blue"><b> Transitional XHTML -
Phase 1</b></font></p>
<p><a name="description" id="description">This document is
transitional XHTML - we'll see how it does in the browsers.</a></p>
<p>The cleanup shouldn't cause too many problems, we hope.</p>
<ul>
<li><a href="javascript:presentCount()">Click me for a
count!</a></li>
<li><a href="query.htm?val1=1&amp;val2=2&amp;val3=3">Click here for
a query!</a></li>
<li><a href="#description">Click here for a description of this
page</a></li>
</ul>
<p>Copyright 2000 by the Wacki HTML Writer <br />
All rights reserved.</p>
</body>
</html>
```

To test it out, send it to the W3C's HTML Validation Service at `http://validator.w3.org/`. The results: Passing! (See Figure 5-2.)

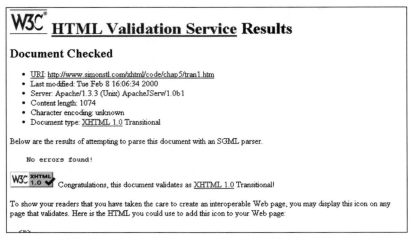

Figure 5-2: This cleaned-up version gets a clean bill of health
from the W3C's HTML Validation Service.

You test this document out in a wide variety of browsers later in the chapter, but
for now you can extend the example a little bit further by removing the script from
the document and storing it in an external file. This enables you to get rid of the
CDATA section since script files don't have to be XML. The new script element references the code file using the src attribute and it looks like this:

```
<script language="javascript" type="text/javascript" src="mycode.js"
></script>
```

While it is acceptable XML practice to use an empty tag instead of the opening
and closing tags, most browsers don't recognize that approach and try to treat the
rest of the document as a script.

The script goes into a separate file named **mycode.js**:

```
function presentCount() {
counter="";
for (i=0; i<10; i++) {
  counter=counter + " " + i;
}
alert (counter);
}
```

The document as a whole now reads:

```
<!DOCTYPE html
 PUBLIC "-//W3C//DTD XHTML 1.0 Transitional//EN"
 "http://www.w3.org/TR/1999/PR-xhtml1-19991210/DTD/xhtml1-
transitional.dtd">
```

```
<html xmlns="http://www.w3.org/1999/xhtml">
<head>
<title>Transitional XHTML - Phase 2</title>
<script language="javascript" type="text/javascript" src="mycode.js"
></script>
</head>
<body bgcolor="#FFFFFF">
<p><font face="Times" size="6" color="blue"><b> Transitional XHTML -
Phase 2</b></font></p>
<p><a name="description" id="description">This document is
transitional XHTML - we'll see how it does in the browsers.</a></p>
<p>The cleanup shouldn't cause too many problems, we hope.</p>
<ul>
<li><a href="javascript:presentCount()">Click me for a
count!</a></li>
<li><a href="query.htm?val1=1&amp;val2=2&amp;val3=3">Click here for
a query!</a></li>
<li><a href="#description">Click here for a description of this
page</a></li>
</ul>
<p>Copyright 2000 by the Wacki HTML Writer <br />
All rights reserved.</p>
</body>
</html>
```

Like its predecessor, this document passes the W3C HTML Validation Service (as shown in Figure 5-3).

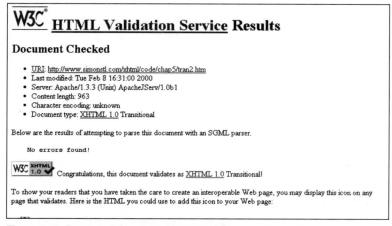

Figure 5-3: This transitional version with external scripts gets a clean bill of health from the W3C's HTML Validation Service.

Remedy 2: The Strict DTD and Entity Replacement

While the files produced using the first approach are valid XHTML, a little more work can produce documents that are easier to manage in the long run. This requires making a few more structural changes to the document and adding some cascading style sheets information. In your first pass, you convert the document to the HTML 4.01 strict DTD without worrying about XHTML. Then you convert it to XML in two slightly different ways. You also try a different approach in the scripts on the first XML pass — one that works well on XML processors but which still fails in most HTML processors.

Converting to strict HTML

You start out by declaring your intentions to use the strict HTML 4.01 DTD by putting the appropriate DOCTYPE declaration at the head of the document:

```
<!DOCTYPE HTML
     PUBLIC "-//W3C//DTD HTML 4.01//EN"
     "http://www.w3.org/TR/html4/strict.dtd">
```

Now the first section of the document, including the HTML opening tag and the HEAD element and its contents, is fine except for one line. The SCRIPT element no longer supports a LANGUAGE attribute — instead, a TYPE attribute containing a MIME content identifier (text/javascript) for the script is required:

```
<HTML>
<HEAD>
<TITLE>Non-XHTML Strict HTML</TITLE>
<SCRIPT TYPE="text/javascript">
function presentCount() {
counter="";
for (i=0; i<10; i++) {
  counter=counter + " " + i;
}
alert (counter);
}
</SCRIPT>
</HEAD>
```

Because this is still regular HTML and not XHTML, the < sign and the uppercase element names in the script are fine. When you read the BODY start tag and the headline, however, you should notice a problem. The BGCOLOR attribute of the BODY element isn't supported by the strict DTD and neither is the FONT [GSL1]element used for the headline.

There are two ways to handle this problem. The first approach simply moves the formatting information to a different place within the elements concerned – the STYLE attribute. This approach, called *in-line styling*, is more of a quick-fix solution. It solves the immediate problem of preserving formatting, but it doesn't make the document any more manageable in the long term. The new BODY start tag and headline look like this:

```
<BODY STYLE="background-color:#FFFFFF">
<P STYLE="color:blue; font-family:Times, serif; font-size:24pt"><b>Non-XHTML Strict HTML</b></p>
```

The second solution separates the style information from the element markup entirely, putting it in its own place inside of the document's head element. This requires two steps. First, you clean up the elements using an H1 element in place of the p element (after all, this is a headline):

```
<BODY>
<H1>Strict XHTML - Phase 1</H1>
```

Next, you add a style element to the head element of the document, containing the same formatting information that appears in the style attributes. The style element uses cascading style sheets syntax to identify the elements to which the formatting is applied and to describe the formatting:

```
<STYLE TYPE="text/css">
BODY {background-color:#FFFFFF }
H1 {color:blue; font-family:Times, serif; font-size:24pt}
</STYLE>
```

Because the information now is stored at the beginning of the document in a style element, you can use that formatting across elements anywhere in the document. While you might have only one H1 element in a given document, it isn't unusual for a document to have many copies of lower-level headings or other components. As phase 2 demonstrates, this approach also enables you to store style information in a form that can be shared across multiple documents. This makes it easy to define and modify a look for a set of documents.

The next few paragraphs are fine as they stand.

```
<P><A NAME="description">This document opens in most HTML browsers,
but it is definitely not XHTML.</A>
<P>The cleanup shouldn't cause too many problems, we hope.
```

The LI elements of the list need to be contained within a UL element. Now it's time to change the approach used by the link that calls the script. You left the javascript in href attributes in the other approach, but you change it here. First you use a span element to replace the a element, and use its onclick attribute to capture the event.

```
<UL>
<LI><SPAN ONCLICK="presentCount()">Click me for a count!</SPAN></LI>
```

 TIP For an explanation of why the javascript usage is discouraged, see http://lists.w3.org/Archives/Public/www-html/2000Feb/0039.html.

Although case is mixed up in the next few LI elements and their contents, these elements require very few changes. You need to replace the ampersands in the query string in the link with the & entity, and you need to add a closing UL tag.

```
<LI><a href="query.htm?val1=1&amp;val2=2&amp;val3=3">Click here for
a query!</a>
<li><a href="#description">Click here for a description of this
page</a>
</UL>
```

The remainder of the document is acceptable as is:

```
<p>Copyright 2000 by the Wacki HTML Writer <br>
All rights reserved.
</BODY>
</HTML>
```

The document as a whole now looks like this:

```
<!DOCTYPE HTML
    PUBLIC "-//W3C//DTD HTML 4.01//EN"
    "http://www.w3.org/TR/html4/strict.dtd">
<HTML>
<HEAD>
<TITLE>Non-XHTML Strict HTML</TITLE>
<SCRIPT TYPE="type/javascript">
function presentCount() {
counter="";
for (i=0; i<10; i++) {
```

```
    counter=counter + " " + i;
}
alert (counter);
}
</SCRIPT>
<STYLE TYPE="text/css">
BODY {background-color:#FFFFFF }
H1 {color:blue; font-family:Times, serif; font-size:24pt}
</STYLE>
</HEAD>
<BODY>
<H1>Strict Non-XHTML HTML</H1>
<P><A NAME="description">This document opens in most HTML browsers,
but it is definitely not XHTML.</A>
<P>The cleanup shouldn't cause too many problems, we hope.
<UL>
<LI><SPAN ONCLICK="presentCount()">Click me for a count!</SPAN></LI>
<LI><a href="query.htm?val1=1&amp;val2=2&amp;val3=3">Click here for
a query!</a>
<li><a href="#description">Click here for a description of this
page</a>
</UL>
<p>Copyright 2000 by the Wacki HTML Writer <br>
All rights reserved.
</BODY>
</HTML>
```

This document passes muster with the W3C's HTML Validation Service, although it certainly isn't XHTML. See Figure 5-4.

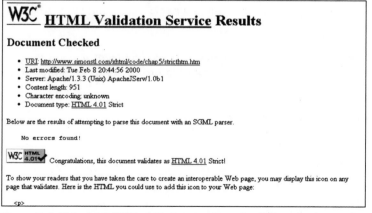

Figure 5-4: This strict HTML 4.01 document meets all the rules imposed by the strict DTD.

Converting to strict XHTML

The conversion to strict HTML does a lot to simplify the process of converting to strict XHTML, but there's still a lot to do. For starters, you use the XML declaration and a different DOCTYPE declaration at the top of this document. The XML declaration enables you to declare the document encoding (which you do again in the head element) and the version of XML used, while the DOCTYPE declaration tells processors that this document will abide by the rules of the XHTML strict DTD:

```
<?xml version="1.0" encoding="UTF-8"?>
<!DOCTYPE html
     PUBLIC "-//W3C//DTD XHTML 1.0 Strict//EN"
     "http://www.w3.org/TR/1999/PR-xhtml1-19991210/DTD/xhtml1-
strict.dtd">
```

Once again, the HTML element needs some modification: making it lowercase. Take the opportunity to add some information about the language this document uses (English) and do so using both the old-style HTML lang attribute and the XHTML xml:lang attribute.

```
<html xmlns="http://www.w3.org/1999/xhtml" lang="en-US"
xml:lang="en-US">
```

The head element gets some extra information as well. While this addition isn't necessary to meet the demands of the strict DTD, it makes sense in the context of the strict approach and provides the strongest possible set of information to satisfy both HTML and XHTML parsers. Add an element identifying the encoding used in this document to HTML browsers:

```
<head>
<title>Strict XHTML - Phase 1</title>
<meta http-equiv='Content-type' content='text/html; charset="UTF-
8"'>
```

You can experiment with the script element in this document using a character entity to represent the < character rather than hiding the script within a CDATA section:

```
<script type="text/javascript">
function presentCount() {
counter="";
for (i=0; i&lt;10; i++) {
  counter=counter + " " + i;
}
alert (counter);
```

```
}
</script>
```

Using entities may prove easier in an XML-only context than with CDATA sections, but it may cause problems (as you'll see) in HTML browsers. You need to add a style element in the head as well.

```
<style type="text/css">
body {background-color:#FFFFFF }
h1 {color:blue; font-family:Times, serif; font-size:24pt}
</style>
</head>
```

You already cleaned up the architecture of the body and h1 elements, so just move them to lowercase.

```
<body>
<h1>Strict XHTML - Phase 1</h1>
```

The next element, the first paragraph, includes an anchor with a NAME attribute. Just like with the transitional version, you need to lowercase this and supplement it with an id attribute. The p element also needs a closing tag at the end of the paragraph.

```
<p><a name="description" id="description">This document is strict
XHTML - we'll see how it does in the browsers.</a></p>
```

(Yes, the text changed yet again.)

The next paragraph just needs you to make its P element into a lowercase p and give it a closing tag:

```
<p>The cleanup shouldn't cause too many problems, we hope.</p>
```

You must put the list item elements that follow in lowercase and give them end tags. The br element following the first list item is unnecessary so you can remove it. Otherwise, just make the markup lowercase and close the li element.

```
<ul>
<li><span onclick="presentCount()">Click me for a count!</span></li>
```

The rest of the conversion can follow the previously established pattern for the transitional DTD. The next two list items need end tags.

```
<li><a href="query.htm?val1=1&amp;val2=2&amp;val3=3">Click here for
a query!</a></li>
```

```
<li><a href="#description">Click here for a description of this
page</a></li>
</ul>
```

At the end, you have a paragraph containing a line break. You need to add a closing tag for the p element and make the br element into an empty tag rather than just a start tag:

```
<p>Copyright 2000 by the Wacki HTML Writer <br />
All rights reserved.</p>
```

Finally, you need to convert the closing tags of the BODY and HTML elements into lowercase to match the start tags:

```
</body>
</html>
```

The results are similar to the strict HTML version, but thoroughly cleaned up.

```
<?xml version="1.0" encoding="UTF-8"?>
<!DOCTYPE html
     PUBLIC "-//W3C//DTD XHTML 1.0 Strict//EN"
     "http://www.w3.org/TR/1999/PR-xhtml1-19991210/DTD/xhtml1-
strict.dtd">
<html xmlns="http://www.w3.org/1999/xhtml" lang="en-US"
xml:lang="en-US">
<head>
<title>Strict XHTML - Phase 1</title>
<meta http-equiv='Content-type' content='text/html; charset="UTF-
8"'>
<script type="text/javascript">
function presentCount() {
counter="";
for (i=0; i&lt;10; i++) {
  counter=counter + " " + i;
}
alert (counter);
}
</script>
<style type="text/css">
body {background-color:#FFFFFF }
h1 {color:blue; font-family:Times, serif; font-size:24pt}
</style>
</head>
<body>
```

```
<h1>Strict XHTML - Phase 1</h1>
<p><a name="description" id="description">This document is strict
XHTML - we'll see how it does in the browsers.</a></p>
<p>The cleanup shouldn't cause too many problems, we hope.</p>
<ul>
<li><span onclick="presentCount()">Click me for a count!</span></li>
<li><a href="query.htm?val1=1&amp;val2=2&amp;val3=3">Click here for
a query!</a></li>
<li><a href="#description">Click here for a description of this
page</a></li>
</ul>
<p>Copyright 2000 by the Wacki HTML Writer <br />
All rights reserved.</p>
</body>
</html>
```

This strict XHTML document passes the W3C Validation Service with no flags raised about its use of the < entity in the script (see Figure 5-5).

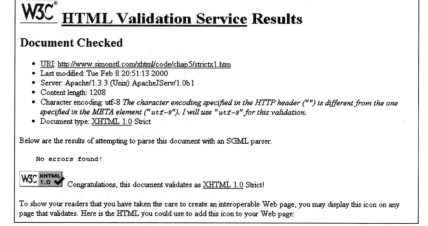

Figure 5-5: This strict XHTML 1.0 document meets all the rules imposed by the strict DTD.

For the final version, take the script and style sheet information out of the document using external files (like you did for the transitional DTD). All of the changes involved take place in the head element.

```
<head>
<title>Strict XHTML - Phase 2</title>
<meta http-equiv='Content-type' content='text/html; charset="UTF-8"'
```

```
/>
<script type="text/javascript" src="mycode.js" ></script>
<link rel="stylesheet" href="mycss.css" type="text/css" />
</head>
```

The script element is reduced to a `type` and `src` attribute, with the script stored in the external file **mycode.js**. The style sheet has to be connected by a different mechanism because the `style` element offers no `src` attribute. The mechanism shown, the `link` element, uses attributes to identify that it is connecting a style sheet, that the style sheet is of type `text/css` (cascading style sheets), and that it is located in the file **mycss.css**. The document as a whole now looks like this:

```
<?xml version="1.0" encoding="UTF-8"?>
<!DOCTYPE html
     PUBLIC "-//W3C//DTD XHTML 1.0 Strict//EN"
     "http://www.w3.org/TR/1999/PR-xhtml1-19991210/DTD/xhtml1-
strict.dtd">
<html xmlns="http://www.w3.org/1999/xhtml" lang="en-US"
xml:lang="en-US">
<head>
<title>Strict XHTML - Phase 2</title>
<meta http-equiv='Content-type' content='text/html; charset="UTF-8"'
/>
<script type="text/javascript" src="mycode.js" ></script>
<link rel="stylesheet" href="mycss.css" type="text/css" />
</head>
<body>
<h1>Strict XHTML - Phase 2</h1>
<p><a name="description" id="description">This document is strict
XHTML - we'll see how it does in the browsers.</a></p>
<p>The cleanup shouldn't cause too many problems, we hope.</p>
<ul>
<li><span onclick="presentCount()">Click me for a count!</span></li>
<li><a href="query.htm?val1=1&amp;val2=2&amp;val3=3">Click here for
a query!</a></li>
<li><a href="#description">Click here for a description of this
page</a></li>
</ul>
<p>Copyright 2000 by the Wacki HTML Writer <br />
All rights reserved.</p>
</body>
</html>
```

Like its many cousins, this version of the document also passes the W3C Validation Service (as shown in Figure 5-6).

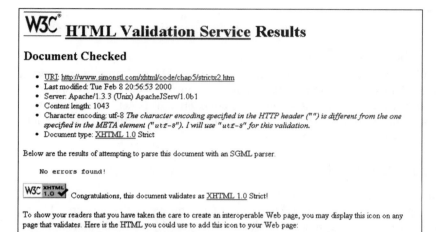

W3C® **HTML Validation Service Results**

Document Checked

- URI: http://www.simonstl.com/xhtml/code/chap5/strictx2.htm
- Last modified: Tue Feb 8 20:56:53 2000
- Server: Apache/1.3.3 (Unix) ApacheJServ/1.0b1
- Content length: 1043
- Character encoding: utf-8 *The character encoding specified in the HTTP header ("") is different from the one specified in the META element ("utf-8"). I will use "utf-8" for this validation.*
- Document type: XHTML 1.0 Strict

Below are the results of attempting to parse this document with an SGML parser.

    No errors found!

Congratulations, this document validates as XHTML 1.0 Strict!

To show your readers that you have taken the care to create an interoperable Web page, you may display this icon on any page that validates. Here is the HTML you could use to add this icon to your Web page:

Figure 5-6: This strict XHTML 1.0 document meets all the rules imposed by the strict DTD while referencing resources that aren't themselves XHTML (or even XML).

Browser Testing

While the W3C's HTML Validation Service is a useful tool for making sure that documents conform to the specification, most of the documents created previously will have at least some problems in existing browsers. To demonstrate the kinds of problems you may encounter as you deploy XHTML, the next few pages show the results of running the original HTML, the strict HTML, and all of their variations through a variety of browsers of different vintages. No browser accepts every version, but you can see trends emerging over time.

The browsers tested here range from the obsolete to the experimental. While very few users still work with Netscape Navigator 1.22 (though it's still used on some older servers), its response to XHTML documents demonstrates how some aspects of the strict approach can make XHTML more palatable to even the oldest of commercial browsers. Newer browsers have an extraordinary number of quirks that suggest Web designers will test their work in multiple browsers for some time to come. Because the Microsoft Internet Explorer versions tend to vary widely on different platforms, I provide samples for both Macintosh and Windows. The Netscape and Amaya browsers display the same results whatever operating system they use, so I show results for Windows NT and Windows 95.

You can run these same sets of tests on your own browser. The test files are available at http://www.simonstl.com/xhtml/code/chap5/.

While the browser tests may not make the browsers look great at handling XHTML, this is hardly a knock on their performance. Most of these were written well before XHTML even began to germinate, so you can't hold them responsible for ideas hatched long after their code was completed. This set of tests provides benchmarks you can use to determine your strategy for creating XHTML documents, not to evaluate browser performance.

Netscape Navigator 1.22/Windows NT 4.0

The original HTML document looks fairly bad in this environment (see Figure 5-7). The script appears on the page. (This is one of the browsers that inspired hiding scripts in the comments approach described in Chapter 3.) Some of the formatting information, notably color, simply isn't supported. Because Netscape 1.22 doesn't support JavaScript, it doesn't run the script.

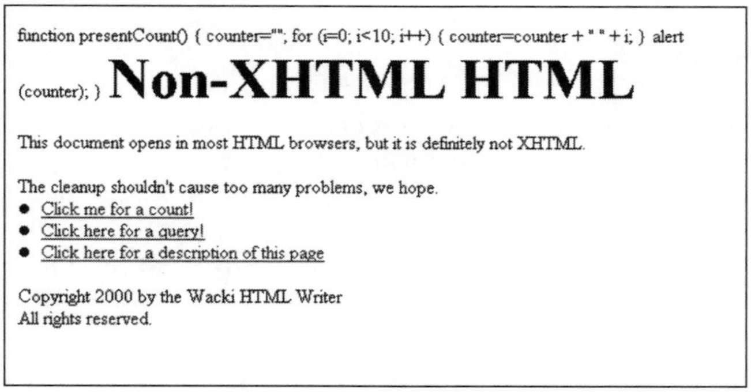

function presentCount() { counter=""; for (i=0; i<10; i++) { counter=counter + " " + i; } alert

(counter); } **Non-XHTML HTML**

This document opens in most HTML browsers, but it is definitely not XHTML.

The cleanup shouldn't cause too many problems, we hope.
- Click me for a count!
- Click here for a query!
- Click here for a description of this page

Copyright 2000 by the Wacki HTML Writer
All rights reserved.

Figure 5-7: The original HTML document

The transitional XHTML document looks a lot better (see Figure 5-8). The headline is a friendlier size. The CDATA section seems to hide the script successfully, but it doesn't run. Clicking the "Click me for a count!" link produces a 404 Not Found Error.

The revised transitional document looks exactly the same as its predecessor (refer to Figure 5-9). The script element's reference to an external script is ignored as was the CDATA section.

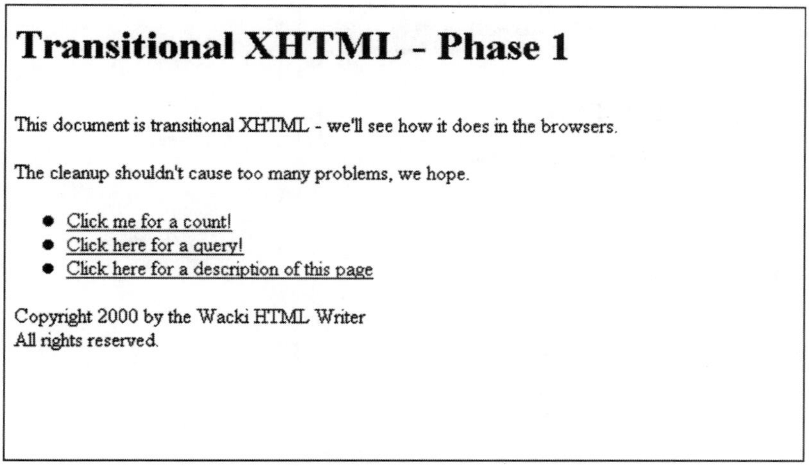

Transitional XHTML - Phase 1

This document is transitional XHTML - we'll see how it does in the browsers.

The cleanup shouldn't cause too many problems, we hope.

- Click me for a count!
- Click here for a query!
- Click here for a description of this page

Copyright 2000 by the Wacki HTML Writer
All rights reserved.

Figure 5-8: The transitional XHTML document

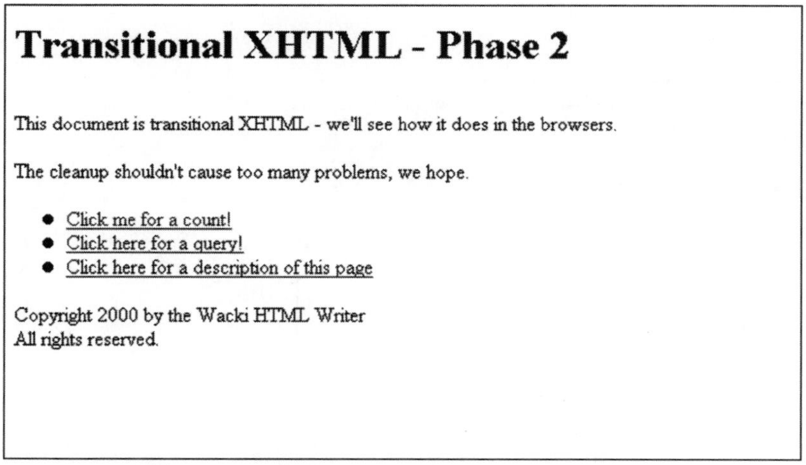

Transitional XHTML - Phase 2

This document is transitional XHTML - we'll see how it does in the browsers.

The cleanup shouldn't cause too many problems, we hope.

- Click me for a count!
- Click here for a query!
- Click here for a description of this page

Copyright 2000 by the Wacki HTML Writer
All rights reserved.

Figure 5-9: The revised transitional document

The strict HTML document shows off its CSS as well as the script (see Figure 5-10). The H1 headline is a little smaller than its FONT counterpart. Meanwhile, the "count" link that produced the 404 Not Found in the other versions is gone.

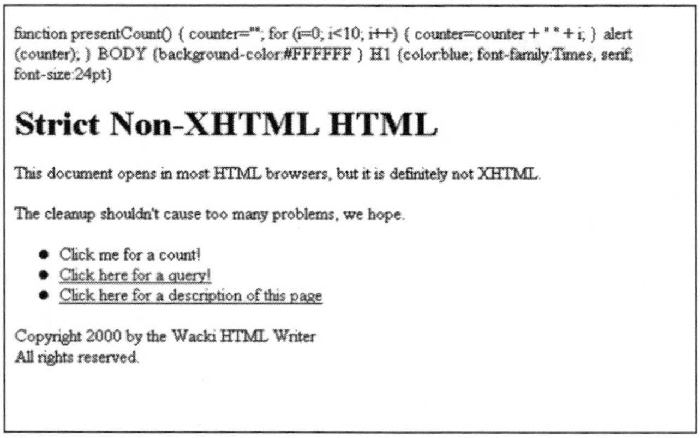

```
function presentCount() { counter=""; for (i=0; i<10; i++) { counter=counter + " " + i; } alert
(counter); } BODY {background-color:#FFFFFF } H1 {color:blue; font-family:Times, serif;
font-size:24pt)
```

Strict Non-XHTML HTML

This document opens in most HTML browsers, but it is definitely not XHTML.

The cleanup shouldn't cause too many problems, we hope.

- Click me for a count!
- Click here for a query!
- Click here for a description of this page

Copyright 2000 by the Wacki HTML Writer
All rights reserved.

Figure 5-10: The strict HTML document

The strict XHTML document looks pretty much like its HTML counterpart, except that the XML declaration appears as well as the script and style information (see Figure 5-11).

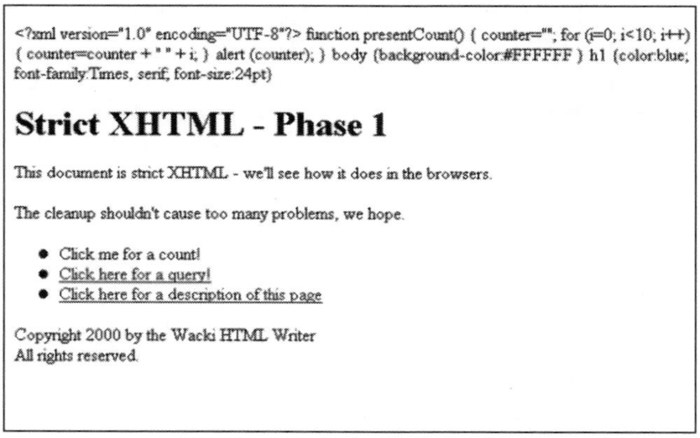

```
<?xml version="1.0" encoding="UTF-8"?> function presentCount() { counter=""; for (i=0; i<10; i++)
{ counter=counter + " " + i; } alert (counter); } body {background-color:#FFFFFF } h1 {color:blue;
font-family:Times, serif; font-size:24pt)
```

Strict XHTML - Phase 1

This document is strict XHTML - we'll see how it does in the browsers.

The cleanup shouldn't cause too many problems, we hope.

- Click me for a count!
- Click here for a query!
- Click here for a description of this page

Copyright 2000 by the Wacki HTML Writer
All rights reserved.

Figure 5-11: The strict XHTML document

The revised strict XHTML document looks much better, although the XML declaration still appears (refer to Figure 5-12). The script and style sheet are ignored.

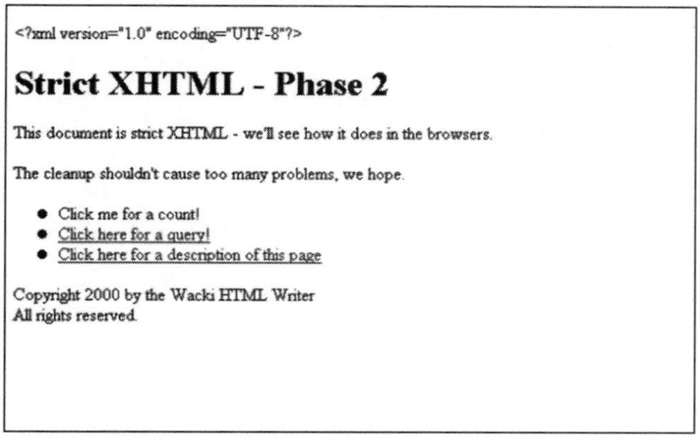

```
<?xml version="1.0" encoding="UTF-8"?>
```

Strict XHTML - Phase 2

This document is strict XHTML - we'll see how it does in the browsers.

The cleanup shouldn't cause too many problems, we hope.

- Click me for a count!
- Click here for a query!
- Click here for a description of this page

Copyright 2000 by the Wacki HTML Writer
All rights reserved.

Figure 5-12: The revised strict XHTML document

Netscape Navigator 2.02/Windows NT 4.0

The original HTML document looks okay and the script works just fine (see Figure 5-13).

Non-XHTML HTML

This document opens in most HTML browsers, but it is definitely not XHTML.

The cleanup shouldn't cause too many problems, we hope.
- Click me for a count!
- Click here for a query!
- Click here for a description of this page

Copyright 2000 by the Wacki HTML Writer
All rights reserved.

Figure 5-13: The original HTML document

The transitional XHTML document looks similar (the headline is a bit smaller), but now the script is broken (see Figure 5-14). The scripting engine chokes on the CDATA sections.

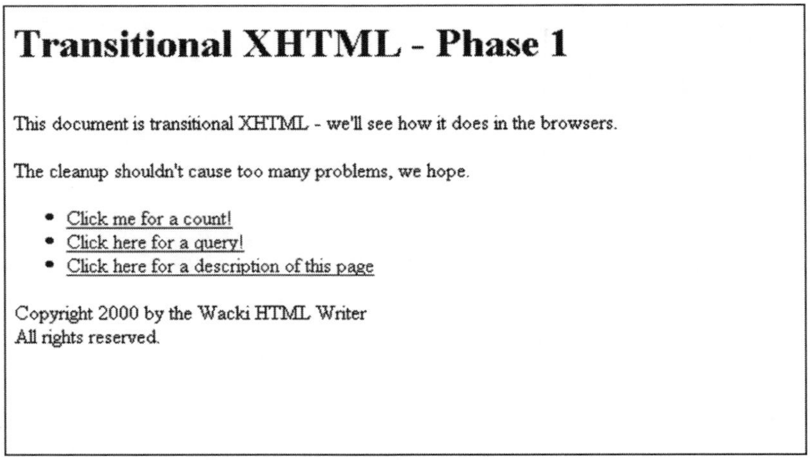

Transitional XHTML - Phase 1

This document is transitional XHTML - we'll see how it does in the browsers.

The cleanup shouldn't cause too many problems, we hope.

- Click me for a count!
- Click here for a query!
- Click here for a description of this page

Copyright 2000 by the Wacki HTML Writer
All rights reserved.

Figure 5-14: The transitional XHTML document

The revised transitional XHTML document looks fine, but the script doesn't work here either (refer to Figure 5-15). Netscape 2.02 doesn't support external script files.

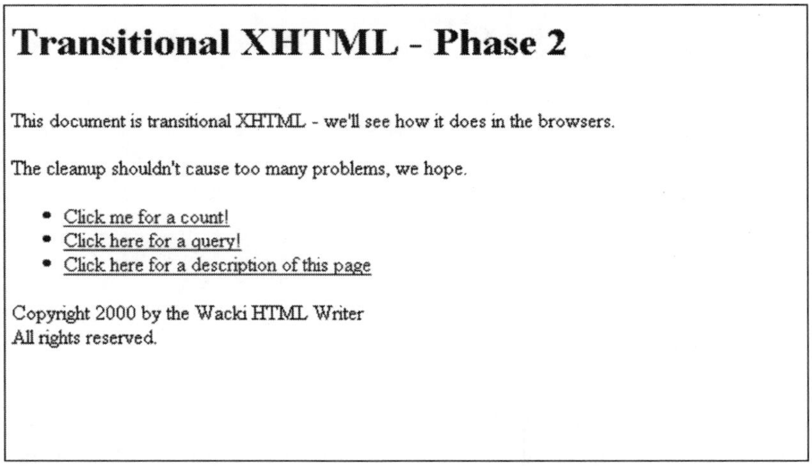

Transitional XHTML - Phase 2

This document is transitional XHTML - we'll see how it does in the browsers.

The cleanup shouldn't cause too many problems, we hope.

- Click me for a count!
- Click here for a query!
- Click here for a description of this page

Copyright 2000 by the Wacki HTML Writer
All rights reserved.

Figure 5-15: The revised transitional XHTML document

The strict HTML document doesn't include color for the headline, which appears a little smaller (see Figure 5-16). The "Click me for a count!" link is broken and the onclick attribute isn't recognized.

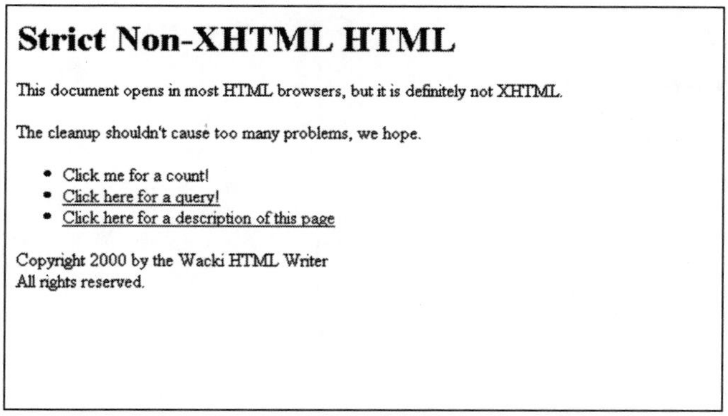

Strict Non-XHTML HTML

This document opens in most HTML browsers, but it is definitely not XHTML.

The cleanup shouldn't cause too many problems, we hope.

- Click me for a count!
- Click here for a query!
- Click here for a description of this page

Copyright 2000 by the Wacki HTML Writer
All rights reserved.

Figure 5-16: The strict HTML document

The strict XHTML document has lots of problems (see Figure 5-17). First, the XML declaration shows up and then the CSS style information appears. Again, the headline has no color and the script doesn't work, reporting an error about parentheses caused by the < entity in the `for` loop.

<?xml version="1.0" encoding="UTF-8"?> body {background-color:#FFFFFF } h1 {color:blue; font-family:Times, serif; font-size:24pt)

Strict XHTML - Phase 1

This document is strict XHTML - we'll see how it does in the browsers.

The cleanup shouldn't cause too many problems, we hope.

- Click me for a count!
- Click here for a query!
- Click here for a description of this page

Copyright 2000 by the Wacki HTML Writer
All rights reserved.

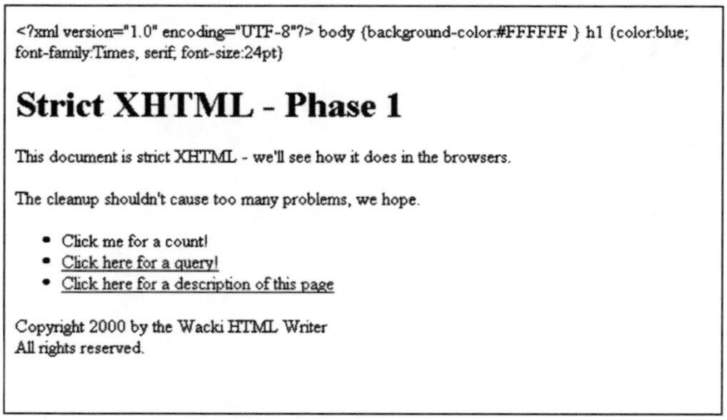

Figure 5-17: The strict XHTML document

The revised strict XHTML document looks a little better, although the XML declaration still shows up (see Figure 5-18). The scripting error disappears because the browser never loads the script; the CSS is not loaded either.

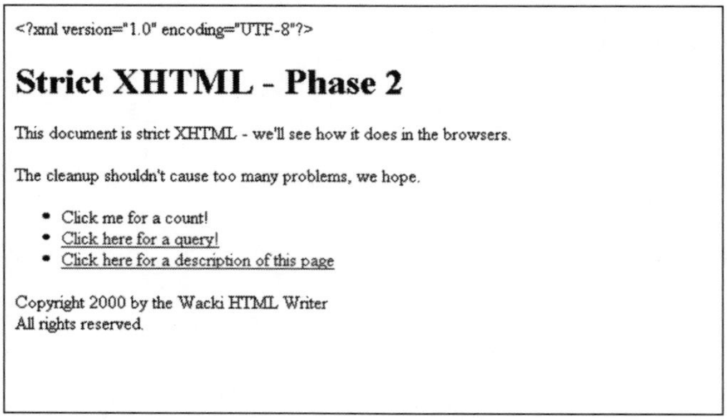

<?xml version="1.0" encoding="UTF-8"?>

Strict XHTML - Phase 2

This document is strict XHTML - we'll see how it does in the browsers.

The cleanup shouldn't cause too many problems, we hope.

- Click me for a count!
- Click here for a query!
- Click here for a description of this page

Copyright 2000 by the Wacki HTML Writer
All rights reserved.

Figure 5-18: The revised strict XHTML document

Netscape Navigator 3.0/Windows NT 4.0

The original HTML document looks and works just fine in this environment (refer to Figure 5-19).

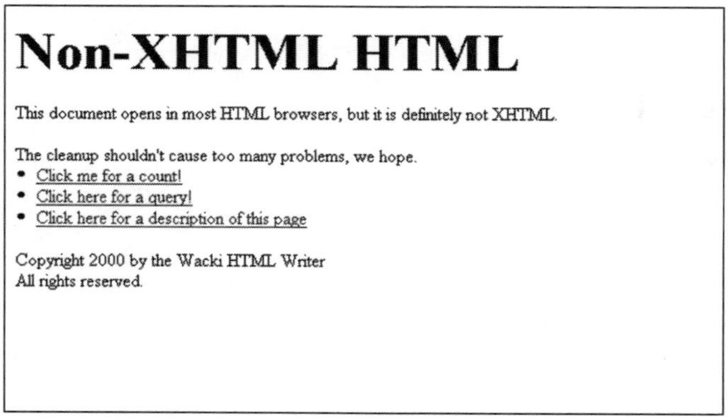

Non-XHTML HTML

This document opens in most HTML browsers, but it is definitely not XHTML.

The cleanup shouldn't cause too many problems, we hope.
- Click me for a count!
- Click here for a query!
- Click here for a description of this page

Copyright 2000 by the Wacki HTML Writer
All rights reserved.

Figure 5-19: The original HTML document

The transitional XHTML document reports an error during loading because of the CDATA section, but otherwise displays fine (see Figure 5-20).

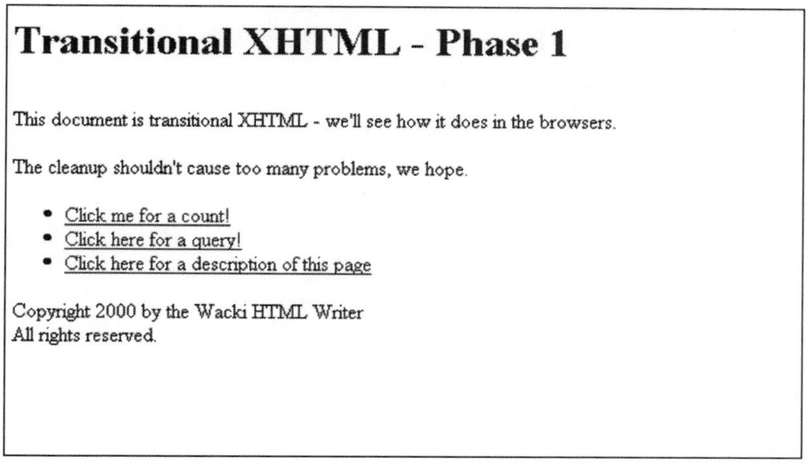

Transitional XHTML - Phase 1

This document is transitional XHTML - we'll see how it does in the browsers.

The cleanup shouldn't cause too many problems, we hope.

- Click me for a count!
- Click here for a query!
- Click here for a description of this page

Copyright 2000 by the Wacki HTML Writer
All rights reserved.

Figure 5-20: The transitional XHTML document

The revised transitional XHTML document only loads briefly and then is replaced by the script file, an apparent mishandling of the script element calling on an external file (see Figure 5-21).

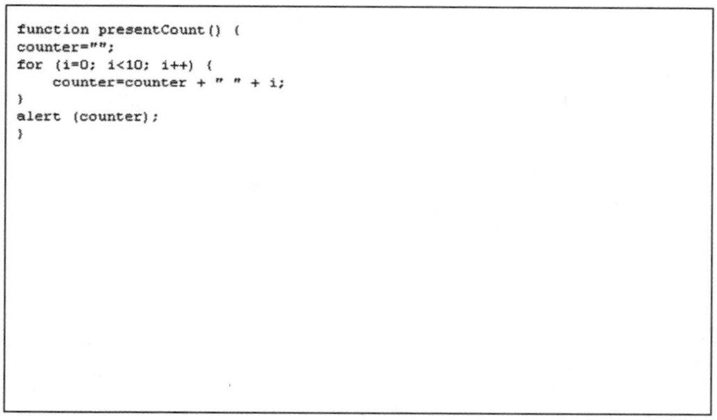

```
function presentCount() {
counter="";
for (i=0; i<10; i++) {
    counter=counter + " " + i;
}
alert (counter);
}
```

Figure 5-21: The revised transitional XHTML document

The strict HTML document looks okay, except that the headline goes black and is a little smaller (see Figure 5-22). Netscape 3.0 was released before cascading style sheets.

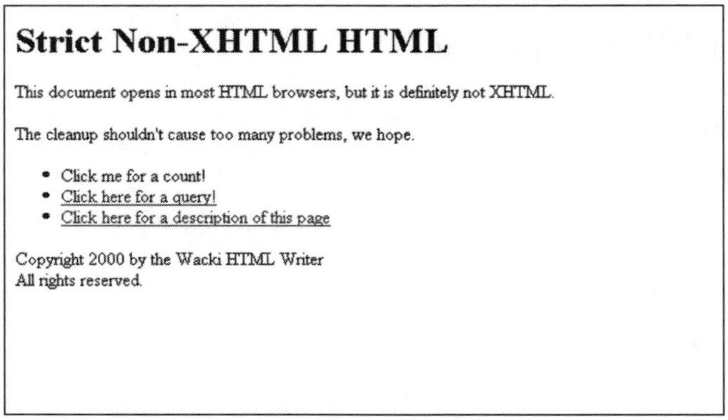

Strict Non-XHTML HTML

This document opens in most HTML browsers, but it is definitely not XHTML.

The cleanup shouldn't cause too many problems, we hope.

- Click me for a count!
- Click here for a query!
- Click here for a description of this page

Copyright 2000 by the Wacki HTML Writer
All rights reserved.

Figure 5-22: The strict HTML document

The strict XHTML document displays its XML declaration and style sheet contents, as well as reports an error about a missing parenthesis brought on by the < entity (see Figure 5-23).

<?xml version="1.0" encoding="UTF-8"?> body (background-color:#FFFFFF) h1 (color:blue; font-family:Times, serif, font-size:24pt)

Strict XHTML - Phase 1

This document is strict XHTML - we'll see how it does in the browsers.

The cleanup shouldn't cause too many problems, we hope.

- Click me for a count!
- Click here for a query!
- Click here for a description of this page

Copyright 2000 by the Wacki HTML Writer
All rights reserved.

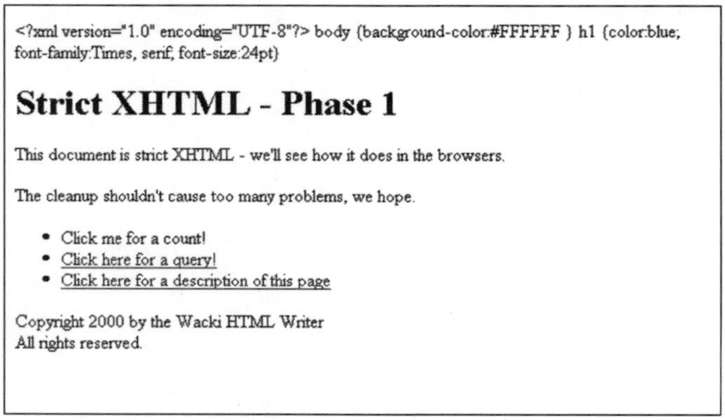

Figure 5-23: The strict XHTML document

The revised strict XHTML document only loads briefly and then is replaced by the script file, falling to the same bug that prevented the revised transitional XHTML document from loading (refer to Figure 5-24).

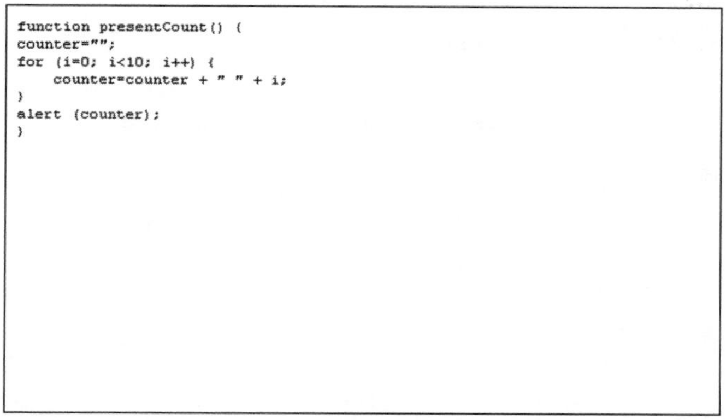

```
function presentCount() {
counter="";
for (i=0; i<10; i++) {
    counter=counter + " " + i;
}
alert (counter);
}
```

Figure 5-24: The revised strict XHTML document

Netscape Communicator 4.7/Windows NT 4.0

The original HTML document looks and works just fine in this environment (see Figure 5-25).

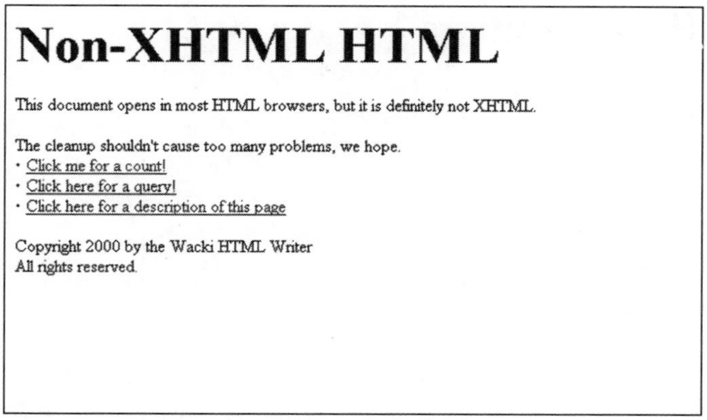

Non-XHTML HTML

This document opens in most HTML browsers, but it is definitely not XHTML.

The cleanup shouldn't cause too many problems, we hope.
· Click me for a count!
· Click here for a query!
· Click here for a description of this page

Copyright 2000 by the Wacki HTML Writer
All rights reserved.

Figure 5-25: The original HTML document

The transitional XHTML document looks fine, but the script doesn't work anymore (see Figure 5-26). No error is reported, however.

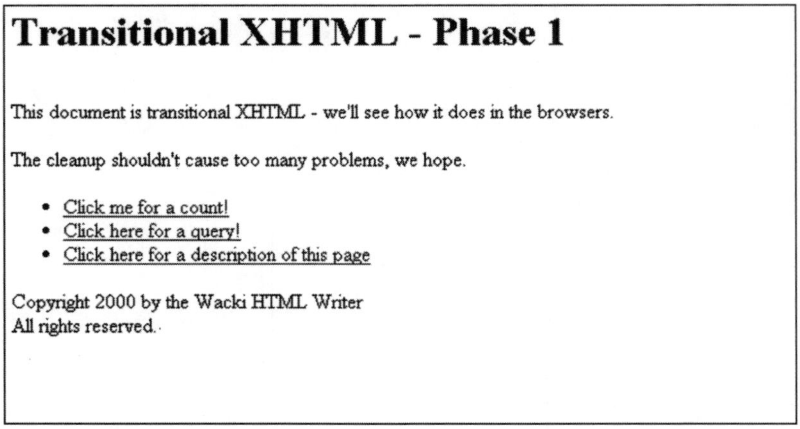

Figure 5-26: The transitional XHTML document

The revised transitional XHTML document looks and works just fine (see Figure 5-27).

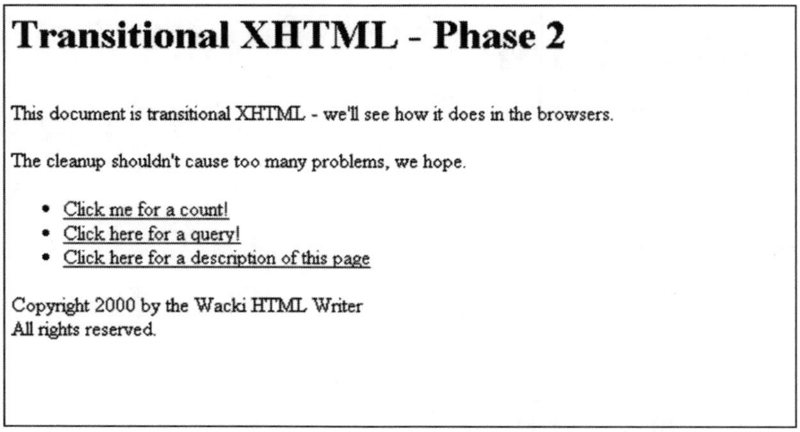

Figure 5-27: The revised transitional XHTML document

The strict HTML document looks okay, although the headline rendering is sized differently (see Figure 5-28). The counting script doesn't work because Communicator doesn't support the onclick attribute for connecting the script to the text.

The strict XHTML document looks like its predecessor HTML document. The counting script still doesn't work (refer to Figure 5-29).

The revised strict XHTML document again looks like its predecessor HTML document. The counting script still doesn't work (see Figure 5-30).

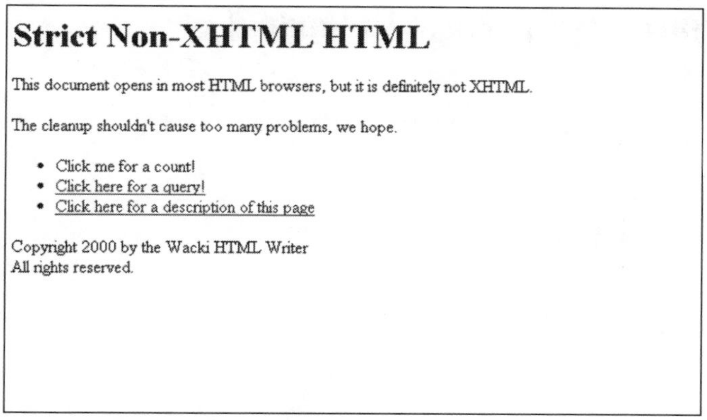

Strict Non-XHTML HTML

This document opens in most HTML browsers, but it is definitely not XHTML.

The cleanup shouldn't cause too many problems, we hope.

- Click me for a count!
- Click here for a query!
- Click here for a description of this page

Copyright 2000 by the Wacki HTML Writer
All rights reserved.

Figure 5-28: The strict HTML document

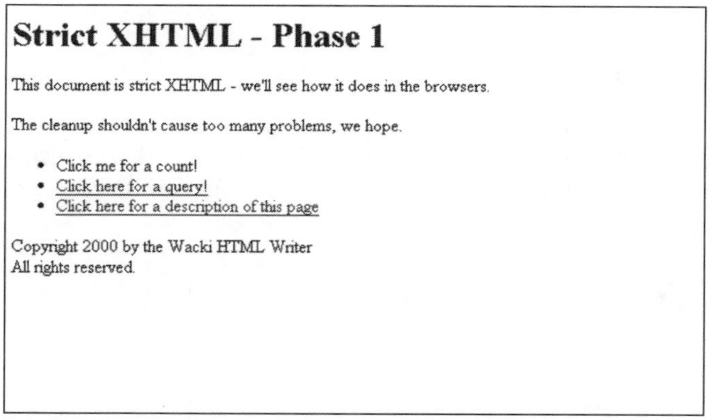

Strict XHTML - Phase 1

This document is strict XHTML - we'll see how it does in the browsers.

The cleanup shouldn't cause too many problems, we hope.

- Click me for a count!
- Click here for a query!
- Click here for a description of this page

Copyright 2000 by the Wacki HTML Writer
All rights reserved.

Figure 5-29: The strict XHTML document

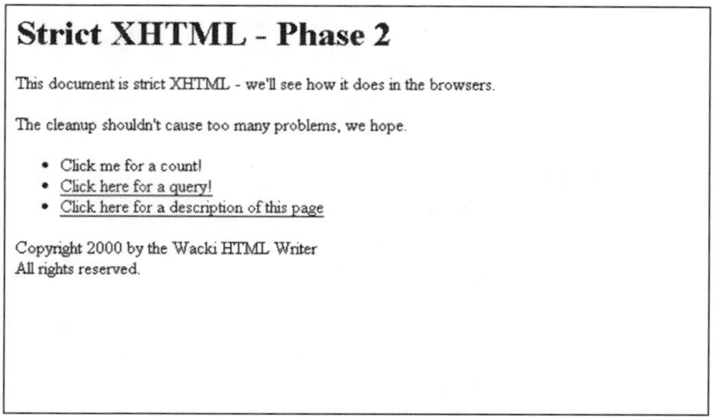

Strict XHTML - Phase 2

This document is strict XHTML - we'll see how it does in the browsers.

The cleanup shouldn't cause too many problems, we hope.

- Click me for a count!
- Click here for a query!
- Click here for a description of this page

Copyright 2000 by the Wacki HTML Writer
All rights reserved.

Figure 5-30: The revised strict XHTML document

Netscape Navigator 6 Preview Release 1/ Windows NT 4.0

The original HTML document displays fine and the script works (see Figure 5-31).

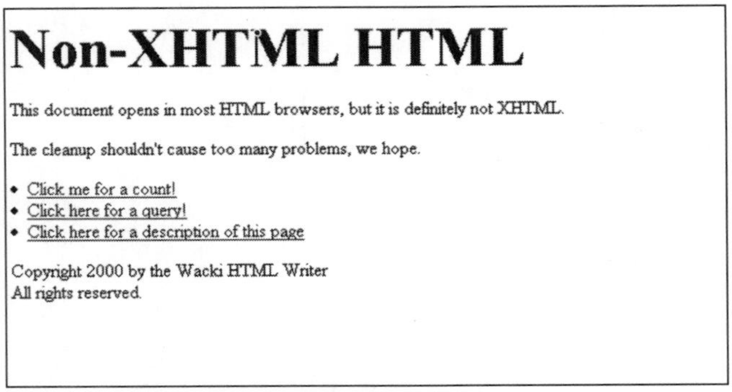

Non-XHTML HTML

This document opens in most HTML browsers, but it is definitely not XHTML.

The cleanup shouldn't cause too many problems, we hope.

- Click me for a count!
- Click here for a query!
- Click here for a description of this page

Copyright 2000 by the Wacki HTML Writer
All rights reserved.

Figure 5-31: The original HTML document

The transitional XHTML document displays fine, but clicking the link to execute the script produces an error brought on by the CDATA section (refer to Figure 5-32).

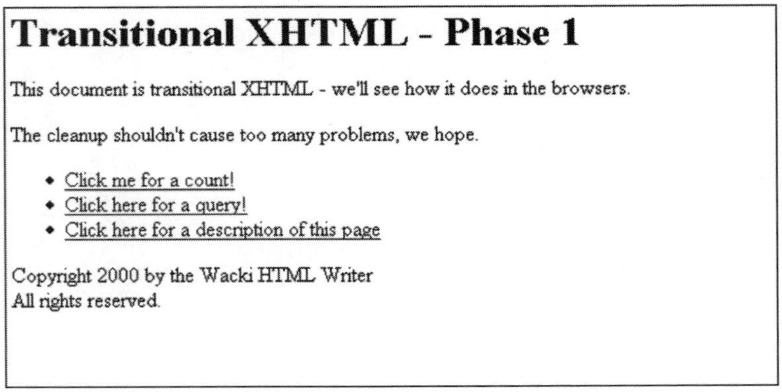

Transitional XHTML - Phase 1

This document is transitional XHTML - we'll see how it does in the browsers.

The cleanup shouldn't cause too many problems, we hope.

- Click me for a count!
- Click here for a query!
- Click here for a description of this page

Copyright 2000 by the Wacki HTML Writer
All rights reserved.

Figure 5-32: The transitional XHTML document

The revised transitional XHTML document works just fine. Moving the script out of the main file brings it back (see Figure 5-33).

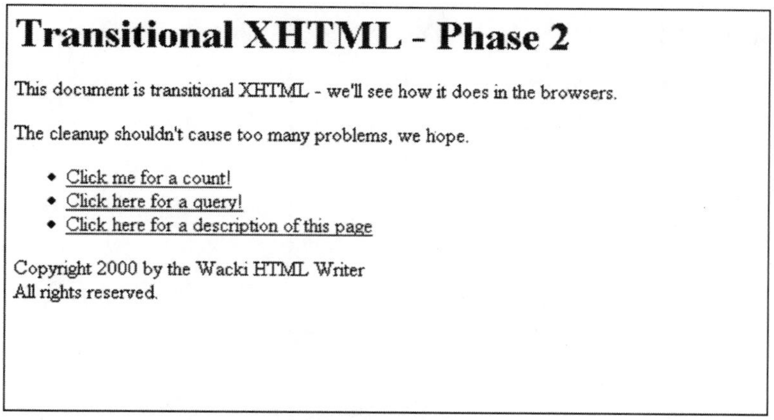

Transitional XHTML - Phase 2

This document is transitional XHTML - we'll see how it does in the browsers.

The cleanup shouldn't cause too many problems, we hope.

- Click me for a count!
- Click here for a query!
- Click here for a description of this page

Copyright 2000 by the Wacki HTML Writer
All rights reserved.

Figure 5-33: The revised transitional XHTML document

The strict HTML document looks and works fine, although the headline looks a bit different (see Figure 5-34). The script does run when you click the "Click here for a count!" text.

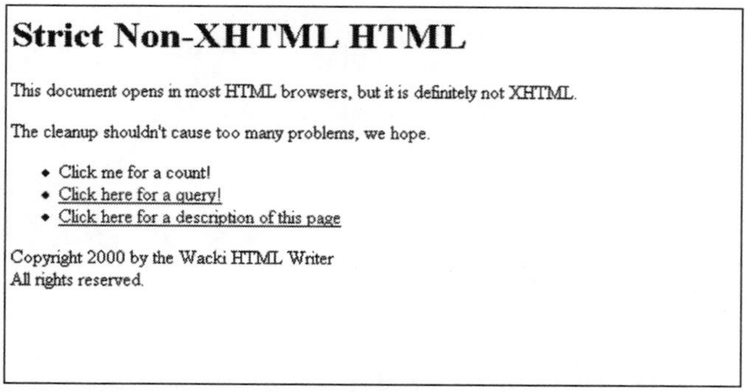

Strict Non-XHTML HTML

This document opens in most HTML browsers, but it is definitely not XHTML.

The cleanup shouldn't cause too many problems, we hope.

- Click me for a count!
- Click here for a query!
- Click here for a description of this page

Copyright 2000 by the Wacki HTML Writer
All rights reserved.

Figure 5-34: The strict HTML document

The strict XHTML document looks and works fine, although the scripting engine doesn't like the < entity reference any more than it likes the CDATA section so it doesn't run the script (see Figure 5-35).

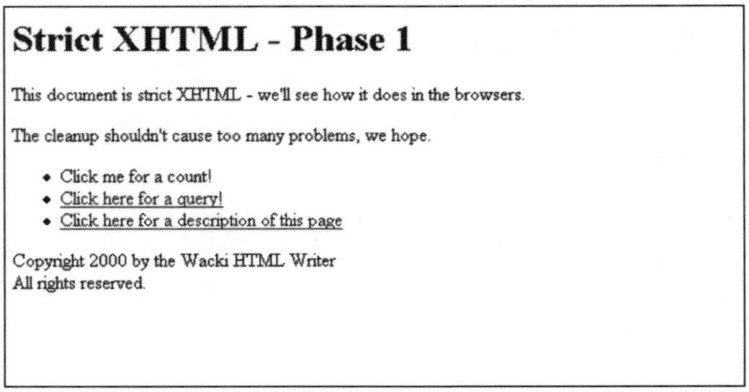

Strict XHTML - Phase 1

This document is strict XHTML - we'll see how it does in the browsers.

The cleanup shouldn't cause too many problems, we hope.

- Click me for a count!
- Click here for a query!
- Click here for a description of this page

Copyright 2000 by the Wacki HTML Writer
All rights reserved.

Figure 5-35: The strict XHTML document

The revised strict XHTML document looks and works fine (see Figure 5-36). The script runs when you click the text.

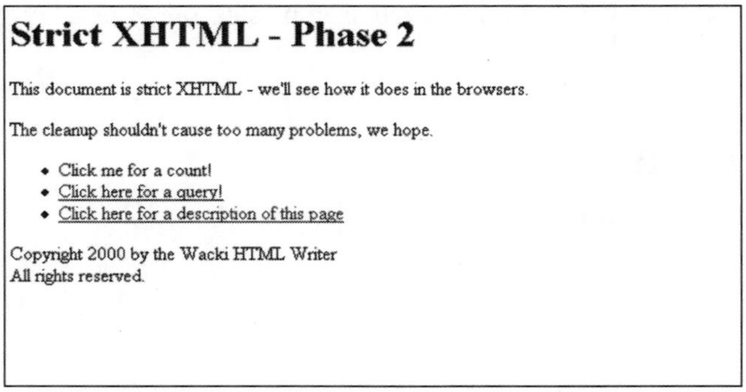

Strict XHTML - Phase 2

This document is strict XHTML - we'll see how it does in the browsers.

The cleanup shouldn't cause too many problems, we hope.

- Click me for a count!
- Click here for a query!
- Click here for a description of this page

Copyright 2000 by the Wacki HTML Writer
All rights reserved.

Figure 5-36: The revised strict XHTML document

Internet Explorer 3.01/MacOS 8.1

The original HTML document looks and works fine in this environment (see Figure 5-37).

The transitional XHTML document looks okay, but the browser reports a script compilation error and doesn't run the counting script because of the CDATA section (refer to Figure 5-38).

The revised transitional XHTML document looks fine, but the script doesn't run (see Figure 5-39). This version of Internet Explorer is too old to support external script files.

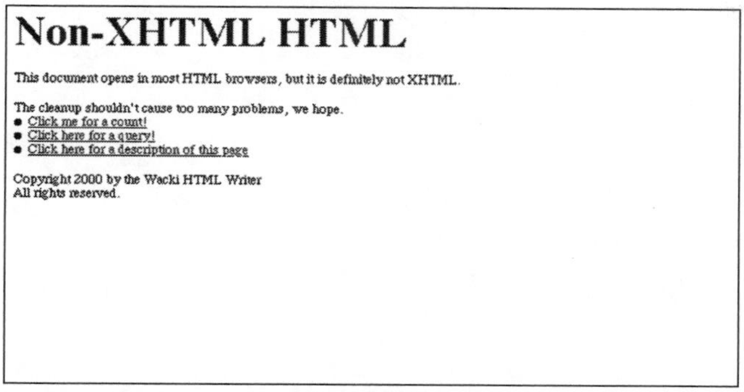

Non-XHTML HTML

This document opens in most HTML browsers, but it is definitely not XHTML.

The cleanup shouldn't cause too many problems, we hope.
- Click me for a count!
- Click here for a query!
- Click here for a description of this page

Copyright 2000 by the Wacki HTML Writer
All rights reserved.

Figure 5-37: The original HTML document

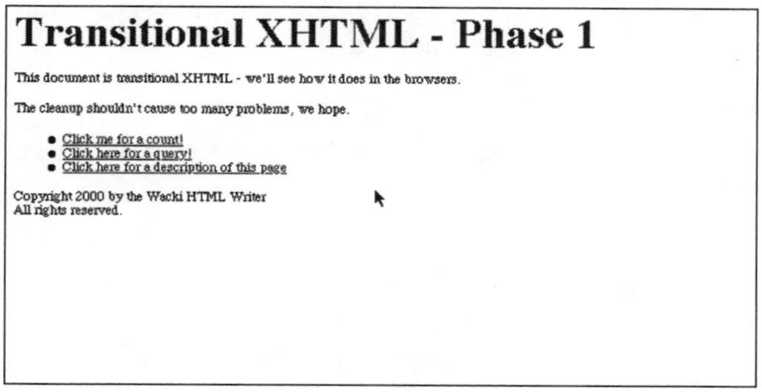

Transitional XHTML - Phase 1

This document is transitional XHTML - we'll see how it does in the browsers.

The cleanup shouldn't cause too many problems, we hope.

- Click me for a count!
- Click here for a query!
- Click here for a description of this page

Copyright 2000 by the Wacki HTML Writer
All rights reserved.

Figure 5-38: The transitional XHTML document

Transitional XHTML - Phase 2

This document is transitional XHTML - we'll see how it does in the browsers.

The cleanup shouldn't cause too many problems, we hope.

- Click me for a count!
- Click here for a query!
- Click here for a description of this page

Copyright 2000 by the Wacki HTML Writer
All rights reserved.

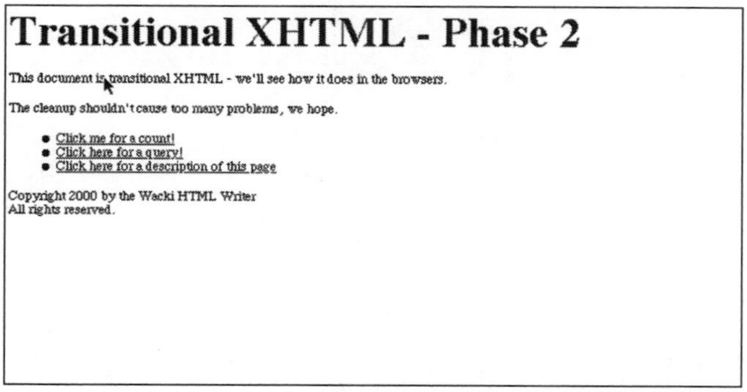

Figure 5-39: The revised transitional XHTML document

The strict HTML document presents a different-looking headline and a gray background (see Figure 5-40). The script doesn't run because the `onclick` attribute isn't supported.

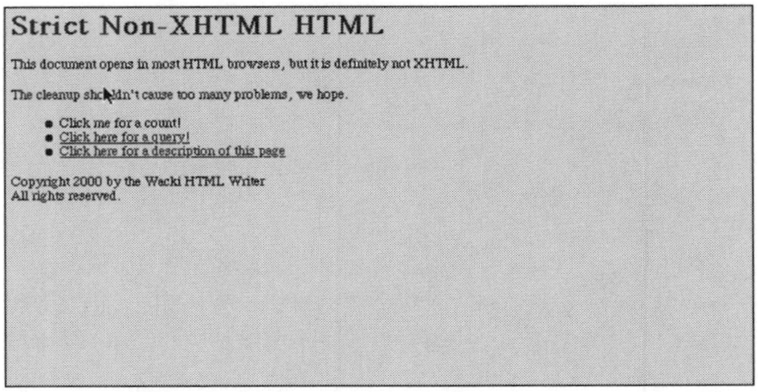

Strict Non-XHTML HTML

This document opens in most HTML browsers, but it is definitely not XHTML.

The cleanup shouldn't cause too many problems, we hope.

- Click me for a count!
- Click here for a query!
- Click here for a description of this page

Copyright 2000 by the Wacki HTML Writer
All rights reserved.

Figure 5-40: The strict HTML document

The strict XHTML document looks like the strict HTML document, except that the XML declaration appears at the top of the page and a compilation error is reported when the page loads (refer to Figure 5-41).

The revised strict XHTML document doesn't report a compilation error — it ignores the external script file — but it also displays the XML declaration at the top of the page (see Figure 5-42).

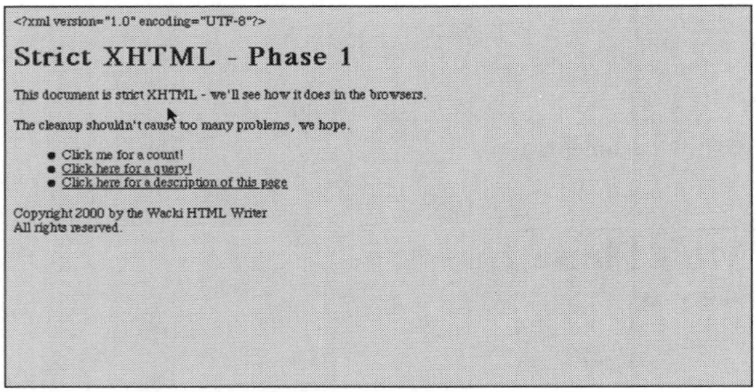

```
<?xml version="1.0" encoding="UTF-8"?>
```

Strict XHTML - Phase 1

This document is strict XHTML - we'll see how it does in the browsers.

The cleanup shouldn't cause too many problems, we hope.

- Click me for a count!
- Click here for a query!
- Click here for a description of this page

Copyright 2000 by the Wacki HTML Writer
All rights reserved.

Figure 5-41: The strict XHTML document

```
<?xml version="1.0" encoding="UTF-8"?>
```

Strict XHTML - Phase 2

This document is strict XHTML - we'll see how it does in the browsers.

The cleanup shouldn't cause too many problems, we hope.

- Click me for a count!
- Click here for a query!
- Click here for a description of this page

Copyright 2000 by the Wacki HTML Writer
All rights reserved.

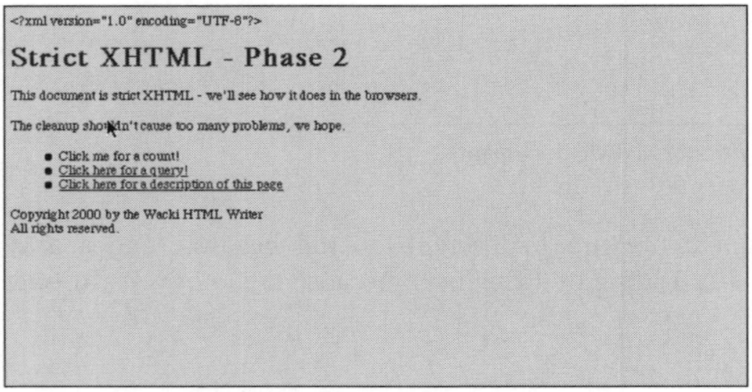

Figure 5-42: The revised strict XHTML document

Microsoft Internet Explorer 4.0/MacOS 8.1

The original HTML document looks and works just fine in this environment (see Figure 5-43).

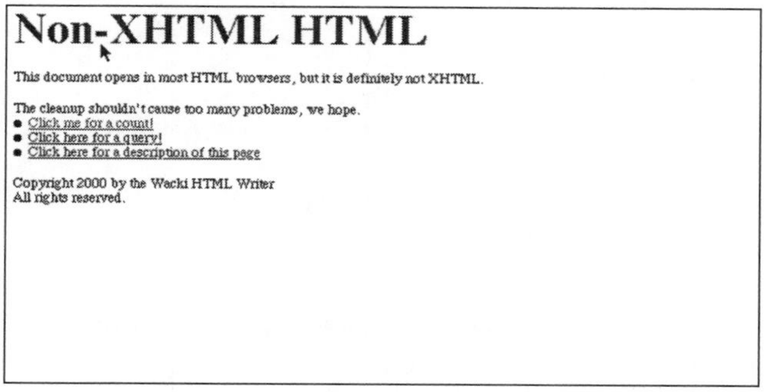

Non-XHTML HTML

This document opens in most HTML browsers, but it is definitely not XHTML.

The cleanup shouldn't cause too many problems, we hope.
- Click me for a count!
- Click here for a query!
- Click here for a description of this page

Copyright 2000 by the Wacki HTML Writer
All rights reserved.

Figure 5-43: The original HTML document

The transitional XHTML document looks fine, but the script reports a compilation error because of the CDATA section (refer to Figure 5-44).

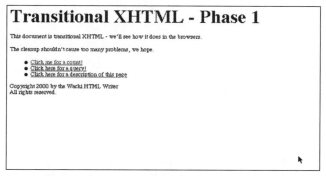

Transitional XHTML - Phase 1

This document is transitional XHTML - we'll see how it does in the browsers.

The cleanup shouldn't cause too many problems, we hope.

- Click me for a count!
- Click here for a query!
- Click here for a description of this page

Copyright 2000 by the Wacki HTML Writer
All rights reserved.

Figure 5-44: The transitional XHTML document

The revised transitional XHTML document looks and works fine (see Figure 5-45).

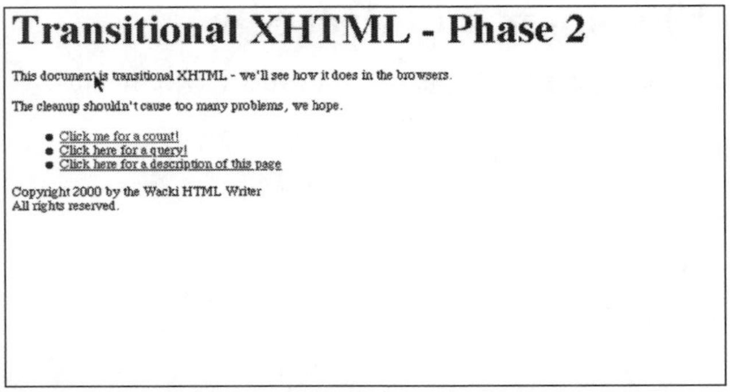

Transitional XHTML - Phase 2

This document is transitional XHTML - we'll see how it does in the browsers.

The cleanup shouldn't cause too many problems, we hope.

- Click me for a count!
- Click here for a query!
- Click here for a description of this page

Copyright 2000 by the Wacki HTML Writer
All rights reserved.

Figure 5-45: The revised transitional XHTML document

The strict HTML document has a different-looking headline, but the script works just fine when you click "Click here for a count!" (see Figure 5-46).

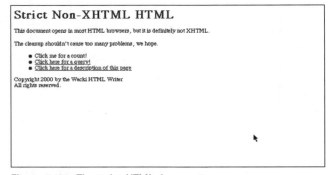

Strict Non-XHTML HTML

This document opens in most HTML browsers, but it is definitely not XHTML.

The cleanup shouldn't cause too many problems, we hope.

- Click me for a count!
- Click here for a query!
- Click here for a description of this page

Copyright 2000 by the Wacki HTML Writer
All rights reserved.

Figure 5-46: The strict HTML document

The strict XHTML document looks like the strict HTML document, but it reports a script compilation error because of the < entity (refer to Figure 5-47).

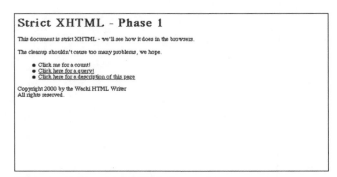

Strict XHTML - Phase 1

This document is strict XHTML - we'll see how it does in the browsers.

The cleanup shouldn't cause too many problems, we hope.

- Click me for a count!
- Click here for a query!
- Click here for a description of this page

Copyright 2000 by the Wacki HTML Writer
All rights reserved.

Figure 5-47: The strict XHTML document

The revised strict XHTML document looks like the strict HTML document and the script works once again (see Figure 5-48).

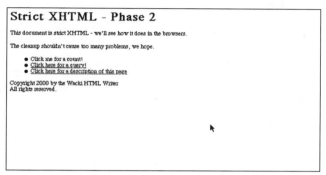

Figure 5-48: The revised strict XHTML document

Microsoft Internet Explorer 4.01/Windows 95

The original HTML document looks and works fine in this environment (refer to Figure 5-49).

Figure 5-49: The original HTML document

The transitional XHTML document looks fine, but it reports an error compiling the JavaScript code because of the CDATA section (see Figure 5-50).

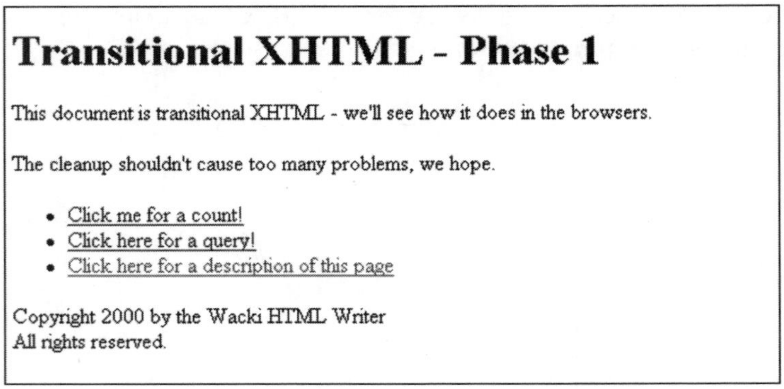

Transitional XHTML - Phase 1

This document is transitional XHTML - we'll see how it does in the browsers.

The cleanup shouldn't cause too many problems, we hope.

- Click me for a count!
- Click here for a query!
- Click here for a description of this page

Copyright 2000 by the Wacki HTML Writer
All rights reserved.

Figure 5-50: The transitional XHTML document

The revised transitional XHTML document looks and works perfectly fine (see Figure 5-51).

The strict HTML document is almost the same, except with a slightly smaller headline (see Figure 5-52). The script works.

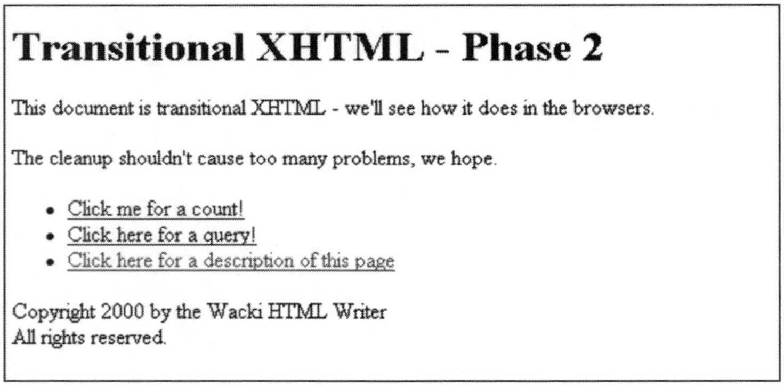

Transitional XHTML - Phase 2

This document is transitional XHTML - we'll see how it does in the browsers.

The cleanup shouldn't cause too many problems, we hope.

- Click me for a count!
- Click here for a query!
- Click here for a description of this page

Copyright 2000 by the Wacki HTML Writer
All rights reserved.

Figure 5-51: The revised transitional XHTML document

Strict Non-XHTML HTML

This document opens in most HTML browsers, but it is definitely not XHTML.

The cleanup shouldn't cause too many problems, we hope.

- Click me for a count!
- Click here for a query!
- Click here for a description of this page

Copyright 2000 by the Wacki HTML Writer
All rights reserved.

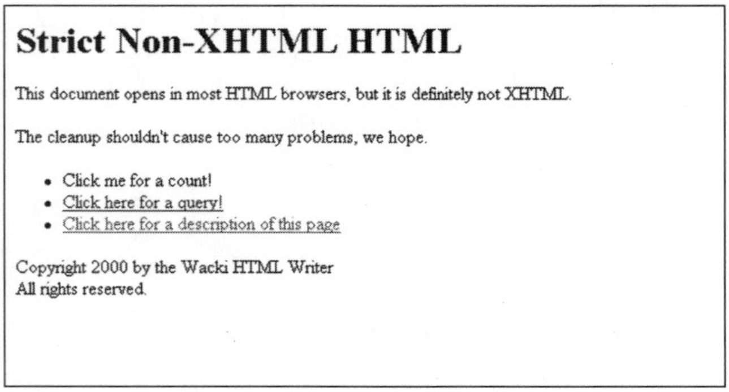

Figure 5-52: The strict HTML document

The strict XHTML document looks like the strict HTML document, but the script doesn't work, and the link disappears as well, because we've taken a different approach (see Figure 5-53).

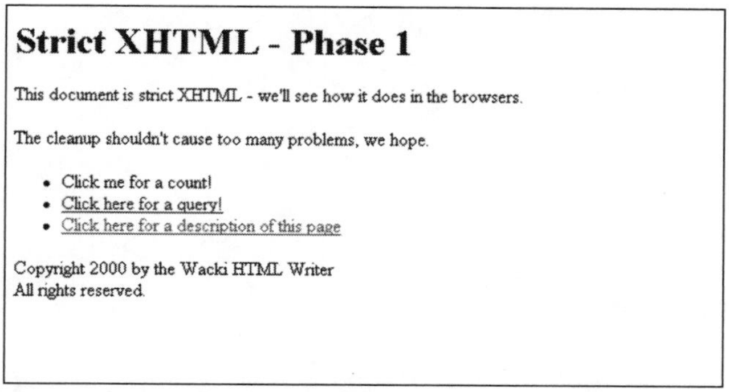

Strict XHTML - Phase 1

This document is strict XHTML - we'll see how it does in the browsers.

The cleanup shouldn't cause too many problems, we hope.

- Click me for a count!
- Click here for a query!
- Click here for a description of this page

Copyright 2000 by the Wacki HTML Writer
All rights reserved.

Figure 5-53: The strict XHTML document

The revised strict XHTML document looks and works like the strict HTML document (refer to Figure 5-54).

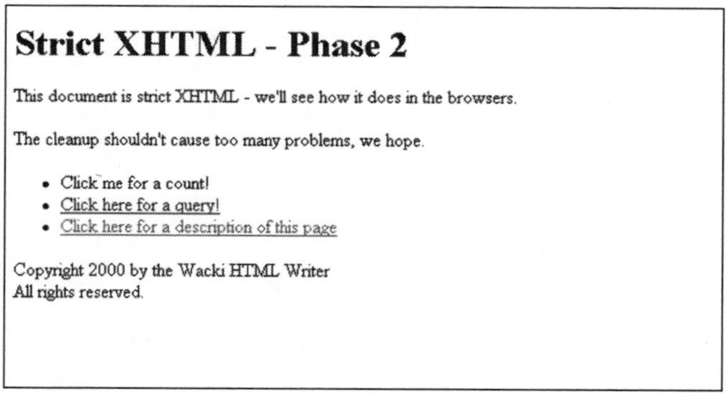

Strict XHTML - Phase 2

This document is strict XHTML - we'll see how it does in the browsers.

The cleanup shouldn't cause too many problems, we hope.

- Click me for a count!
- Click here for a query!
- Click here for a description of this page

Copyright 2000 by the Wacki HTML Writer
All rights reserved.

Figure 5-54: The revised strict XHTML document

Microsoft Internet Explorer 5.01/Windows NT 4.0

The original HTML document looks and works fine, although the description link is marked read because it connects to the same page (refer to Figure 5-55).

The transitional XHTML document looks like the original HTML document (see Figure 5-56). The script doesn't produce an error when the page is loaded, but it doesn't run.

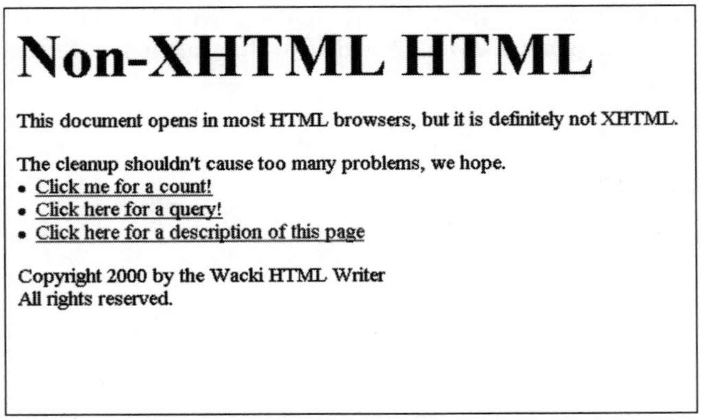

Non-XHTML HTML

This document opens in most HTML browsers, but it is definitely not XHTML.

The cleanup shouldn't cause too many problems, we hope.
- Click me for a count!
- Click here for a query!
- Click here for a description of this page

Copyright 2000 by the Wacki HTML Writer
All rights reserved.

Figure 5-55: The original HTML document

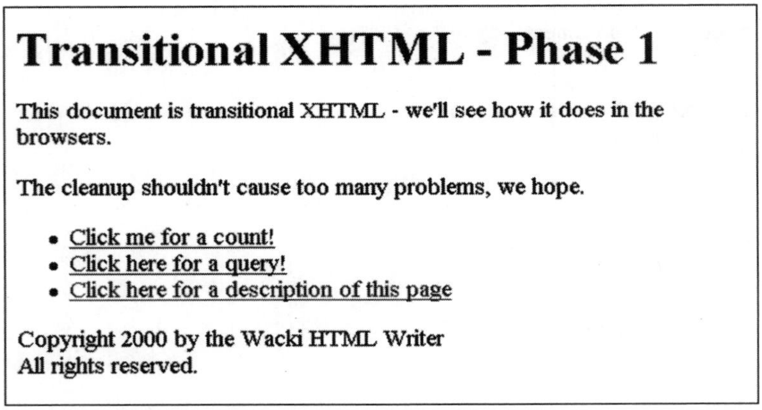

Transitional XHTML - Phase 1

This document is transitional XHTML - we'll see how it does in the browsers.

The cleanup shouldn't cause too many problems, we hope.

- Click me for a count!
- Click here for a query!
- Click here for a description of this page

Copyright 2000 by the Wacki HTML Writer
All rights reserved.

Figure 5-56: The transitional XHTML document

The revised transitional XHTML document looks fine and the script runs fine (see Figure 5-57).

The strict HTML document has a different-looking headline, but otherwise everything works fine (see Figure 5-58).

The strict XHTML document looks like the strict HTML document, but the script produces an error message because of the < entity reference (refer to Figure 5-59).

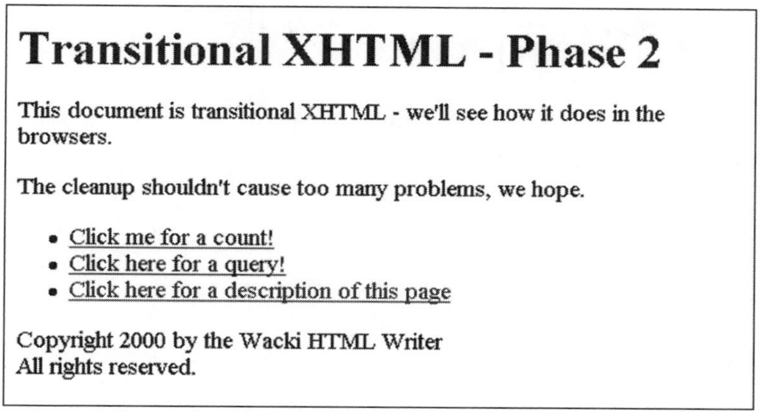

Transitional XHTML - Phase 2

This document is transitional XHTML - we'll see how it does in the browsers.

The cleanup shouldn't cause too many problems, we hope.

- Click me for a count!
- Click here for a query!
- Click here for a description of this page

Copyright 2000 by the Wacki HTML Writer
All rights reserved.

Figure 5-57: The revised transitional XHTML document

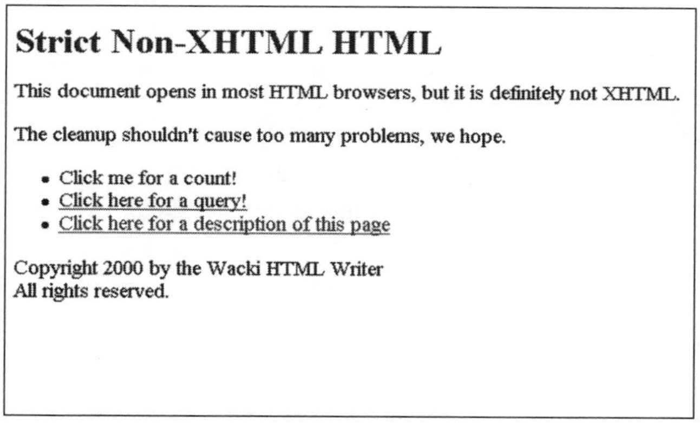

Strict Non-XHTML HTML

This document opens in most HTML browsers, but it is definitely not XHTML.

The cleanup shouldn't cause too many problems, we hope.

- Click me for a count!
- Click here for a query!
- Click here for a description of this page

Copyright 2000 by the Wacki HTML Writer
All rights reserved.

Figure 5-58: The strict HTML document

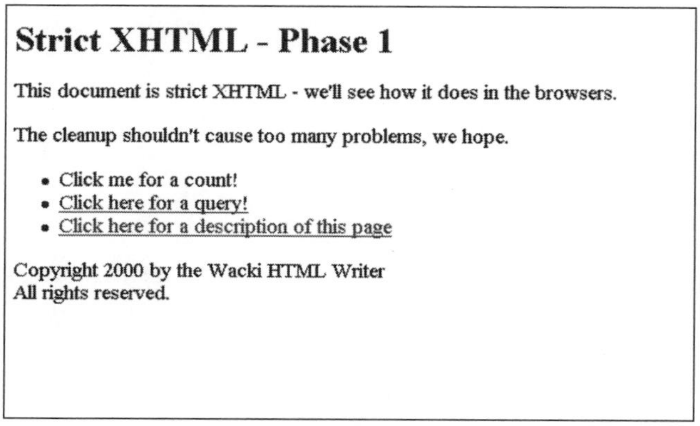

Strict XHTML - Phase 1

This document is strict XHTML - we'll see how it does in the browsers.

The cleanup shouldn't cause too many problems, we hope.

- Click me for a count!
- Click here for a query!
- Click here for a description of this page

Copyright 2000 by the Wacki HTML Writer
All rights reserved.

Figure 5-59: The strict XHTML document

The revised strict XHTML document looks like the strict HTML document and the script works fine (see Figure 5-60).

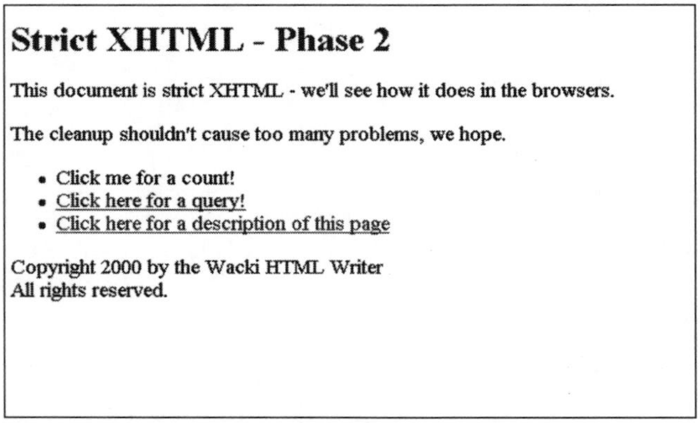

Strict XHTML - Phase 2

This document is strict XHTML - we'll see how it does in the browsers.

The cleanup shouldn't cause too many problems, we hope.

- Click me for a count!
- Click here for a query!
- Click here for a description of this page

Copyright 2000 by the Wacki HTML Writer
All rights reserved.

Figure 5-60: The revised strict XHTML document

Opera 3.62/Windows NT

The original HTML document mostly looks fine, except that the last paragraph is formatted more like a list item because of the missing end tag for the UL element (see Figure 5-61). The script works.

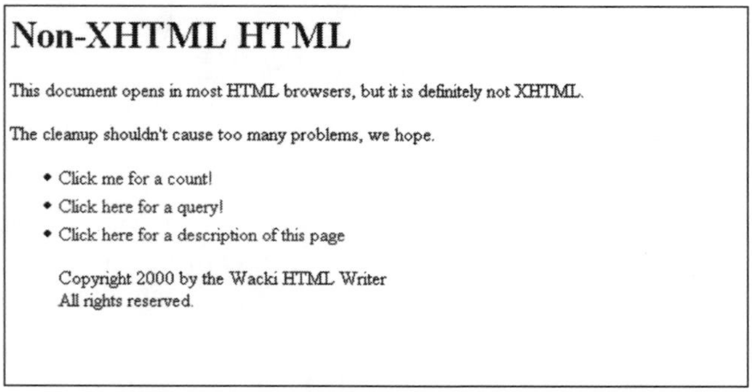

Non-XHTML HTML

This document opens in most HTML browsers, but it is definitely not XHTML.

The cleanup shouldn't cause too many problems, we hope.

- Click me for a count!
- Click here for a query!
- Click here for a description of this page

    Copyright 2000 by the Wacki HTML Writer
    All rights reserved.

Figure 5-61: The original HTML document

The transitional XHTML document looks cleaner than the original HTML, having fixed the list item formatting (see Figure 5-62). The JavaScript engine, however, chokes on the CDATA section and reports an execution failure.

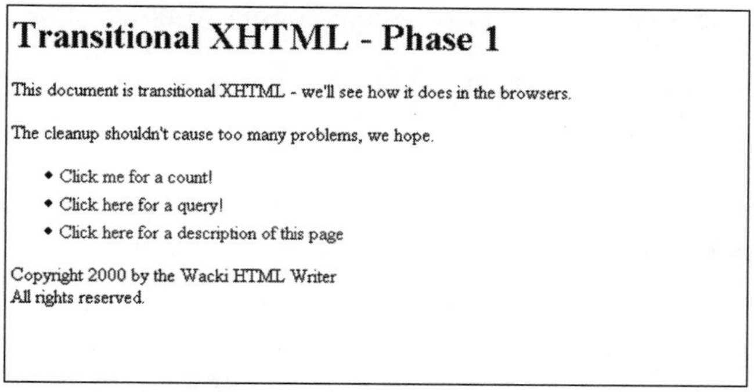

Transitional XHTML - Phase 1

This document is transitional XHTML - we'll see how it does in the browsers.

The cleanup shouldn't cause too many problems, we hope.

- Click me for a count!
- Click here for a query!
- Click here for a description of this page

Copyright 2000 by the Wacki HTML Writer
All rights reserved.

Figure 5-62: The transitional XHTML document

The revised transitional XHTML document looks and works just fine (see Figure 5-63).

The strict HTML document looks fine, but the script doesn't work because Opera doesn't support the `onclick` attribute (refer to Figure 5-64).

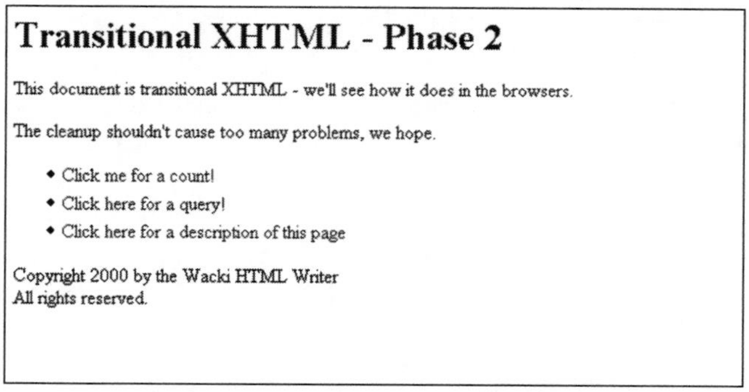

Transitional XHTML - Phase 2

This document is transitional XHTML - we'll see how it does in the browsers.

The cleanup shouldn't cause too many problems, we hope.

- Click me for a count!
- Click here for a query!
- Click here for a description of this page

Copyright 2000 by the Wacki HTML Writer
All rights reserved.

Figure 5-63: The revised transitional XHTML document

Strict Non-XHTML HTML

This document opens in most HTML browsers, but it is definitely not XHTML.

The cleanup shouldn't cause too many problems, we hope.

- Click me for a count!
- Click here for a query!
- Click here for a description of this page

Copyright 2000 by the Wacki HTML Writer
All rights reserved.

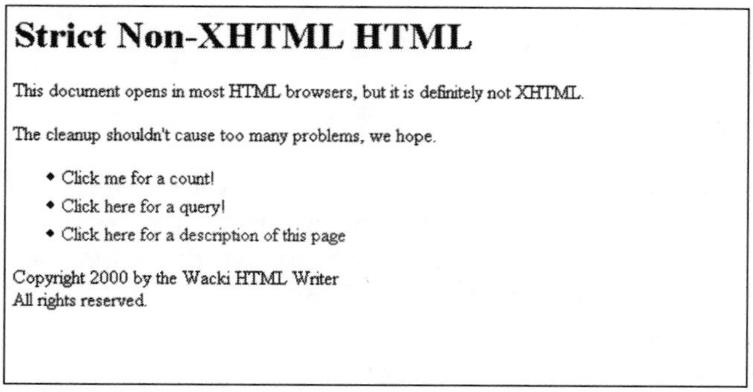

Figure 5-64: The strict HTML document

The strict XHTML document looks fine, but the script doesn't work again (see Figure 5-65).

The revised strict XHTML document looks fine, but the script still doesn't work (refer to Figure 5-66).

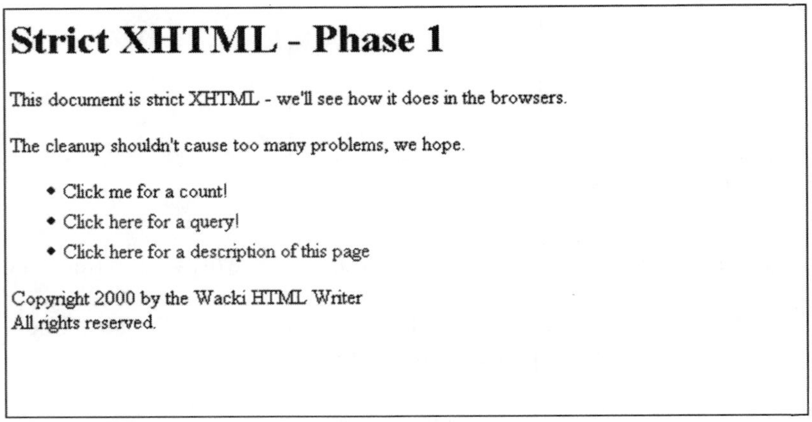

Strict XHTML - Phase 1

This document is strict XHTML - we'll see how it does in the browsers.

The cleanup shouldn't cause too many problems, we hope.

- Click me for a count!
- Click here for a query!
- Click here for a description of this page

Copyright 2000 by the Wacki HTML Writer
All rights reserved.

Figure 5-65: The strict XHTML document

Strict XHTML - Phase 2

This document is strict XHTML - we'll see how it does in the browsers.

The cleanup shouldn't cause too many problems, we hope.

- Click me for a count!
- Click here for a query!
- Click here for a description of this page

Copyright 2000 by the Wacki HTML Writer
All rights reserved.

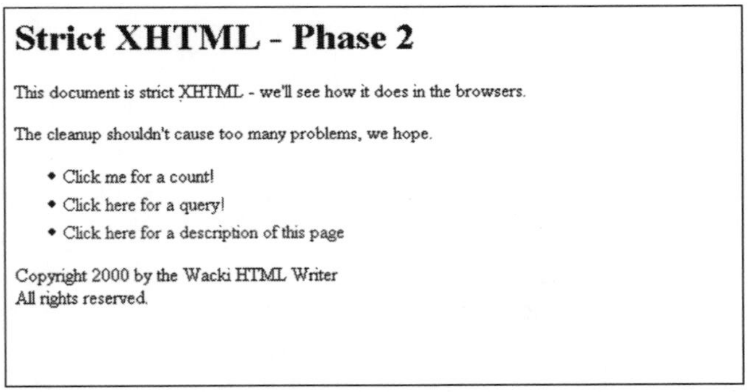

Figure 5-66: The revised strict XHTML document

Amaya 2.4/Windows NT

The original HTML document looks okay, although Amaya interprets the size of the headline generously (see Figure 5-67). Like Opera, Amaya formats the last paragraph like a list item because the UL element isn't closed. Amaya doesn't support JavaScript, so the script doesn't work in any of these versions.

The transitional XHTML document has a more reasonable size for the headline, and the paragraph is restored to its proper location (see Figure 5-68).

The revised transitional XHTML document looks like its predecessor (see Figure 5-69).

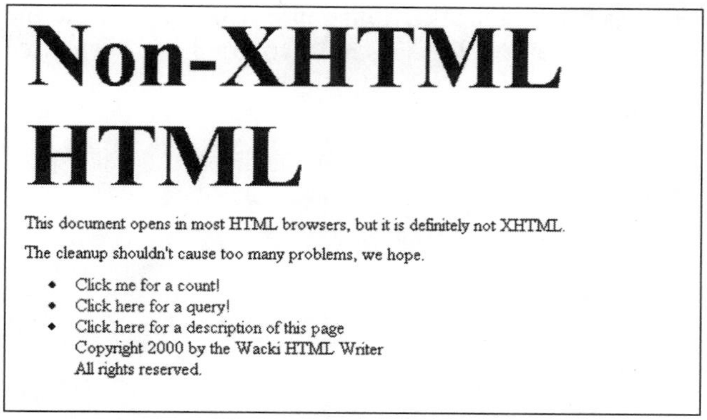

Non-XHTML HTML

This document opens in most HTML browsers, but it is definitely not XHTML.

The cleanup shouldn't cause too many problems, we hope.

- Click me for a count!
- Click here for a query!
- Click here for a description of this page
  Copyright 2000 by the Wacki HTML Writer
  All rights reserved.

Figure 5-67: The original HTML document

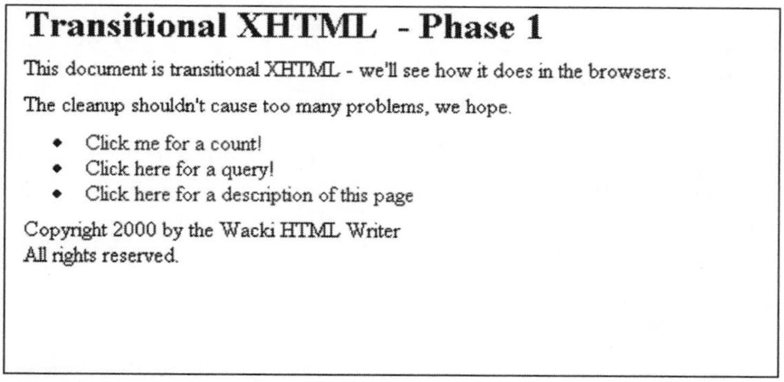

Transitional XHTML - Phase 1

This document is transitional XHTML - we'll see how it does in the browsers.

The cleanup shouldn't cause too many problems, we hope.

- Click me for a count!
- Click here for a query!
- Click here for a description of this page

Copyright 2000 by the Wacki HTML Writer
All rights reserved.

Figure 5-68: The transitional XHTML document

Transitional XHTML - Phase 2

This document is transitional XHTML - we'll see how it does in the browsers.

The cleanup shouldn't cause too many problems, we hope.

- Click me for a count!
- Click here for a query!
- Click here for a description of this page

Copyright 2000 by the Wacki HTML Writer
All rights reserved.

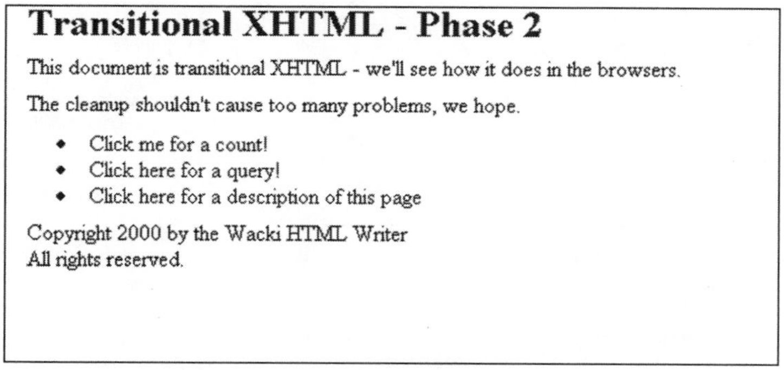

Figure 5-69: The revised transitional XHTML document

The strict HTML document has a much smaller (but more reasonable) headline than its predecessors (refer to Figure 5-70). The list and paragraph are formatted correctly.

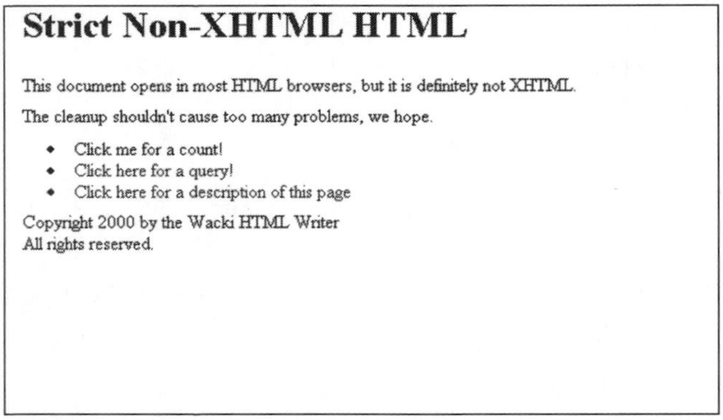

Strict Non-XHTML HTML

This document opens in most HTML browsers, but it is definitely not XHTML.

The cleanup shouldn't cause too many problems, we hope.

- Click me for a count!
- Click here for a query!
- Click here for a description of this page

Copyright 2000 by the Wacki HTML Writer
All rights reserved.

Figure 5-70: The strict HTML document

The strict XHTML document looks like the strict HTML document (see Figure 5-71). Because there isn't a scripting engine here, nothing can go wrong with the JavaScript interpretation.

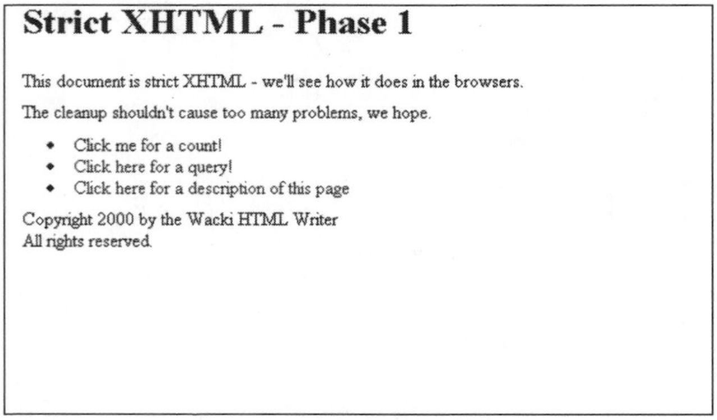

Strict XHTML - Phase 1

This document is strict XHTML - we'll see how it does in the browsers.

The cleanup shouldn't cause too many problems, we hope.

- Click me for a count!
- Click here for a query!
- Click here for a description of this page

Copyright 2000 by the Wacki HTML Writer
All rights reserved.

Figure 5-71: The strict XHTML document

The revised strict XHTML document looks like the strict HTML document (see Figure 5-72).

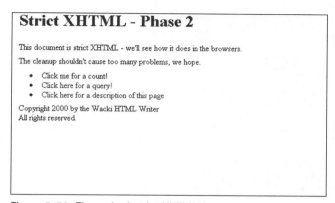

Strict XHTML - Phase 2

This document is strict XHTML - we'll see how it does in the browsers.

The cleanup shouldn't cause too many problems, we hope.

- Click me for a count!
- Click here for a query!
- Click here for a description of this page

Copyright 2000 by the Wacki HTML Writer
All rights reserved.

Figure 5-72: The revised strict XHTML document

Lynx 2.8.2/Windows 95

The original HTML document looks okay in Lynx, which discards most of the formatting information to support its plain-text approach (refer to Figure 5-73). Clicking the script results in a "badly-formed URL" message because Lynx doesn't support JavaScript.

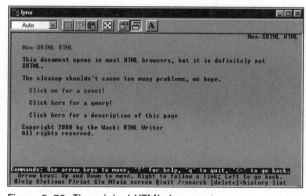

Figure 5-73: The original HTML document

The transitional XHTML document looks the same as the original document, except for tighter spacing on the list items (see Figure 5-74).

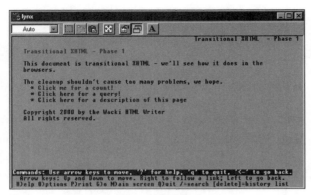

Figure 5-74: The transitional XHTML document

The revised transitional XHTML document looks the same as the original document, except for tighter spacing on the list items (see Figure 5-75).

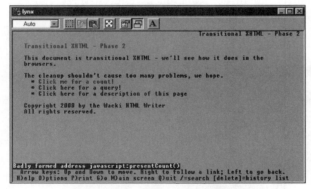

Figure 5-75: The revised transitional XHTML document

The strict HTML document now has a centered headline because of the H1 element (refer to Figure 5-76). Lynx ignores CSS information as well as scripts, so none of the color information is supported. The onclick attribute isn't supported, so "Click me for a count!" isn't highlighted or navigable in any way.

The strict XHTML document looks like the strict HTML document (see Figure 5-77). Lynx ignores the XML declaration as well as the script.

The revised strict XHTML document looks like its predecessor (see Figure 5-78).

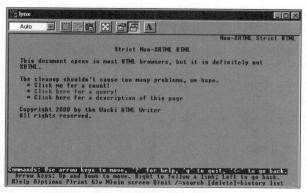

Figure 5-76: The strict HTML document

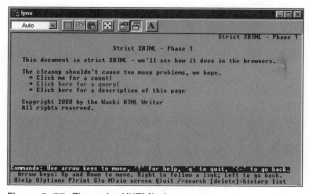

Figure 5-77: The strict XHTML document

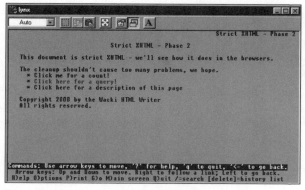

Figure 5-78: The revised strict XHTML document

Lessons

Creating XHTML that meets the W3C's specs clearly is not enough to achieve interoperability with older browsers. While you probably can disregard some of the experiments in very old browsers, there are still some tools with serious problems that you shouldn't ignore — and some issues (such as the use of CDATA sections in scripts) are here to stay. Although most designers now expect at least version 3 or version 4 functionality in their pages, the preceding examples demonstrate that even those browsers aren't really enough to handle full-fledged XHTML. In addition, many programs use toolkits for integrating browser functionality that support more or less the equivalent of Netscape 1 or 2.

Complying with both the W3C standards and the compatibility limitations of existing browsers is yet another painful challenge for Web developers, much like the early problems with JavaScript, dynamic HTML, and cascading style sheets. Making any of these technologies work in a mixed environment is difficult, and there are very few completely pure communities of users working with only the latest browsers.

The test suite does demonstrate some strategies to avoid when creating XHTML pages that have to work in older browsers. First, it's easiest to move scripts outside of the document. Although Netscape 3.0 has some problems with this strategy, script elements stored inside the body element rather than the head seem to get around this problem. (It's acceptable to the XHTML DTD, although it's not exactly best practice in documents with lots of scripts at the front of the document.) Similarly, cascading style sheets information should be stored in external files because it keeps their contents from cluttering the top of the document. It may delay browser rendering if style sheet retrieval is slow, but it does make file management easier.

The XML declaration causes problems in many older browsers. (In some embedded browser tools, it even keeps documents from displaying at all.) Although leaving out the XML declaration effectively restricts documents to using UTF-8 or UTF-16, this may not pose a problem if you have tools for editing documents in these encodings. Java uses UTF-8 by default, and various Microsoft tools are capable of exporting Unicode text in these formats. If your pages can get by using the ASCII subset of characters — basically American English — your files will be UTF-8 compatible automatically. Users of the common Latin-1 or other character encodings may want to upgrade their tools so that they can save their files to UTF-8 or UTF-16 if the XML declaration display issue is a serious concern.

Chapter 6

Reading the XHTML DTDs: A Guide to XML Declarations

ALTHOUGH THE W3C has long had document type definitions (DTDs) for HTML, few developers actually use those DTDs as a foundation for learning HTML. XHTML 1.0 simplifies those DTDs with the slightly friendlier XML syntax – they previously used SGML's more complex syntax – and the increased emphasis on validation may lead developers to explore them more closely. Making good use of XHTML 1.1 requires some level of understanding of DTDs, so getting started now is a good idea. Fortunately, XHTML doesn't use every tool XML provides; figuring out XHTML is easier than learning all about XML.

The W3C is moving slowly toward its new XML Schemas standard for describing document structures. You'll want to learn XML Schemas when they're ready, but the DTDs described in this structure provide a solid foundation for figuring them out.

You can work with XHTML 1.0 without any comprehension of the DTD because the rules for element and attribute usage are the same as those for HTML 4.0. However, if you plan on using validating parsers with XHTML 1.0, you should know about DTDs to figure out some of the error messages you may encounter. In addition, understanding DTDs can help you out considerably with XHTML 1.1 and its modular approach.

Because you don't necessarily need to understand DTD syntax to use XHTML, you're welcome to bail out of this chapter if you prefer, and come back to it if and when you need it.

The W3C wrote the XHTML DTDs for its own convenience, making them more manageable (and at an abstract level, more readable) — but at the cost of requiring some cross-referencing to figure out exactly what's included in a particular element or attribute. As a result, the XHTML DTDs aren't recommended reading for developers without an XML or SGML background. The following sections introduce the different kinds of declarations used within the XHTML DTDs in their simpler forms, building up to the more complex rules used to assemble the XHTML 1.0 DTDs.

If you want a guide to creating and reading XML DTDs in all their glory, try *XML: A Primer, 2nd Edition* by Simon St. Laurent (IDG Books, 1999). For even more details on XML technicalities, see *XML Elements of Style* (McGraw-Hill, 1999), also by Simon St.Laurent.

Element Type Declarations

Every valid document needs one or more *element type declarations,* which describe element names used within a document and content that appears within a given element. If an element name appears in a document and there is no corresponding element type declaration, validating parsers report an error. (Some parsers also halt processing, although that isn't required.) Similarly, if an element appears in a context where it's not supposed to appear, validating parsers report errors.

The syntax for element type declarations is simple:

<!ELEMENT *elementName contentModel*>

Element names must begin with letters, underscores, or colons, and they may contain letters, underscores, colons, digits, hyphens, and periods. Element names beginning with xml (or any case variation on that, such as XmL or XML) are reserved for the use of the W3C. The use of colons is discouraged *except* for use with namespaces, which Chapter 4 describes.

Content models can be a lot more complicated, enabling designers to specify intricate combinations of elements and text. There are four basic types of content models available: EMPTY, ANY, structured content models, and mixed content models.

Element type declarations *don't* provide any background on what the element is for, what contexts it may be used in, or what its appearance in a given context might mean. You have to provide that information separately, typically in documentation. Element type declarations only describe a small, but important, set of element properties: name and allowed contents.

The EMPTY content model

The *EMPTY content model* is the simplest model available. EMPTY elements may either use empty element tags or a set of start and end tags with no content whatsoever (not even whitespace) between them. However, they may (and usually do) store information in attributes, which are declared separately. The img and br elements are both examples of elements with EMPTY content models, and their declarations are very similar:

```
<!ELEMENT img EMPTY>
<!ELEMENT br EMPTY>
```

The ANY content model

The *ANY content model* is nearly as simple as the EMPTY model. Elements declared as ANY can contain any mix of text and (declared) elements. The ANY content model is never used within XHTML 1.0, but it sometimes appears in XML documents that contain XHTML content (perhaps followed by a comment):

```
<!ELEMENT documentation ANY>
<!--Please note: XHTML is the preferred content for the
documentation element, but other models may be used.-->
```

XML developers frown on the widespread use of ANY, seeing it as introducing serious weaknesses, but you may use it appropriately in your own DTDs at the beginning of a project or to preserve spaces for future extensions.

Structured content models

Structured content models provide most of the sophistication available to element type declarations. They enable developers to specify complex sets of possible content using a compact notation. While they're limited to element-only content — mixed content models, described next, enable you to add text — you can use structured content models to create complex frameworks that house text-containing elements. XHTML uses all the options available, for instance, to describe the fairly complex set of structures that can be a table:

```
<!ELEMENT table
   (caption?, (col*|colgroup*), thead?, tfoot?, (tbody+|tr+))>
```

Decoding this requires an understanding of how the various punctuation marks interact with the element names to describe structures. Table 6-1 describes these marks — called *sequence* and *occurrence indicators* — and their meanings.

Table 6-1 SYMBOLS FOR DESCRIBING ELEMENT CONTENT STRUCTURES

Symbol	Symbol Type	Description	Example	Example Notes
|	Vertical bar	Indicates a choice ("or")	thisone | thatone	Either thisone or thatone must appear.
,	Comma	Requires elements or groups to appear in specified sequence	thisone, thatone	thisone must appear, followed by thatone.
?	Question mark	Makes the element type it follows optional, but only one may appear	thisone?	thisone may appear, but only once if it does appear.
	No symbol	One, and only one, must appear	thisone	thisone must appear exactly once.
*	Asterisk	Allows any number to appear in a sequence, even zero	thisone*	thisone may appear; multiple appearances (or zero appearances) of thisone are acceptable.
+	Plus sign	Requires at least one to appear; more may appear sequentially.	thisone+	thisone must be present at least once; multiple thisone elements may appear.
( )	Parentheses	Groups elements so that groups may be given the preceding sequence and occurrence indicators.	(thisone | thatone), whichone	Either thisone or thatone (but not both) may appear, followed by whichone.

Using this decoder key, you can translate the content model of the table element type's declaration and its pieces into English. The outside parentheses just enclose the entire content model – a requirement for structured content model declarations.

The first item inside the parentheses, `caption?`, indicates that a `caption` element may appear once as the first element inside the `table` element (but it is optional). The comma following `caption?` indicates that the other items following it must appear in sequence. The next chunk provides some options:

```
(col*|colgroup*)
```

This grouping means that either `col` or `colgroup` elements may appear after the caption and before the `thead` (if they appear), but that `col` and `colgroup` elements may not be mixed within a given table element. This chunk of markup says that *either* zero or more `col` elements *or* zero or more `colgroup` elements may appear at this point. If the developers of the XHTML standard had wanted to allow `col` and `colgroup` elements to be mixed, they could have written:

```
(col|colgroup)* <!--this is not the route XHTML chose-->
```

This says that zero or more instances of the `col` or `colgroup` elements may appear, without prohibiting both from appearing in a single sequence.

A comma follows the `(col*|colgroup*)` grouping, followed by `thead?`. Like `caption?`, this allows the `thead` element to appear zero or one times. The comma following then permits `tfoot?` to indicate the possible appearance of a `tfoot` element zero or one times.

The last portion of the content model is similar to the `(col*|colgroup*)` grouping, but with a slight change:

```
(tbody+|tr+)
```

Again, either `tbody` or `tr` elements may appear in this location within the content model. However, at least one instance of one of these elements is required for a valid document. This is the only required content within a table element. No instance of the `table` element may appear without containing at least a `tbody` or a `tr` element.

Mixed content models

Most of HTML's elements contain *mixed content models*, which enable document authors to mix text and elements together to create Web pages. Mixed content models in XML come in two varieties. The simpler variety enables you to create elements that may contain only text: The `title` element, for example, may contain only text:

```
<!ELEMENT title (#PCDATA)>
```

PCDATA stands for *parsed character data*, the only one of SGML's textual types that XML supports. You can write the same declaration like this:

```
<!ELEMENT title (#PCDATA)*>
```

The asterisk is optional when a text-only element is declared, but the asterisk makes it more consistent with other mixed content models.

Mixed content models that describe the mixture of text and elements are more complicated. They look like structured content models, using the | and * indicators, but you are very limited in how you can use them. The general syntax for an element type declaration using mixed content of this kind looks like this:

```
<!ELEMENT elementName (#PCDATA | child1 | child2 | ...)*>
```

Mixed content models only enable you to list a set of elements that may appear mixed with text, but you cannot specify their sequence or the number of times they may appear. For example, if a very simple paragraph element only contains text mixed with bold and italic elements, the declarations might look like this:

```
<!ELEMENT bold (#PCDATA)>
<!ELEMENT italic (#PCDATA)>
<!ELEMENT paragraph (#PCDATA | bold | italic)*>
```

Based on those declarations, all of the paragraphs shown here are legal:

```
<paragraph>There's just text in this one!</paragraph>
<paragraph><bold>This one's bold!</bold></paragraph>
<paragraph><italic>This one's italic!</italic></paragraph>
<paragraph><bold>This one's part bold</bold> and <italic>part
italic!</italic></paragraph>
<paragraph><italic>This one's part italic</italic> and <bold>part
bold - </bold> and then <bold>bold again!</bold></paragraph>
```

Mixed declarations are used throughout the XHTML 1.0 DTDs; to understand their usage there, you need to know about parameter entities (which I cover later in this chapter).

Attribute List Declarations

Attribute list declarations enable you to specify attributes that you can use on particular element types. Every element in XHTML has at least one core set of attributes so attribute list declarations (sometimes abbreviated `ATTLIST` declarations) are an important part of the XHTML 1.0 DTDs. You have more options for attribute list declarations than element type declarations in XML, but fortunately the XHTML 1.0 specification stays away from the most complicated types of attributes.

The basic syntax for an attribute list declaration looks like this:

```
<!ATTLIST elementName
   attName    attType    default
   attName    attType    default
   ... >
```

Multiple attribute list declarations may appear for a single element type, although the first definition of a particular attribute for a given element is the one that gets used in repeated definitions. Any number of attributes may be defined for a particular element in a given attribute list declaration, even none:

```
<!ATTLIST myElement>
```

Attribute names are subject to the same rules as element names: they must begin with letters, underscores, or colons, and may contain letters, underscores, colons, digits, hyphens, and periods. Attribute names beginning with `xml` (or any case variation on that, such as `xMl` or `XML`) are reserved for the use of the W3C. Furthermore, the use of colons is discouraged *except* for use with namespaces. The simplest type of attribute is the `CDATA` type, an abbreviation for *Character DATA*. The simplest default is the keyword `#IMPLIED`, which doesn't supply any default value for the attribute. A very simple attribute declaration might look like this:

```
<!ATTLIST myElement
   note    CDATA    #IMPLIED>
```

The following sections discuss the attribute types and default options in more detail.

Types of attributes

XML provides a variety of attribute types that often define the attribute's role within a document, although they provide only a weak set of constraints. XHTML uses six of the 10 attribute types provided by XML 1.0, as listed in Table 6-2.

TABLE 6-2 ATTRIBUTE TYPES USED IN XHTML 1.0

Type	Explanation
CDATA	The attribute may contain only text (character data).
ID	The value of the attribute must be unique in identifying the element. If two attributes within a document of type ID have the same value, the parser should return an error. (Note that attributes of type ID may not have default values or fixed values.) The only elements in XHTML that have the type ID are named id. The value of ID-type attributes must begin with a letter or underscore, and may contain letters, underscores, colons, digits, hyphens, and periods.
IDREF, IDREFS	The value of the attribute must refer to an ID value declared elsewhere in the document. If the value of the attribute doesn't match an ID value within the document, validating parsers should return an error. IDREFS is similar, but it allows multiple values separated by whitespace — again, all the values must correspond to the value of an ID-type attribute in the document.
NMTOKEN	The value of the attribute may contain only letters, digits, periods, dashes, underscores, or colons. (NMTOKENS, which isn't used in the XHTML DTDs, resembles NMTOKEN but it allows multiple values separated by whitespace.)
Enumerated, for example, thisone | thatone	The value of the attribute must match one of the values listed. Values must appear in parentheses and be separated by OR (|) symbols.

Let's take a look at how these attributes are used by exploring subsets of the declarations employed in the XHTML DTD. The DTD uses parameter entities, covered later in this chapter, and smaller examples are easier to work with, so we'll create examples that are easy to read but aren't the exact quote from the XHTML DTD. Also, as you'll see, the W3C uses parameter entities to specify expectations for attribute content that can't be expressed using the basic types.

Attributes of type CDATA appear throughout the XHTML DTDs. CDATA is the loosest model, accommodating all kinds of needs while setting very few expectations. CDATA attribute types can hold URLs, numeric information, style information — basically anything that can be expressed as text. A subset of the attribute list declaration for the img element, for example, might look like this:

```
<!--These are compatible with the XHTML DTDs but do not represent
the complete declarations from the XHTML DTD-->
```

```
<!ATTLIST img
  src      CDATA       #REQUIRED
  alt      CDATA       #REQUIRED
  height      CDATA       #IMPLIED
  width      CDATA       #IMPLIED
>
```

The src attribute, which takes a URL, is represented as CDATA. The alt attribute, which contains text to display if the image isn't loaded, also is represented as CDATA despite the differences between its content and that of the src attribute. The height and width attributes, which accept lengths, also use CDATA. CDATA can handle all of these different types because it places so few restrictions on its content.

The XHTML 1.0 Recommendation names all of its attributes of type ID as id and makes them available to every single element in the DTD. To add the ID element to the img element, you just use this:

```
<!ATTLIST img
  id     ID      #IMPLIED
>
```

Or add this to the preceding list:

```
<!--These are compatible with the XHTML DTDs but do not represent
the complete declarations from the XHTML DTD-->
<!ATTLIST img
  src      CDATA       #REQUIRED
  alt      CDATA       #REQUIRED
  height   CDATA       #IMPLIED
  width    CDATA       #IMPLIED
  id       ID          #IMPLIED
>
```

The IDREF and IDREF attribute types are used more sparingly. The label element, which enables the creation of labels for all elements in a document, has a for attribute that should contain an ID value describing the content being labeled:

```
<!--This is compatible with the XHTML DTDs but does not represent
the complete declarations from the XHTML DTD-->
<!ATTLIST label
  for      IDREF       #IMPLIED
```

This mechanism allows the label to refer to one and only one element in a document — the one that has an id attribute value matching that of the label's for attribute.

IDREFS are used similarly, although they permit a single attribute to refer to multiple ID values. XHTML 1.0 uses IDREFS to allow table cells to point to the header labels that describe them:

```
<!--This is compatible with the XHTML DTDs but does not represent
the complete declarations from the XHTML DTD-->
<!ATTLIST td
 headers        IDREFS      #IMPLIED
>
<!ATTLIST th
 headers        IDREFS      #IMPLIED
>
```

Complex tables sometimes sprout multiple levels of headers; this can help manage table reorganization or analysis. For instance, XHTML uses the NMTOKEN attribute type to restrict content to a single word. In the a, map, and object elements, NMTOKEN is used to restrict the value of name attributes to the same rules that apply to id attributes:

```
<!--This is compatible with the XHTML DTDs but does not represent
the complete declarations from the XHTML DTD-->
<!ATTLIST a
 name        NMTOKEN        #IMPLIED
 id            ID           #IMPLIED
>
<!ATTLIST map
 name        NMTOKEN        #IMPLIED
 id            ID           #IMPLIED
>
<!ATTLIST object
 name        NMTOKEN        #IMPLIED
 id            ID           #IMPLIED
>
```

XHTML uses *enumerated attributes* to restrict the values for an attribute to a small set of permitted choices, presented as a list. Enumerated attributes appear throughout the DTDs. The use of an enumerated attribute type to restrict values is useful especially for input elements in which the type attribute defines the "real" meaning of the element:

```
<!--This is compatible with the XHTML DTDs but does not represent
the complete declarations from the XHTML DTD-->
<!ATTLIST input
 type    (text | password | checkbox | radio | submit | reset | file
| hidden | image | button)  "text"
>
```

Enumerated types also are used for certain attributes (such as the ismap attribute for img elements, which can have only one value if enumerated types are used):

```
<!ATTLIST img
 ismap     (ismap)    #IMPLIED>
```

If the img element should be treated as an image map, the document creator should use the ismap attribute shown here:

```
<img src='whatever.png' ismap='ismap' />
```

If the image isn't a map, the img element shouldn't have an ismap attribute at all as shown here:

```
<img src='whatever.png' />
```

XHTML 1.0 doesn't use the NMTOKENS, NOTATION, ENTITY, or ENTITIES attribute types at all. However, their use is not prohibited in XML DTDs that are designed to include or be included by XHTML. If you encounter these types in a DTD you use with XHTML, consult the documentation for that DTD regarding their proper use.

Defaulting attribute values

XML 1.0 also provides a set of tools for specifying what happens if an attribute isn't declared within an element. Four different possibilities exist, including "the attribute just isn't there"; "the attribute must be there, period"; and "the attribute has this value, period." A small set of keywords and the capability to include values in quotes, shown in Table 6-3, provide the tools XHTML 1.0 uses to define the rules for attribute values.

TABLE 6-3 ATTRIBUTE DEFAULTS

Default	Explanation
#REQUIRED	Indicates to the parser that this attribute must have a value in all instances of the element. Failure to include the attribute results in errors if a validating parser processes the document.
#IMPLIED	Allows the parser to ignore this attribute if no value is specified. Basically, nothing happens if the attribute isn't defined.

Continued

TABLE 6-3 ATTRIBUTE DEFAULTS *(Continued)*

Default	Explanation
#FIXED "*value*"	Announces that element instances that provide a value for this attribute must specify *value*. If an element instance doesn't include this attribute explicitly, its value is presumed to be the value specified.
"*defaultvalue*"	Provides a default value for the attribute. If the attribute is not declared explicitly in an element instance, the attribute is assumed to have a value of *defaultvalue*.

You already have seen a few uses of these choices in the preceding declarations. In the img element, for instance, the src and alt attributes are required (#REQUIRED); meanwhile, most of the rest of its attribute content is optional (#IMPLIED):

```
<!--These are compatible with the XHTML DTDs but do not represent
the complete declarations from the XHTML DTD-->
<!ATTLIST img
 src      CDATA     #REQUIRED
 alt      CDATA     #REQUIRED
 height      CDATA     #IMPLIED
 width     CDATA     #IMPLIED
 id      ID     #IMPLIED
>
```

The XHTML 1.0 DTDs only use fixed attributes in a very few cases, notably on the html element for its namespace declaration:

```
<!--This is compatible with the XHTML DTDs but does not represent
the complete declarations from the XHTML DTD-->
<!ATTLIST html
 xmlns    CDATA     #FIXED 'http://www.w3.org/1999/xhtml'
>
```

This, combined with the XHTML 1.0's exhortation to always include the xmlns attribute on the html element of XHTML documents, means that only:

```
<html xmlns='http://www.w3.org/1999/xhtml'>...</html>
```

is legal, and not:

```
<html xmlns='http://www.example.com/1999/xhtml'>...</html>
```

The last option, a simple default value in quotes, appears in a few cases in which defaults are supplied easily. For example, the `form` element needs a method and `enctype` (encoding type) value and these have commonly used values.

```
<!--This is compatible with the XHTML DTDs but does not represent
the complete declarations from the XHTML DTD-->
<!ATTLIST form
 action    CDATA       #REQUIRED
 method    (get|post)   "get"
 enctype   CDATA       "application/x-www-form-urlencoded"
>
```

The `form` element is useless without a place to send the information, so the `action` attribute is required. No default is possible because it is different for every form. On the other hand, you can default to the `get` HTTP method. This method then sends all data using the content-type `application/x-www-form-urlencoded`, making these good candidates for defaulting.

Parameter Entity Declarations

Sorting out parameter entities is critical to being able to read the XHTML 1.0 and 1.1 DTDs. *Parameter entities* enable DTD creators to define information within a DTD that can be reused repeatedly by reference to their names. The W3C does this for several reasons — sometimes to describe the content of an attribute more precisely than XML 1.0 allows and sometimes to avoid making the same declarations over and over. This second strategy reduces the size of the DTD and makes it more manageable, while still keeping the same content. The third reason for using parameter entities is modularization. External parameter entities enable DTD creators to reference content in other files for inclusion in the DTD. In XHTML 1.0, this is used only to include the three sets of entity descriptions that are stored outside the core DTDs; but it becomes a major part of XHTML's strategy for modularizing XHTML.

First, let's explore internal parameter entities. They have this general syntax:

```
<!ENTITY % entityName "entityContent">
```

Entity names follow the same rules as element and attribute names: they must begin with letters, underscores, or colons and may contain letters, underscores, colons, digits, hyphens, and periods. Entity names beginning with `xml` (or any case variation on that, such as `XMl` or `XML`) are reserved for the use of the W3C. The Namespaces Recommendation discourages the use of colons.

The content of an internal parameter entity usually is fragments of declarations, intended for use within other declarations. This content also can consist of complete declarations, but fragments that start in one declaration and end in another are prohibited. All of the internal parameter entities used in the XHTML 1.0 DTDs are fragments of declarations. The simplest ones just provide more clarification about the kind of content a particular CDATA-type attribute should include:

```
<!ENTITY % Number "CDATA">
  <!-- one or more digits -->
<!ENTITY % URI "CDATA">
  <!-- a Uniform Resource Identifier, see [RFC2396] -->
```

When used in an attribute declaration, these entities provide some additional description to help developers figure out how to use an attribute:

```
<!ATTLIST pre
 width      %Number;   #IMPLIED
>
```

Parameter entities are included by prefixing their name with a percent sign (%) and following them with a semicolon, as shown in the preceding example. In this case, a parser interprets the %Number; parameter entity to produce this declaration:

```
<!ATTLIST pre
 width      CDATA      #IMPLIED
>
```

Developers reading the DTD, however, can figure out that width should be specified as a number (of characters) rather than in a string like "2 and 1/4 inches". The URI parameter entity is used similarly throughout the specification:

```
<!ATTLIST img
 src       %URI;      #REQUIRED
 longdesc  %URI;      #IMPLIED
 usemap    %URI;      #IMPLIED
>
```

All of these attributes should include URIs pointing to appropriate resources. This information is intended for human consumption. The parser converts all this to:

```
<!ATTLIST img
 src           CDATA    #REQUIRED
 longdesc      CDATA    #IMPLIED
 usemap        CDATA    #IMPLIED
>
```

This also may enable the W3C to update these types more easily in future versions of XML that support more data types. But for now it just documents usage.

The XHTML DTD uses a similar strategy to describe some similar enumerations, such as those for shapes:

```
<!ENTITY % Shape "(rect|circle|poly|default)">
```

Instead of repeating this list of shapes, using entities allows the XHTML DTD to include more readable things like this:

```
<!ATTLIST area
 shape     %Shape;     "rect">
```

The XHTML DTDs include some parameter entities describing sets of attributes that are applied commonly. For instance, the i18n (for internationalization, which has 18 letters between the 'i' and the 'n') parameter entity is used repeatedly, assigning language and text-direction values.

```
<!ENTITY % LanguageCode "NMTOKEN">
  <!-- a language code, as per [RFC1766] -->
<!ENTITY % i18n
 "lang     %LanguageCode; #IMPLIED
 xml:lang  %LanguageCode; #IMPLIED
 dir       (ltr|rtl)  #IMPLIED"
 >
```

The i18n entity includes declarations for the lang, xml:lang, and dir attributes, which are ready for use within any attribute list declaration. Note that nesting parameter entities within parameter entities is perfectly acceptable—%LanguageCode; is replaced with NMTOKEN during the parsing of the DTD. The i18n entity is used like this:

```
<!ELEMENT title (#PCDATA)>
<!ATTLIST title %i18n;>
```

The parser expands the %i18n; to:

```
<!ELEMENT title (#PCDATA)>
<!ATTLIST title
 lang     %LanguageCode; #IMPLIED
 xml:lang %LanguageCode; #IMPLIED
 dir      (ltr|rtl)  #IMPLIED >
```

and then to:

```
<!ELEMENT title (#PCDATA)>
<!ATTLIST title
 lang     NMTOKEN #IMPLIED
 xml:lang NMTOKEN #IMPLIED
 dir      (ltr|rtl)   #IMPLIED >
```

This produces an attribute list declaration for the title element that supports the lang, xml:lang, and dir attributes for internationalization.

The W3C takes a similar approach to element content models, bundling many of them into entities for easy reference. For example, header (h1-h6) elements can appear in the same places within a document so they create a heading entity that enables you to choose among any of these attributes:

```
<!ENTITY % heading "h1|h2|h3|h4|h5|h6">
```

If an element only contains headings and text, you can create a declaration like this one:

```
<!ELEMENT myMixedHeadlinesElement (#PCDATA | %heading;)*>
```

The parser then expands this declaration to:

```
<!ELEMENT myMixedHeadlinesElement (#PCDATA | h1|h2|h3|h4|h5|h6)*>
```

This declaration enables you to mix text and heading elements. The XHTML DTD doesn't use this approach because headings are only one kind of block element and other types may appear in the same places. Instead, the heading entity is aggregated with other entities for other kinds of block elements:

```
<!ENTITY % block
    "p | %heading; | div | %lists; | %blocktext; | fieldset | table">
```

Then this is aggregated with even more options for different use cases:

```
<!ENTITY % Block "(%block; | form | %misc;)*">
<!ENTITY % Flow "(#PCDATA | %block; | form | %inline; | %misc;)*">
<!ENTITY % form.content "(%block; | %misc;)*">
```

You then may use these content models within element declarations:

```
<!ELEMENT div %Flow;>
```

which expands to:

```
<!ELEMENT div (#PCDATA | %block; | form | %inline; | %misc;)*>
```

which then expands to a much larger declaration as all of the parameter entities are resolved, letting the div element contain many different possible element types.

External parameter entities, at least the way XHTML 1.0 uses them, are much simpler. (Chapters 13 and 14 cover their use in XHTML 1.1.) External parameter entities are used to reference the files containing all the declarations for general entities (such as) for inclusion in processing. For example, use this to include the Latin-1 entity set:

```
<!ENTITY % HTMLlat1 PUBLIC
   "-//W3C//ENTITIES Latin 1 for XHTML//EN"
   "xhtml-lat1.ent">
%HTMLlat1;
```

The public identifier for the entity set, created by the W3C, provides a formal description. Meanwhile, a URI (relative to the XHTML DTDs themselves) tells the parser where to find the actual file. Declaring this entity alone isn't enough to include that file because the %HTMLlat1; does that. The parser retrieves the file and inserts its contents at that point in the DTD.

General Entity Declarations

XHTML supports the same set of general entities that HTML 4.0 supports. Unlike parameter entities, *general entities* are meant for use within XHTML documents instead of the XHTML DTD. The mechanism used to create those entities works much like the parameter entity mechanism, using similar syntax — only the percent sign is missing:

```
<!ENTITY entityName "entityContent">
```

Again, entity names follow the same rules as element and attribute names: they must begin with letters, underscores, or colons and may contain letters, underscores, colons, digits, hyphens, and periods. Entity names beginning with xml (or any case variation on that, such as XMl or XML) are reserved for the use of the W3C. The Namespaces Recommendation discourages the use of colons. General and parameter entities may have the same names within a single DTD without conflict, but an entity declared as a general entity cannot be referenced as a parameter entity and vice-versa.

The entity declarations used by the XHTML DTDs reference decimal values for Unicode characters, with documentation describing each entity. For example:

```
<!ENTITY nbsp   " "> <!-- no-break space = non-breaking space,
                U+00A0 ISOnum -->
```

The W3C provides three sets of these declarations for the Latin-1 character set, symbols, and special characters. To reference any of these entities within an XHTML document, just prefix the name of the entity with an ampersand (&) and follow it with a semicolon (;). This is the same way HTML always handles entities. For example:

```
These words will stay on the same 
;line.
```

To see a complete list of the characters available in Unicode, see *The Unicode Standard* from the Unicode Consortium (published by Addison-Wesley). While the XML 1.0 specification references Unicode 2.0, the Unicode 3.0 specification is on the horizon and probably will replace Unicode 2.0 eventually. For a friendlier introduction to Unicode, see *Unicode: A Primer*, by Tony Graham (IDG Books, 2000.)

While XML 1.0 supports external parameter entities and enables you to create your own internal entity sets, HTML browsers do not support this usage. Probably only those XHTML processors that are built on validating XML processors will support these entities. For more details, see your favorite XML reference.

If you build your own XML DTDs, you can include the XHTML entity sets easily. Just include a line like this:

```
<!ENTITY % HTMLlat1 PUBLIC
    "-//W3C//ENTITIES Latin 1 for XHTML//EN"
    "http://www.w3.org/TR/xhtml1/DTD/xhtml-lat1.ent">
```

in your DTD. Each set of entities has its own declaration. Not all XML parsers retrieve external resources so make sure you use a validating parser if you employ this approach.

Comments

You can use comments in DTDs pretty much as you use them in documents. Just as comments can't appear within tags in a document, they also can't appear inside of declarations in the DTD. Comments typically are positioned (before, or sometimes to the side) with the declarations they describe. Anything that appears between <!-- and --> is a comment, meant for human consumption only. Often, comments are your guides in the XHTML DTD for the "whys" of particular constructions, especially for some of the odder parts.

Chapter 7

Exploring the XHTML DTDs

THE XHTML DTDs MAY LOOK daunting initially, but being able to read them can help you produce cleaner XHTML. Hopefully, you'll encounter fewer errors and be able to understand the ones you find better because you'll have access to the rules processors use to evaluate your documents. Understanding the DTD syntax described in Chapter 6 is an important start to decoding the particular declarations. However, you still should keep a copy of HTML 4.01 (or a friendlier HTML reference) around for fuller descriptions of the meaning and usage of this vocabulary, as well as the XHTML 1.0 spec itself. This chapter explores the DTDs and how they specify and organize the declarations so that you may have an easier time if and when you need to read them.

 You can access the HTML 4.01 specification from the W3C at http://www.w3.org/TR/html401. If you compare the HTML 4.01 DTDs with the XHTML 1.0 DTDs, you can see significant reorganization. However, the results of the declarations within those DTDs are almost identical.

 If a detailed exploration of the XHTML declarations isn't your highest priority, you can skip this chapter and return to it when you need it.

Choosing Your DTD

XHTML 1.0 provides three DTDs that describe different sets of XHTML elements and attributes. They reflect the three choices provided in HTML 4.0: strict, transitional, and frameset. The *strict* DTD is probably the one that the W3C would like to see developers adhere to, but *transitional* and *frameset* DTDs reflect the reality of HTML usage much more accurately. Appendix A lists the elements included in the three different DTDs, along with notes regarding attributes.

If you're creating documents from scratch, have some understanding of cascading style sheets (covered in Chapter 8), and don't need frames, the strict DTD is probably the best way to go. (If you need frames, you definitely have to use the frameset DTD.) If you're converting older HTML documents to XHTML, odds are good that you need to use the transitional DTD to accommodate many of the tools used in the graphic design-oriented world of much of Web development (such as the FONT element and the use of tables for layout). While it is possible to convert documents that use these tools to strict XHTML, it may require a lot more effort to maintain the look of your documents. If you don't have the time to choose a DTD for every document, transitional or frameset is probably your best choice for minimizing validation errors.

To identify the DTD for a given document, you must use a DOCTYPE declaration in the prologue of your document. The XHTML 1.0 Recommendation provides three options, one for each DTD. They look much like their HTML 4.01 predecessors, although their names are slightly different and the HTML root element is now html.

For the strict DTD, this HTML 4.01 declaration:

```
<!DOCTYPE HTML
      PUBLIC "-//W3C//DTD HTML 4.01//EN"
      "http://www.w3.org/TR/html4/strict.dtd">
```

becomes this XHTML 1.0 declaration:

```
<!DOCTYPE html
      PUBLIC "-//W3C//DTD XHTML 1.0 Strict//EN"
      "http://www.w3.org/TR/xhtml1/DTD/xhtml1-strict.dtd">
```

For the transitional DTD, this HTML 4.01 declaration:

```
<!DOCTYPE HTML
      PUBLIC "-//W3C//DTD HTML 4.01 Transitional//EN"
      "http://www.w3.org/TR/html4/loose.dtd">
```

becomes this XHTML 1.0 declaration:

```
<!DOCTYPE html
      PUBLIC "-//W3C//DTD XHTML 1.0 Transitional//EN"
      "http://www.w3.org/TR/xhtml1/DTD/xhtml1-transitional.dtd">
```

And for the frameset DTD, this HTML 4.01 declaration:

```
<!DOCTYPE HTML
      PUBLIC "-//W3C//DTD HTML 4.01 Frameset//EN"
      "http://www.w3.org/TR/html4/frameset.dtd">
```

becomes this XHTML 1.0 declaration:

```
<!DOCTYPE html
    PUBLIC "-//W3C//DTD XHTML 1.0 Frameset//EN"
    "http://www.w3.org/TR/xhtml1/DTD/xhtml1-frameset.dtd">
```

Whichever declaration you choose, it must appear after the XML declaration (if there is one) and before the root element of the document. If your document passes through a validating parser, it checks your document to make sure that its contents conform to the rules laid out in the DTD.

The XHTML 1.0 Recommendation doesn't say anything about using another XML feature, the internal subset of the DOCTYPE declaration. While its use isn't prohibited, you should avoid using it with XHTML documents.

Starting Out

All three DTDs follow roughly the same layout, with a few sections more or less depending on the particular DTD you read. The first few sections of a DTD are often the most frustrating (they often put people off) because they lay groundwork for later declarations rather than make concrete declarations. Reading somewhat abstract collections of declarations outside of their context for page after page may not feel rewarding, but it's important to understand these preliminaries in order to make sense of the concrete declarations.

While these preliminaries are important in XHTML 1.0, they will become even more important when XHTML is modularized in XHTML 1.1. Then you may need to choose which modules are used in documents. Understanding how these pieces fit together is critical as the specification is broken into smaller pieces.

Including character entities

After some introductory comments, the three XHTML DTDs all start by referencing the entity sets—*character mnemonic entities*—supported by HTML: Latin-1, Symbols, and Special. Because these entity sets are stored in separate files, the DTDs can reference them easily without requiring a special set for each DTD. (It also means that other XML applications can reference the XHTML entity sets easily without needing to incorporate the entire DTD.) The declaration for the Latin-1 set, immediately followed by a reference including the material referenced by the declaration, looks like:

```
<!ENTITY % HTMLlat1 PUBLIC
  "-//W3C//ENTITIES Latin 1 for XHTML//EN"
  "xhtml-lat1.ent">
%HTMLlat1;
```

The entity declaration creates a parameter entity named HTMLlat1. HTMLlat1 references a set of declarations using two different identifiers, including a public identifier (-//W3C//ENTITIES Latin 1 for XHTML//EN) that applications can use if they already know what these entities are and don't want to retrieve information from the URL. Applications that don't understand the public identifier, like most XML processors, can use the URL to retrieve the full set of declarations. Either way, documents that use the XHTML DTDs may use the full set of entities.

The URLs for the entity set locations are given as local URLs. If you want to reference these sets in your own XML declarations, use the full form: http://www.w3.org/TR/xhtml1/DTD/xhtml-lat1.ent. You also may want to create a local copy — not all users of your XML DTDs may have access to the Internet or the W3C site. The copyright statement at the top of the DTD makes it clear that this kind of usage is acceptable.

Imported names

In the next section of each of the DTDs, the W3C defines some parameter entities that are used within attribute list declarations as data types. As noted in Chapter 6, the CDATA attribute type doesn't provide very many restraints on the kinds of textual information that an attribute may contain. The XHTML DTD uses parameter entities to provide more meaningful descriptions of attribute content than are available in "pure" XML 1.0, and to identify to what those descriptions refer. For each of these names, a comment follows a parameter entity declaration:

```
<!ENTITY % Character "CDATA">
  <!-- a single character from [ISO10646] -->
```

This declaration, for instance, creates the Character parameter entity; meanwhile, the comment tells developers that attributes declared using this parameter entity must contain a single character as defined in ISO 10646.

Appendix E of the XHTML 1.0 specification mostly omits the specs listed in square brackets, but they are available at http://www.w3.org/TR/xhtml1/#refs. If you need to look up the RFCs, see http://www.rfceditor.org. For more on ISO 10646, see the XML 1.0 references at http://www.w3.org/TR/REC-xml#sec-existing-stds.

Many of the types are defined more simply, without referring to outside specifications. The Number entity, for instance, is described as "one or more digits." The Shape entity doesn't have a description, but its declaration limits it to a small set of well-known types:

```
<!ENTITY % Shape "(rect|circle|poly|default)">
```

The transitional and frameset DTDs include two additional entities, ImgAlign and Color, which support formatting properties left out of the strict DTD. These entities are declared in a slightly different style, with their descriptive comments preceding the declaration rather than following it. These DTDs also provide a list of commonly supported colors in comments, although they aren't formally a part of the DTD that an XML parser understands.

Generic attributes

The next section of each of the DTDs defines entities describing numerous attributes that are applied to many different elements. For the most part, all three DTDs define the same set of attributes for their elements. This section, in a sense, defines the framework with which the W3C wants developers to build XHTML applications. It contains the hooks for styling, internationalization, and scripting – all key tools for moving beyond static Web pages built for Western organizations. The generic attributes make XHTML more active and more inclusive at the same time.

The first entity, coreattrs, defines a set of attributes that can be applied to any XHTML element in the body of an XML document. The id attribute uniquely identifies elements – even when a name attribute is available – as discussed in Chapter 4. Style sheets use the class attribute to provide formatting with a slightly finer grain than is possible using the same style for every element of a given type. The style attribute enables developers to apply cascading style sheets' tools for in-line styling to XHTML elements, specifying formatting on a per-element basis. Finally, the title attribute enables you to supply a human-readable name to any element in a document.

The next entity (i18n) supports internationalization, and its contents are applied to every element in XHTML. The lang and xml:lang attributes, described in Chapter 4, are both available. (Indeed, you have to use them both every time you use one in conformant XHTML 1.0.) The dir attribute enables you to specify whether you want the text presented left-to-right (ltr) or right-to-left (rtl).

The next two sets of entities define attributes used to connect XHTML elements to user interfaces and the scripts that respond to user activities. The `events` entity defines a set of attributes that connect scripts to particular user-driven events, such as `onclick` and `onkeypress`, and is employed widely on elements in the body of HTML documents. The `focus` entity provides additional hooks for elements that can receive and lose user-interface focus. (Oddly enough, the `focus` entity is never used anywhere in the three DTDs, although its contents appear regularly.)

Then, three of these entities — `coreattrs`, `i18n`, and `events` — are combined into a single large `attrs` attribute for use on many of the textual elements. The transitional and frameset DTDs also declare the `TextAlign` entity, which defines the `align` formatting attribute for many of the block-level elements.

Text elements

The next few sections define element content for various parts of XHTML. The first, text elements, defines content that is used throughout the set of elements that present text. In this section, the first large differences between the strict and the transitional and frameset DTDs become clearly apparent. While all of the DTDs declare the same set of entities, the strict DTD omits many of the content models permitted by the other DTDs' `special` and `fontstyle` entities and effectively abolishes `iframe`, `u`, `s`, `strike`, `font`, and `basefont` from the XHTML vocabulary. This isn't new — it happened in HTML 4.0 — but it's an indicator of the direction the W3C wants to see developers take, moving away from explicit formatting in markup to a more abstracted approach applying style sheets to the structures formed by that markup.

The rest of the text elements entities, culminating in the `Inline` entity, describe different content models that can appear inside textual content. This section defines markup that you can use inside of paragraphs and other block-level elements. One entity, `misc`, provides support for content that may appear in both the textual and block-level contexts, such as `ins`, `del`, `script`, and `noscript`.

Block-level elements

The next section describes structures that operate at a higher level than the text elements, creating the structures in which those text elements can appear. Here the three DTDs almost converge, defining sets of block-level elements that fit into the relatively neat categories of `heading`, `lists`, and `blocktext`, and then adding the `p`, `div`, `fieldset`, and `table` element types for a main block element. The strict DTD leaves out `isindex`, `menu`, `dir`, `center`, and `noframes`, which appear in the other two DTDs.

These element models then combine with the `misc` entity and `form` element to create the `Block` entity. Remember, XML's case sensitivity means that `block` and `Block` are completely different things. For cases in which an element may contain either block-level or textual content, this section also defines the `Flow` entity. This entity adds the `inline` entity and text to the combination of components that make up `Block`. The `Flow` entity functions in elements that step outside the usual block-text distinctions and permit either form to appear.

Content models for exclusions

This is one of the odder sections of the XHTML 1.0 DTDs. Effectively, it declares content models for particular elements using models much like those in the block-level area – but with minor changes explained in comments. This section of the DTD is the result of the switch to XML. Older versions of HTML used a feature of SGML, called exclusions, to specify rules such as "no a element can contain another a element." XML dropped that feature for the sake of simplicity. As a result, this section of the DTD redefines a few of the models from the previous section in terms of needs for particular elements – a, pre, form, and button. There are also some differences among the DTDs. The content model for Form, for instance, includes the Block model in the strict DTD but the Flow model in the transitional and frameset DTDs.

Building Structure: Element and Attribute Declarations

After all of these preliminaries, it's finally time to make some real declarations, creating the elements and attributes partly described by the entities established so far. This portion of the DTD is broken down into segments that reflect groupings of element types, foreshadowing to some extent the modularization process that XHTML 1.1 will perform. If you have trouble getting your XHTML documents to validate, you need to explore this portion of the DTD to track down the content models you need to support. The three DTDs have slightly different sets of declarations, as noted next.

Document structure

The top-level declaration needed to create an XHTML document is the html element. The html element's role as a container gives it a very simple structure in the strict and transitional DTDs – it can contain a single head element and a single body element with only the internationalization and namespace declaration for attributes. In the frameset DTD, however, the content model changes dramatically to a head element and a frameset element, which limits the use of the frameset DTD to documents that use frames or the noframes element. Effectively, frames are segregated from the rest of XHTML. Strict and transitional documents may appear within those frames, although the strict DTD is missing some key tools for working with frames (such as the target attribute).

Document head

The head element primarily is a container for *metadata* – information describing the document that follows. Some of this metadata (such as style sheets) may be applied to the document as part of the presentation; other parts help systems outside the document to categorize the document and reference it appropriately. While the contents of the head element are similar in all three DTDs, some subtle differences are important to note. The strict DTD omits the long-deprecated isindex element, as well as the target attribute that allows the base and link elements to specify a target frame in addition to a URI.

This section also defines a script element that may appear in either the head or the body element and a noscript element that may appear only in the body. The declaration for noscript in the strict DTD only permits the use of block elements, while the version in the other DTDs allows anything defined in the Flow entity, including both block and in-line elements.

The declaration for the head element in all three DTDs demonstrates how XML sometimes requires complex notation to state something as simple as "one title element and any of the rest in any order."

Frames (frameset and transitional only)

This section follows the document head section in both the transitional and frameset DTDs, and is omitted entirely in the strict DTD. The transitional DTD only declares two elements — the iframe and noframes elements. Meanwhile, the frameset DTD declares those and the frameset and frame elements — the two core elements for creating frame-based Web sites. The noframes element, used in a transitional document, may contain any elements appearing in the Flow entity, while the frameset DTD restricts its content to body.

Document body

This next section creates the body and div elements in all three DTDs. The body element receives two event attributes — onload and onunload. This is in addition to the event attributes used for other HTML elements, which provide support for scripts that run when the document is opened and closed. In the strict DTD, only block elements may appear directly inside the body element, while the transitional and framset DTDs permit anything listed in the Flow parameter entity. The most significant general difference among the DTDs is the strict DTD's omission of the formatting properties (notably bgcolor) supported by the other DTDs. Similarly, the strict DTD's version of the div element omits the TextAlign entity that provides the align attribute (another formatting feature).

In HTML 4.0, onunload and onload were commonly written onUnload and onLoad. In XHTML, they must be entirely lower-case.

Paragraphs and headings

The next two sections describe some of the core components of XHTML: the p element and the h1-h6 heading elements that together formed the backbone of HTML documents since the very beginning of the Web. All of these elements are defined so that they may contain only in-line elements (as defined in the Inline entity, described in the preceding Text Elements section.). The transitional and frameset DTDs also provide use of the align attribute through the TextAlign entity.

Lists

The list section defines XHTML's ordered, unordered, and definition lists. In the strict DTD, the declarations are very simple; they apply only the core attributes (defined in the attrs entity) using the Inline and Flow entities to identify content models for list items. In the transitional and frameset DTDs, the type, compact, and start attributes give document authors a lot more control over how they can present the lists.

Other elements

The next few sections of the DTDs define elements that don't fit easily into categories. The horizontal rule (hr), preformatted text (pre), block quotation (blockquote), centering (center, which only appears in the transitional and framework DTDs), and insert and delete editing elements (ins and del) are defined here.

Anchor element

The anchor element (a), another difficult element to categorize, comes next. The a element defines its content model using the a.content entity (defined in the section for exclusions). Its hyperlinking features are defined using its attributes, which are the same in all the DTDs except that the strict DTD doesn't allow the target attribute to identify the frame in which content should appear.

 Strange though it may seem, the a element is one of the most likely elements to face significant change in the immediate future as the XLink standard is integrated with XHTML.

In-line elements

The in-line elements section defines an enormous number of XHTML element types, all of them intended for use within text. Almost all of them are defined using the attrs entity for their attributes and the Inline entity for their content. The transitional and frameset DTDs include the u, s, strike, basefont, and font elements, which were deprecated in HTML 4.0 and aren't present in the strict DTD. Similarly, the br element loses the clear attribute, commonly used in complex layouts.

Objects and applets

The next two sections define the somewhat similar object and applet elements for including software objects and Java applets within XHTML documents. The strict DTD omits a few formatting descriptions from the object element and completely omits the applet element — considering it to be a duplication of the object element's functionality. At the same time, the object element loses the formatting-oriented hspace, vspace, and border attributes. Also worth noting, although without significant impact in XHTML 1.0, is a suggestion to drop the param element. The W3C's *Resource Description Framework (RDF)* allows more flexibility in representing information and could eventually permit attributes to replace param elements in the object element. This isn't, however, implemented in any of the DTDs.

Images and image maps

The next two sections define elements for images (img) and client-side image maps (map and area). The img element receives a few extra formatting attributes in the transitional and frameset DTDs, while the area element loses the target attribute in the strict DTD.

Forms

XHTML 1.0 provides the same form support as HTML 4.0. Apart from a slight change to prevent form elements from containing other form elements (which is prohibited), most of these declarations are fairly simple. As usual, the transitional and frameset DTDs provide additional formatting options.

Tables

XHTML 1.0 provides the same table support as HTML 4.0. Most of these declarations are fairly simple, although the table element is notable for prohibiting direct textual content. (If you have any text floating in your table elements that isn't contained by another element, be sure to remove it!) As usual, the transitional and frameset DTDs provide additional formatting attributes, such as bgcolor, height, width, and some alignments.

Beyond the XHTML DTDs

While the XHTML DTDs describe an enormous amount of document structure, there remain a few key parts of XHTML that can't be contained neatly within the DTD. XML DTDs only permit elements to describe their own content — they aren't, for instance, allowed to prohibit content within the elements they contain. To enforce such requirements, the W3C includes a normative (required) appendix to the XHTML 1.0 specification, "Element Prohibitions" (`http://www.w3.org/TR/xhtml1/#prohibitions`). While validating XML parsers won't catch these problems, XHTML applications should check for these situations.

In a significant sense, the XHTML 1.0 DTDs represent only one piece of a complex specification. While learning to read the DTDs can give you lots of insight into how the W3C is implementing XHTML, there's a reason that these formal declarations are relegated to an appendix. They are an important part of the specification — the appendix is, in fact, normative — but they provide only part of the XHTML picture.

Chapter 8

Style Sheets and XHTML

Cascading Style Sheets (CSS) is an enormously powerful tool that has been slow to catch on in the HTML development world. Whether or not you use (or like) CSS, the continuing evolution of CSS is deeply intertwined with the work moving forward on XHTML so learning about CSS can help you understand XHTML as well as implement it. Fortunately, CSS isn't very difficult once you master a few key structures and learn to apply its vocabulary. There are some real problems with existing CSS implementations that I cover later in this chapter, but future XHTML work probably should make as much use of CSS as possible.

Cascading style sheets is an enormous specification in itself, worth a book or three on its own. This chapter gets you started in CSS, but you'll want to find additional information if you move into CSS in a big way. The latest information on cascading style sheets from the W3C is available at `http://www.w3.org/Style/CSS/`. The discussions in this chapter focus on CSS Level 1 and CSS Level 2, both of which are stable as paper specifications if not completely implemented. The ongoing development of CSS Level 3 is likely to bring some significant changes to the XHTML landscape, and is definitely worth following. For a current list of CSS work, see `http://www.w3.org/Style/CSS/current-work`.

Separating Format from Content

CSS was one of the W3C's earliest efforts at separating formatting information from document structure in HTML. This recurring theme has been at the heart of most W3C HTML activity since HTML 4.0's start, and CSS is a critical ingredient in implementing that project. By providing a simple set of tools that exercise much more thorough control over presentation than HTML itself, CSS was supposed to lure developers away from the millions of FONT tags used in HTML documents. CSS is the carrot; HTML 4.0's (and XHTML's) deprecation of the FONT element is the stick.

CSS offers document designers a number of key features that are nearly impossible to implement effectively with straight HTML (even if the FONT element is used). CSS also provides reusability. The formatting descriptions applied to documents can be applied to any document with the same vocabulary. CSS even lets you create style sheets that address particular situations within a given vocabulary, specifying formatting based on nested element structures or attribute values. You can make tens of thousands of HTML documents use the same formatting just by connecting one line of code in each document to the same CSS style sheet. This also makes it easy to change formatting across all of those documents because changes made to the master style sheet are reflected in all the documents that use it. Managing presentation is much simpler when all it takes is a change in a style sheet rather than a search-and-replace across thousands of documents.

Keep your style sheet documents in a safe place! Any time your documents refer to a central style sheet, you can use that resource to modify the presentation for all your documents. It makes it easier for you to make the changes, but attackers potentially could modify the style sheet to graffiti your pages. See the first part of David Megginson's "When XML Gets Ugly" presentation at http://www.megginson.com/ugly/index.html for some of the attacks you should watch out for.

Although a single master style sheet for a site is attractive, sometimes you need to change a presentation for a particular unit of an organization, a certain document, or even a certain element. The "cascade" in Cascading Style Sheets enables you to handle this problem easily without requiring constant cut-and-paste to create customized style sheets. Style sheets and documents can reference multiple style sheets, and CSS provides a set of rules for resolving where to use each style. HTML and XHTML provide extra hooks — the class and style attributes — for connecting style-based formatting to particular elements. (The hooks aren't as necessary in XML, where developers have more control over the vocabulary.)

Cascading Style Sheets also enables designers to get out of the complex business of formatting HTML generated by server-side programs. Rather than having to edit templates filled with programming code, designers can agree with programmers on what the output of those programs should look like and then design style sheets to match without getting directly involved in the code. On the client side, CSS makes it easy for programmers to reach into the formatting created by document designers and change it when appropriate; thus, designers do not have to build styling specific to a page. While designers and programmers sometimes have to work closely together in both client- and server-side development (and sometimes they're the same person), CSS makes it easy to divide responsibilities cleanly.

Finally — although this isn't implemented widely in browsers — CSS offers mechanisms that enable users to specify how content should be formatted. Combined with the emphasis on accessibility that has influenced much of the CSS process, this enables readers to access information in a format that's comfortable for them. Some readers need larger font sizes, while others just want to get the information in as compact a form as possible. Still other readers need aural (audio) presentation of the content — either because they can't see it or because, for instance, they're driving their cars and checking the news. Some designers grit their teeth at the prospect of users changing their carefully built designs, but for many users this critical issue determines the Web's usefulness for them.

The CSS Processing Model

Cascading Style Sheets takes what is known as an *annotative* approach to formatting documents. Rather than convert one document into another (the *transformative* approach of XSL), CSS processors add the information from the style sheets into the structures' browsers and other tools used to present information.

Like HTML, CSS assumes that the content contained within element structures is meant for display while attributes are meant to provide additional information that shouldn't be displayed directly as part of the text flow. Effectively, style sheet information is treated as additional markup, much like attributes, and primarily modifies the presentation of the information already in the document, not its content.

CSS2 and CSS3 provide some simple tools for modifying content, but nothing complex or especially powerful, at least as compared to XSLT's transformation capabilities. CSS3 also provides tools for connecting scripts to elements through style sheets. Despite these extra tools, the preceding description holds very well for most current CSS activity.

Cascading style sheets that deal with HTML or XHTML can build on the understandings browsers already have about the presentation semantics for the HTML vocabulary. H1 elements typically are rendered in larger type than H2 elements, LI elements are rendered as indented bulleted (or numbered, depending on context) list items, and so on. For HTML and XHTML, CSS enables designers to fine-tune those already understood rules. In some cases, CSS also enables designers to break the rules completely, using tricks such as CSS positioning to place content in particular locations on the screen or in a document window.

For a clear picture of the "understood" presentation semantics of the HTML vocabulary, see the non-normative (effectively unofficial) style sheet in Appendix A of the CSS2 specification (http://www.w3.org/TR/REC-CSS2/sample.html). You also can use this style sheet to display XHTML documents in XML browsers that lack a clear understanding of the HTML vocabulary. It even includes rules for aural presentation!

Because browsers already have rules for how they present HTML built into their code, designers can specify as much or as little formatting information as they like. Also, it's possible to create documents and style sheets that degrade gracefully. Browsers that don't understand CSS, or that only understand a portion of the CSS vocabulary used in a style sheet, are capable of presenting a basic view of the document to users. This is very useful when creating HTML documents that must be viewed on older browsers (the 3.x generation) or on text-only browsers such as Lynx. The demonstration of various browser capabilities in Chapter 5 shows some real limitations of this approach, but the degradation is becoming more graceful with the most recent browsers. Some features, such as positioning or the tools for adding content, will never degrade gracefully. However, they may be useful for certain projects (notably intranet development) in which the application developers can expect users to have more recent browsers.

CSS style sheets are built out of lists of rules. While there are some hierarchies to these lists (more on this later in the chapter), the lists of rules generally are built out of two parts. The first part is the *selector*, which identifies to which elements a given rule applies. The second part, composed of properties, describes the formatting that a particular set of elements should receive. The general syntax looks like this:

```
selector {propertyName1: propertyValue1;
    propertyName2: propertyValue2;
    etc...}
```

Using Selectors

Cascading style sheets often are separate from the elements or even documents they format, so style sheets need to have a way of identifying which elements need which formatting. Selectors provide a flexible layer of abstraction that makes it easy to apply properties to individual element types, as well as groups and subsets of element types. Selectors describe the parts of a document that should receive particular formatting and they make it easy to create style sheets that work across a set of documents; they do not describe document structures in general.

There are many different coding styles for selectors, all built on the same syntax. Repeated declarations within a style sheet using the same selector are perfectly acceptable, and multiple selectors can target the same element. Unlike XML document type definitions, there is no requirement that a given document conform to the structure described by a style sheet. If a selector is used that doesn't have a match in a given document, the rule is ignored. These fairly relaxed rules make it possible to create sophisticated style sheets that fit tightly across documents with extremely varied structures.

The simplest selector is just an element name, indicating that all elements with that name should receive the styling properties specified in the braces:

```
h1 {font-family:serif}
```

In this case, all h1 elements are rendered in the browser's default serif typeface — Times or Times New Roman, typically. If you want to apply the same properties to h1, h2, and h3 elements, you can write:

```
h1 {font-family:serif}
h2 {font-family:serif}
h3 {font-family:serif}
```

Or, to reduce the size of this, you can take advantage of another feature of CSS selectors: commas. This single declaration has the same meaning as the three preceding declarations:

```
h1, h2, h3 {font-family:serif}
```

If you want to specify particular formatting for elements that are contained by other elements, CSS selectors enable you to specify containment relationships. If, for example, you want the content of em elements to appear in a sans-serif typeface when used within unordered lists and in a serif typeface when used within ordered lists, you can use these two declarations:

```
ul em {font-family:sans-serif}
ol em {font-family:serif}
```

Because there isn't a comma, these selectors express containment. In CSS Level 2, you can tighten the focus slightly by specifying that rules apply only to direct children rather than just descendants. For example, if you want to create rules to format list items in a particular way for ordered and unordered lists, you can use:

```
ul>li { properties }
ol>li { properties }
```

If needed, you can use the asterisk (*) as a wildcard in place of an element name in any of the preceding declarations.

Another common approach uses attribute values to select particular elements for styling. XHTML's class element was designed specifically for styling, enabling document authors to specify particular types within the generic HTML vocabulary.

There are two ways to use class information. First, you can use class information in combination with element name information. If some p elements have a class value of aside, you can specify properties for them with syntax like this:

```
p.aside { properties }
```

If you have multiple element types that all use the aside class value—div elements, for instance—you can specify the class value without specifying the element name and create a selector that applies to all of them:

```
.aside { properties }
```

Similarly, CSS enables you to select elements by ID value—the id attribute value in XHTML. This feature is most common in one-off style sheets intended for a single document, typically a dynamic HTML document. It works much like the selector for class, except that it uses # instead of a period. If you want to apply styling to the element with the ID "Section12", you can create a declaration that looks like this:

```
#Section12 { properties }
```

If you want to limit that styling to p elements that have the ID "Section12", you can write:

```
p#Section12 { properties }
```

While these are the most common selectors, CSS offers many more possibilities (as shown in Table 8-1).

TABLE 8–1 CSS LEVEL 1 AND 2 SELECTORS

Selector	Meaning	CSS Level
elementName	Selects all elements named elementName	1, 2
elementName1 elementName2	Selects all elements named elementName2 that are contained (not necessarily directly) within elements named elementName1	1, 2

Selector	Meaning	CSS Level
`elementName1, elementName2[, element Name3...]`	Selects any elements that match any `elementName` in the list	1, 2
`elementName1> elementName2`	Selects all `elementName2` elements that are direct children (not just descendants) of `elementName1` elements	2
`elementName1+ elementName2`	Selects `elementName2` elements that follow (and are siblings of, not children, of) `elementName1` elements	2
`* (asterisk)`	Selects all elements, regardless of their name or content. You can use the asterisk in place of an element name anywhere within a selector. While it typically does not stand by itself for all elements, it can be very useful for describing paths through tree structures. `p * b`, for instance, would select all b elements that were children of children of a p element.	2

Continued

TABLE **8-1** CSS LEVEL 1 AND 2 SELECTORS *(Continued)*

Selector	Meaning	CSS Level
[attName]	Selects elements that specify a value (the particular value doesn't matter) for the attribute attName	2
[attName= "attValue"]	Selects elements that have the particular value attValue for the attribute attName	2
[attName~= "attValue"]	Selects elements when the value attValue is contained anywhere in a list (separated by whitespace) of tokens in the attribute attName	2
[attName|= "attValue"]	Selects elementName elements with attributes named attName when their value begins with attValue followed by a hyphen (used to select particular language types)	2
.className	Selects elementName elements (if specified) that contain an attribute named class (XHTML or HTML) or CLASS (HTML only) whose value is className	1, 2 (HTML and XHTML only)
#IDvalue	Selects elementName elements that contain an attribute of type ID (in HTML, named ID) whose value is Idvalue. In XHTML, this selector references elements named id.	1, 2

Selector	Meaning	CSS Level
:first-child	Selects elements when they are the first child elements to appear inside their parent elements	2
:link	Selects elements when they represent hypertext links that the user has not visited yet	1, 2
:visited	Selects elements when they represent hypertext links that the user has visited already	1, 2
:active	Selects hypertext links while the user is activating them. Enables you to specify a different look for the link during the clicking process.	1, 2
:hover	Selects elements when the user holds the mouse cursor over them. Used for highlighting links, typically.	2
:focus	Selects elements when they have the focus, typically when a user enters information in a form	2
:lang (language)	Selects element content of the language specified. The CSS2 specification suggests that this will work in conjunction with the xml:lang attribute for identifying	2

Continued

TABLE 8-1 CSS LEVEL 1 AND 2 SELECTORS *(Continued)*

Selector	Meaning	CSS Level
`:lang(language)` *continued*	element language content. This should work safely with the XHTML `xml:lang` attribute.	
`:before`	This selector inserts content (using the `content` property) before the element described by the rest of the selector. This must appear at the end of a selector, after other selectors target to which elements this applies.	2
`:after`	This selector inserts content (using the `content` property) after the element described by the rest of the selector. This must appear at the end of a selector, after other selectors target to which elements this applies.	2
`:first-line`	Selects the first line of the content identified by the rest of the selector	2
`:first-letter`	Selects the first letter of the content identified by the rest of the selector	2

No single browser currently supports the entire range of CSS1 and CSS2 selectors, but support is improving. Most Level 1 selectors are implemented, although older tools may not handle even all of Level 1. Check online for the latest information regarding implementation. *Web Review* maintains a chart at http://webreview.com/pub/guides/style/css2select.html.

The W3C is developing even more selectors for CSS3. See http://www.w3.org/TR/CSS3-selectors for the latest developments, though it will be a long while before we see these new features in production browsers..

Formatting Content with Properties

While selectors do a great job of picking out content that needs formatting, designers (as opposed to Web site managers) like CSS mostly because of the large number of available formatting properties. CSS offers properties that support nearly any presentation of a document desired, and yet more properties are in development as part of the CSS3 activity. CSS properties enable you to describe precisely how you want the pieces of your document formatted and to override the rules by which HTML is presented normally.

Table 8-2 provides a list of commonly used CSS properties, although it isn't complete — the full list is enormous, and growing larger. This list should, however, provide you with a taste of what's possible.

TABLE 8-2 CSS LEVEL 1 AND 2 FORMATING PROPERTIES

Property	Notes	Acceptable Values	Level
background	Specifies all the possibilities for a background in one value. A *combination* property, meaning that it contains many values describing the background.	A collection of the values for the other background properties	1, 2
background-attachment	Specifies whether the background scrolls with the content or remains fixed in one place	scroll, fixed, inherit	1, 2
background-color	Background color for the element	A color name (such as white) or hex representation (such as #FFFFFF for white)	1, 2
background-image	Background image of an element	URL identifying the image	1, 2
background-repeat	Identifies whether the background should repeat	repeat, repeat-x, repeat-y, no-repeat, inherit	1, 2
border	Specifies all the possibilities describing the border of the element in one value	A collection of the values for the other border properties	1, 2
border-bottom-color	Sets color value for bottom border	Color name or hex value	2
border-bottom-style	Sets the style for the border on the bottom of the block	none (default), dotted, dashed, solid, double, groove, ridge, inset, outset	2

Property	Notes	Acceptable Values	Level
border-bottom-width	Sets width for the border on the bottom of the block	thin, medium, thick, or an explicit measurement	1, 2
border-color	Sets color value for entire border	Color name or hex value	1, 2
border-left-color	Sets color value for left border	Color name or hex value	2
border-left-style	Sets style of the border on the left of the block	none (default), dotted, dashed, solid, double, groove, ridge, inset, outset	2
border-left-width	Sets width of the border on the left of the block	thin, medium, thick, or an explicit measurement	1, 2
border-right-color	Sets color value of right border	Color name or hex value	2
border-right-style	Sets style for the border on the right of the block	none (default), dotted, dashed, solid, double, groove, ridge, inset, outset	2
border-right-width	Sets width of the border on the right of the block	thin, medium, thick, or an explicit measurement	1, 2

Continued

TABLE 8-2 CSS LEVEL 1 AND 2 FORMATING PROPERTIES *(Continued)*

Property	Notes	Acceptable Values	Level
border-style	Sets the style for the entire border	none (default), dotted, dashed, solid, double, groove, ridge, inset, outset	1, 2
border-top-color	Sets color of top border	Color name or hex value	2
border-top-style	Sets style of the border on top of the block	none (default), dotted, dashed, solid, groove, ridge, double, inset, outset	2
border-top-width	Sets width for the border on top of the block. Also acts as default if other border-*-width settings not explicitly set.	thin, medium, thick, or an explicit measurement	1, 2
clear	Specifies if floating blocks are allowed along the sides of an object	none, left, right, both, or inherit	1, 2
color	Takes color value for element foreground	Color name or hex value	1, 2
content	Enables designers to insert content into a document. Used with the :before and :after pseudo-element selectors.	Textual content for insertion	2

Property	Notes	Acceptable Values	Level
direction	Identifies the direction of text flow. Important for internationalization	ltr (left-to-right), rtl (right-to-left), or inherit (Inherit only works in CSS; don't try this in XHTML attributes directly.)	2
display	Provides a basic description of how an element should be formatted.	block, inline, listItem, none, run-in, compact, marker, inherit, table, inline-table, table-row-group, table-header-group, table-footer-group, table-row, table-column-group, table-column, table-cell, or table-caption	1, but much enhanced in 2
float	Makes a block float	none, left, right, or inherit	1, 2
font	Specifies all the possibilities for font choice in a single value. A *combination* property.	A collection of the values for the other font properties	1, 2

Continued

TABLE 8-2 CSS LEVEL 1 AND 2 FORMATTING PROPERTIES *(Continued)*

Property	Notes	Acceptable Values	Level
font-family	Identifies the font or font family for an element	serif, sans-serif, and monospace are common; also can be a particular family name (Arial, Times, and so on), although not all fonts are available on all computers, and spaces in font names require quotations around the name.	1, 2
font-size	Sets the font size for an element	May use small, medium, or large as well as point sizes	1, 2
font-style	Sets the style of the font in which style refers to the level and type of italicizing	normal, italic, or oblique	1, 2
font-variant	Used to create small-caps formatting	normal or small-caps	1, 2
font-weight	Specifies a *weight* — level of boldness — for the element content	Integer values from 100 to 900 (if supported), or normal, bold, bolder, or lighter	1, 2

Continued

Property	Notes	Acceptable Values	Level
height	Specifies the height of the element; used for positioning elements in a space, typically a browser window	measurement	1, 2
left	Specifies the position of the left edge of the element from the left edge of the window; used for positioning elements in a space, typically a browser window	measurement	2
letter-spacing	Provides additional (or reduced) spacing between letters within the text	measurement	1, 2
line-height	Specifies distance between baselines of text, allowing line spacing within blocks of text	Can be normal, a number to multiply by point size, an absolute measurement, or a percentage (Absolute measurements cause printing problems in some older browsers.)	1, 2
list-style-image	Allows display of an image—rather than a standard bullet character—as a bullet. With a URI, enables you to customize list presentation beyond the options of list-style-type.	Takes a URI, none, or inherit	1, 2

TABLE 8-2 CSS LEVEL 1 AND 2 FORMATTING PROPERTIES *(Continued)*

Property	Notes	Acceptable Values	Level
list-style-position	Specifies how bullets should be placed into a list of bulleted items	Takes inside, outside, or inherit	1, 2
list-style-type	Sets the default bullet appearance (If an image is specified, it overrides this setting.)	disk, circle, square, decimal, or inherit	1, 2
margin	Specifies all margin properties in a single property. A *combination* property.	A collection of the values for the other margin properties	1, 2
margin-bottom	Specifies how much empty space to leave below the bottom of the element	measurement	1, 2
margin-left	Specifies how much empty space to leave to the left of the element	measurement	1, 2
margin-right	Specifies how much empty space to leave to the right of the element	measurement	1, 2
margin-top	Specifies how much empty space to leave above the top of the element	measurement	1, 2
overflow	Describes what to do if an element's contents go beyond the height and width specified	Can be visible or scroll	2
padding	Specifies all padding properties in a single property. A *combination* property.	A collection of the values for the other padding properties	1, 2

Property	Notes	Acceptable Values	Level
padding-bottom	Specifies how much empty space to leave between the bottom edge of the content and the bottom of the element	measurement	1, 2
padding-left	Specifies how much empty space to leave between the right edge of the content and the left of the element	measurement	1, 2
padding-right	Specifies how much empty space to leave between the right edge of the content and the right of the element	measurement	1, 2
padding-top	Specifies how much empty space to leave between the top edge of the content and the top of the element	measurement	1, 2
page	Identifies pages for printing	Takes an identifier or auto (the default)	2
page-break-after	Specifies how page breaks (in printouts, not onscreen) should come after the appearance of the element	auto, always, avoid, left, right, and inherit	2
page-break-before	Specifies how page breaks (in printouts, not onscreen) should come before the appearance of the element	auto, always, avoid, left, right, and inherit	2

Continued

TABLE 8-2 CSS LEVEL 1 AND 2 FORMATTING PROPERTIES *(Continued)*

Property	Notes	Acceptable Values	Level
page-break-inside	Specifies how page breaks (in printouts, not onscreen) should be handled within the element	auto, always, left, right, avoid, and inherit	2
text-align	Specifies horizontal text alignment	left, right, center, or justify	1, 2
text-decoration	Specifies additional marking (typically lines) for the element text. If you want to recreate the HTML BLINK element in strict XHTML, you need this property.	none, underline, overline, line-through, or blink	1, 2
text-indent	How much to indent the text of the first line of an element	measurement or percentage	1, 2
text-transform	Permits the transformation of text into different cases	none (default), capitalize, uppercase, lowercase, or inherit	1, 2
top	Specifies the position of the top edge of an element relative to the top edge of the window. Used for positioning elements in a space, typically a browser window.	Usually a measurement; also can be auto or inherit	2

Property	Notes	Acceptable Values	Level
vertical-align	Specifies how element content should be aligned relative to the baseline of the text. Used in creating subscripts and superscripts.	baseline (default), sub, super, top, text-top, middle, bottom, text-bottom, or a percentage or measurement above the baseline	1, 2
visibility	Whether or not to render an object transparently. Unlike display:none, this doesn't prevent child elements from appearing.	inherit, collapse, visible, and hidden	2
white-space	pre tells the browser to respect all whitespace in the element content, including line breaks, without requiring tags. nowrap tells the browser not to break lines unless explicitly told to with a , <P>, or other line break-forcing element.	normal, inherit, pre, or nowrap	1, 2
width	Specifies the width of an image	a measurement	1, 2
word-spacing	Specifies additional spacing between words. Sometimes useful for letting background patterns show through text, or for fitting text to a particular space.	a measurement, normal, or inherit	1, 2
z-index	Identifies the z-layer of a positioned block for (somewhat) three-dimensional positioning; higher values are layered on top of lower values.	any integer	2

Now that you have a set of tools to work with, take a look at some simple examples based on the strict XHTML example used (sometimes successfully) in Chapter 5.

```
<?xml version="1.0" encoding="UTF-8"?>
<!DOCTYPE html
   PUBLIC "-//W3C//DTD XHTML 1.0 Strict//EN"
   "http://www.w3.org/TR/xhtml1/DTD/xhtml1-strict.dtd">
<html xmlns="http://www.w3.org/1999/xhtml" lang="en-US" xml:lang="en-US">
<head>
<title>Strict XHTML - Phase 2</title>
<meta http-equiv='Content-type' content='text/html; charset="UTF-8"' />
<script type="text/javascript" src="mycode.js" ></script>
<link rel="stylesheet" href="mycss.css" type="text/css" />
</head>
<body>
<h1>Strict XHTML - Phase 2</h1>
<p><a name="description" id="description">This document is strict XHTML - we'll
see how it does in the browsers.</a></p>
<p>The cleanup shouldn't cause too many problems, we hope.</p>
<ul>
<li><span onclick="presentCount()">Click me for a count!</span></li>
<li><a href="query.htm?val1=1&amp;val2=2&amp;val3=3">Click here for a
query!</a></li>
<li><a href="#description">Click here for a description of this page</a></li>
</ul>
<p>Copyright 2000 by the Wacki HTML Writer <br />
All rights reserved.</p>
</body>
</html>
```

The original style sheet was quite simple:

```
body {background-color:#FFFFFF }
h1 {color:blue; font-family:Times, serif; font-size:24pt}
```

The body element is given a white background, while the headline is presented in blue type – preferably in Times, but alternatively in a typeface with serifs using 24-point type. This should produce results (in a CSS-aware browser) that look like Figure 8-1:

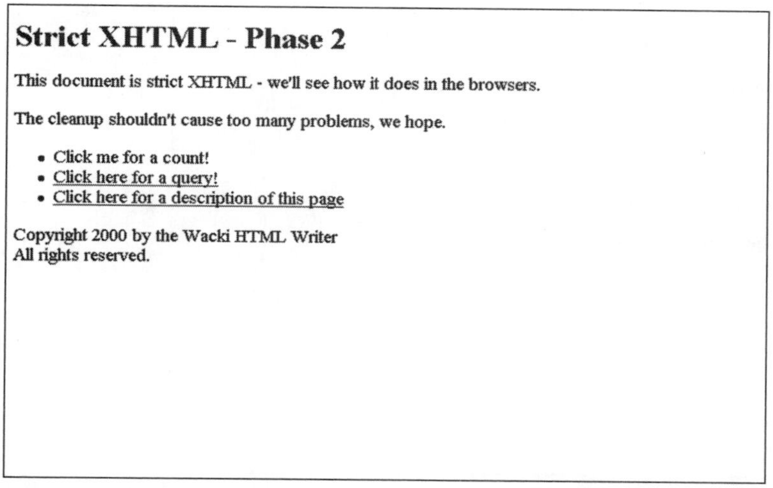

Strict XHTML - Phase 2

This document is strict XHTML - we'll see how it does in the browsers.

The cleanup shouldn't cause too many problems, we hope.

- Click me for a count!
- Click here for a query!
- Click here for a description of this page

Copyright 2000 by the Wacki HTML Writer
All rights reserved.

Figure 8-1: The strict XHTML document, opened in a CSS-aware browser, has the specified blue 24-point headline with a white background.

When you created this style sheet in Chapter 5, you only tried to recreate some simple effects you built using the FONT element in the old HTML. Now that it's converted, you can modify the style sheet to show off some of the capabilities CSS provides. You can start by specifying more information about the text presentation. Then change the paragraph and list text to sans-serif type and make the body text bigger.

```
body {background-color:#FFFFFF }
h1 {color:blue; font-family:Times, serif; font-size:24pt}
p {font-family:sans-serif; font-size:14pt}
li {font-family:sans-serif; font-size:12pt}
```

By adding two lines of very simple style information, you change the presentation significantly (as shown in Figure 8-2).

Without changing the document, you also can change the way links are presented using the :link, :visited, and :active pseudo-classes.

```
body {background-color:#FFFFFF }
h1 {color:blue; font-family:Times, serif; font-size:24pt}
p {font-family:sans-serif; font-size:14pt}
li {font-family:sans-serif; font-size:12pt}
a:link {color:green; font-weight:bold}
a:visited {color:brown; font-weight:normal}
a:active {background-color:yellow}
```

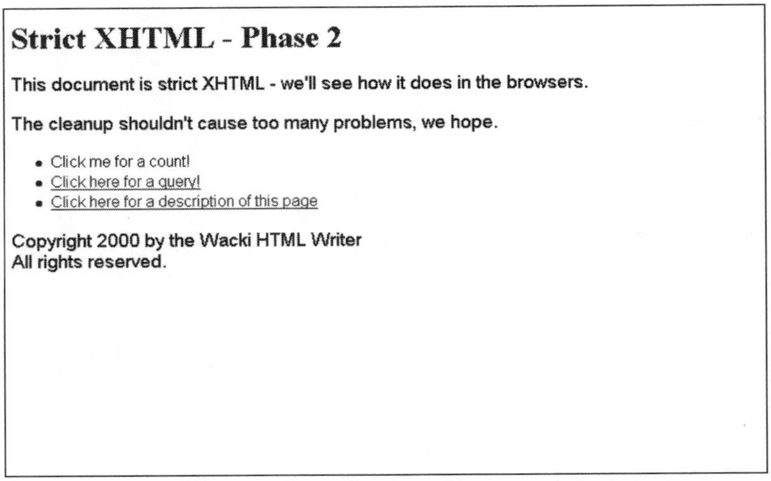

Strict XHTML - Phase 2

This document is strict XHTML - we'll see how it does in the browsers.

The cleanup shouldn't cause too many problems, we hope.

- Click me for a count!
- Click here for a query!
- Click here for a description of this page

Copyright 2000 by the Wacki HTML Writer
All rights reserved.

Figure 8-2: All of the content in the strict XHTML document is styled by CSS now, although it still has the foundation provided by the HTML vocabulary.

The new properties make the links more interesting, as shown in Figures 8-3 through 8-5.

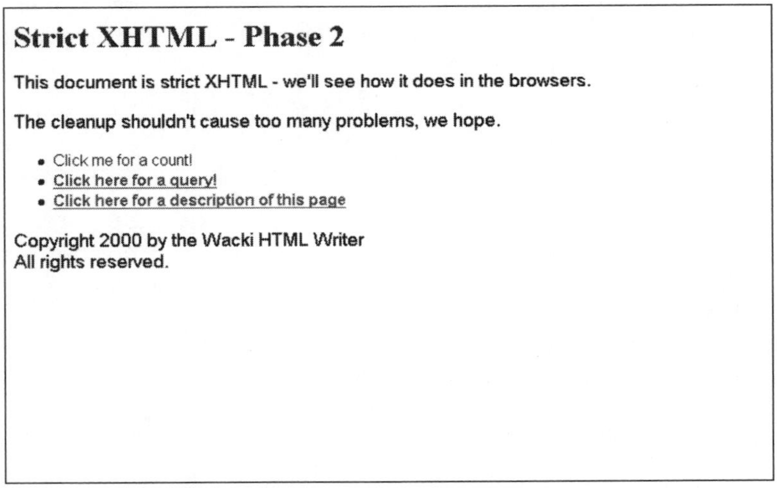

Strict XHTML - Phase 2

This document is strict XHTML - we'll see how it does in the browsers.

The cleanup shouldn't cause too many problems, we hope.

- Click me for a count!
- Click here for a query!
- Click here for a description of this page

Copyright 2000 by the Wacki HTML Writer
All rights reserved.

Figure 8-3: The links in the document appear in a different color now, waiting for people to click them. Note that while no underline is specified, it appears because of the rules for HTML vocabularies.

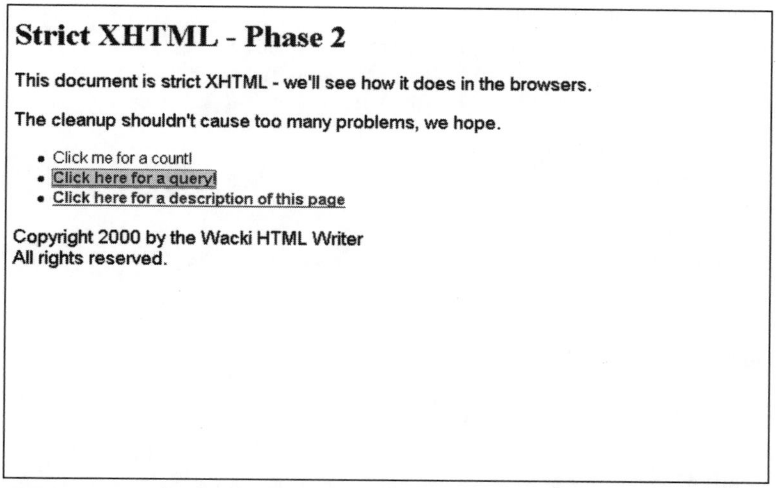

Strict XHTML - Phase 2

This document is strict XHTML - we'll see how it does in the browsers.

The cleanup shouldn't cause too many problems, we hope.

- Click me for a count!
- Click here for a query!
- Click here for a description of this page

Copyright 2000 by the Wacki HTML Writer
All rights reserved.

Figure 8-4: When you click a link (but before you release the button), it is highlighted in yellow.

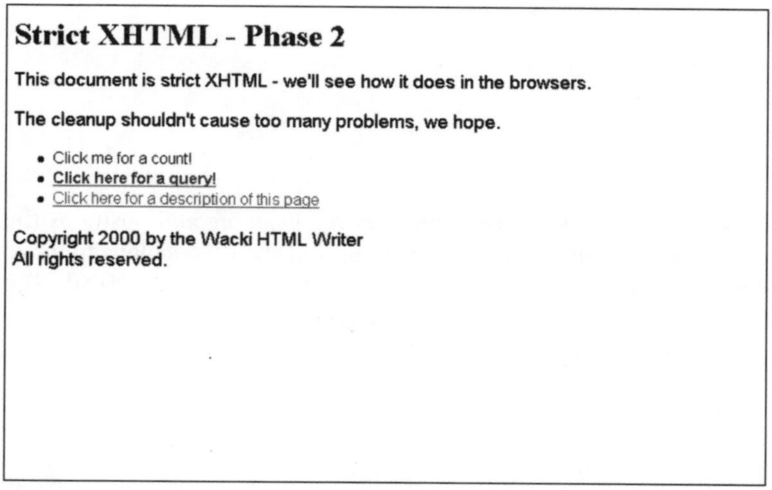

Strict XHTML - Phase 2

This document is strict XHTML - we'll see how it does in the browsers.

The cleanup shouldn't cause too many problems, we hope.

- Click me for a count!
- Click here for a query!
- Click here for a description of this page

Copyright 2000 by the Wacki HTML Writer
All rights reserved.

Figure 8-5: After you select a link, the boldface disappears and the link is presented in a different color.

To demonstrate some of CSS's more sophisticated capabilities, you now create a demonstration document that has a few more hooks with which you can work. The following document is fairly simple strict XHTML, but it provides a foundation for experiments.

```
<?xml version="1.0" encoding="UTF-8"?>
<!DOCTYPE html
```

```
PUBLIC "-//W3C//DTD XHTML 1.0 Strict//EN"
"http://www.w3.org/TR/xhtml1/DTD/xhtml1-strict.dtd">
<html xmlns="http://www.w3.org/1999/xhtml" lang="en-US"
xml:lang="en-US">
<head>
<title>CSS Positioning Demo</title>
<meta http-equiv='Content-type' content='text/html; charset="UTF-8"'
/>
<link rel="stylesheet" href="funkcss.css" type="text/css" />
</head>
<body>
<div id="header">Headline</div>
<div id="fragment1">Fragment 1</div>
<div id="fragment2">Fragment 2</div>
<div id="fragment3">Fragment 3</div>
<div id="fragment4">Fragment 4</div>
<div id="fragment5">Fragment 5</div>
<div id="fragment6">Fragment 6</div>
<div id="fragment7">Fragment 7</div>
<div id="fragment8">Fragment 8</div>

<div id="paragraph">This paragraph contains more text and some
<em>emphasis</em> as well.</div>
</body>
</html>
```

You start with a simple style sheet that modifies the headline and positions the first and second fragments. Positioning is a critical part of the W3C's plans to move beyond frame-based Web interfaces, as well as a key tool for dynamic HTML. The first fragment gets positioned in absolute terms relative to the document as a whole, while the second fragment gets positioned relative to where it would appear.

```
body {background-color:#FFFFFF }
div#header {font-size:24pt; font-family:serif; color:blue}
div#fragment1 {position:absolute; top:175px; left:150px}
div#fragment2 {position:relative; top:175px; left:100px}
```

You employ two different kinds of measurement here. The pt measurements are points (used for characters), while the px measurements are pixels (used more frequently to specify locations for blocks of content). Later, you use percentage measures as well. Figure 8-6 shows the results:

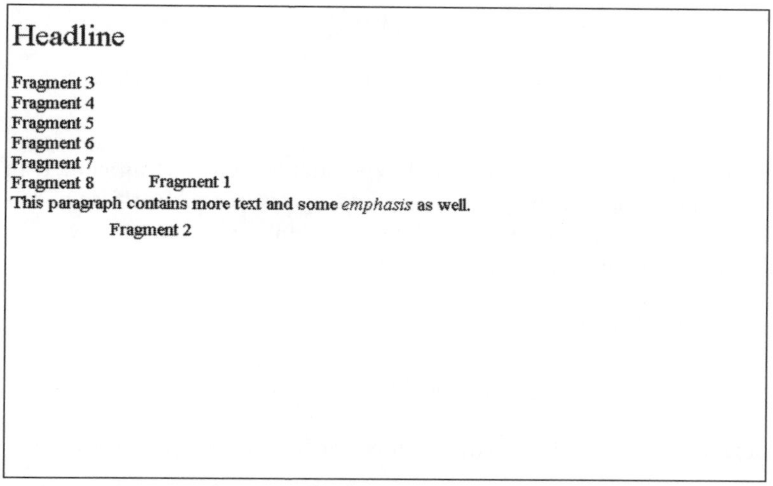

```
Headline

Fragment 3
Fragment 4
Fragment 5
Fragment 6
Fragment 7
Fragment 8            Fragment 1
This paragraph contains more text and some emphasis as well.
              Fragment 2
```

Figure 8-6: Relative and absolute positioning

Now let's modify some more CSS properties for the other fragments and for the div elements in general. Start with the previous style sheet:

```
body {background-color:#FFFFFF }
div#header {font-size:24pt; font-family:serif; color:blue}
div#fragment1 {position:absolute; top:175px; left:150px}
div#fragment2 {position:relative; top:175px; left:100px}
```

Next, you do some basic formatting on fragments 3 through 5. For fragment 3, you transform its content to uppercase with the text-transform property. For fragment 4, you widen the spacing between characters using the letter-spacing property and center fragment 5 using the text-align property.

```
div#fragment3 {text-transform:uppercase;}
div#fragment4 {letter-spacing:3pt;}
div#fragment5 {text-align:center;}
```

For fragments 6 and 7, you use the margin properties, padding properties, and borders to demonstrate how CSS handles these. For fragment 6, you set a left margin of 25 points to move the text to the right; then you set a bottom margin of 50 points to move the text that follows much farther away. The border then shows the area that the browser considers the content of the element. For fragment 7, you set a left margin of 50 points, but a right margin of 25 percent of the browser window. Fifty points of padding — all around the element because you're using the combination property — expands the space occupied by the fragment, and the groove border shows you how the browser handles this set of properties.

```
div#fragment6 {margin-left:25pt; margin-bottom:50pt; border-style:
double;}
div#fragment7 {margin-left:50pt; margin-right:25%; padding:50pt;
border-style:groove;}
```

Now modify the presentation for the last few elements, setting fragment 8 to appear on the right-hand edge of the page. The paragraph is in sans-serif type, distinguishing it from its div counterparts. For the em element, however, you override only the default italic – making it bold but not italic.

```
div#fragment8 {text-align:right;}
p {font-family:sans-serif;}
em {font-weight:bold; font-style:normal;}
```

Figure 8-7 shows the results of this strange brew of formatting properties.

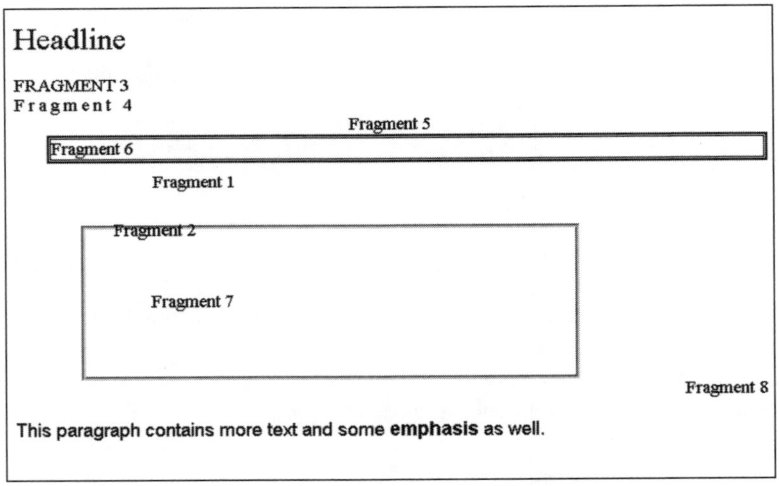

Figure 8–7: Adding more formatting information definitely changes the look of the document. Note the difference between the use of margins (fragment 6) and padding (fragment 7).

While this demonstrates many of the capabilities of CSS, making CSS useful requires case-by-case examination of your documents in combination with the XHTML strategies you choose. If you plan to use strict XHTML, CSS is an invaluable tool. Even if you use transitional or frameset XHTML, however, you may find it easier to apply CSS properties from style sheets rather than scatter formatting information throughout your documents.

Rules for Rules

The *cascade* in Cascading Style Sheets describes a set of rules determining how CSS properties get applied. Documents can reference multiple style sheets with multiple `link` elements, and those style sheets may in turn reference other style sheets through CSS `@import URL` statements. Documents also may include style sheets directly within a `style` element, elements within HTML and XHTML documents may specify additional styling by describing properties in the `style` attribute, and users may (at least in theory) tell their browsers to present documents using style sheets of their choice. All of these options provide enormous flexibility, but they make a clear set of rules critical.

CSS2 lays these rules out in Section 6: Assigning Property Values, Cascading, and Inheritance (`http://www.w3.org/TR/REC-CSS2/cascade.html`). The specification first describes *inheritance*, the rules for handling styling of elements contained by other elements. Then it describes the interaction among user agent (typically browser), user, and author style sheets. Users should be able to create style sheets and override the style sheets that come with documents (the author style sheets), but CSS provides an `!important` mechanism that enables the creators of author style sheets to override user preferences. The `!` mechanism is somewhat controversial, partly because `!` usually means 'not', and partly because the rules for processing it changed between CSS Level 1 and CSS Level 2. At this point, most software doesn't provide a mechanism for applying user style sheets, which favors the theory that authors should be able to override the browser defaults.

As for the many style sheet documents that may contribute to the presentation of a given document, the general rule is that the last declaration wins and imported style sheets are considered to come before the document content that actually imports them. The last style sheet linked into an HTML or XHTML document is effectively dominant. Style sheets may build on older style sheets by importing them and then overriding or supplementing the rules they contain. Another somewhat complex set of rules describes how to choose among rules set by different selectors based on how specifically they target a given element. Styling describing an `ID` is more specific than styling describing a class of elements, which may be more specific than styling describing how to format all elements of a given name. The rules are a little strange, but they typically make sense in practice.

Application Issues

The worst problems for developers using CSS stem from implementation in various browsers, not from the complexity of the specification itself. While the W3C's www-style mailing list periodically tears apart pieces of the specifications, most of the difficulties involve various levels of support for CSS functionality in different browsers. Even when features are implemented, often details don't work as expected or as advertised. CSS today is also a very browser-oriented technology, although there are editors that support and use cascading style sheets on various levels. In addition, browser-orientation is pretty natural to XHTML.

As Chapter 5 reveals, older browsers have plenty of problems with XHTML already; using CSS helps in some of these cases and hurts in others. While CSS seems like a natural part of the XHTML family of standards in the long term, it will be a bumpy transition while browsers improve and users slowly upgrade.

If you have questions about the structure of CSS or why it does things in a particular way, as opposed to simple implementation issues, the www-style mailing list maintained by the W3C is an excellent resource. Archives are available at `http://lists.w3.org/Archives/Public/www-style/`, and subscription information is available at `http://www.w3.org/Mail/ Request`.

If you need to find out which browsers support certain features of CSS, *Web Review* maintains an excellent listing at `http://webreview.com/pub/ guides/style/style.html`. To test out a particular browser's conformance to CSS, visit the W3C's CSS Test Suite (CSS1 only at present) at `http://www.w3.org/Style/CSS/Test/`. To check that your own CSS is written properly, visit the W3C's CSS Validation Service at `http://jigsaw. w3.org/css-validator/`.

Is XSL for XHTML?

Supporters of Extensible Stylesheet Language (XSL) promote it as far more powerful than CSS, especially for print media. You can apply XSL to any XML, including XHTML. XSL's capability to reorganize and rebuild documents is attractive in some situations, and some classes of applications may find it necessary.

There are some real costs to XSL, however. As of this writing, the specification for the formatting objects remains in development, although Chapter 12 explores the complete transformation vocabulary (XSL Transformations, or XSLT). While the XSL Formatting Objects vocabulary is fairly similar to cascading style sheets, the mechanisms involved in XSL's transformative approach are much more like programming than those in cascading style sheet's more descriptive approach. Designers who already have a background in programming may find XSL exciting, but others may find it intimidating.

XSL support probably will come to browsers eventually, although it isn't clear if support for XSL will be any smoother than that for CSS. In any case, it's likely that XSL support will be delayed as CSS support has been—making this transition, if it takes place, a slow one. For now, while it's wise to keep an eye on XSL developments, you probably will do better to leverage the already friendly relations between HTML (and XHTML) and CSS.

Part III

Making the Big Jump

CHAPTER 9
Using XHTML in Traditional HTML Applications

CHAPTER 10
The Big Clean-Up: Fixing Static HTML
(The Easy Part)

CHAPTER 11
The Big Clean-Up: Fixing HTML Generating Code
(The Hard Part)

Chapter 9

Using XHTML in Traditional HTML Applications

BEFORE MOVING INTO the much more complicated terrain of converting older HTML content to the newer XHTML rules, let's take a look at how the shift to XHTML affects day-to-day Web development and the construction of new content. Web development has been in nearly constant flux since its beginnings, and developers are accustomed to (if perhaps tired of) the challenges that come with every new standard and every new browser. Some of the challenges XHTML presents are familiar, although a few new twists brought on by XHTML's view of processing beyond the browser make new demands.

Lessons from Previous Technology Shifts

XHTML is the latest in a long line of technologies that have changed the way the Web works. Some of those technologies have bounced off the Web, proving too complex or too finicky for Web developers to use easily or reliably. Other technologies — such as in-line images (presented as part of the document), image maps, JavaScript, cookies, and dynamic HTML — have become part of the mainstream of Web development. All of these technologies have had some bumps as they entered the market, largely caused by the widespread use of older software, but the solutions they presented solved enough real problems for developers to use them. As newer software has appeared and become more widespread, compatibility issues have eased — although new issues continue to emerge.

Perhaps the single clearest message from the past is that waiting solves problems. The sample XHTML document shown in Chapter 5 works much more easily in the latest-and-greatest browsers, although it's still not quite perfect. The next round of browsers, after developers have a chance to look at XHTML and make some changes to accommodate it, very likely will cure that problem. Similarly, developers of authoring tools shouldn't find it too difficult to move up to XHTML, although it likely will take a revision.

For developers, however, the authoring tools and viewers are only part of the process. JavaScript drove a lot of people who focused on making their sites look good into some degree of programming, while cascading style sheets has proven important to developers using dynamic HTML. Dynamic HTML has forced designers to coordinate their work with developers creating scripts; over time, the skill set for building Web sites has broadened considerably.

Fortunately, XHTML 1.0 is a relatively nondisruptive technology. It makes certain older technologies, notably Cascading Style Sheets and dynamic HTML, easier to use reliably. It does require some minor tweaks in authoring tools and some style changes for those who hand-code their own pages. Like JavaScript, XHTML 1.0 adds extra junk to pages in certain browsers (as demonstrated in Chapter 5), but you usually can avoid those problems by sticking to a slightly smaller subset of XHTML than the W3C provides. Unlike some previous technologies, XHTML generally will degrade gracefully because it isn't really making new demands of older browsers.

As a management challenge, XHTML 1.0 should rate very low on the difficulty scale. Developer retraining shouldn't require more than presenting a fairly short list of guidelines and insisting that authors test their pages — validate them — before making them public. Even in the early stages of XHTML 1.0 adoption when browsers haven't learned yet to treat XHTML as anything different than HTML, XHTML 1.0 likely will provide more cultural problems (You mean I really have to add all those end tags, and use lower case?) than technical difficulties.

Making Certain Nothing Looks Different (to the User)

Chapter 5's testing of valid XHTML in older browsers may have looked frightening, but in fact it points the way toward making XHTML work smoothly in HTML environments. Fortunately, Netscape 1.22 has faded from the list of browsers most organizations still support; those organizations that still consider it important tend not to use the features (such as style sheets and JavaScript) that give it problems. Based on the testing done in that chapter, describing the functionality subset considered safe isn't very difficult.

Scripts and style sheets are stored best outside of the document. XHTML's shift from hiding scripts in comments (`<!-- -->`) to hiding scripts in CDATA sections (`<![CDATA[ ]]>`) creates problems for even the latest browser releases. Admittedly, Netscape 3.0 had some trouble with a script file referenced from a `script` element inside the `head` element, but it does better with `script` elements that appear inside the `body` element. Style sheets stored in document head elements caused problems in some older browsers; but in the very worst case, external style sheets were ignored. Storing scripts and style sheets in external files has additional advantages because it becomes much easier to use them in multiple pages, even across a site, and make changes to all of them from a single location. Editors and other tools can focus on a particular syntax, rather than dealing with three or four different systems at once.

The other XHTML-specific issue that has caused a lot of trouble, even for newer browsers, is the XML declaration. The XML declaration is critical in certain cases for XML parsing, but it goes unused by HTML browsers. If you choose to leave XML declarations off your XHTML document, especially if you go so far as to prohibit their use, you should note the encoding problems that working with an encoding declaration may cause for XML parsers (as described in the next section of this chapter).

Apart from these significant compatibility issues, the rest of the guidelines for using XHTML in an HTML production environment flow in two general streams: enforcing the syntactical restrictions of XHTML and choosing a strategy regarding which document type definition to use for documents. The syntactical part isn't so difficult. The following list provides a quick start:

- Every document must have a `DOCTYPE` declaration before its `html` element, and the document must be validated successfully against the type specified in that declaration.

- The `html` element must include the `xmlns` attribute with the XHTML namespace declaration.

- All element and attribute names must be in lowercase.

- Every start tag (`<name>`) must have an end tag (`</name>`).

- All empty elements — such as `hr`, `br`, and `img` — must be represented using syntax such as `<name></name>` or `<name />`.

- All attribute values must be enclosed in single or double quotes.

This part of the explanation isn't so difficult, even when there are additional issues such as XHTML 1.0's rules for transitioning from `name` to `id` attributes and supplementing the `lang` attribute with `xml:lang`. It's a good idea to encourage developers to talk about elements rather than tags in an effort to clarify that structure is more important than markup, but generally XHTML 1.0's syntactical policing isn't that difficult to enforce.

The harder choices come from XHTML 1.0's insistence on the inclusion of the `DOCTYPE` declaration and its provision of three different DTDs. While the transitional DTD maximizes compatibility with older HTML and reflects the way most authoring tools create HTML, it's fairly clear that the long-term future of XHTML in the W3C's vision is that of the strict DTD. XHTML 1.1 and its likely successors base their primary form on the strict DTD, though their modularization includes (unused) support for frames and other features. While developers can add their own modules to a driver file to support the functionality in the transitional and frameset DTDs — it's likely that someone will, if not the W3C — those modules aren't likely to receive any kind of official blessing.

How much does "official blessing" matter in this case? Past experience suggests that browser makers support features when it seems convenient to them, not because the W3C says so. The more standards-friendly approach of the Mozilla project may change this, but it's unlikely that the mainstream of browser development will purge `frame` or `font` elements anytime soon.

For a vision of a small HTML that goes well beyond the strict DTD, see the W3C's XHTML Basic at `http://www.w3.org/TR/xhtml-basic/`. You should keep in mind that pure XHTML Basic implementations likely will be used only in environments with very limited processing such as appliances, personal digital assistants (PDAs), and cell phones. If your developers feel constrained by the strict DTD, you can use this as a handy rhetorical device to demonstrate that a smaller subset is possible.

If your organization or your site supports a wide variety of different HTML approaches, you may find it easiest not to make a decision and simply require that document authors choose a given DTD and apply it on a per-document basis. This provides maximum flexibility and enables Web developers to transition at their own pace, without forcing them to change their vocabulary as well as their syntax.

If you plan to take advantage of the W3C's ongoing XHTML development, however, you may find it easiest to stay within the confines of the strict DTD. The capabilities provided by Cascading Style Sheets more than make up for the formatting information provided by the transitional DTD. Developers have to learn CSS, or perhaps use a standardized style sheet across all of their documents, imposing some additional costs on organizations in which CSS isn't already in widespread use. While switching to the strict DTD may cause some differences in appearance from pages created using other forms of HTML or XHTML, you can control those differences using CSS.

If switching to the strict DTD sounds impossible because your site uses frames, you can use the frameset DTD exclusively for defining framesets and rely on the strict DTD for all of the documents inside of those frames. The Strict DTD doesn't include the `target` attribute, which may limit how well your framesets work, however.

Supporting the Widest Possible Base in XML

While making good use of existing HTML skills and browsers is important, making your documents acceptable to XML parsers is the other half of the XHTML transition. In the short term, minimizing transition costs for older HTML software is a worthy goal; but you should ensure that your documents do in fact make the transition to XML. As previously noted, the XML declaration presents problems for many older browsers — but it is critical for XML processing of documents in many commonly used encodings. Dropping this declaration may keep your documents from being processed by search engines, stored in document repositories, or even read by users of XML-based clients.

Although HTML does use it, the encoding declaration in the XML declaration is critically important to XML parsing. In fact, the encoding declaration is important for all cases in which non-Unicode character encodings are used. XML parsers should be capable of auto-detecting the UTF-8 (which includes basic ASCII) and UTF-16 encodings, but they may not be capable of detecting other commonly used encodings such as ISO-Latin-1 and Shift-JIS. This means that leaving off the XML declaration requires you to store documents in UTF-8 or UTF-16 if interoperability with XML parsers is important. Some tools can create and manage documents in these encodings, while others can't.

 It's a safe bet that any XML-oriented or Java-based tool can handle UTF-8 and UTF-16 character encodings. Other programs and environments may vary.

Until Unicode support becomes more widespread, you may find it worth your effort to explore some strategies to ensure your XHTML is acceptable to XML parsers. If you can stand to have the declaration appear at the top of the page in some browsers (especially if you work in an environment that doesn't use those problem browsers), keeping the declaration is a good idea. If you work with pure ASCII documents, they can pass as UTF-8 and the declaration isn't required. Users of the Latin-1 character set can replace all of the Latin-1 characters that aren't in ASCII with their equivalents in the Latin-1 entity set — all of HTML's built-in entities remain available. Users of other character encodings are faced with converting their documents to UTF-8 or UTF-16, or using numeric character references throughout their documents — not an especially readable or efficient approach, but one that does have the virtue of reliability.

TIP

XHTML developers working with Asian character encodings, particularly Chinese, may want to visit Academica Sinica's *Chinese XML Now!* Web site at `http://www.ascc.net/xml/`. The site includes a Frequently Asked Questions list and a section on XHTML. In addition, it has a version of the Tidy XHTML clean-up program customized to work with Chinese and Japanese encodings.

If your documents are generated dynamically, you also may be able to check the software requesting documents and add or leave out the declaration on a case-by-case basis. It requires extra processing, but it supports the widest possible range of both XML and HTML clients and tools.

Balancing Needs and Retraining

If you're reading this book because you need to apply XHTML to your own one-person projects, you probably already made some decisions about the compatibility trade-offs. If you're using XHTML as part of a larger project, the decision-making process is likely to be a lot more difficult because different participants with different needs have very different perspectives about the usefulness of these trade-offs.

Moving from HTML to XHTML 1.0 involves changing some habits and looking more closely at features such as character encodings, which most developers take for granted. Some Web designers may chafe at the syntactical restrictions imposed by XHTML, while others (particularly those who work with dynamic HTML and cascading style sheets) may observe many of the restrictions already. Spreading the gospel of XHTML isn't always easy, especially at this early stage when tools (even XML-oriented tools) are far more HTML-oriented than XHTML-oriented.

If you decide that the potential of XML is worth the trouble of making some changes, make certain that those changes are explained to everyone involved in your Web development organization. With luck, an explanation of the benefits and the direction the W3C is taking HTML can give developers more motivation to change their habits. However, you may find it necessary to make all the accommodations possible – notably using the transitional DTD and leaving off the XML declaration – to keep HTML developers comfortable with the brave new world of XHTML.

Chapter 10

The Big Clean-Up: Fixing Static HTML (The Easy Part)

CHAPTER 4 BRIEFLY EXPLAINS how HTML becomes XHTML. This chapter actually goes over some of the best methods of converting an entire site from HTML to XHTML. It may or may not be worthwhile to convert every site, so we'll start by exploring the cases where it is most useful, and then move on to techniques and tools that can simplify the process.

Why Convert Existing XHTML?

Before we get started, you may be asking yourself "Why should I want to covert my Web site that works perfectly fine in HTML to this newfangled XHTML?" Most likely your curiosity is piqued if you've made it this far into the book. However, let me give you some answers to better soothe your fears and to justify to management why you should make the jump to XHTML.

XHTML provides two main improvements over HTML:

◆ Cleaner structures (which make things such as dynamic HTML and styling a lot easier)

◆ The ability to use tools developed for XML

Cleaner structures are basic conveniences that demonstrate how it's a lot easier for a browser to reference parts of a document reliably. Plus, they avoid some of the crazier cross-browser hopscotching caused by different interpretations of structures. (Guessing what a document author intended is harder when parts are missing or misplaced.)

The ability to use XML tools opens the field to a lot of new possibilities from Scalable Vector Graphics for graphics and layout, to MathML for math, to SMIL for multimedia, to MyML for my stuff and "YourML" for your stuff and "HisML" and "HerML" and "TheirML."

It's not just that developers will be able to extend the HTML vocabulary. They will be able to do it in controllable ways and in a context in which clients, servers, and peers can negotiate the kind of information they accept and make smarter decisions than are possible with today's browser and object sniffing techniques.

XHTML is also much more reusable than HTML. If you need to convert your documents to Wireless Markup Language or some other presentation variant, you can use scripts and the DOM, Extensible Stylesheet Language Transformations (XSLT), or other XML-based tools to handle the conversion. You can move from one structure to another without having to read the markup byte by byte and guess what's supposed to happen.

Finally, XHTML enables you to do things such as use XML repositories for your documents, opening up easier and more powerful referencing, fragmenting, and searching possibilities. Instead of storing your static documents as plain old files, XML repositories let you store your documents based on the XML structure. It's easier to have multiple people editing (and versioning) a document using such tools, and analyzing your Web site can become a lot easier.

Some examples of situations in which converting is beneficial include:

◆ Customers who want the older content delivered as XHTML so they can use XML processing tools on it. (Say you're converting a Web site to a print book, and they want to use XSLT to convert it to PDF under their control.)

◆ New storage requirements. Somebody orders the site moved into an XML-aware content management system perhaps to support versioning of documents or for new functionality such as you can add by using Zope, a powerful Web applications builder.

◆ Downtime (it happens once in a while). XHTML conversion can be a good, nonintrusive project for developers when they're stuck waiting for clients.

Starting with Your HTML Document

Find a document authored in HTML. This document should be somewhat complex because you don't want to work with something that only has two lines beyond the basic HTML structure (at least not to use as your primary learning page). If you don't have a page in mind, you can find the HTML page used in this example at http://www.zotgroup.com/development/test-suites/xhtml10/html-to-xhtml.html.

Here's the code:

```
<HTML>
<HEAD>
<TITLE>BK's Home Page</TITLE>
</HEAD>
<BODY bgcolor=#ffffff>
<FONT color=red><H1 align=center>BK's Home Page</H1></FONT>
```

```
This is the homepage of BK DeLong. Enjoy your visit!<P>

My EverQuest Friends:<BR>
<A href="http://www.attrition.org/eq/crimen/"><B>Crimen
Talionis</A></B><BR>
MacIntyre<BR>
Kiekre<BR>
Krimzor<BR>
Catya<P>

<HR>
B.K. DeLong<BR>
<A href="mailto:bkdelong@zotgroup.com">bkdelong@zotgroup.com</A>
</BODY>
</HTML>
```

Pretty nasty HTML. For beginners who didn't learn HTML with a background knowledge of SGML and thought it was used for *designing* pages, this is pretty typical of a person's first Web site. (I'm sure this is quite similar to my initial Web site.) Now clean it up. You're not going to clean up your HTML in the order that you build an XHTML file from scratch necessarily. Instead start with the easiest things to check first.

Step 1: All elements are lowercase

The most tedious thing you have to do with your HTML files is to make sure that all the elements are lowercase. The only text that should be uppercase is your own content. This difficult task can be made easier by some of the authoring tools discussed toward the end of this chapter.

Once you're finished, the file should look like this:

```
<html>
<head>
<title>BK's Home Page</title>
</head>
<body bgcolor=#ffffff>
<font color=red><h1 align=center>BK's Home Page</h1></font>

This is the homepage of BK DeLong. Enjoy your visit!<p>

My EverQuest Friends:<br>
<a href="http://www.attrition.org/eq/crimen/"><b>Crimen
Talionis</a></b><br>
MacIntyre<br>
Kiekre<br>
```

```
Krimzor<br>
Catya<p>

<hr>
B.K. DeLong<br>
<a href="mailto:bkdelong@zotgroup.com">bkdelong@zotgroup.com</a>
</body>
</html>
```

Step 2: All attribute values must have quotes

This is another easy step, although it can be tedious. Spotting all non-quoted attributes can be tough, too. You may have to rely on the validation process to uncover the ones you can't find.

```
<html>
<head>
<title>BK's Home Page</title>
</head>
<body bgcolor="#ffffff">
<font color="red"><h1 align="center">BK's Home Page</h1></font>

This is the homepage of BK DeLong. Enjoy your visit!<p>

My EverQuest Friends:<br>
<a href="http://www.attrition.org/eq/crimen/"><b>Crimen
Talionis</a></b><br>
MacIntyre<br>
Kiekre<br>
Krimzor<br>
Catya<p>

<hr>
B.K. DeLong<br>
<a href="mailto:bkdelong@zotgroup.com">bkdelong@zotgroup.com</a>
</body>
</html>
```

You're getting there.

Step 3: All elements must end

Now that you've completed some of the most basic cleanup of your HTML document, you need to start fixing the actual structure. A document isn't considered well formed or valid if elements that are started aren't closed. Cleanly authored

XHTML (as with any markup language) makes it a lot easier to figure out what's going on in the document, so logically this is the next step of your cleanup.

Basically, there are three elements in your HTML document that you need to address. The two easiest are the "empty" elements `<hr>` and `<br>`. All that you need to add to them is a space along with a backslash (/) so they look like this: `<br />`. Is the space required? No, but many of the older browser versions view a `<br/>` as the text BR/ and not a `<br>` element. The browser doesn't know what a BR/ element is, but it recognizes it if a space separates the BR and the backslash.

The other element that needs closure is the `<p>` element. The first rule of markup is that it's meant to denote context and not design or layout. So technically, the `<p>` element should not be at the end of the paragraph to create a carriage return. The `<p>` element should appear at the beginning of a paragraph with a `</p>` at the end.

After making these changes, you now have better formed HTML with which to work.

```
<html>
<head>
<title>BK's Home Page</title>
</head>
<body bgcolor="#ffffff">
<font color="red"> <h1 align="center">BK's Home Page</h1></font>

<p>This is the homepage of BK DeLong. Enjoy your visit!</p>

<p>
My EverQuest Friends:<br />
<a href="http://www.attrition.org/eq/crimen/"><b>Crimen
Talionis</a></b><br />
MacIntyre<br />
Kiekre<br />
Krimzor<br />
Catya
</p>

<hr />
B.K. DeLong<br />
<a href="mailto:bkdelong@zotgroup.com">bkdelong@zotgroup.com</a>
</body>
</html>
```

Step 4: All elements must be in the right place

You must remedy a few problems still remaining with this document.

First, you cannot have a header element, `<h1>`, contained by a `<font>` element. It's not legal according to the XHTML 1.0 DTD (even the transitional one). To fix this, place the `<font>` element inside the `<h1>`:

```
<h1 align="center"><font color="red">BK's Home Page</font></h1>
```

While this is not required for making your document well formed or valid — because the `<font>` element is deprecated in favor of style sheets — you should change the line to read:

```
<h1 style="text-align:center;color:red">BK's Home Page</h1>
```

You also need to fix the way you use the `<b>` element in the "My EverQuest Friends" list. Most people know by now that you can't have an element overlap another element in XHTML. The line in question currently reads like this:

```
<a href="http://www.attrition.org/eq/crimen/"><b>Crimen
Talionis</a></b><br />
```

You should modify it to look like this:

```
<a href="http://www.attrition.org/eq/crimen/"><b>Crimen
Talionis</b></a><br />
```

Again, the `<b>` element deals with the style of text. While it's not required, I recommend changing the `<b>` element to a `<strong>` element that better denotes its context. If you want to change its style inlined, then the line should look like this:

```
<a href="http://www.attrition.org/eq/crimen/" style="font-weight:
bold">Crimen Talionis</a><br />
```

Step 5: Adding XHTML declarations and definitions

At this point, your core document structure is as XHTMLized as possible. Now you need to add the headers that identify this document as XHTML instead of HTML.

First, you need to declare the XHTML namespace. As you may remember from previous chapters, you do this by adding the `xmlns` attribute to the `<html>` element:

```
<html xmlns="http://www.w3.org/1999/xhtml">
```

Next, you need to make sure you declare the correct DOCTYPE for XHTML. Are you using strict, frameset, or transitional? In this case, I think you should stick with transitional — especially if you keep the <b> and <font> elements:

```
<!DOCTYPE html PUBLIC "-//W3C//DTD XHTML 1.0 Transitional//EN"
"http://www.w3.org/TR/xhtml1/DTD/xhtml1-transitional.dtd">
```

Last, and this is not required of an XHTML document, add in the XML declaration. I strongly encourage you to put this into all XHTML documents so you keep in the habit of using it with other XML documents. The only issue worth mentioning with this declaration is that it may appear in older browsers.

```
<?xml version="1.0"?>
```

Your final XHTML document should look like this now:

```
<?xml version="1.0"?>
<!DOCTYPE html PUBLIC "-//W3C//DTD XHTML 1.0 Transitional//EN"
"http://www.w3.org/TR/xhtml1/DTD/xhtml1-transitional.dtd">
<html xmlns="http://www.w3.org/1999/xhtml">
<head>
<title>BK's Home Page</title>
</head>
<body bgcolor="#ffffff">
<h1 align="center" style="color:red">BK's Home Page</h1>

<p>This is the homepage of BK DeLong. Enjoy your visit!</p>

<p>
My EverQuest Friends:<br />
<a href="http://www.attrition.org/eq/crimen/" style="font-
weight:bold">Crimen Talonis</a><br />
MacIntyre<br />
Kiekre<br />
Krimzor<br />
Catya
</p>

<hr />
B.K. DeLong<br />
<a href="mailto:bkdelong@zotgroup.com">bkdelong@zotgroup.com</a>
</body>
</html>
```

Notice that the DOCTYPE declaration in the beginning of the document is uppercase. This is allowable because it isn't actually "part of the document." However the "html" identifier in the DOCTYPE declaration should be in lowercase to correspond with the <html>.

Using a Tool to Convert Your HTML Documents to XHTML

Now that I've walked you through how to convert your HTML to XHTML manually, I'm going to drive you crazy by telling you that there is a program that does it for you.

HTML Tidy

HTML guru Dave Raggett has written a program called HTML Tidy that "tidies up" your HTML by fixing all the previously detailed problems, including:

◆ Misplacement of elements

◆ Uppercase versus lowercase elements and attributes

◆ Quotes around attribute values

◆ Adding correct XHTML declarations and namespaces when prompted

You can download this small application from its Web site (http://www.w3.org/People/Raggett/tidy/) and use it to auto-convert your own HTML. This has been ported to many platforms, and on the HTML Tidy Web site you can find the pre-compiled binaries for almost any operating system you are running.

To convert your HTML document to XHTML using Tidy, all you have to do is make sure **tidy.exe** (the application name) is accessible from your HTML files directory. Then use the following line:

```
tidy -asxml -clean filename.html > filename.xhtml
```

Running Tidy without any flags lowercases all elements and attributes, ensures all attribute values have quotes, and checks that the HTML is well formed with no stray elements. The -asxml flag adds in all the XHTML features including the namespace declaration, the XHTML DOCTYPE declaration, and the XML declaration. It also makes sure all the "empty" elements are formatted correctly for XHTML. Finally, the -clean flag converts <font> elements and center attributes to their CSS counterparts. Unfortunately, you have to do a little more tweaking if you want to have it do the same with elements such as <b>. Because Tidy has to fix the formatting of the

<b> element and put both tags in the correct location, it doesn't convert it to CSS. Another run through Tidy and the problems are fixed.

If you're comfortable with Tidy directly modifying your original document, you can add the -modify flag to make all changes in the source document.

Let's take a look at what HTML Tidy does to your original HTML document:

```
<?xml version="1.0"?>
<!DOCTYPE html PUBLIC "-//W3C//DTD XHTML 1.0 Transitional//EN"
    "http://www.w3.org/TR/xhtml1/DTD/xhtml1-transitional.dtd">
<html xmlns="http://www.w3.org/1999/xhtml">
<head>
<meta name="generator" content="HTML Tidy, see www.w3.org" />
<title>BK's Home Page</title>
<style type="text/css">
 h1.c1 {color: red; text-align: center}
</style>
</head>
<body bgcolor="#ffffff">
<h1 class="c1">BK's Home Page</h1>

This is the homepage of BK DeLong. Enjoy your visit!

<p> My EverQuest Friends:<br />
 <a href="http://www.attrition.org/eq/crimen/"><b>Crimen
Talionis</b></a><br />
 MacIntyre<br />
 Kiekre<br />
 Krimzor<br />
 Catya</p>

<hr />
<b>B.K. DeLong<br />
 <a href="mailto:bkdelong@zotgroup.com">
bkdelong@zotgroup.com</a></b>
</body>
</html>
```

 Notice that HTML Tidy has taken the CSS and converted it into a class reference as opposed to entering it inline. This is because there is only one <h1> in the document and therefore it can have a global style reference.

There have been many concerns that use of HTML Tidy for an HTML to XHTML conversion can screw up some complex pages. Let's take a look at the UMass News Office Web site (`http://www.umass.edu/newsoffice`) and its complex HTML to find out what happens during this conversion (see Figure 10-1).

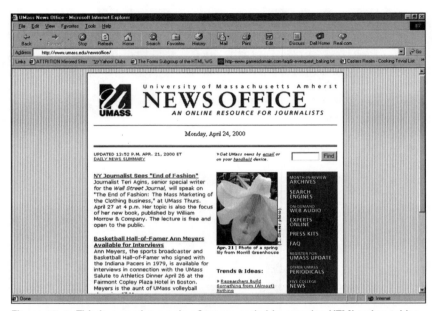

Figure 10-1: This is a good example of a page coded in complex HTML using tables for precise layout.

```
<html>
<head>
<title>UMass News Office</title>
<meta http-equiv="Content-Type" content="text/html; charset=
iso-8859-1">
<SCRIPT language="JavaScript">
<!-- Begin
var day="";var month="";
var ampm="";var ampmhour="";
var myweekday="";var year="";
var oneDate = new Date()
mydate = new Date();
myday = mydate.getDay();
mymonth = mydate.getMonth();
myweekday= mydate.getDate();
weekday= myweekday;
myyear= mydate.getFullYear();  <!--- THIS LINE CHANGES      ---->
```

```
year = myyear;
myhours = mydate.getHours();
ampmhour  =  (myhours > 12) ? myhours - 12 : myhours;
ampm =  (myhours >= 12) ? ' PM' : ' AM';
mytime = mydate.getMinutes();
myminutes =  ((mytime < 10) ? ':0' : ':') + mytime;
if(myday == 0)
day = " Sunday, ";
else if(myday == 1)
day = " Monday, ";
else if(myday == 2)
day = " Tuesday, ";
else if(myday == 3)
day = " Wednesday, ";
else if(myday == 4)
day = " Thursday, ";
else if(myday == 5)
day = " Friday, ";
else if(myday == 6)
day = " Saturday, ";
if(mymonth == 0) {
month = "January ";}
else if(mymonth ==1)
month = "February ";
else if(mymonth ==2)
month = "March ";
else if(mymonth ==3)
month = "April ";
else if(mymonth ==4)
month = "May ";
else if(mymonth ==5)
month = "June ";
else if(mymonth ==6)
month = "July ";
else if(mymonth ==7)
month = "August ";
else if(mymonth ==8)
month = "September ";
else if(mymonth ==9)
month = "October ";
else if(mymonth ==10)
month = "November ";
else if(mymonth ==11)
month = "December ";
// End -->
```

```
</SCRIPT>
</head>
<body bgcolor="#FFFFFF" background="images/bkg.gif" link="#003887"
vlink="#006666" alink="#006666">
<!==================== RED MARGIN TABLE COLOR = 640000 WIDTH = 620
CELLPADDING=2 ==================>
<table width="600" border="0" cellspacing="0" cellpadding="2"
align="center">
<tr bgcolor="#640000" align="center" valign="top">
<td height="0">
     <table width="100%" border="0" cellpadding="5"
bgcolor="#ffffff" align="center">
       <tr align="center" valign="top">
<td height="0">
           <table width="98%" border="0" cellspacing="7"
align="center">
             <tr align="left">
               <td width="103" valign="top" bgcolor="#FFFFFF"><img
src="images/logo_head.gif" width="102" height="100" alt="UMass
Logo"></td>
               <td width="183" valign="top" bgcolor="#FFFFFF">
                 <div align="right"><img src="images/news_head.gif"
width="180" height="99"></div>
                 </td>
                 <td colspan="2" valign="top" bgcolor="#FFFFFF">
                   <div align="left"><img src="images/mass_head.gif"
width="297" height="99"></div>
                   </td>
               </tr>
             <tr align="left">
               <td colspan="4" height="2" valign="top"
bgcolor="#FFFFFF">
                 <div align="left"><font size="-7"> <img
src="images/1pt.gif" width="600" height="1" alt="&quot;&quot;"
border="0">
                   </font></div>
                 </td>
               </tr>
             <tr align="left">
               <td height="2" bgcolor="#FFFFFF" colspan="4">
                 <div align="center"> <font face="Sabon, Times New
Roman, Palatino, serif" size="3">
                   <script>
```

```
<!--//
document.write()
document.write(day + month);
document.write(myweekday + ", " + year);<!----------------------
THIS LINE CHANGES      ----->
// -->
</script>
                    </font></div>
              </td>
            </tr>
            <tr align="left">
              <td colspan="4" height="2" valign="top"
bgcolor="#FFFFFF">
                  <div align="left"><img src="images/2pt.gif"
width="600" height="5" alt="&quot;&quot;" border="0">
                  </div>
              </td>
            </tr>
            <tr align="left"> <!=========== UPDATE TIME/DATE STAMP
GOES HERE ==========================>
                  <td colspan="2" bgcolor="#FFFFFF" height="0"
valign="top"><font face="Verdana, Arial, Helvetica, sans-serif"
size="1">UPDATED
                  12:52 P.M. APR. 21, 2000 ET<br>
                  <a href="summary/index.html">DAILY NEWS
SUMMARY</a></font></td>
                  <td bgcolor="#FFFFFF" height="0" valign="top">
                  <div align="left"><font size="1" face="Arial,
Helvetica, sans-serif"><font face="Verdana, Arial, Helvetica, sans-
serif" size="1">&#187;</font>
                  <font face="Verdana, Arial, Helvetica, sans-
serif"><i>Get
                  UMass news by <a href="update/">email</a> or on
your <a href="pda/">handheld</a>
                  device.</i></font></font></div>
              </td>
              <td bgcolor="#FFFFFF" height="0" valign="top"
align="right">
                  <form action="http://cronos.oit.umass.edu/cgi-
bin/query" name="">
                  <font face="Verdana, Arial, Helvetica, sans-
serif" size="1">
                      <input type=hidden name=mss value=simple>
                      <input type=hidden name=pg value=q>
```

```
                    <input type=hidden name=what value=web>
                    <input type=hidden name=fmt value=.>
                    <input type=hidden name=who value="This form
queries News Office pages.">
                    <input type=hidden name=filter
value="url:http://www.umass.edu/newsoffice">
                    <input type="text" name="q" size="8" value="">

                    <input type=submit name="Submit" value="Find">
                      </font>
                   </form>
                 </td>
               </tr>
               <tr align="left">
                 <td colspan="2" valign="top" rowspan="2"
bgcolor="#FFFFFF" height="0">
                    <p align="left"><font size="2" face="Verdana,
Arial, Helvetica, sans-serif"><b><a
href="archive/2000/042100fashion.html">NY
                    Journalist Sees &quot;End of
Fashion&quot;</a></b><br>
                    Journalist Teri Agins, senior special writer for
the <i>Wall
                    Street Journal,</i> will speak on "The End of
Fashion: The
                    Mass Marketing of the Clothing Business," at
UMass Thurs.
                    April 27 at 4 p.m. Her topic is also the focus
of her new
                    book, published by William Morrow & Company. The
lecture is
                    free and open to the public. </font></p>
                    <p align="left"><font size="2" face="Verdana,
Arial, Helvetica, sans-serif"><a
href="archive/2000/042000meyers.html"><b>Basketball
                    Hall-of-Famer Ann Meyers<br>
                    Available for Interviews</b></a><br>
                    Ann Meyers, the sports broadcaster and
Basketball Hall-of-Famer
                    who signed with the Indiana Pacers in 1979, is
available for
                    interviews in connection with the UMass Salute
to Athletics
```

```
                        Dinner April 26 at the Fairmont Copley Plaza
Hotel in Boston.
                        </font><font face="Verdana, Arial, Helvetica,
sans-serif" size="2">Meyers
                        is the aunt of UMass volleyball champion Jill
Meyers. </font>
                        </p>
                        <p align="left"><font size="2" face="Verdana,
Arial, Helvetica, sans-serif"><b><a
href="archive/2000/042000capsule.html">UMass
                        to Dedicate Time Capsule</a></b><br>
                        UMass will dedicate its Year 2000 Time Capsule
in a campus
                        celebration May 1 at 4 p.m. on the library lawn.
In addition
                        to a brief dedication ceremony, the event will
feature music,
                        T-shirts, food, and prizes, as well as an
opportunity for
                        students to have their photographs taken for
placement in
                        the time capsule.</font> </p>
                        </td>
                    <td width="160" valign="top" bgcolor="#FFFFFF"
height="0">
                        <p align="left"><font size="1" face="Verdana,
Arial, Helvetica, sans-serif"><b><img src="photos/iris.jpg"
width="160" height="188"><br>
                        Apr. 21</b><b> |</b> Photo of a spring lily from
Morrill Greenhouse
                        </font></p>
                        <p><font size="1" face="Verdana, Arial, Helvetica,
sans-serif"><b><font size="2"><br>
                        Trends &amp; Ideas:</font><br>
                        <br>
                        </b>&#187; <a
href="http://www.umass.edu/newsoffice/archive/2000/041200research.ht
ml">Researchers
                        Build Something from (Almost)
Nothing</a></font></p>
                        <p><font size="1" face="Verdana, Arial, Helvetica,
sans-serif">&#187;
                        <a
```

```
href="archive/2000/041200williams.html">Student Wins Prestigious
               Goldwater Scholarship</a> </font></p>
               <p><font size="1" face="Verdana, Arial, Helvetica,
sans-serif">&#187;
               <a
href="archive/2000/041100suspend.html">Chancellor Orders
               Security Cameras</a> </font></p>
               </td>
            <td width="123" valign="top" bgcolor="#660000"
height="0">
               <div align="right">
               <p align="left"><a href="archive/"><img
src="images/btn_mir.gif" width="119" height="37" border="0"
alt="Archives"></a><br>
               <a href="engines/"><img
src="images/btn_engine.gif" width="119" height="38" border="0"
alt="Search Engines"></a><a href="audio/"><img
src="images/btn_audio.gif" width="119" height="35" border="0"
alt="Web Audio"></a><br>
               <a href="experts/"><img
src="images/btn_exp.gif" width="119" height="37" border="0"
alt="Experts Online"></a><br>
               <a href="prkit/"><img
src="images/btn_photo.gif" width="119" height="25" border="0"
alt="Press Kits"></a><br>
               <a href="hfiles/faq.html"><img
src="images/btn_faq.gif" width="119" height="26" border="0"
alt="Frequently Asked Question"></a><br>
               <a href="update/"><img
src="images/btn_updt.gif" width="119" height="35" border="0"
alt="UMass Update"></a><br>
               <a href="pubs/"><img src="images/btn_pubs.gif"
width="119" height="37" border="0" alt="UMass Periodicals"></a><br>
               <a href="http://www.fivecolleges.edu"><img
src="images/btn_5col.gif" width="119" height="35" border="0"
alt="Five College News"></a><br>
               <a href="hfiles/staff.html"><img
src="images/btn_staff.gif" width="119" height="25" border="0"
alt="Ask an Editor"></a><br>
               <a href="hfiles/feedback.html"><img
src="images/btn_feedback.gif" width="119" height="26" border="0"
alt="Feedback"></a>
               </div>
               </td>
```

```
          </tr>
          <tr bgcolor="#FFFFFF" align="left">
            <td width="165" height="0" valign="top"
bgcolor="#CCCC99">
              <table width="100%" border="0" cellspacing="6"
cellpadding="0">
                <tr>
                  <td><font face="Verdana, Arial, Helvetica,
sans-serif" size="1"><a href="hfiles/foia.html">Guide
                    to the FOIA &amp; Mass. Public Document
Laws</a></font></td>
                </tr>
                <tr>
                  <td><font face="Verdana, Arial, Helvetica,
sans-serif" size="1"><a href="hfiles/tools.html">Media/Reference
                    Links</a></font></td>
                </tr>
                <tr>
                  <td><font face="Verdana, Arial, Helvetica,
sans-serif" size="1"><a href="hometn/index.html">Hometown
                    News</a></font></td>
                </tr>
                <tr>
                  <td><font face="Verdana, Arial, Helvetica,
sans-serif" size="1"><a href="newsline/1299.html">News
                    Office News<i>Line</i></a></font></td>
                </tr>
              </table>
            </td>
            <td width="123" height="0" valign="top"
bgcolor="#FFCC66">
              <div align="left">
                <p align="center"><a
href="http://www.campaign.umass.edu"><img
src="images/campaign_btn.gif" width="123" height="39" alt="News from
Campaign UMass" border="0"></a><font size="1" face="Verdana, Arial,
Helvetica, sans-serif"><br>
                  <br>
                  </font><font size="2" face="Verdana, Arial,
Helvetica, sans-serif"><a
href="archive/2000/041400campaign.html"><font size="1">Campaign
                    Tops <br>
                    $100 Million Mark</font></a><b></b></font></p>
              </div>
```

```
              </td>
            </tr>
            <tr align="left">
              <td colspan="4" valign="top" bgcolor="#FFFFFF">
                <div align="center"><img src="images/3pt.gif"
width="600" height="2" alt="&quot;&quot;" border="0"></div>
              </td>
            </tr>
            <tr align="left">
              <td colspan="4" valign="top" bgcolor="#FFFFFF"
height="0">
                <p><img src="images/sm_logo.gif" width="72"
height="63" align="left" alt="UMass Logo" border="0"><font
size="2"><br>
                  This is an <a
href="http://www.umass.edu/umhome/official.html">Official
                  Publication</a> of the University of
Massachusetts Amherst
                  Campus.</font></p>
                <p><font size="2">Copyright &copy; 1997-2000. <a
href="hfiles/about.html">About
                  this site</a> | <a
href="hfiles/usage.html">Usage Agreement</a>
                  | <a
href="http://www.umass.edu/umhome/index.html">UMass Home
                  Page</a></font></p>
              </td>
            </tr>
          </table>
        </td>
      </tr>
    </table>
  </td>
</tr>
</table>
</body>
</html>
```

After a quick run through Tidy (which cleans up some odd comment syntax as well), the difference is negligible with the exception of two small spacing problems (see Figure 10-2).

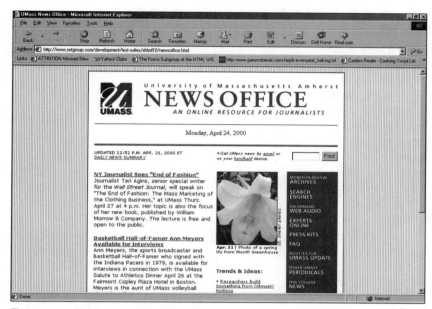

Figure 10-2: This is the same page converted to XHTML by HTML Tidy. See any differences visually?

Here is the same code after its run through Tidy:

```
<?xml version="1.0"?>
<!DOCTYPE html PUBLIC "-//W3C//DTD XHTML 1.0 Transitional//EN"
    "http://www.w3.org/TR/xhtml1/DTD/xhtml1-transitional.dtd">
<!-- saved from
url=(0043)http://www.umass.edu/newsoffice/nonova.html -->
<html xmlns="http://www.w3.org/1999/xhtml">
<head>
<meta name="generator" content="HTML Tidy, see www.w3.org" />
<title>UMass News Office</title>
<meta http-equiv="Content-Type"
content="text/html; charset=iso-8859-1" />
<script type="text/javascript" language="JavaScript">
<!-- Begin
var day="";
var month="";
var ampm="";
var ampmhour="";
```

```
var myweekday="";
var year="";
var oneDate = new Date()
mydate = new Date();
myday = mydate.getDay();
mymonth = mydate.getMonth();
myweekday= mydate.getDate();
weekday= myweekday;
myyear= mydate.getFullYear();  <!----  THIS LINE CHANGES        ----->
year = myyear;
myhours = mydate.getHours();
ampmhour  =  (myhours > 12) ? myhours - 12 : myhours;
ampm =  (myhours >= 12) ? ' PM' : ' AM';
mytime = mydate.getMinutes();
myminutes =  ((mytime < 10) ? ':0' : ':') + mytime;

if(myday == 0)
day = " Sunday, ";
else if(myday == 1)
day = " Monday, ";
else if(myday == 2)
day = " Tuesday, ";
else if(myday == 3)
day = " Wednesday, ";
else if(myday == 4)
day = " Thursday, ";
else if(myday == 5)
day = " Friday, ";
else if(myday == 6)
day = " Saturday, ";
if(mymonth == 0) {
month = "January ";}
else if(mymonth ==1)
month = "February ";
else if(mymonth ==2)
month = "March ";
else if(mymonth ==3)
month = "April ";
else if(mymonth ==4)
month = "May ";
else if(mymonth ==5)
month = "June ";
else if(mymonth ==6)
month = "July ";
```

```
else if(mymonth ==7)
month = "August ";
else if(mymonth ==8)
month = "September ";
else if(mymonth ==9)
month = "October ";
else if(mymonth ==10)
month = "November ";
else if(mymonth ==11)
month = "December ";
// End -->
</script>
<meta content="MSHTML 5.50.3825.1300" name="GENERATOR" />
</head>
<body vlink="#006666" alink="#006666" link="#003887"
bgcolor="#ffffff" background="newsoffice_files/bkg.gif">
<table cellspacing="0" cellpadding="2" width="600" align="center"
border="0">
<tbody>
<tr valign="top" align="middle" bgcolor="#640000">
<td height="0">
<table cellpadding="5" width="100%" align="center"
bgcolor="#ffffff" border="0">
<tbody>
<tr valign="top" align="middle">
<td height="0">
<table cellspacing="7" width="98%" align="center" border="0">
<tbody>
<tr align="left">
<td valign="top" width="103" bgcolor="#ffffff"><img height="100"
alt="UMass Logo" src="newsoffice_files/logo_head.gif"
width="102" /></td>
<td valign="top" width="183" bgcolor="#ffffff">
<div align="right"><img height="99"
src="newsoffice_files/news_head.gif" width="180" /></div>
</td>
<td valign="top" bgcolor="#ffffff" colspan="2">
<div align="left"><img height="99"
src="newsoffice_files/mass_head.gif" width="297" /></div>
</td>
</tr>

<tr align="left">
<td valign="top" bgcolor="#ffffff" colspan="4" height="2">
<div align="left"><font size="-7"><img height="1" alt='""'
```

```
src="newsoffice_files/1pt.gif" width="600" border="0" />
</font></div>
</td>
</tr>

<tr align="left">
<td bgcolor="#ffffff" colspan="4" height="2">
<div align="center"><font
face="Sabon, Times New Roman, Palatino, serif" size="3">
<script type="text/javascript">
<!--//
document.write()
document.write(day + month);
document.write(myweekday + ", " + year);<!---THIS LINE CHANGES--->
// -->
</script>
</font></div>
</td>
</tr>

<tr align="left">
<td valign="top" bgcolor="#ffffff" colspan="4" height="2">
<div align="left"><img height="5" alt='"""'
src="newsoffice_files/2pt.gif" width="600" border="0" /></div>
</td>
</tr>

<tr align="left">
<td valign="top" bgcolor="#ffffff" colspan="2" height="0"><font
face="Verdana, Arial, Helvetica, sans-serif" size="1">UPDATED 12:52
P.M. APR. 21, 2000 ET<br />
<a href="http://www.umass.edu/newsoffice/summary/index.html">DAILY
NEWS SUMMARY</a></font></td>
<td valign="top" bgcolor="#ffffff" height="0">
<div align="left"><font face="Arial, Helvetica, sans-serif"
size="1"><font face="Verdana, Arial, Helvetica, sans-serif"
size="1">&raquo;</font> <font
face="Verdana, Arial, Helvetica, sans-serif"><i>Get UMass news by
<a href="http://www.umass.edu/newsoffice/update/">email</a> or on
your <a href="http://www.umass.edu/newsoffice/pda/">handheld</a>
device.</i></font></font></div>
</td>
<td valign="top" align="right" bgcolor="#ffffff" height="0">
<form name="" action="http://cronos.oit.umass.edu/cgi-bin/query">
```

```
<font face="Verdana, Arial, Helvetica, sans-serif" size="1"><input
type="hidden" value="simple" name="mss" /> <input type="hidden"
value="q" name="pg" /> <input type="hidden" value="web"
name="what" /> <input type="hidden" value="." name="fmt" /> <input
type="hidden" value="This form queries News Office pages."
name="who" /> <input type="hidden"
value="url:http://www.umass.edu/newsoffice" name="filter" /> <input
size="8" name="q" /> <input type="submit" value="Find"
name="Submit" /></font></form>
</td>
</tr>

<tr align="left">
<td valign="top" bgcolor="#ffffff" colspan="2" height="0"
rowspan="2">
<p align="left"><font face="Verdana, Arial, Helvetica, sans-serif"
size="2"><b><a
href="http://www.umass.edu/newsoffice/archive/2000/042100fashion.htm
l">
NY Journalist Sees "End of Fashion"</a></b><br />
Journalist Teri Agins, senior special writer for the <i>Wall Street
Journal,</i> will speak on "The End of Fashion: The Mass Marketing
of the Clothing Business," at UMass Thurs. April 27 at 4 p.m. Her
topic is also the focus of her new book, published by William
Morrow &amp; Company. The lecture is free and open to the
public.</font></p>

<p align="left"><font face="Verdana, Arial, Helvetica, sans-serif"
size="2"><a
href="http://www.umass.edu/newsoffice/archive/2000/042000meyers.html
">
<b>Basketball Hall-of-Famer Ann Meyers<br />
Available for Interviews</b></a><br />
Ann Meyers, the sports broadcaster and Basketball Hall-of-Famer who
signed with the Indiana Pacers in 1979, is available for interviews
in connection with the UMass Salute to Athletics Dinner April 26 at
the Fairmont Copley Plaza Hotel in Boston.</font> <font
face="Verdana, Arial, Helvetica, sans-serif" size="2">Meyers is the
aunt of UMass volleyball champion Jill Meyers.</font></p>

<p align="left"><font face="Verdana, Arial, Helvetica, sans-serif"
size="2"><b><a
href="http://www.umass.edu/newsoffice/archive/2000/042000capsule.htm
l">
UMass to Dedicate Time Capsule</a></b><br />
```

UMass will dedicate its Year 2000 Time Capsule in a campus
celebration May 1 at 4 p.m. on the library lawn. In addition to a
brief dedication ceremony, the event will feature music, T-shirts,
food, and prizes, as well as an opportunity for students to have
their photographs taken for placement in the time
capsule.</font></p>
</td>
<td valign="top" width="160" bgcolor="#ffffff" height="0">
<p align="left"><font face="Verdana, Arial, Helvetica, sans-serif"
size="1"><b><img height="188" src="newsoffice_files/iris.jpg"
width="160" />
Apr. 21</b><b> |</b> Photo of a spring lily from Morrill
Greenhouse</font></p>

<p><font face="Verdana, Arial, Helvetica, sans-serif" size="1"><b>
<font size="2">
Trends & Ideas:</font>

</b>» <a
href="http://www.umass.edu/newsoffice/archive/2000/041200research.ht
ml">
Researchers Build Something from (Almost) Nothing</a></font></p>

<p><font face="Verdana, Arial, Helvetica, sans-serif" size="1">
» <a
href="http://www.umass.edu/newsoffice/archive/2000/041200williams.ht
ml">
Student Wins Prestigious Goldwater Scholarship</a></font></p>

<p><font face="Verdana, Arial, Helvetica, sans-serif" size="1">
» <a
href="http://www.umass.edu/newsoffice/archive/2000/041100suspend.htm
l">
Chancellor Orders Security Cameras</a></font></p>
</td>
<td valign="top" width="123" bgcolor="#660000" height="0">
<div align="right">
<p align="left"><a href="http://www.umass.edu/newsoffice/archive/">
<img height="37" alt="Archives" src="newsoffice_files/btn_mir.gif"
width="119" border="0" /></a>
<a href="http://www.umass.edu/newsoffice/engines/"><img height="38"
alt="Search Engines" src="newsoffice_files/btn_engine.gif"
width="119" border="0" /></a><a
href="http://www.umass.edu/newsoffice/audio/"><img height="35"
alt="Web Audio" src="newsoffice_files/btn_audio.gif" width="119"

```
border="0" /></a><br />
<a href="http://www.umass.edu/newsoffice/experts/"><img height="37"
alt="Experts Online" src="newsoffice_files/btn_exp.gif" width="119"
border="0" /></a><br />
<a href="http://www.umass.edu/newsoffice/prkit/"><img height="25"
alt="Press Kits" src="newsoffice_files/btn_photo.gif" width="119"
border="0" /></a><br />
<a href="http://www.umass.edu/newsoffice/hfiles/faq.html"><img
height="26" alt="Frequently Asked Question"
src="newsoffice_files/btn_faq.gif" width="119"
border="0" /></a><br />
<a href="http://www.umass.edu/newsoffice/update/"><img height="35"
alt="UMass Update" src="newsoffice_files/btn_updt.gif" width="119"
border="0" /></a><br />
<a href="http://www.umass.edu/newsoffice/pubs/"><img height="37"
alt="UMass Periodicals" src="newsoffice_files/btn_pubs.gif"
width="119" border="0" /></a><br />
<a href="http://www.fivecolleges.edu/"><img height="35"
alt="Five College News" src="newsoffice_files/btn_5col.gif"
width="119" border="0" /></a><br />
<a href="http://www.umass.edu/newsoffice/hfiles/staff.html"><img
height="25" alt="Ask an Editor"
src="newsoffice_files/btn_staff.gif" width="119"
border="0" /></a><br />
<a href="http://www.umass.edu/newsoffice/hfiles/feedback.html"><img
height="26" alt="Feedback" src="newsoffice_files/btn_feedback.gif"
width="119" border="0" /></a></p>
</div>
</td>
</tr>

<tr align="left" bgcolor="#ffffff">
<td valign="top" width="165" bgcolor="#cccc99" height="0">
<table cellspacing="6" cellpadding="0" width="100%" border="0">
<tbody>
<tr>
<td><a href="http://www.umass.edu/newsoffice/hfiles/foia.html">
<font face="Verdana, Arial, Helvetica, sans-serif" size="1">Guide
to the FOIA &amp; Mass. Public Document Laws</font></a></td>
</tr>

<tr>
<td><a href="http://www.umass.edu/newsoffice/hfiles/tools.html">
<font face="Verdana, Arial, Helvetica, sans-serif" size="1">
Media/Reference Links</font></a></td>
```

```
</tr>

<tr>
<td><a href="http://www.umass.edu/newsoffice/hometn/index.html">
<font face="Verdana, Arial, Helvetica, sans-serif" size="1">
Hometown News</font></a></td>
</tr>

<tr>
<td><a href="http://www.umass.edu/newsoffice/newsline/1299.html">
<font face="Verdana, Arial, Helvetica, sans-serif" size="1">News
Office News<i>Line</i></font></a></td>
</tr>
</tbody>
</table>
</td>
<td valign="top" width="123" bgcolor="#ffcc66" height="0">
<div align="left">
<p align="center"><a href="http://www.campaign.umass.edu/"><img
height="39" alt="News from Campaign UMass"
src="newsoffice_files/campaign_btn.gif" width="123"
border="0" /></a><font face="Verdana, Arial, Helvetica, sans-serif"
size="1"><br />
<br />
</font><a
href="http://www.umass.edu/newsoffice/archive/2000/041400campaign.ht
ml">
<font face="Verdana, Arial, Helvetica, sans-serif" size="2"><font
size="1">Campaign Tops<br />
$100 Million Mark</font></font></a></p>
</div>
</td>
</tr>

<tr align="left">
<td valign="top" bgcolor="#ffffff" colspan="4">
<div align="center"><img height="2" alt='""'
src="newsoffice_files/3pt.gif" width="600" border="0" /></div>
</td>
</tr>

<tr align="left">
<td valign="top" bgcolor="#ffffff" colspan="4" height="0">
```

```
<p><img height="63" alt="UMass Logo"
src="newsoffice_files/sm_logo.gif" width="72" align="left"
border="0" /><font size="2"><br />
This is an <a href="http://www.umass.edu/umhome/official.html">
Official Publication</a> of the University of Massachusetts Amherst
Campus.</font></p>

<p><font size="2">Copyright &copy; 1997-2000. <a
href="http://www.umass.edu/newsoffice/hfiles/about.html">About this
site</a> | <a
href="http://www.umass.edu/newsoffice/hfiles/usage.html">Usage
Agreement</a> | <a href="http://www.umass.edu/umhome/index.html">
UMass Home Page</a></font></p>
</td>
</tr>
</tbody>
</table>
</td>
</tr>
</tbody>
</table>
</td>
</tr>
</tbody>
</table>
</body>
</html>
```

HTML-Kit

If handling the files one at a time is still too much for you, consider downloading a program from `Chami.com` called HTML-Kit. This program, while not a WYSIWYG tool, offers Web developers complete control over their HTML documents. HTML-Kit's creators also were smart enough to integrate HTML Tidy as a push-button function. This enables you to load up your documents and, using a menu option, convert your HTML to XHTML. You can download the program at `http://www.chami.com/html-kit/`.

Java Tidy

Software developer Andy Quick (`http://www3.sympatico.ca/ac.quick/`) migrated HTML Tidy into a JavaBean to allow for more versatility and to make it easier to add as a component to any commercial or in-house development package. You can download a copy at http://www3.sympatico.ca/ac.quick/jtidy.html.

BBTidy

Web developers using the Macintosh platform will appreciate BBTidy (http://www.geocities.com/SiliconValley/1057/tidy.html), a plug-in to the ever-popular BBEdit Web editing environment that does much the same that the HTML Tidy feature in HTML-Kit does.

Batch conversion

Unfortunately, no program can spider through a site and auto-convert it from HTML to XHTML. However, using HTML Tidy, you can do it directory by directory. Providing you use the -modify or -m flag to make the HTML-to-XHTML conversion take place within the source document, you can use wildcards with Tidy. To convert a whole directory of documents, use the following line:

```
tidy  -asxml -clean -modify *.html
```

This line converts every .html document in the directory to XHTML.

Document Validation

Whether you perform the conversion process by hand or use a program, nothing is infallible. HTML Tidy has not been tested fully to see if it produces 100 percent valid and well-formed XHTML in each and every instance – and in hand-coding, there's always one or two things someone overlooks. That's why it is very important to use a validation tool to check your documents and be absolutely sure.

The best Web-based solution for XHTML validation is the W3C Validation Service (http://validator.w3.org). This is a great way to see what you're missing in your conversion process. Just make sure you have one of the three XHTML DOCTYPE declarations or it will validate your document as HTML.

Another valuable validating tool comes as part of the Mozquito Factory XHTML-FML authoring environment – discussed in detail in Chapter 18 – in which one button checks a document's well-formedness and another button checks its validity.

Chapter 11

The Big Clean-Up: Fixing HTML Generating Code (The Hard Part)

As HORRIBLE A TASK as updating static HTML pages may seem, static documents at least have the advantage of predictability. Once a document is converted to XHTML, it stays XHTML unless someone actually modifies it. Code that generates HTML isn't nearly as predictable. You may think you've found all the glitches in the HTML it generates, and converted it to XHTML, but variations in how the code runs with different data may mean you have to come back for more. If you really want to generate conformant XHTML, you may find it more convenient to change some aspects of your coding style rather than just fix the existing code. XHTML's stricter syntactical rules impose discipline that hasn't existed in Web applications before and they make "best practices" considerably more important now than in the past.

Y2K Revisited?

Programmers recently survived an exercise in code archaeology and repair – cleaning up Year 2000 bugs – but the costs of that project were enormous. While failure to convert to XHTML isn't likely to shut off the world's power, disrupt emergency services, or devastate the world economy, the cleanup process is nearly as complicated as the work that was done on Y2K. Even though Web applications are newer, many of them have been written in an immense hurry by developers who since have moved on to other projects. Some developers, especially those fond of writing "obfuscated" code, have created large amounts of code that does what it's supposed to but is difficult to manage or modify.

Proper coding practice may have been understood better in the relatively short period the Web has existed than in the period when most of the code that wasn't Y2K-compliant was written – but those practices haven't been honored necessarily. *Hack-and-slash code*, cut-and-pasted out of various examples, has been popular on the Web (even encouraged). (*Mea culpa*: I've done plenty of this kind of code hacking myself.) Because HTML browsers have been forgiving devices, there just hasn't been a need to make sure that all the i's are dotted and the t's crossed. When it looks okay in a few dominant browsers and it doesn't crash the server, a project is often ready to go. The distinction between prototype and deliverable has blurred considerably.

Even for situations in which proper coding practice is followed and program behaviors are well understood and manageable, corner-cutting often occurs that makes it difficult to move programs from HTML to XHTML. Designers seeking to shrink their file sizes have figured out HTML's rules (and the rules in browsers) regarding when and where end tags are needed and how best to shrink small amounts of whitespace in a quest for the smallest possible files. These kinds of shortcuts make sense when generating pages on a large scale — and XHTML slightly raises the cost of document generation because it requires the use of end tags — but they make it more difficult to switch an application from generating HTML to generating XHTML.

If you or your organization chooses to switch to XHTML, you most likely have a lot of work to do. The difficulty level of that work depends on the kind of code you have to deal with — not so much which language it is written in or what environment it runs in, but how it was structured and documented. You may want to survey the code you have before deciding whether to make the leap in order to have some estimate of the costs compared with the benefits. You may not have a choice, of course, if your customers or your organization want to apply XML-based tools to the documents you create. Then you just have to dig in.

Preliminaries

Some of the changes you need to make to your code are minor, even cosmetic, although the implications of the choices you make may be more complex. For your code to be conformant XHTML, you need to label it as such with a DOCTYPE declaration, an XHTML namespace, and possibly an XML declaration. Adding these pieces to code generation isn't very difficult (usually), but they may determine and modify some of your future paths through the application.

If your documents are delivered using a character encoding other than UTF-8 or UTF-16, you should consider using the XML declaration. That declaration may appear in some older browsers — as shown in Chapter 5 — but you have to decide whether including the declaration is better or worse than converting your code to generate UTF-8 or UTF-16 documents. You can go without the declaration entirely, but that omission results in garbled transmission of documents to applications unable to guess the document encoding. The charset parameter used in HTTP transmissions may be helpful here, but it doesn't last beyond the length of the transmission and leads to possible problems if users save files and then try to open or retransmit them.

Choosing a DOCTYPE for generated code may be harder than choosing a DOCTYPE for static code because generated HTML may come up differently depending on circumstance. Developers who already have code that produces variations (typically for different brands and versions of browsers) may have to examine the code they produce to see how well (indeed if) it can fit any of the W3C XHTML DTDs. Sites built using features that XHTML doesn't support (such as Netscape's LAYER element or Microsoft's XML element) may face some serious choices between a lot of work to produce genuinely conformant documents or less work combined with a prayer that the code never goes near a validating XML parser.

Otherwise, the same rules apply to choosing a DOCTYPE for generated HTML as apply to static HTML. Sites that use frames have to use the frameset DOCTYPE, while sites that use the font element or align attribute have to use the transitional DOCTYPE declaration. Only sites that conform tightly to the strict set of rules should use the strict DOCTYPE declaration. Sites that generate relatively simple HTML (or had designers who were especially picky about writing to the W3C standards) probably have the best luck meeting this requirement.

Adding the XHTML namespace to your html element shouldn't be that difficult, fortunately. You also may want to add language information (using the lang and xml:lang attributes) to the html element if you know what language your generated documents contain.

Pitfalls: Case-Sensitivity

One of the easiest and most obvious changes in XHTML – the mandated shift to lowercase element and attribute names – can be one of the most frustrating for developers, at least for those who use uppercase markup in their code. While search-and-replace isn't that difficult when working with static HTML documents, where it's clear what represents markup and what doesn't, it can be a hassle inside of a program. Developers converting code from HTML to XHTML generation need to watch out for a variety of details that can disrupt the transition.

Variable and object names that include HTML element names can become inadvertent victims of quick search-and-replace approaches, possibly disrupting interactions with other program modules that don't generate HTML directly. Many developers rely on case for visual cues to make their code more readable – lowercase for names in the program and uppercase for the generated markup. That approach no longer works, although it can be reversed. Similarly, developers need to make sure that their case changes are thorough and that they modify code using HTML element and attribute names as arguments – not just code that creates elements and attributes.

Programs that have gone to extreme lengths to separate markup from code, perhaps even creating tables of markup vocabularies, will be the easiest to change over. Programs that freely mix code and content (like most Active Server Pages and Java Server Pages) will be more difficult. This relatively simple-sounding change can impose some real costs, depending on the style of coding used. (If your code already uses lowercase, you can count yourself as very lucky!)

Pitfalls: Well–Formedness

Generated markup that passes the "it looks okay in a browser" test may conceal some serious structural problems that prevent its easy use as XHTML. HTML permits a wide variety of syntactical variations that can't parse as XHTML (such as omitted end tags) and browsers allow many more possibilities (such as meaningless or repeated end tags and omitted quotes around attribute values). Depending on how your code was written, sorting out these issues may be extremely easy or frustratingly difficult. "Off-by-one" bugs, where loops end in slightly the wrong place, can complicate matters significantly, especially if those errors only appear in certain contexts.

Most of these difficulties arise because HTML generation code typically sees its job as the creation of a text stream. The approach described in Chapter 13, which creates document trees and then converts them to text, is much safer; but this approach also represents a significant change from common practice. Because most tools for generating HTML documents are really tools for generating text files, with various levels of awareness of HTML and HTTP, developers are largely on their own when it comes to making sure their documents are well structured.

There are a number of common situations in which these problems occur. The paragraph element p often is used like the line break element br. Many early HTML developers treated p elements like the paragraph marks used in word processors to mark the ends of paragraphs, effectively treating p as a larger line break than br and not a container for paragraphs. The fragment shown here demonstrates this style:

```
This is paragraph number one.<p>
This is paragraph number two.<p>
This is paragraph number three.<p>
This is paragraph number four.<p>
```

Cleaning this problem out of text-generating code may be as simple as adding a slash (/) to the end tag and a <p> to the start of the paragraph in a template. Or it may mean tracking down the code that creates the paragraph and prefacing it with an extra tag. Another possibility is replacing <p> with </p><p>, although that may create an extra paragraph start tag at the end and leave off a <p> at the beginning of the series.

List items have a similar problem, although typically in reverse. Many developers treat the <li> start tag as a stand-in for a bullet or number, not a container for a list item. As a result, code can look like this:

```
<ul>
<li> Item One
<li> Item Two
<li> Item Three
</ul>
```

In a template-based approach, adding the closing `</li>` may not be difficult. In code that generates text explicitly, fixing this probably requires adding an extra bit of code that inserts the end tag where appropriate.

Lists and tables share some code-structuring problems. Both are generated by code looping over incoming information; processing comes to an end when the information ends or when the information is no longer appropriate. Because you can skip some of the code at the end of the loop that generates these structures, it's possible that end tags for one or more elements won't be generated ever. Developers familiar with the need to close table elements already have some experience with this problem. (Many browsers don't display tables that don't have a clearly marked end.) XHTML conformance requires the table itself to be closed, as well as the cells, headers, and rows — and they must be closed in the sequence they were opened. Maintaining a stack of open elements isn't necessary, but it may become critical if your code takes multiple paths through the same information.

XHTML elements that have no textual content, such as `img` and `br`, can cause problems in code that treats these empty elements as start tags and nothing more. If your code uses generic mechanisms to build start tags (taking element and attribute name-value pairs as arguments, for instance), you may need to add logic that checks the element name to see if it should be an empty tag or if it enables developers to specify it as an empty tag. The latter approach is more flexible, but also more prone to errors.

Web developers also use a number of techniques that may not cause problems in the environments they originally were built for, but that may cause problems if your XHTML documents move into a more XML-oriented environment. *Server-side includes*, for example, use HTML comments to store information that the server processes. Comments are a convenient mechanism for doing this because users don't see extra content should a server fail to include the content, unless they search the source for comments. Server-side includes — at least those that don't reference content that can disrupt well-formedness by including content with unbalanced markup, — should continue to work during a transition to XHTML. They may not prove portable however, if your document templates are parsed as XML before reaching the server-side include engine. XML provides other mechanisms for this kind of content referencing, called *entities*, but XHTML doesn't support the creation of external entities explicitly. Server-side includes are probably here to stay, but you may want to watch them closely — perhaps parsing content before shipping it to the users — if you perform major surgery on your code-generation architecture.

Pitfalls: Valid XHTML

While making generated HTML well formed is difficult, making it valid XHTML is even more difficult. While some developers may check their results against the HTML 4.0 DTDs (using tools such as the W3C's HTML Validation Service), most don't; and the discipline of conforming to a particular document structure is a fairly new introduction for most Web developers. It isn't difficult to generate valid XHTML, but retrofitting older code can be tricky.

The problems involved in generating valid XHTML do not differ much from the problems involved in converting legacy HTML static documents to XHTML. Like their static document-creating counterparts, a lot of Web developers left out features such as the `html`, `head`, and `body` elements unless they had a particular use for them in their code. Title support and the use of `meta` elements to identify pages to search engines does mean that the `head` element commonly appears.

Adding the basic structure of an XHTML document to code that left it out typically isn't that difficult — most developers don't try to specify the `title` element in the body of their document anyway. Starting a document with a `DOCTYPE` declaration and properly XHTMLized `html` element is reasonably easy, as is making sure that the document ends with `</body></html>`.

On the other hand, there's no simple way to ensure that your generated documents comply with the XHTML DTDs. Even code that generates document structures, as described in Chapter 13, may have a hard time testing the implications for document validity of adding a particular element or attributes. Furthermore, text generators can't do it at all until the document is complete. Generating valid XHTML (actually, any kind of valid XML) requires building the code that writes the documents around the DTD in some form. It doesn't mean that you can use a DTD's description of a document structure to generate code — most likely it means that the developers creating a particular document generation system need to be aware of the DTD and understand how the documents they create relate to that DTD.

Working within the constraints provided by DTDs isn't that difficult for new projects, although it requires programmers to have a much higher-level understanding of the markup vocabulary with which they are working. For legacy projects, however, developers need both that understanding and a thorough knowledge of how the old code worked. Cosmetic cleanups may catch gross errors, and even get past the well-formedness problems associated with old code, but document structure issues may require more cleanup. Making sure that block elements and inline elements mingle properly — or that all of the constraints on form structures are obeyed — may require a lot of testing and an eye for detail.

True XHTML conformance demands valid documents. But HTML parsers and non-validating XML environments may find it acceptable for your documents to be well formed XHTML that doesn't conform to a particular DTD. It won't pass a test from the W3C's Validation Service or any other validating XML parser, however.

Testing, Testing, Testing

Whatever strategy you use for cleaning up your legacy code, the best way to make sure it works is to test it out against a broad range of possible situations. This does not differ much from the traditional testing of HTML code against as many browsers as possible to determine if the code looks right, but it's a slightly more formal process that probably is better accomplished with XML parsers than with armies of machines running browsers. (Hopefully, XHTML and more standards-compliant browsers will reduce the need for the old-style testing in the long run.)

Most of the tools for checking well-formedness or validity examine a single document at a time — excellent for small-scale work, but not especially useful if you need to check 4,000 pages or even 4,000 variations of a single code generation. Fortunately, options for testing multiple documents are starting to appear. The Web Design Group's *WDG HTML Validator*, available at `http://www.htmlhelp. com/tools/validator/`, is a Web-based tool for validating HTML and XHTML documents and sites. It includes a batch mode (`http://www.htmlhelp. com/tools/validator/batch.html`) that accepts a list of URLs and reports on the conformance of all of those documents. (There seems to be a limit of 60, but it's a start.)

You also can build your own tools on top of existing XML parsers, although hopefully more tools of this kind will become widely available as more developers transition to XHTML.

TIP Liam Quinn, the maintainer of the WDG HTML Validator, also maintains a list of other validation tools at `http://www.htmlhelp.com/links/ validators.htm`.

Tools alone are not likely to solve all of your testing problems. Testing for XHTML conformance is a process you usually need to perform at multiple stages of development. In addition, it may require placeholders at various points in the process for incomplete work. Because the validation process doesn't provide any simple means of "validating only this far into the document, but don't worry about the missing pieces," it may be difficult to use automated testing processes on intermediate phases of work. In these cases, at least until someone develops a more controllable set of testing tools, a human being who reads markup and compares it to a thorough understanding of XHTML 1.0's structures probably presents a better approach to testing.

Strategies for Managing XHTML Generation Code

Generating XHTML is a more demanding process than generating HTML, if only because XHTML comes with a much stricter set of rules. Meeting these demands doesn't have to mean hours of bug-hunting every time you build a complex program, but it may mean that you have to modify the way you write your programs. (No requirement forces you to change, but adhering to these rules may prove easier in the long run.) Pretty much all of the techniques that work with HTML work with XHTML, but you may want to incorporate more of an XHTML-orientation into your generation code choices.

Text

Working with HTML and XHTML documents as text is, in some ways, the easiest approach. In other ways, it is definitely the hardest approach. Text is the foundation of markup documents. Working at that level can be straightforward, but it also denies you the privilege of working with information at a higher level (such as the container structures created by XHTML). Writing code that generates raw text — which just happens to be XHTML — requires a lot of attention to detail, especially as XHMTL is much less forgiving of errors.

Text-generation strategies may be useful, especially for projects that need to create more than one version of a document. Fundamentally, every environment that generates XHTML generates text. It's just a matter of what kinds of abstractions are in use. Probably the easiest way to update text-generating code for the new challenges of XHTML is to add some of those layers of abstraction, separating code that generates markup from code that address content. As the abstraction proceeds, you then can add extra logic that ensures that markup is properly balanced or conforms to a required structure. Most programmers already do this to some extent so they can reuse code; in essence, it may just be a matter of refocusing existing work.

Templates

Template systems, such as Active Server Pages (ASP) and Java Server Pages (JSP), enable developers to mix logic for creating content and structure with general templates that provide an overall framework. In some ways, these approaches are much like the text-generating systems described previously — but they have both advantages and disadvantages over that straightforward approach. Templates typically are easier to read and modify, especially for cases in which the generated content is a small portion of the document. At the same time, however, the interaction between the generated code and the information already stored in the template can cause problems that look like they are in the code but are in fact in the template and vice-versa.

Using PHP Scripting in XHTML Files

There are a few environments in which using XHTML can be difficult because of conflicts between XHTML syntax and the syntax of the development environment. If you use PHP scripting to generate XHTML documents, you may encounter a problem. Including the XML declaration (`<?xml?>`) throws off the PHP processor. Because it can rely on the `<?` as its placemark for where to begin processing, you have two options in authoring your XHTML.

The first option is to exclude the XML declaration completely. It's not required in an XHTML document, so this isn't a problem. Having it in the first place is just a good markup habit. The other option is to always use `<?php` as its placemark to begin parsing. That way, `<?xml?>` can't throw it off. Disabling the 'short open tag' setting may require coordination with your Web site hosting company if you don't have administrative control over your server.

 Although Extensible Stylesheet Language Transformations (XSLT) are template-based document generators, the rules they follow are much stricter than those used by the technologies described here.

The XML 1.0 specification already faced similar issues with general entities, which enabled developers to include content (including markup) by reference. The solution XML 1.0 enforces is a requirement that all general entities that contain markup must be well formed. If an entity includes a start tag for an element, it must include an end tag for that element. All of the structures inside of a general entity must be nested and marked up properly. You can't use general entities to specify parts of markup, such as half a start tag or just an end tag.

Taking a similar approach to code generation can solve most of the problems caused by unexpected interactions between the template and the generated content, and should make it easier to track down the origin of such problems when they do occur. The strategies suggested for text-generating code also apply in large part to template-based XHTML generation. Creating layers of abstraction that go beyond creating streams of characters can help make the code portion of these template-based systems easier to work with, and may make it more reusable across documents and projects.

While template-based systems can produce XHTML, the templates themselves frequently are not XHTML (or even XML) because of their use of constructions such as <%. Among other things, this may force you to store templates separately from XHTML documents if you use an XML-based document management facility. The XML-Apache project is building a template language called *XML Server Pages (XSP)* that does use XML documents for their templates, but they are well ahead of most template systems in their zeal for well formed templates. See `http://xml.apache.org/cocoon/wd-xsp.html` for a draft of XSP.

Modularization

In general, the most thorough long-term approaches to making XHTML generation clean and maintainable involve creating code modules that do simple things reliably and then connecting these modules to create documents. Reliability is perhaps the most important change moving from HTML to XHTML development, and that reliability is of a somewhat different type. In the HTML world, the code had to produce content that looked consistent in a given browser or browsers; in the XHTML world, the code has to produce content that is structurally – as well as visually – consistent. While an occasional missing end-paragraph tag doesn't cause problems in an HTML browser, it can bring a halt to XHTML processing.

Breaking down the larger problem of building a document into the smaller problems of creating particular structures is one way to make sure that the small problems are solved consistently. It also enhances reusability and makes it easier to update the small problem solutions without interfering with the overall logic of the document.

Several HTML generation systems – such as CGI.pm (the CGI module for Perl) and the Java Servlet Library – already use modules that generate markup based on arguments passed to them through function calls. When developers rely on these modules exclusively, rather than mixing them with explicit text-generation code, then updating a system to use XHTML is easy. You just update the module system to an XHTML-compliant version.

Module systems that generate XHTML are starting to appear — notably a new version of CGI.pm — but it may be a while before these generic systems consistently produce XHTML instead of HTML. If it isn't clear from the documentation, you may want to contact the developer maintaining the markup generation system you are using.

Even if you do not use one of these systems, you may find it worthwhile to modularize your own code as much as possible. By separating your document logic from the small-scale element logic, you can build more flexible systems that enable you to make changes in one place without disrupting work throughout the system. You also may be able to create new systems that build on this modularity by replacing the code that built XHTML documents with code that produces Wireless Markup Language (WML) documents, as described in Chapter 18.

In addition to containing side effects, adding modularity to your code should help you future-proof it to some extent. XHTML 1.0 marks the first major structural change to HTML since its inception, and developers thus far have been able to rely on older code working just fine in newer browsers. While XHTML 1.0 may be the first change to break that understanding, it certainly will not be the last. XHTML 1.1 won't instantly break XHTML 1.0 processing, but it adds new functionality that may require substantial change to both document-generation code on the server and document-processing code on the client. By modularizing your code, you position yourself to take advantage of the new possibilities XHTML 1.1 will create for extending the HTML vocabulary.

XHTML 2.0 is also on the horizon, although probably much further out. XHTML 2.0 may involve significant destruction and reconstruction of some parts of the HTML vocabulary, including linking functionality and other processing that involves external resources. If you move the code that handles the details of such work into a separate module, you can make changes easily when the time comes.

Finally, modularization opens up a significant new possibility in markup generation – one that goes well beyond the simple case-switch logic used by many applications to generate documents customized for different browsers. With the advent of technologies such as Composite Capabilities/Preference Profiles (CC/PP), discussed in Chapter 14, programs need to be capable of generating the same document in several different forms and choosing the appropriate set of modules for a given application. Text-generation and template-based systems will need to handle this customization with an enormous number of if-then or case-switch statements. Meanwhile, modular frameworks may be capable of setting a few variables and letting the code work itself out more smoothly, thereby turning modules on and off as appropriate.

These various kinds of future-proofing may require a different mindset than the one that has proven so successful at creating large numbers of HTML applications at low cost. Despite the potential of higher development costs per module, however, this new mindset promises long-term upgradability and a much easier task for programmers who need to manage and reuse code over the long term.

Part IV

Moving Forward into XML

CHAPTER 12
Using XSL to Generate (X)HTML

CHAPTER 13
Integrating the Document Object Model with XHTML Generation

CHAPTER 14
Moving to Modules: Creating Extensible Document Structures with XHTML 1.1

CHAPTER 15
Fragmenting XHTML

CHAPTER 16
Extending XHTML

CHAPTER 17
XHTML Inside XML: Using XHTML in an XML Context

Chapter 12

Using XSL to Generate (X)HTML

WHILE XML HAS INHERITED an enormous amount of familiar infrastructure from the world of Web development, its SGML ancestry has brought with it some tools and innovations that may seem strikingly unfamiliar to Web developers. Extensible Stylesheet Language (XSL) and Extensible Stylesheet Language Transformations (XSLT) originally were developed as industrial-strength formatting tools, but they have application to XHTML work as well. XSLT is probably more interesting to developers who want to work with the HTML vocabulary because XSL is largely about the creation of a markup vocabulary to replace HTML for formatting.

This chapter shows you what XSL has to offer XHTML developers, but it's not a full-scale XSL tutorial. XSL, even just XSLT, is an enormous subject worthy of its own book-length treatment. You may want to explore Elliotte Rusty Harold's *XML Bible* (IDG Books, 1999) for a thorough introduction to XPath and XSLT. Ken Holman has a complete set of training materials available through `http://www.cranesoftwrights.com/training/index.htm`; the first and last two chapters are available as free downloads.

The XSL specification is available at `http://www.w3.org/TR/xsl/`. The XSLT specification, which you apply in this chapter, is available at `http://www.w3.org/TR/xslt`. The XPath specification, which XSLT uses, is available at `http://www.w3.org/TR/xpath`. If you need XSL help, the XSL-List (at `http://www.mulberrytech.com/xsl/xsl-list/index.html`) is a great place to start.

Introduction to XSL

While XSL has been much slower in development than XML, the ideas behind it coalesced around the same time as XML itself. XML's roots are in SGML, while XSL's roots are in a styling language for SGML — the *Document Style Semantics and Specification Language (DSSSL)*. While XML was largely a simplification of SGML, XSL has proven more of an inheritor and reinterpreter of DSSSL. In effect, XSL

215

makes some aspects of DSSSL that hadn't received much use (transformations) more central to the project and reconciles DSSSL's model for document formatting to some extent with the W3C's cascading style sheets.

XSL is in some ways a competitor to CSS, although its proponents consider them different enough that they don't compete officially. While CSS describes formatting for particular structures within a document, XSL describes a transformation from the original document to a set of formatting objects – possibly reorganizing, filtering, or even discarding the original structures along the way. While CSS is annotative, XSL is transformative. CSS works well in environments in which documents are either static or generated by code that isn't format-specific; XSL, on the other hand, assumes that it has much more work to do in building a document.

Extensible Stylesheet Language Transformations (XSLT) processors take an XML document as an input, the origin tree, and create a result tree based on the template rules provided in the style sheet. That result tree may contain *XSL Formatting Objects* (often called *XSL-FOs*) or it may contain other information, typically HTML or XHTML. The output is already a tree, and the XSLT processor has to reserialize it anyway, so converting it to XHTML is easy. Effectively, XSLT provides a simple way to convert XML documents to XHTML, making it easy to present content from XML documents to browsers that know nothing of XML itself. (XSLT input documents must be XML – you can't use this tool on HTML that doesn't conform to XHTML's rules.)

XSL Formatting Objects provide an explicit XML vocabulary for describing formatted text. XSL-FOs are still in development at the W3C and haven't received wide implementation (at least in browsers) yet. For the latest specification, see http://www.w3.org/TR/xsl/. When they're ready, XSL will provide a complete formatting solution, using XSLT transformations to convert documents into formatting objects describing information presentation.

The other possibility that XSLT opens, but which isn't implemented widely yet, is sending XML information to clients. The clients then perform the XSLT transformation locally. Most servers process multiple, simultaneous requests, while most browsers more or less are idle. This redistributes processing for better server response. So far, however, Microsoft is the only vendor actively pursuing this strategy; the old version of XSLT that Microsoft currently supports is decidedly different from the standard. (The Mozilla project is pursuing standard XSLT support, although that remains in the early stages.) For now, most XSLT processing has to take place on the server where developers have more control over the environment.

XSLT processing is fairly resource-intensive, requiring the construction of object trees in memory. This can become a burden for servers that process large numbers of requests or process very large documents. There are several strategies for avoiding this bottleneck—from buying more hardware, to sending processing to the client when possible, to aggressively caching the result documents produced by transformations in order to avoid processing the same document and style sheet combinations repeatedly. In some cases, batch processing can make conversions before users actually retrieve the files and keep the server load minimal.

 XSLT is new enough that it isn't a standard feature of most server environments yet, although this is changing slowly. There are a number of different XSLT processors available, most of which conform to the W3C Recommendation closely. Many of them are freely distributed or open source, requiring only some integration with your processing environment. For a list of XSLT processors, see `http://www.xslinfo.com/`. News on recent developments in XSLT is available at `http://xmlhack.com/list.php?cat=2`.

Basic Transformation Principles

XSLT style sheets are XML documents that combine an XSLT vocabulary with the vocabulary that the information is transformed into—in this case, XHTML. (In some cases, an extension vocabulary for a particular processor also may appear.) The XSLT vocabulary defines the rules for processing, while the other vocabulary provides parts and structures that are assembled into the result document.

Preliminaries

An `xsl:stylesheet` element can contain the entire style sheet:

```
<?xml version="1.0"?>
<xsl:stylesheet
    xmlns:xsl="http://www.w3.org/1999/XSL/Transform"
    version="1.0">
...stylesheet...
</xsl:stylesheet>
```

An `xsl:transform` element used the same way may be substituted for `xsl:stylesheet`; technically, neither of these elements is necessary. It's also a good idea to define any namespaces you plan to use in the result document here. An XSLT style sheet can be any XML document, and only elements using the XSL namespace are processed. Despite that incredible flexibility, let's stick to a more conservative approach.

The next piece you need for XHTML creation is the `xsl:output` element, which enables you to specify the type of output you're creating and provides access to the `DOCTYPE` declaration.

```
<xsl:output method="xml" indent="yes"
    doctype-public="http://www.w3.org/TR/xhtml11/DTD/xhtml1-
strict.dtd"
    doctype-system="-//W3C//DTD XHTML 1.0 Strict//EN"    omit-xml-
declaration="yes" />
```

While most XSLT processors provide an `html` output method, this leaves off end tags (or empty tags) for empty elements and may leave off end tags for some elements with content. Using the `xml` output method must suffice until developers begin supporting XHTML explicitly.

 While XSL processors produce valid XHTML using the `xml` setting, they don't do things such as insert the space before the `/>` of an empty tag to produce `<br/>` instead of `<br />`. You can do a search-and-replace after the transformation to add the space, or add dummy attributes (like `class=""`) to keep older browsers from choking on the empty tags. If you're doing batch processing, rather than generating files on the fly, you also can use the Tidy program (described in Chapter 10) on the results to add the needed space.

The `indent` attribute is handy if you want to produce more readable markup, but it doesn't have much effect on the output seen in the browser window because of the way HTML and XHTML discard extra whitespace. The next two attributes, `doctype-public` and `doctype-system`, are critical if you're creating strictly conforming XHTML because they enable you to specify the public and system identifiers of the XHTML vocabulary you're using. The example here uses the identifiers for the XHTML 1.0 strict DTDs, but you can replace these with values for the transitional or frameset DTDs or with XHTML 1.1 (and beyond identifiers when they become available).

The last attribute, `omit-xml-declaration`, keeps the XML declaration from appearing at the front of the document when its value is set to `yes`. If you generate XHTML that has to go to a wide range of browsers, particularly older browsers that sometimes display the XML declaration at the top of the screen, this is probably a good idea. If you're less interested in backward compatibility and more interested in forward compatibility with more character encodings for internationalization, you should set this value to `no`.

Creating the result document

Now that you've specified the overall form of the result document, you need to start describing its content. XSLT enables you to specify content using a mix of the result document and XSLT-specific elements and attributes that build the document from information in the source document. XSLT provides some default behavior that sets the processor to explore the document tree until it finds a match, and a rule that copies the text of nodes. For the first example, you override those rules and create a style sheet that completely ignores the content of the source tree and just produces XHTML:

```
<?xml version="1.0"?>
<xsl:stylesheet
    xmlns:xsl="http://www.w3.org/1999/XSL/Transform"
    version="1.0">

<xsl:output method="xml" indent="yes"
    doctype-public="http://www.w3.org/TR/xhtml1/DTD/xhtml1-
strict.dtd"
    doctype-system="-//W3C//DTD XHTML 1.0 Strict//EN"
    omit-xml-declaration="yes" />

<xsl:template match="/">
<html xmlns="http://www.w3.org/1999/xhtml" xml:lang="en-US"
lang="en-US">
<head>
<title>Hello World!</title>
</head>
<body>
<h1>Hello World!</h1>
<p>Hello World!</p>
</body>
</html>
</xsl:template>

</xsl:stylesheet>
```

The output looks like this:

```
<!DOCTYPE html PUBLIC "http://www.w3.org/TR/xhtml1/DTD/xhtml1-
strict.dtd" "-//W3C//DTD XHTML 1.0 Strict//EN">
<html xml:lang="en-US" lang="en-US"
xmlns="http://www.w3.org/1999/xhtml">
<head>
<title>Hello World!</title>
```

```
</head>
<body>
<h1>Hello World!</h1>
<p>Hello World!</p>
</body>
</html>
```

While this simple example isn't convincing, it does provide a foundation for future work. The output is notable for several things, including the proper handling of the XML declaration (which you said you don't want) and the DOCTYPE, which you set. Also notable is the change in the sequence of attributes on the html element — attribute order isn't considered important in XML, HTML, or XHTML, and XSLT doesn't preserve it either.

The xsl:template element does the real work; it specifies both the content to which they should be applied and the results that should be included. Because you just replaced the entire document, you match against the root element (/, an XPath expression). This bit of code then replaces the root element and the output is generated.

Although they don't appear in the style sheet, there are also default rules built into XSLT (in Section 5.8) that get tested — but only if none of the explicit rules match. The first is this:

```
<xsl:template match="*|/">
    <xsl:apply-templates/>
</xsl:template>
```

The match attribute uses XPath notation to say that the template should apply to any element (*) or (|) of the root element (/) of the document. The xsl:apply-templates element inside the xsl:template element tells the XSLT processor to check the rest of the document for possible templates that apply to the content of the document. This allows recursive processing of documents because the explicit rules provided in the style sheet can begin with content further into the document than the root element, and some content may be skipped.

The second rule is normally this:

```
<xsl:template match="text()|@*">
    <xsl:value-of select="."/>
</xsl:template>
```

By default, this applies to all text nodes (text()) and the contents of all attributes (@*) and includes their content in the document. The xsl:value-of element retrieves that information, using the select attribute value (.) to get the content from the current node. (There is also a default rule that drops processing instructions and comments from the original document.)

The XSLT implementation in Internet Explorer 5.5, apart from using a slightly different syntax, also doesn't support these default rules. Future versions may provide better support.

On just this small foundation, you can create some XSLT style sheets that do real work. You can take a simple XML document and convert it into an XHTML table. Start with an XML document describing a set of books:

```
<catalog>
<book>
<author>Simon St.Laurent</author>
<title>XML Elements of Style</title>
<pubyear>2000</pubyear>
<publisher>McGraw-Hill</publisher>
<isbn>0-07-212220-X</isbn>
<price>$29.99</price>
</book>
<book>
<author>Elliotte Rusty Harold</author>
<title>XML Bible</title>
<pubyear>1999</pubyear>
<publisher>IDG Books</publisher>
<isbn>0764532367</isbn>
<price>$49.99</price>
</book>
<book>
<author>Robert Eckstein</author>
<title>XML Pocket Reference</title>
<pubyear>1999</pubyear>
<publisher>O'Reilly and Associates</publisher>
<isbn>1-56592-709-5</isbn>
<price>$8.95</price>
</book>
<book>
<author>Kevin Dick</author>
<title>XML: A Manager's Guide</title>
<pubyear>1999</pubyear>
<publisher>Addison-Wesley</publisher>
<isbn>0201433354</isbn>
<price>$29.95</price>
</book>
<book>
```

```
<author>Simon St.Laurent</author>
<title>XML: A Primer, 2nd Ed.</title>
<pubyear>1999</pubyear>
<publisher>IDG Books</publisher>
<isbn>0-7645-3310-X</isbn>
<price>$19.99</price>
</book>
<book>
<author>Simon St.Laurent</author>
<title>Building XML Applications</title>
<pubyear>1999</pubyear>
<publisher>McGraw-Hill</publisher>
<isbn>0-07-134116-1</isbn>
<price>$49.99</price>
</book>
</catalog>
```

The style sheet includes a rule to build the HTML document as a whole, including a table element, and then rules to build rows and cells:

```
<?xml version="1.0"?>
<xsl:stylesheet
    xmlns:xsl="http://www.w3.org/1999/XSL/Transform"
    xmlns="http://www.w3.org/1999/xhtml"
    version="1.0">
<xsl:output method="xml" indent="yes"
    doctype-public="http://www.w3.org/TR/xhtml1/DTD/
xhtml1-strict.dtd"
    doctype-system="-//W3C//DTD XHTML 1.0 Strict//EN"
    omit-xml-declaration="yes" />

<xsl:template match="/">
<html xmlns="http://www.w3.org/1999/xhtml" xml:lang="en-US"
lang="en-US">
<head>
<title>Catalog</title>
</head>
<body>
<h1>Books</h1>
<table>
<xsl:apply-templates/>
</table>
</body>
```

```
</html>
</xsl:template>

<xsl:template match="book">
<tr><xsl:apply-templates/></tr>
</xsl:template>

<xsl:template match="book/*">
<td><xsl:apply-templates/></td>
</xsl:template>

</xsl:stylesheet>
```

The first rule matches the root element (/) and builds an XHTML document framework, just like the previous example. In this case, however, the rule adds a table element and includes an xsl:apply-templates rule to let the XSL processor build the table from the rest of the document.

The second rule matches any book elements it encounters and builds table rows (tr elements) to contain their content. Again, xsl:apply-templates lets the processor continue to work on the contents of the book element.

The last rule matches any child element of any book element (book/*) and enables you to avoid the task of creating rules for the author, title, pubyear, and other elements specifically. These become the table cells (td elements), and xsl:apply-templates is applied yet again.

When applied to the document, the results form the following code (shown in the browser in Figure 12-1).

```
<!DOCTYPE html PUBLIC "http://www.w3.org/TR/xhtml1/DTD/xhtml1-
strict.dtd" "-//W3C//DTD XHTML 1.0 Strict//EN">
<html xml:lang="en-US" lang="en-US"
xmlns="http://www.w3.org/1999/xhtml">
<head>
<title>Catalog</title>
</head>
<body>
<h1>Books</h1>
<table>
<tr>
<td>Simon St.Laurent</td>
<td>XML Elements of Style</td>
<td>2000</td>
<td>McGraw-Hill</td>
<td>0-07-212220-X</td>
```

```
<td>$29.99</td>
</tr>
<tr>
<td>Elliotte Rusty Harold</td>
<td>XML Bible</td>
<td>1999</td>
<td>IDG Books</td>
<td>0764532367</td>
<td>$49.99</td>
</tr>
<tr>
<td>Robert Eckstein</td>
<td>XML Pocket Reference</td>
<td>1999</td>
<td>O'Reilly and Associates</td>
<td>1-56592-709-5</td>
<td>$8.95</td>
</tr>
<tr>
<td>Kevin Dick</td>
<td>XML: A Manager's Guide</td>
<td>1999</td>
<td>Addison-Wesley</td>
<td>0201433354</td>
<td>$29.95</td>
</tr>
<tr>
<td>Simon St.Laurent</td>
<td>XML: A Primer, 2nd Ed.</td>
<td>1999</td>
<td>IDG Books</td>
<td>0-7645-3310-X</td>
<td>$19.99</td>
</tr>
<tr>
<td>Simon St.Laurent</td>
<td>Building XML Applications</td>
<td>1999</td>
<td>McGraw-Hill</td>
<td>0-07-134116-1</td>
<td>$49.99</td>
</tr>
</table>
</body>
</html>
```

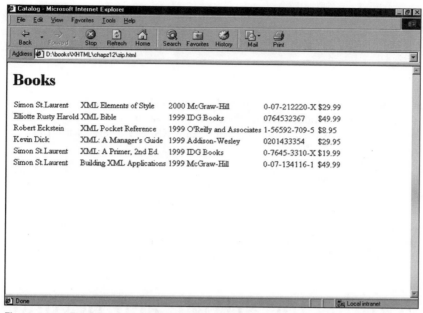

Figure 12-1: The XSL-generated XHTML as it appears in a Web browser

This example is pretty simple because it doesn't need to create or access any attributes. To make these entries referenceable, use the ISBN of each book to create an id attribute on the table row. You only need to change the rule that handles the book element, although you reach into the isbn element to create the attribute.

```
<xsl:template match="book">
<tr>
<xsl:attribute name="id">
<xsl:value-of select="./isbn"/>
</xsl:attribute>
<xsl:apply-templates/></tr>
</xsl:template>
```

The xsl:attribute element enables you to add attributes to the current element — in this case the tr element. The xsl:value-of element fills in the content based on its select attribute's value. The select attribute's value is "./isbn", meaning to start from the current source tree node and find a child isbn element. The xsl:apply-templates element then lets the rest of the processing continue as usual. The new entries in the table now look like this:

```
<tr id="0-07-212220-X">
<td>Simon St.Laurent</td>
<td>XML Elements of Style</td>
```

```
<td>2000</td>
<td>McGraw-Hill</td>
<td>0-07-212220-X</td>
<td>$29.99</td>
</tr>
```

Similarly, you can reach into attributes for their values using XPath's @name syntax for referencing attributes. Remember, attribute values are added by default to your content because of the default rules built into XSLT. You may want to override this behavior, as shown here:

```
<xsl:template match="@*">
</xsl:template>
```

This lets the default rule for text apply, but it prevents attributes from showing up.

XSLT offers an enormous number of options that build on these basic structures and enable you to sort, recombine, split up, or modify your content.

Applications for XHTML and Beyond

XSLT's applicability to traditional Web applications is limited by its demand for an XML source document. If your organization hasn't deployed XML already, this may be of limited use as far as XHTML *production* is concerned. Despite that limitation, however, you may find XSLT useful for managing and modifying your XHTML content. XHTML is after XML, and therefore ripe for processing with XSLT, if you find it appropriate.

Perhaps ironically, documents created with cascading style sheets in mind, which make great use of the class attribute, are almost as easy to work with in XSLT as are XML documents with semantic element names. Because XSLT enables you to specify rules that are dependent on attribute values and names as well as elements, you can "harvest" the semantic content (if any) of your existing XHTML documents. At the same time, you may be able to convert them to other XML formats — from your own vocabularies to more generic vocabularies such as XSL Formatting Objects, Scalable Vector Graphics (SVG), or *Synchronized Multimedia Integration Language (SMIL)*. The more markup information your documents contain, and the more regularly it is applied, the better your chances of applying XSLT to such work.

Even if you don't have plans to do this, and you generate all your Web documents from databases, you may be able to put XSLT to work as a layer of abstraction between your final documents and the data sources that populate them. If you work with multiple databases, and especially if they are distributed widely, you may find it useful to have the databases or some kind of middleware send you their information as sets of XML documents. They can accomplish this either in reply to queries, in advance, or both in some of kind caching approach. Then you can use XSLT to knit the results together into a final format.

Chapter 13

Integrating the Document Object Model with XHTML Generation

ALTHOUGH HTML DEVELOPERS have used the Document Object Model (DOM) on the client in some form since about 1997 when the earliest dynamic HTML implementations appeared, its use on the server opens up new horizons in document generation. At the same time, the DOM makes it very easy to create conformant XHTML. Using the DOM to generate documents may not be appropriate in every situation: It takes a very different approach than text generation or templates, and may require retooling as well as rethinking the programming model. For cases in which it does fit, however, the DOM promises to make XHTML conformance much easier while making program structures easier to design formally.

Building Trees, Not Streams

One main change exists between the text generation covered in Chapter 11 and the object model generation covered in this chapter. The former treats XHTML documents as a stream of text and the latter treats them as a tree of components. (The XSLT approach described in Chapter 12 holds an intermediate position between these two extremes.) Streams of text require few resources and you can generate them relatively efficiently. Conversely, trees require more resources and they sometimes cost more processing power. However, they open up new possibilities for developers who need to push the envelope.

Object trees inherently have more overhead than streams of bytes because they contain structural information that takes extra storage and processing. On the other hand, that structural information makes the tree both navigable and modifiable so that it can change the beginning of a document after its end is completed. Navigability and modifiability are the hallmarks of dynamic HTML development on the client, but these same features are useful on the server as well.

Tree models are not an innovation appearing only with XHTML. Similar models have been used to generate HTML code for years, notably in Java Servlet implementations (which use their own model, not necessarily the DOM). Trees make especially good sense in XML processing where document structures are built entirely as collections of nodes containing other nodes — in computer science parlance, a *tree*. The

XML specification requires that document syntax must conform to this structure, and XML best practices have followed this lead. XSLT, described in Chapter 12, uses a tree model in its rules for processing documents; meanwhile, cascading style sheets and XPointer provide various tools for describing locations within these tree structures.

Tree models provide two main advantages to developers building XHTML applications. First, they offer a large degree of modularity to insulate developers from the bugs caused by mistaken textual outputs. Second, they provide a much greater degree of flexibility that enables developers to create an initial tree and then modify it as necessary — perhaps even transforming it into a different structure altogether or reducing it to a small fragment. If you need this kind of reliability and flexibility, and can accept the greater memory and processing demands needed by these tree structures, then you may find it useful to generate documents through the DOM.

The DOM Level 1 specification, which includes all the functionality you use in this chapter, is available at `http://www.w3.org/TR/REC-DOM-Level-1`. If you're feeling curious, DOM Level 2 is available from `http://www.w3.org/TR/DOM-Level-2`. Information on further DOM development is available at `http://www.w3.org/DOM/`.

DOM Implementations

The Document Object Model, as specified by the W3C, comes in several *Levels*, all of which provide scripts and programs to sets of document information through an API. The DOM API is officially specified through a CORBA IDL file (you don't need to know anything about that to use the DOM), but is more commonly used in its Java and JavaScript translations. The DOM doesn't specify everything about document processing and handling — for example, the W3C only addresses loading documents, creating new documents, and saving documents in the Level 3 work that's just getting started.

As a result of this approach, the world of DOM implementations is somewhat fragmented. Besides the differences among the Java, JavaScript, and CORBA versions of the DOM, it's extremely difficult to write complete DOM code for multiple environments. While the core document generation may remain the same, the beginning and end of the process may vary substantially as you move DOM code from environment to environment and even from server to browser and back again.

Fortunately, the basic principles are pretty safe. If you learn the fundamentals of manipulating the DOM within an Active Server Pages (ASP) environment, you can transfer a substantial amount of that knowledge to work using Java XML parsers from Sun, IBM, Apache, and others, or the JavaScript processing built into Mozilla/Netscape Navigator 6. The basic concepts are the same across all of these systems, and the implementations should (hopefully) converge as the W3C releases more complete standards and developers build on those standards. The next section takes a look at the basic principles in one environment, ASP, while pointing out how the surrounding script may differ in other environments.

The DOM comes in various flavors as well as Levels. In this chapter, you work with the Core of the DOM Level 1 to generate code. More HTML-specific functionality is available in the HTML portion of the DOM Level 1. However, that functionality tends to be more appropriate to client-side dynamic HTML applications and usually isn't supported in the tools used to generate XML — even with an HTML vocabulary.

DOM Examples

While the following examples use Active Server Pages as their development environment, they mostly use ASP as a programming environment and ignore its capability to create templates. While you can mix and match the DOM and template approaches, the surrounding material in the template may compromise the reliability of the markup created through the code. This is especially true if that template includes other generated content. Because the DOM Level 1 doesn't support "editing DocumentType" nodes, you still have to use the template portion for the XML declaration (if appropriate) and DOCTYPE declaration (required for XHTML 1.0 conformance).

Even if you don't use ASP or don't like ASP, the following examples include a lot of basic DOM vocabulary and usage that is applicable to developing in other environments.

You create your first DOM-based XHTML document as a classic "Hello World." The code you create builds an XHTML document that looks like this:

```
<?xml version="1.0" encoding="UTF-8"?>
<!DOCTYPE html
    PUBLIC "-//W3C//DTD XHTML 1.0 Strict//EN"
    "http://www.w3.org/TR/xhtml1/DTD/xhtml1-strict.dtd">
```

```
<html xmlns="http://www.w3.org/1999/xhtml" xml:lang="en-US"
lang="en-US">
<head>
<title>Hello World!</title>
</head>
<body>
<h1>Hello World!</h1>
<p>Hello World!</p>
</body>
</html>
```

Because of the DOM's limitations, you have to create a shell for the XML declaration and the `DOCTYPE` that looks like this:

```
<%@LANGUAGE=JavaScript%><?xml version="1.0" encoding="UTF-8"?>
<!DOCTYPE html
    PUBLIC "-//W3C//DTD XHTML 1.0 Strict//EN"
    "http://www.w3.org/TR/xhtml1/DTD/xhtml1-strict.dtd">
<!--Document-generating code goes here-->
```

Because most ASP implementations default to VBScript, and you're using the JavaScript bindings of the DOM from the specification, you need to tell ASP that you're using JavaScript. The XML declaration has to follow immediately because it is treated as a processing instruction (and likely ignored) if whitespace is included. The next portion of the code creates a document object you can manipulate using Microsoft's syntax. (The DOM Level 1 doesn't provide a standard mechanism for this process.)

```
<% var myDoc=Server.CreateObject("Microsoft.XMLDOM");
```

Once you have a document, you need to create a root element (in this case, `html`). The `createElement()` method takes an element name for its argument and returns an element object you then can manipulate.

```
var htmlNode=myDoc.createElement("html");
```

The `html` element needs some attributes to declare the namespace and the languages you are using here. Once you have the `html` element, you can use the `setAttribute` method to create the `xmlns`, `xml:lang`, and `lang` attributes and set their values.

```
htmlNode.setAttribute("xmlns"," http://www.w3.org/1999/xhtml");
htmlNode.setAttribute("xml:lang","en-US");
htmlNode.setAttribute("lang","en-US");
```

The `html` element now exists, and it has a full complement of attributes, but you probably should establish it as the root element for the document.

```
myDoc.documentElement=htmlNode;
```

Now that you have an `html` element, it's time to create the rest of the document content. To do that, you create elements and text nodes and then attach the text nodes and element nodes to their parents. While it isn't very important which sequence you create the nodes in, that sequence of the code typically reflects the order of the document to keep debugging from getting too confusing. Let's start with the `head` and `title` elements:

```
var headNode=myDoc.createElement("head");
var titleNode=myDoc.createElement("title");
var titleText=myDoc.createTextNode("Hello World!");
titleNode.appendChild(titleText);
headNode.appendChild(titleNode);
htmlNode.appendChild(headNode);
```

You build the `head` element by creating all of its nodes separately and then adding them to their appropriate container elements. The `createElement` and `createTextNode` methods create elements and text respectively, while the `appendChild` method establishes the connections between these nodes.

```
var bodyNode=myDoc.createElement("body");
var h1Node=myDoc.createElement("h1");
var h1Text=myDoc.createTextNode("Hello World!");
var paraNode=myDoc.createElement("p");
var paraText=myDoc.createTextNode("Hello World!");
h1Node.appendChild(h1Text);
paraNode.appendChild(paraText);
bodyNode.appendChild(h1Node);
bodyNode.appendChild(paraNode);
htmlNode.appendChild(bodyNode);
```

Finally, you write out the XML document you've modeled using the `xml` method of the `myDoc` object. This is a Microsoft addition to the DOM API:

```
Response.write(myDoc.xml); %>
```

The result (as seen in a Web browser) is shown in Figure 13-1, while the generated code producing that result appears in Figure 13-2.

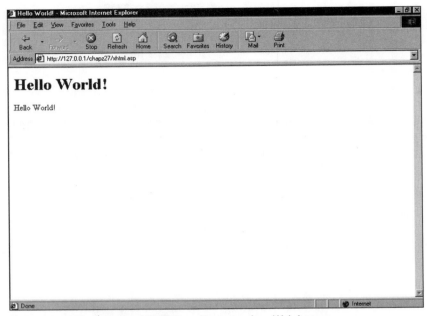

Figure 13-1: The generated XHTML as it appears in a Web browser

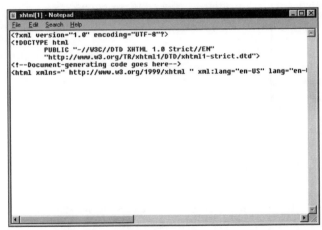

Figure 13-2: The generated code, close up. Note the absence
of line breaks in the content created by the DOM tree.

The xml method produces XML content with no additional whitespace. If you
need whitespace, you can create text nodes containing it.

This approach is hardly limited to generating XHTML whose content is known in
advance. It also works easily with material coming from databases, forms, or other

possibilities. The next example uses a static XHTML form to collect information and passes it to an XHTML-generating script.

```
<?xml version="1.0" encoding="UTF-8"?>
<!DOCTYPE html
     PUBLIC "-//W3C//DTD XHTML 1.0 Strict//EN"
     "http://www.w3.org/TR/xhtml1/DTD/xhtml1-strict.dtd">
<html xmlns="http://www.w3.org/1999/xhtml" xml:lang="en-US"
lang="en-US">
<head><title>Forms to XHTML</title></head>
<body><h1>Address Collector</h1>
<form action="genxhtml.asp" method="POST">
<p>First Name:<input type="text" name="firstname" size="20" /></p>
<p>Last Name:<input type="text" name="lastname" size="30" /></p>
<p>Address 1:<input type="text" name="address1" size="40" /></p>
<p>Address 2:<input type="text" name="address2" size="40" /></p>
<p>City:<input type="text" name="city" size="25" />
State/Province:<input type="text" name="state" size="25" /></p>
<p>ZIP/Postal Code:<input type="text" name="postalcode" size="15" />
Country:<input type="text" name="country" size="25" /></p>
<p><input type="submit" name="Submit" /></p>
</form>
</body></html>
```

The recipient of this form information uses the DOM to insert the material into an XHTML document. Most of the techniques used look like those in the previous example, but explanations of a few differences follow the code:

```
<%@LANGUAGE=JavaScript%><?xml version="1.0" encoding="UTF-8"?>
<!DOCTYPE html
     PUBLIC "-//W3C//DTD XHTML 1.0 Strict//EN"
     "http://www.w3.org/TR/xhtml1/DTD/xhtml1-strict.dtd">
<%
var myDoc=Server.CreateObject("Microsoft.XMLDOM");
var htmlNode=myDoc.createElement("html");
htmlNode.setAttribute("xmlns","http://www.w3.org/1999/xhtml");
htmlNode.setAttribute("xml:lang","en-US");
htmlNode.setAttribute("lang","en-US");
myDoc.documentElement=htmlNode;

var headNode=myDoc.createElement("head");
var titleNode=myDoc.createElement("title");
var titleText=myDoc.createTextNode("Address of " +
Request.Form.item("firstname") + " " + Request.Form.item("lastname") );
titleNode.appendChild(titleText);
```

```
headNode.appendChild(titleNode);
htmlNode.appendChild(headNode);

var bodyNode=myDoc.createElement("body");

var nameNode=myDoc.createElement("p");
var firstNameNode=myDoc.createElement("span");
firstNameNode.setAttribute("class","firstName");
var firstNameText=myDoc.createTextNode(Request.Form.item
("firstname"));
firstNameNode.appendChild(firstNameText);
var nameSeparatorNode=myDoc.createTextNode(" ");
var lastNameNode=myDoc.createElement("span");
firstNameNode.setAttribute("class","lastName");
var lastNameText=myDoc.createTextNode(Request.Form.item
("lastname"));
lastNameNode.appendChild(lastNameText);
nameNode.appendChild(firstNameNode);
nameNode.appendChild(nameSeparatorNode);
nameNode.appendChild(lastNameNode);
bodyNode.appendChild(nameNode);

var addressNode=myDoc.createElement("div");
addressNode.setAttribute("class","address");

var line1Node=myDoc.createElement("p");
line1Node.setAttribute("class","line1");
var line1Text=myDoc.createTextNode(Request.Form.item("address1"));
line1Node.appendChild(line1Text);
addressNode.appendChild(line1Node);

var line2Node=myDoc.createElement("p");
line2Node.setAttribute("class","line2");
var line2Text=myDoc.createTextNode(Request.Form.item("address2"));
line2Node.appendChild(line2Text);
addressNode.appendChild(line2Node);

var cityNode=myDoc.createElement("span");
cityNode.setAttribute("class","city");
var cityText=myDoc.createTextNode(Request.Form.item("city"));
cityNode.appendChild(cityText);
addressNode.appendChild(cityNode);

citySeparatorNode=myDoc.createTextNode(", ");
addressNode.appendChild(citySeparatorNode);
```

```
var stateNode=myDoc.createElement("span")
stateNode.setAttribute("class","state");
var stateText=myDoc.createTextNode(Request.Form.item("state"));
stateNode.appendChild(stateText);
addressNode.appendChild(stateNode);

postalSpaceNode=nameSpaceNode.cloneNode(false);
addressNode.appendChild(postalSpaceNode);

var postalNode=myDoc.createElement("span");
postalNode.setAttribute("class","postalcode");
var
postalText=myDoc.createTextNode(Request.Form.item("postalcode"));
postalNode.appendChild(postalText);
addressNode.appendChild(postalNode);

var countryNode=myDoc.createElement("p");
countryNode.setAttribute("class","country");
var countryText=myDoc.createTextNode(Request.Form.item("country"));
countryNode.appendChild(countryText);
addressNode.appendChild(countryNode);

bodyNode.appendChild(addressNode);

htmlNode.appendChild(bodyNode);

Response.write(myDoc.xml)
%>
```

In creating the title for the document, you combine multiple fields from the form into a single string of text that becomes a single text node:

```
var titleText=myDoc.createTextNode("Address of " +
Request.Form.item("firstname") + " " + Request.Form.item("lastname")
);
```

This works well because the title element contains only text. If it were mixed text and elements, it would require a more complicated approach (which I demonstrate the next time you use the name information):

```
var nameNode=myDoc.createElement("p");
nameNode.setAttribute("class","name");
var firstNameNode=myDoc.createElement("span");
firstNameNode.setAttribute("class","firstName");
```

```
var firstNameText=myDoc.createTextNode(Request.Form.item
("firstname"));
firstNameNode.appendChild(firstNameText);
var nameSeparatorNode=myDoc.createTextNode(" ");
var lastNameNode=myDoc.createElement("span");
lastNameNode.setAttribute("class","lastName");
var lastNameText=myDoc.createTextNode(Request.Form.item
("lastname"));
lastNameNode.appendChild(lastNameText);
nameNode.appendChild(firstNameNode);
nameNode.appendChild(nameSeparatorNode);
nameNode.appendChild(lastNameNode);
bodyNode.appendChild(nameNode);
```

This chunk of code is notable for a number of reasons. First, because the name appears on a single line, the entire name is contained in a single p element. Meanwhile, the first name and last name are contained in span elements. The name can be constructed like it is in the title — just text — but using span elements and class attributes preserves additional information about the content and makes it possible to style parts of the name differently or address them as a group through client-side dynamic HTML. Also worth noting is the creation of the name separator node — even though it's just a space, it has to be created and appended explicitly. Later in the code, a different separator appears:

```
citySeparatorNode=myDoc.createTextNode(", ");
addressNode.appendChild(citySeparatorNode);
```

Companies that want to please the post office, rather than use a popular form, can change the comma-space to just a space. Between the state and postal code, however, you can do something different:

```
postalSpaceNode=nameSpaceNode.cloneNode(false);
addressNode.appendChild(postalSpaceNode);
```

Suppose you want the space between the state and postal code to be the same as the space between the first and last names, but the same node can't have multiple parents. To avoid this complication, use the cloneNode() method; this method returns a new copy of the node's contents. By passing it the argument false, it only returns a simple copy of the node without dredging through possible layers of element content. You only want a space — this is a very simple node — so the argument doesn't matter very much. Yes, this might seem excessively complicated. On the other hand, it also helps ensure that your documents will be clean XML, every single time.

If you enter the information shown in Figure 13-3, you get the results shown in Figure 13-4.

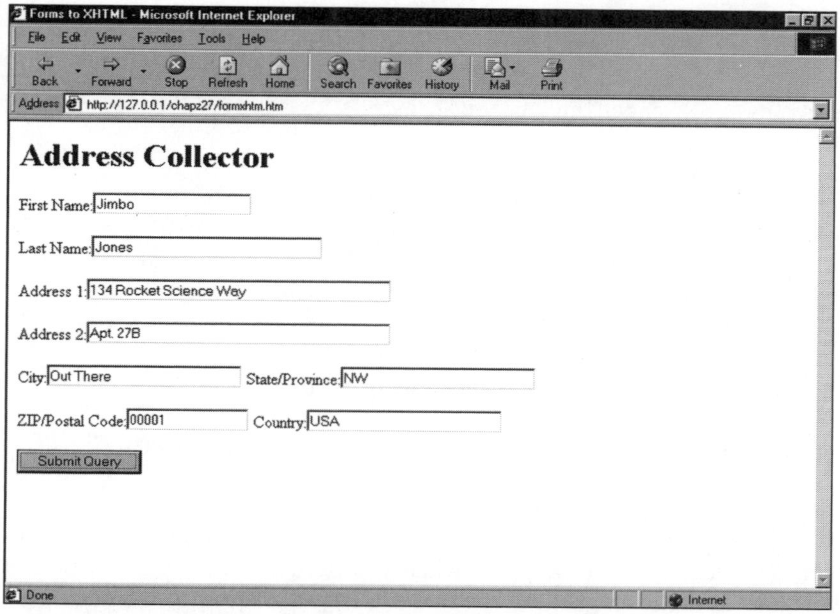

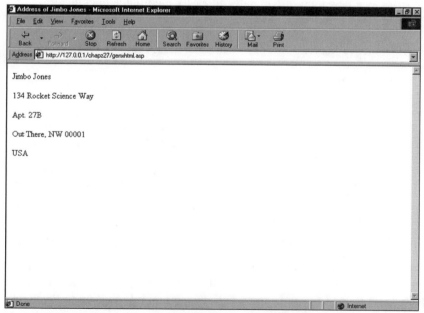

Figure 13-3: Forms can pass information to XHTML-generating code.

Figure 13-4: The results of the code generation, rendered simply.

The XHTML produced by the generator is once again without whitespace for the most part, although whitespace does appear where you explicitly add it:

```
<?xml version="1.0" encoding="UTF-8"?>
<!DOCTYPE html
    PUBLIC "-//W3C//DTD XHTML 1.0 Strict//EN"
    "http://www.w3.org/TR/xhtml1/DTD/xhtml1-strict.dtd">
<html xmlns="http://www.w3.org/1999/xhtml" xml:lang="en-US"
lang="en-US"><head><title>Address of Jimbo
Jones</title></head><body> <p class="name"><span
class="firstName">Jimbo</span> <span
class="lastName">Jones</span></p><div class="address"><p
class="line1">134 Rocket Science Way</p><p class="line2">Apt.
27B</p><span class="city">Out There</span>, <span
class="state">NW</span> <span class="postalcode">00001</span>
<p class="country">USA</p></div></body></html>
```

So far, this seems like an enormous amount of work to produce a relatively minor result. The benefits start to appear when you need to do more sophisticated things with your document structure, such as add entire sections to the document or transform one kind of document into another. In the next example, you add your address information to an existing XHTML document, using XHTML documents within the DOM as a new kind of template, an easily modifiable document.

The template you use looks like this:

```
<html xmlns="http://www.w3.org/1999/xhtml" xml:lang="en-US"
lang="en-US">
<head><title>Your Prize</title></head>
<body>
<div />
<p>Dear Fool,</p>
<p>You have won a million, trillion dollars!!!!! In laminated game
money, that is. Please contact us to collect your prize at +1 888
555 1212. Shipping and handling fees of up to ten thousand dollars
may be required to collect your prize.</p>
<p><strong>Hahahaha!</strong></p>
<p>the prize committee (we prys your money away from you!)</p>
</body></html>
```

While it may or may not be a legal letter to send someone (although it's an obvious parody), it is almost conformant XHTML. Next, you modify the DOM code you've been using to load this document, add the address information to the empty div element, and put it out as a letter.

While it is preferable to include the DOCTYPE declaration in the template, the ASP engine and the XML parser seem to choke on XHTML documents that contain DOCTYPE declarations loaded as XML. We'll have to put that information into the script once again.

Most of the code is the same as the DOM code used to generate the preceding address. The main difference lies at the start of the code where you load the template document and use it as a base.

```
<%@LANGUAGE=JavaScript%><?xml version="1.0" encoding="UTF-8"?>
<!DOCTYPE html
    PUBLIC "-//W3C//DTD XHTML 1.0 Strict//EN"
    "http://www.w3.org/TR/xhtml1/DTD/xhtml1-strict.dtd">
<%
sourceFile=Server.MapPath("prizexhtm2.xml");
var myDoc=Server.CreateObject("Microsoft.XMLDOM");
myDoc.async=false;
myDoc.load(sourceFile);
var changeNode=myDoc.getElementsByTagName("div").item(0);

var nameNode=myDoc.createElement("p");
nameNode.setAttribute("class","name");
var firstNameNode=myDoc.createElement("span");
firstNameNode.setAttribute("class","firstName");
var firstNameText=myDoc.createTextNode(Request.Form.item
("firstname"));
firstNameNode.appendChild(firstNameText);
var nameSeparatorNode=myDoc.createTextNode(" ");
var lastNameNode=myDoc.createElement("span");
lastNameNode.setAttribute("class","lastName");
var
lastNameText=myDoc.createTextNode(Request.Form.item("lastname"));
lastNameNode.appendChild(lastNameText);
nameNode.appendChild(firstNameNode);
nameNode.appendChild(nameSeparatorNode);
nameNode.appendChild(lastNameNode);
changeNode.appendChild(nameNode);

var addressNode=myDoc.createElement("div");
addressNode.setAttribute("class","address");


var line1Node=myDoc.createElement("p");
```

```
line1Node.setAttribute("class","line1");
var line1Text=myDoc.createTextNode(Request.Form.item("address1"));
line1Node.appendChild(line1Text);
addressNode.appendChild(line1Node);

var line2Node=myDoc.createElement("p");
line2Node.setAttribute("class","line2");
var line2Text=myDoc.createTextNode(Request.Form.item("address2"));
line2Node.appendChild(line2Text);
addressNode.appendChild(line2Node);

var cityNode=myDoc.createElement("span");
cityNode.setAttribute("class","city");
var cityText=myDoc.createTextNode(Request.Form.item("city"));
cityNode.appendChild(cityText);
addressNode.appendChild(cityNode);

citySeparatorNode=myDoc.createTextNode(", ");
addressNode.appendChild(citySeparatorNode);

var stateNode=myDoc.createElement("span")
stateNode.setAttribute("class","state");
var stateText=myDoc.createTextNode(Request.Form.item("state"));
stateNode.appendChild(stateText);
addressNode.appendChild(stateNode);

postalSpaceNode=nameSeparatorNode.cloneNode(false);
addressNode.appendChild(postalSpaceNode);
var postalNode=myDoc.createElement("span");
postalNode.setAttribute("class","postalcode");
var
postalText=myDoc.createTextNode(Request.Form.item("postalcode"));
postalNode.appendChild(postalText);
addressNode.appendChild(postalNode);

var countryNode=myDoc.createElement("p");
countryNode.setAttribute("class","country");
var countryText=myDoc.createTextNode(Request.Form.item("country"));
countryNode.appendChild(countryText);
addressNode.appendChild(countryNode);

changeNode.appendChild(addressNode);

Response.write(myDoc.xml);
%>
```

The main activity in this script that differs from the prior example is in the code at the beginning that loads the template:

```
sourceFile=Server.MapPath("prizexhtm2.xml");
var myDoc=Server.CreateObject("Microsoft.XMLDOM");
myDoc.async=false;
myDoc.load(sourceFile);
var changeNode=myDoc.getElementsByTagName("div").item(0);
```

The technique for loading files is a Microsoft extension, once again unspecified by the W3C DOM specs. Basically, this code creates a full path to a file in the same folder as the script, which is used as a template. The XML parser then parses that file — setting `myDoc.async` to `false` ensures that the entire document is loaded before processing continues. Then you grab the empty `div` element so that you can put the information you receive from the form into that element.

The form that you use to gather the information is identical to the one used in the previous example, but the results are quite different (as shown in Figure 13-5).

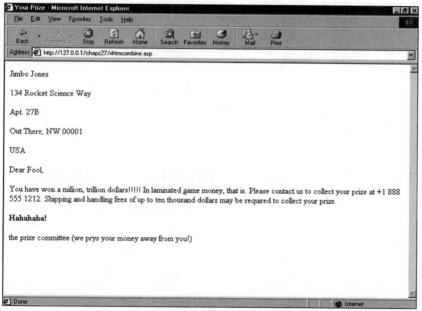

Figure 13-5: The results of the code generation, rendered in the context of a template.

The source code behind that generation is also interesting. It shows some inconsistencies in how the Microsoft XML parser handles whitespace from documents it loads as opposed to whitespace from documents created through code.

```
<?xml version="1.0" encoding="UTF-8"?>
<!DOCTYPE html
     PUBLIC "-//W3C//DTD XHTML 1.0 Strict//EN"
     "http://www.w3.org/TR/xhtml1/DTD/xhtml1-strict.dtd">
<html xmlns="http://www.w3.org/1999/xhtml" xml:lang="en-US"
lang="en-US">
     <head><title>Your Prize</title></head>
     <body>
         <div><p class="name"><span class="firstName">Jimbo</span>
<span class="lastName">Jones</span></p><div xmlns=""
class="address"><p class="line1">134 Rocket Science Way</p><p
class="line2">Apt. 27B</p><span class="city">Out There</span>, <span
class="state">NW</span> <span class="postalcode">00001</span><p
class="country">USA</p></div></div>
         <p>Dear Fool,</p>
         <p>You have won a million, trillion dollars!!!!! In
laminated game money, that is. Please contact us to collect your
prize at +1 888 555 1212. Shipping and handling fees of up to ten
thousand dollars may be required to collect your prize.</p>
         <p><strong>Hahahaha!</strong></p>
         <p>the prize committee (we prys your money away from
you!)</p>
     </body></html>
```

While these examples are fairly simple, you can apply the same mechanisms to tasks such as building tables around information from database or XML document structures, rearranging document content, or deleting pieces from a document.

Making Logic and Structure Mobile

The Document Object Model and the code it tends to produce are both somewhat unwieldy, but the results can trim unwieldy projects down to size. The Document Object Model lurks at the boundary between HTML and XML, developed with an eye toward the former but quite useful for tasks involving the latter. On the browser, you may want to take advantage of its features for addressing the HTML vocabulary and various understandings built around that vocabulary. On the server, you can use it to create documents from an XML perspective. XHTML requires an understanding of both of these perspectives, so the DOM is a natural fit.

Perhaps the most important thing about the DOM is that it enables you to partition your applications among different systems however you find appropriate. In this regard, it is much like Extensible Stylesheet Transformations (XSLT) described in the last chapter — but to some extent, it is even more powerful. Because the tree structures created by parsing documents into a DOM remain manipulatable, and aren't simply the output of a transformation, the DOM offers flexibility that goes well beyond the simple document generation just shown (although not well implemented across browsers yet).

You could move (if appropriate) the scripts for creating documents and combining documents to client browsers, which then would run the same code on the browser and generate the same document. The Microsoft-specific features used to create and output the document would need updating (as even Internet Explorer uses slightly different syntax for these), but the core logic is easily transferred. (Hopefully, the development of DOM Level 3 will complete this picture and make the logic fully transferable.

This combination of features, some of which are admittedly promises, may mean that XHTML and the DOM finally will make the old promises of dynamic HTML viable. Building applications that run inside of (and outside of) browsers using the data transmitted over the Web for more sophisticated things than pop-up outlines and drag-and-drop games will be a lot easier, even in situations that require support for multiple browser environments.

Chapter 14

Moving to Modules: Creating Extensible Document Structures with XHTML 1.1

WHILE MOST OF THE BOOK up to this point has repeated the mantra "XHTML is just like HTML, only cleaner," it's time to move into some of the more radical possibilities this giant cleanup has made possible for XHTML. The housecleaning performed so far is only the start — a full remodeling of HTML is on the way. The W3C firmly believes that XHTML is the future of HTML, and it has some large plans hinging on XHTML's development.

To get a clearer picture of what the W3C has in mind for XHTML, explore the HTML Working Group Roadmap at http://www.w3.org/TR/xhtml-roadmap/. This document describes the end of development on HTML as well as the next few steps — roughly a year's worth of plans — for XHTML 1.1 and XHTML 2.0.

Different Needs, Different Tools

HTML is running out of steam. As the Web reaches beyond browsers on PCs, HTML is proving both too large (for cell phones) and too small (for many sophisticated applications). The one-size-fits-all approach that has suited HTML so well is causing problems as the Web continues to succeed. Although HTML has never been forced into a single size, with browser-specific variants and the three DTDs approach of HTML 4.0 and XHTML 1.0, HTML as a whole is both too enormous and too limited.

When HTML first appeared, browsers were relatively small and easy to fit on a single disk or embed into a tiny computer. But after a few rounds of competition, they've grown enormous. (The Opera browser has avoided bloat, but it's a very clear exception to the rule.) Part of this expansion has to do with the ever-growing tendency to expand browsers beyond simple HTML processing. But a considerable amount of the extra code has been necessary to process new features added to HTML over the years.

Opera, and now Mozilla (the code base for Netscape Navigator 6 and beyond), was built from the ground up with the latest features in mind. Meanwhile, the older versions of Netscape Navigator — and to some extent Internet Explorer — include a lot of code that layers new functionality on top of old. This isn't necessarily a bad thing — at least until the browser size reaches some serious bloat — because it helps browser vendors get their products out the door and keeps costs down. Over time, however, the changing nature of the Web browser market has piled new code inefficiencies into browsers.

The browser orientation of HTML has also had an effect on the expectations of those who design for Web pages. Even in cases in which developers carefully check their sites across multiple versions of browsers on multiple platforms, there always has been an underlying assumption that a large core of HTML is available on every product calling itself a browser. As browsers have grown more sophisticated, developer expectations have risen. Most sites today, for instance, assume that users have browsers that support tables — once a risky proposition. Many sites assume that browsers support JavaScript, and a lot of sites assume that users have various plug-ins such as Flash or Acrobat.

Vendors who want to bring the Web to devices with less capability than personal computers — such as television set-top boxes, personal digital assistants (PDAs), cell phones, and more — are stuck in a world where most people are developing content that requires much larger software for meaningful processing. It's difficult to stuff Internet Explorer 5 or Netscape Navigator 4 into a cell phone while keeping the costs of the product reasonable.

When WebTV first appeared, Web designers sounded off for months on various mailing lists. They complained about the company's compromises to put HTML content onto television screens and bemoaned missing features. A fair number of people didn't find WebTV acceptable as a candidate for serious Web design. Nonetheless, WebTV remains on store shelves and in people's homes, Microsoft has bought out the company, and similar alternatives for low-cost home browsing continue to appear.

Cell phones, and to a lesser extent PDAs, face an even more difficult situation. They have neither the screen real estate nor the luxury of a large box that sits in a single location. With their tiny screens and lightweight processors, these devices can't process HTML's many complexities efficiently — nor can they display the full content of what they process even if that were easy. Combine these difficulties with the tiny amount of bandwidth available through their typically wireless connectivity, and cell phones are left stranded by HTML in its present form. Vendors have had to develop their own HTML subsets and infrastructures to cope with these problems, as described in Chapter 17, and HTML is only catching up now.

Going the other direction, Web browsers today make very little use of the processing capability available on client machines. While they may have sizable memory and processing footprints as a result of their code for interpreting and presenting HTML, Web browsers act largely as passive presenters for server-side processing.

While you can start Java applets and ActiveX controls from within HTML, and plug-ins can add functionality, none of these really work within HTML itself. They all need information in their own formats, and developing these tools typically means building an HTML shell and then working on anything but HTML.

To some extent, recent browser generations have built stronger HTML processing capabilities into their cores. The development of the Document Object Model (DOM) is a milestone, providing a standardized way for scripts to access information that arrives in HTML (or XHTML or XML) and to modify that information. It's now possible to build sophisticated interfaces that help users find information within documents, or change document presentations to meet different user needs. You also can achieve some processing of information, although that processing is performed on a document-by-document or site-by-site basis. These capabilities are all custom coded right now, and they rely on tools that aren't implemented widely yet.

Netscape woke up Microsoft and earned its undying enmity at one point in the browser wars by proclaiming that browsers would replace operating systems. This announcement directly threatened Microsoft's primary source of profits. Browsers still don't live up to Marc Andreesen's 1996 claim that, "The only difference technically between Netscape's Navigator browser and a traditional operating system is that Navigator will not include device drivers." ("Netscape's Andreesen Eyes Internet OS," *PC Week*, June 17, 1996.)

This "big browser" vision hasn't come to pass, although Microsoft's own version of operating system-browser integration has brought it to court. In large part, though, what has kept it from appearing isn't the Department of Justice or Netscape's collapsing market share. It's simply because HTML hasn't proved a very good foundation for these endeavors. Operating systems are environments for processing any kind of information with a variety of interfaces, while browsers are environments for presenting documents with a relatively limited set of interfaces and inefficient scripting logic to boot. Making these kinds of visions possible, whatever the vendor politics, requires adding new functionality to the foundation of the browser universe – HTML.

The Master Plan: Fragmenting and Extending HTML

The W3C has been trapped in something of a dilemma since it first started its work. While the W3C exists "to lead the World Wide Web to its full potential by developing common protocols that promote its evolution and ensure its interoperability," a large part of its appeal has rested on its authority to codify an "official" flavor of HTML. Web developers looked to the W3C to produce standards they could hold browser vendors to, while the W3C saw itself largely as a research lab pushing the envelope on experimental technologies. The fact that the same browser vendors who were making users crazy were the primary participants and funders of the W3C probably hasn't helped, either.

At the same time that the W3C wants to maintain its role and its reputation as the sole home of HTML, lots of proposals both inside and outside of the W3C have been itching to add new features to HTML. In some cases, such as Microsoft's addition of an xml element in Internet Explorer 5, they simply have moved forward with their own plans. In other cases – such as the W3C's hopes of adding Synchronized Multimedia Integration Language (SMIL), MathML, or Scalable Vector Graphics (SVG) to browser vocabularies – they've remained mostly stuck, unable to convince vendors to build these standards into their browsers.

Some of the problems lie in the politics of standards creation and adoption, which can range from the pleasant to the poisonous. It isn't clear that Microsoft, currently dominating the browser market, has much to gain from fully supporting the W3C specifications that it helped to create. Meanwhile, Netscape – trying to recover from a few years of free-fall – has embraced the W3C's standards (some of them at least) emphatically in Mozilla. While the competitive nightmares of the browser wars create incompatibilities, the incentives for accepting and implementing open standards tend to disappear when competition fades.

Escaping from this trap requires taking a different perspective on the Web and Web infrastructures. The business environment behind the Web isn't likely to change in a substantial way, so perhaps making relatively small changes in the technical infrastructure can create new openings for enhanced capabilities. Plug-ins and similar infrastructures (ActiveX controls, Java applets, and so on) have been adjuncts to HTML so far – only used in a limited number of situations and typically acting on information that comes from outside the HTML document itself.

XHTML modularization squares the circle, providing vendors with a standardized way of creating their own extension vocabularies while developing an opening in the infrastructure that makes it possible for those uninterested in building their own browsers to make substantial contributions. Modularizing XHTML doesn't guarantee that developers will follow up on W3C standards with modular browsers, but it might add incentives for doing so. At the very least, XHTML modularization provides a framework that developers can use on the server side for integrating XML and HTML vocabularies; and perhaps the client-side tools will catch up as well.

By embracing the diversity the W3C originally was hailed for quashing, and by enabling developers to add to the mix in a much more controlled way than was possible when vendors just threw in their own elements and attributes, the W3C hopes to open HTML up without polluting it. The W3C isn't defining any kind of program infrastructure to support modularization, but hopefully some kind of infrastructure will emerge that supports modularization in an unambiguous and widely useful way.

Didn't Namespaces Solve Everything?

Another W3C Recommendation, Namespaces in XML, provides developers with a set of tools for identifying elements and attributes as HTML elements, SVG elements, MathML elements, or My elements. Browsers can home in on this information, and present the information in a way that reflects the element type correctly. Among other things, this means that users can drop `html:img` elements into XML documents for use with Internet Explorer 5 and Netscape 6 and actually get images to appear in the browser window.

As powerful and as useful as namespaces are, however, they don't address an enormous number of issues. Two critical problems are context and registration. Context issues arise when vocabularies are mixed, while registration problems emerge when you use namespaces in environments that don't have a way of dealing with them. XHTML modularization is designed to address the context issues. The registration issues remain for another set of tools described at the end of this chapter.

Context issues typically arise from the nested nature of XML documents. If all the pieces in a document can stand alone (as separate paragraphs, for instance), then an application shouldn't have any significant difficulties processing information as a series of standalone pieces. But if a fragment from one vocabulary is dropped into another vocabulary, it isn't clear how an application should handle it. For example, the following elements are derived from XHTML and SVG:

```
<html xmlns="http://www.w3.org/1999/xhtml" lang="en-US"
xml:lang="en-US" xmlns:svg = 'http://www.w3.org/2000/svg-20000303-
stylable'>
<head><title>random</title>
<body>
<p>This is an HTML paragraph with a mysterious SVG path in it.
<svg:path d="M 80 75 L 100 100 L 140 110 z"/></p>
</body></html>
```

Perhaps the browser will draw the path within the paragraph block, or perhaps it will ignore it. If the browser draws the path, does it start at the end of the paragraph's text content? Or does the browser treat the paragraph block as its natural container and use that as its starting point? While the semantics of an HTML `p` element and an SVG `path` element are well understood in their "home" contexts, dropping them into other contexts strips them of some of their meaning.

XHTML 1.0 already recognizes this to a significant extent, although it includes demonstrations of how mixing and matching vocabularies might work. The conformance rules for strictly conformant XHTML documents (in section 3.1.1) require the use of document type definitions and demand that the document must validate against the formal description that DTD provides. While the examples that immediately follow (in section 3.1.2) show a non-conformant document, the W3C makes clear that "Future work by W3C will address ways to specify conformance for documents involving multiple namespaces."

XHTML 1.1 is effectively that future work. The next few chapters provide the details of how XHTML sorts out context and processing, describing how XHTML 1.1 fragments itself into smaller pieces and how you can create your own pieces to add to the mix. First, though, let's take a detour to explore some issues that haven't been resolved yet — but which will need fixing for these visions to succeed.

New Issues: Content Negotiation & Context Tangles

Breaking XHTML down into parts makes it possible for applications to support both subsets and supersets of the HTML vocabulary. This allows the cell phones and PDAs to do less, and enables application developers on more powerful platforms to do more. At the same time, however, fragmentation introduces significant new complexities — some of which threaten the rough unity the Web has enjoyed up until now.

The first, and probably easier problem, involves creating ways for devices to identify which fragments of the HTML vocabulary they support. To this point, HTML has been identified using the MIME content type identifier text/html. This single identifier is no longer sufficient. In many ways, it hasn't been sufficient for a long while. Web developers have had to create a lot of workarounds for figuring out how to customize their content to different browser capabilities.

On the server side, it's common practice to "sniff out" browser versions using the User-Agent field of HTTP transactions. Once a server learns which kind of browser is on the receiving end of a request, it can generate browser-specific content or simply transfer the browser to a more appropriate view of the information. In extreme cases, users receive messages telling them to update their browsers or replace them with something entirely different.

Knowing which browser is in use isn't always enough, either. Users have significant control over their browsers, and can do things such as turn off (or never install) Java, ActiveX, JavaScript, and various plug-ins. You can use client-side code, typically JavaScript, to sniff for more detailed information within the browser, and either customize information there or send information back to the server. This approach is typically combined with the server-side sniffing because some browsers don't support JavaScript (such as Lynx) or don't permit JavaScript to inspect the browser environment (such as older versions of Internet Explorer for the Macintosh.)

These strategies only work well, however, when there is a relatively limited number of possibilities. If instead of hundreds of browser and version combinations there are thousands, the costs of looking up information rise accordingly. If instead of a few environment issues within browsers there are hundreds or thousands that need checking, and browsers don't all support checking through JavaScript, you may not be able to perform this checking efficiently. Some kind of new infrastructure must make efficient transfers between servers and clients possible.

This isn't an entirely new problem, although the potential scale of XHTML's use and the clear breakdown in older technologies for handling HTML makes it more ominous. The *Internet Engineering Task Force (IETF)* has discussed content negotiation issues for a long time. Other groups, such as the *Wireless Application Protocol (WAP) Forum*, have developed specialized solutions that meet their own needs. It's much easier to mandate content negotiation in a situation involving WAP, where a single organization controls the infrastructure design from end to end. Making content negotiation work on the XHTML and HTTP Web will be a long and slow process.

The W3C is developing a set of tools called Composite Capabilities/Preference Profiles (CC/PP), based on two Notes submitted in July 1999. As of this writing, the project is still developing requirements. However, the two Notes and the current requirement drafts at least present a rough picture of the work that lies ahead – and perhaps a vision of the Web as it will look in a few years. The W3C is working with both the WAP Forum and the IETF to create this architecture, which hopefully will ensure that lots of issues are resolved, although it may slow down the development process. Once the issues are resolved, of course, there will be a long period of integration with existing systems and gradual upgrades if CC/PP is widely accepted.

Unlike the rest of the XHTML infrastructure, CC/PP is a project of the W3C's Mobile Access activity. For the latest on their work, see `http://www.w3.org/Mobile/Activity`. A public mailing list, "www-mobile", is also available for discussions of CC/PP and other Mobile Access work. You can find information on how to subscribe at `http://www.w3.org/Mail/Request` and you can view the archives at `http://lists.w3.org/Archives/Public/www-mobile/`.

CC/PP provides a framework that client devices can use to describe their capabilities and configuration to servers. (There isn't any similar framework that servers can use to describe their capabilities to clients.) CC/PP uses an XML syntax and Resource Description Framework (RDF) structures to create property lists describing a particular client's capabilities and identifying more generic features such as memory capacity. The requirements document emphasizes three key aspects of CC/PP: flexibility, extensibility, and distribution.

You can access the CC/PP Requirements and Architecture draft at `http://www.w3.org/TR/CCPP-ra/`. This discussion is based on the 28 February 2000 draft of that document.

CC/PP is purely about descriptions. Those descriptions must be flexible enough for use with a wide variety of different devices and types of devices, extensible enough to support future needs, and capable of being distributed across networks rather than centralized on servers. (This last point represents a major change from the server-side sniffing techniques just described.) CC/PP is not a protocol — it is only a container, a document format, which can function in a variety of protocols. It includes some features, such as partial descriptions to indicate changed configurations, which need significant support by protocols, however.

The examples in the CC/PP Note (`http://www.w3.org/TR/NOTE-CCPP`) describe hardware and software capabilities, but they don't have anything to do with XHTML. Part of making CC/PP useful for identifying client capabilities with XHTML will be the development of an RDF vocabulary describing different XHTML modules and indicating whether a given client supports them. This shouldn't be difficult for modules built into XHTML 1.1, where the W3C controls the naming conventions and rules, but it may prove more complex for extension modules built outside of the W3C process.

The simplest use for CC/PP is negotiation between a client and a server. CC/PP documents give clients a way of describing formally to servers what information they can handle. If a client only supports XHTML Basic (`http://www.w3.org/TR/xhtml-basic`), there isn't much point in a server sending that client documents marked up for framesets. On the other end, servers may be capable of sending application-specific information that goes beyond XHTML if they know that a given client can actually process it. Instead of guessing about different types of "browsers," servers can customize their presentations for particular application instances.

CC/PP descriptions are useful in a variety of different circumstances. Because the descriptions emanate from each client, may be customized as necessary, and may pass through multiple systems on the way from client to server, it should be possible to create chains of processors that support different capabilities. While proxy servers primarily function for caching and security today, CC/PP descriptions should make it possible to create new kinds of proxy servers that manage and transform information flows among clients and servers with different capabilities.

A cellular provider might, for instance, set up a proxy server that accepts CC/PP information from its customers, and then customize the information it retrieves over the Web to meet the needs and capabilities of customer phones. This proxy approach would give customers a choice of which phones to buy. It also would enable them to turn features on and off, while still ensuring that they weren't wasting expensive bandwidth and connection time on content that their phones couldn't process. The Web servers hosting the information might never see the cell phone CC/PP profiles, and instead receive a profile for the proxy server (or no profile at all, if the infrastructure does not exist.)

Alternatively, proxy servers could add information to incoming material if clients had special-purpose tools they could recognize. Perhaps a company distributes news feeds to its customers, but annotates them with secure messages regarding corporate relationships. Static Web pages might get transformed into forms designed to enable key people to redistribute information across a network. Proxy servers might generate extra information, like that described by *XML Document Navigation Language* (XDNL – `http://www.w3.org/TR/xdnl/`), which makes it easier for users of devices with small screens or limited bandwidth to handle large documents.

Making this work will require a lot more infrastructure than just the descriptions. It's already clear that CC/PP won't work with the older HTTP 1.0 protocol that many older browsers and Web servers still use, and making CC/PP work with the HTTP 1.1 protocol will require some design and implementation work on building extensions. The W3C Note, "CC/PP exchange protocol based on HTTP Extension Framework" (http://www.w3.org/TR/NOTE-CCPPexchange) outlines one possibility for making this work, but it may take further work on HTTP before it becomes reality. The W3C and the IETF are working on a generic extension framework (described in the experimental RFC 2774 at ftp://ftp.isi.edu/in-notes/rfc2774.txt). This work probably will have to be completed and implemented before further integration of CC/PP with existing Web architectures is possible.

TIP If you want to explore the HTTP Extension Framework and start building your own tools for testing CC/PP, you may want to try out the W3C's own Jigsaw server (http://www.w3.org/Jigsaw/). Written in Java (and open source at that), Jigsaw is a Web server with support for the HTTP Extension Framework. You can build your own extensions to Jigsaw to explore the possibilities. It also provides proxying capabilities and Java Servlet support.

Even if the W3C, WAP Forum, and IETF can settle the description issues and thoroughly integrate them with the Web infrastructure, modules still raise some thorny problems. Describing modules as atomic units makes it all sound easy, but modules can twist around one another and modify one another's contents in ways that make the interactions difficult to describe. Programs built to handle a given module may not be capable of handling the combination of that module with other modules.

In many cases, this provides necessary functionality. For example, implementing frames (a task the W3C isn't taking on for XHTML 1.1) requires the addition of target attributes to a variety of link elements. While the frameset, frame, and noframes elements are critical to frame-based development, the target attribute is needed for complex frame-based interfaces to work properly. It isn't clear how software components built to handle a minimal XHTML module for linking will handle the additional information stored in target attributes. Integrating the software pieces is more difficult than declaring the extra attributes.

Similarly, developers who want to use the W3C's own XLink, with its attribute-based approach to describing hyperlinks, may need to add these attributes to XHTML element types. Software components built without any knowledge of XLink need to support some kind of dispatching to get the XLink information to a component that can handle it. Right now (although admittedly XLink remains a working draft), the W3C does not define any architecture for handling these kinds of tasks.

Attribute issues are perhaps an irritant, but element content models are another critical area where new problems can arise. Using Scalable Vector Graphics (SVG) within XHTML documents requires creating places within the XHTML where SVG may appear. Because XHTML 1.1 modules parameterize their content models (as described in Chapter 15), it isn't difficult to modify those content models and (legitimately) slip SVG content into XHTML documents. Again, this is relatively simple to do in document type declarations, but much more difficult in software components.

It may be a while before all of these issues get straightened out. In the meantime, XHTML 1.1 is just getting started and is full of promise for a more powerful Web. If the W3C and its allies can navigate these complicated waters, the end results should make the Internet far more accessible and useful. In turn, the Web will move from being an important part of the computing world to being an important and very ordinary part of the world.

Chapter 15

Fragmenting XHTML

THE THEORY BEHIND FRAGMENTATION, presented in the previous chapter, sounds pretty good. Fragmentation appears to be a cure to the many ills of the Web, pointing the way forward to new XML vocabularies and new possibilities. The concrete implementation details of XHTML 1.1, however, look rather scary. Contained in three drafts with a total of about 180 pages, the XHTML 1.1 specs are a daunting collection of rules (and the application of those rules) that applies to the XHTML vocabulary. Fortunately, while the rules make use of XML's funkier tools, the way they actually work isn't very painful and developers may be able to avoid the frightening details.

 The content of this chapter is based on the 5 January 2000 Last Call Working Drafts of the XHTML 1.1 specifications. Some content may change between the time of this writing and the final approval of the specifications by the W3C, so you should check to find out the current or final status of these issues.

XHTML as Framework

Unlike its predecessors, XHTML 1.1 provides an architectural framework for syntax rather than a simple concrete implementation. XHTML 1.1's architecture for defining modules is effectively a layer on top of XML 1.0's rules for creating DTDs, and its own implementation of the XHTML vocabulary is a layer on top of that one. To simplify all of these layers and their interactions, XHTML 1.1 has these three separate documents defining it:

- ◆ *Building XHTML Modules* (http://www.w3.org/TR/xhtml-building) provides the formal framework on which the XHTML modules (and other modules) are built.

- ◆ *Modularization of XHTML* (http://www.w3.org/TR/xhtml-modularization) describes how you implement XHTML 1.1 using that framework.

- ◆ *XHTML 1.1 - Module-based XHTML* (http://www.w3.org/TR/xhtml11) describes how you create XHTML 1.1 documents using these modules.

In a sense, XHTML is two separate parts defined in three specs. The first part is the framework — how to create the modules (defined in *Building XHTML Modules*) and how to reassemble them as documents (defined in *XHTML 1.1 - Module-based XHTML*). The second part is the implementation that *Modularization of XHTML* — and to some extent *XHTML 1.1 - Module-based XHTML* — defines. This chapter walks through the framework on the way to the implementation explanation, breaking down each component of XHTML while staying within its general bounds.

The framework combines a set of rules for creating modules and different kinds of descriptions of those modules, as well as a set of rules for integrating those modules to create a larger whole. The process of breaking XHTML into modules uses the former set of tools, while documents that use just XHTML rely on the latter.

Abstract Modules

XHTML prescribes both formal and informal ways to describe modules. *Abstract modules* are documents intended purely for human consumption, helping readers avoid the tangle of parameter entity processing needed by the formal tools for describing modules. This level of description is useful both for documentation and planning, forcing developers to specify what their modules contain in a format that goes beyond the prickly formal tools of DTDs and XML Schemas. Abstract modules are not required for conformance to the XHTML 1.1 specifications, but their use can make creating and using XHTML 1.1 modules much easier.

 Abstract modules are defined in Section 4 of *Building XHTML Modules*, available at `http://www.w3.org/TR/xhtml-building/abstraction.html#s_abstraction`.

Abstract modules are basically tables with some supporting textual content. The tables consist of lists of elements with columns for attributes and minimal content models. Because some elements may be defined with *content sets*, such sets may be described in ways that aren't explicitly included in the table. Content sets are typically used repeatedly in multiple elements, so this special treatment probably makes sense. No such provision is made for sets of attributes, however. (One exception: using `Common` as an identifier for a core set of attributes in the XHTML 1.1 DTDs.)

Within those tables, XHTML uses a semiformal syntax that looks like an extended (and reduced) version of XML DTD syntax. Element and attribute names are used within the tables, along with a small set of other syntactic conventions (listed in Table 15-1). They look very much like the DTD indicators described in Chapter 6, but there are some significant differences.

TABLE 15-1 SYMBOLS FOR DESCRIBING ELEMENT CONTENT STRUCTURES IN ABSTRACT MODULE CONVENTIONS

Expression	Description	Example	Example Notes
a | b	Indicates a choice — 'a or b'.	thisone | thatone	Either thisone or thatone must appear.
a , b	Requires elements or groups to appear in specified sequence: a, then b.	thisone, thatone	thisone must appear, followed by thatone. (If this appears in regard to attributes, sequence is not enforced.)
a - b	Allows the contents of expression a to appear, minus the elements in expression b.	(thisone | thatone) - thatone	Allows thisone (only) to appear. This is used more commonly with content sets than with explicit listings of content models.
a	One, and only one, instance of a must appear.	thisone	thisone must appear exactly once.
a?	Makes a optional, and may appear zero or one times.	thisone?	thisone may appear, but only once if it does appear.
a*	Allows a to appear zero or more times.	thisone*	thisone may appear; multiple appearances (or zero appearances) of thisone are acceptable.
a&	When this appears in the element name column, it indicates that the module adds attributes to this element type.	thisone&	Attributes are added to the thisone element type.
a+	Requires at least one a to appear; a may appear one or more times.	thisone+	thisone must be present at least once; multiple thisone elements may appear.

Continued

TABLE 15-1 SYMBOLS FOR DESCRIBING ELEMENT CONTENT STRUCTURES IN ABSTRACT MODULE CONVENTIONS *(Continued)*

Expression	Description	Example	Example Notes
( )	Groups elements so that they may be given the preceding sequence and occurrence indicators.	(thisone | thatone), whichone, (hisone | herone)*	Either thisone or thatone (but not both) may appear, followed by whichone, which may then be followed by any combination of hisone and herone.
(*a* | *b* | *c*) or (*type*)	Provides an enumerated list specifying acceptable values for the attribute or the attribute type.	(thisone | thatone) thatone.	The attribute may have only these values: thisone or thatone.
EMPTY	Specifies an empty content model. May be used only to describe content Elements with EMPTY. Content models may still have attributes.	EMPTY	No content is allowed inside the element.
PCDATA	Specifies that text may appear in an element content model. May be used only to describe content.	PCDATA*	Text may appear inside the content model. (The asterisk is optional, but I recommend parentheses and vertical bars if this is mixed with other element types.)

A very simple abstract module might look like Table 15-2:

TABLE 15-2 A SUPER SIMPLE ABSTRACT MODULE

Element	Attribute	Minimal Content Model
textElement	Common	PCDATA

This describes the element type `textElement`, which uses the XHTML `Common` set of attribute declarations (defined at `http://www.w3.org/TR/xhtml-modularization/xhtml_modules.html#s_basicattributes`) and contains only text. Most modules undoubtedly are more complex than this one, but sometimes only a single element is needed to add functionality.

Before you move on to a more complicated example, you should note some of the pieces that are missing from the abstract module descriptions created in accordance with the *Building XHTML Modules* draft. No information is provided about namespaces. This is reasonable when working strictly within XHTML where all the parts share a common namespace. However, omitting namespaces is probably not such a good idea when creating extensions to XHTML (as you do in the next chapter). While the prefixes may appear in the element names, the URIs they map to need to be documented somewhere. Also missing is an explanation of how you should integrate this module with other modules. It isn't clear how to use this module and its components appropriately within an XHTML framework. This kind of documentation should form an important supplement to the abstract module framework described in the specification itself.

Keeping those warnings in mind, take a look at one of the abstract modules defined in *Modularization of XHTML* to see how these tools are used (see sidebar). The Forms Module is fairly complex, but familiar to most HTML developers, and it contains a variety of content models. While its actual content may change on the path to becoming a W3C recommendation, it has some excellent examples of the abstract module syntax in action and shows how additional textual content can fill in the gaps of an abstract module. Let's start with the module in the sidebar (from Section 4.5.2), and then explore its pieces.

Module from Modularization of XHTML, Section 4.5.2

The Forms Module provides all of the forms features found in HTML 4.0. Specifically, the Forms Module supports:

Element	Attributes	Minimal Content Model
form	Common, accept (ContentTypes), accept-charset (Charsets), action (URI), method ("get" | "put"), enctype (ContentType)	(Heading | Block - form | fieldset)+

Continued

Module from Modularization of XHTML, Section 4.5.2
(Continued)

Element	Attributes	Minimal Content Model
input	Common, accept (ContentTypes), accesskey (Character), alt (CDATA), checked ("checked"), disabled ("disabled"), maxlength (Number), name (CDATA), readonly ("readonly"), size (Number), src (URI), tabindex (Number), type ("text" | "password" | "checkbox" | "radio" | "submit" | "reset" | "file" | "hidden" | "image"), value (CDATA)	EMPTY
select	Common, disabled ("disabled"), multiple ("multiple"), name (CDATA), size (Number), tabindex (Number)	(optgroup | option)+
option	Common, disabled ("disabled"), label (Text), selected ("selected"), value (CDATA)	PCDATA
textarea	Common, accesskey (Character), columns (Number), disabled ("disabled"), name (CDATA), readonly ("readonly"), rows (Number), tabindex (Number)	PCDATA

Element	Attributes	Minimal Content Model
button	Common, accesskey (Character), disabled ("disabled"), name (CDATA), tabindex (Number), type ("button" | "submit" | "reset"), value (CDATA)	(PCDATA | Heading | List | Block - Form | Inline - Formctrl)*
fieldset	Common	(PCDATA | legend | Flow)*
label	Common, accesskey (Character), for (IDREF)	(PCDATA | Inline - Inline - label)*
legend	Common, accesskey (Character)	(PCDATA | Inline)+
optgroup	Common, disabled ("disabled"), label (Text)	

This module defines two content sets:

Form

form | fieldset

Formctrl

input | select | textarea | label | button

When this module is used, it adds the Form content set to the Block content set and it adds the Formctrl content set to the Inline content set as these are defined in the Basic Text Module.

The Forms Module is a superset of the Basic Fjorms Module. These modules may not be used together in a single document type.

Let's start by examining the attributes of the Form element type. The first entry, Common, refers to the set of attributes described earlier. The next few entries describe their content types using the parameter entities described in Chapter 7, such as ContentType and CharSet, and URI:

```
accept (ContentTypes), accept-charset (Charsets), action (URI)
```

This isn't the approach suggested in the *Building XML Modules* draft, but these documents are meant for human consumption so this is probably fine as long as you have some way of finding out what they mean. In the HTML and PDF versions of the *Modularization of XHTML* draft, this information is provided through cross-references and in Section 4.1.3. The method attribute, which only accepts two values, indicates this through the use of the vertical bar:

```
method ("get" | "put")
```

Another technique employed here that isn't documented in the *Building XML Modules* draft is the use of quotes around the possible values for the attribute. This isn't done inside of XML 1.0 DTDs, but it is necessary here to differentiate these attribute values from the names used for attribute types.

The Minimal Content Model for the form element type uses several content sets and some of the tools described in the preceding sidebar table:

```
(Heading | Block - form | fieldset)+
```

The content model for the form element type may include elements from the Heading content set (defined in Section 4.2.2, the Basic Text Module, along with Block, Inline, and Flow). Elements from the Block content set are also welcome, with the exception of the form element itself. The fieldset element, defined within this module, also may appear inside the form element type. Because the final character is a + rather than a *, at least one child element from this range of choices must appear.

The input element type is notable for its use of the EMPTY content type, while most of the other elements in this module allow text (PCDATA) along with other choices. The two content sets defined here, Form and Formset, are used inside of the module only to exclude their content (using the - indicator) rather than to add them to content models. At the same time, however, the notes at the bottom make clear that the module adds these content sets to the Block and Inline content sets defined in Section 4.2.2. As with XML 1.0, you should treat the names used for content sets and elements as case-sensitive: the form element type and the Form content set are not the same thing.

Another important aspect to consider in the notes at the bottom of the module is the potential for conflict with the Basic Forms Module, which defines (in Section 4.5.1) a subset of the larger Forms module. Including both can cause validation problems as the declarations conflict. Reading the fine print can keep you out of trouble when you put together the W3C's own modules, and you should make sure to include such documentation in your own abstract modules as well.

XML DTD Modules

DTD modules are better defined than abstract modules, although not quite as flexible. Because they use the formal syntax of XML 1.0 DTDs (as described in Chapter 6), DTD modules have all the capabilities and all the limitations of any XML DTD. XHTML 1.1 DTD modules are also more complex than the average XML DTD, using a set of naming conventions that takes full advantage of parameter entities to create customizable descriptions of document structures. *Parameterization* is extremely powerful, but it does take some getting used to.

XHTML 1.1 DTD modules are a lot harder to read than many XML DTDs. If you can't penetrate the formal description of a given module, the abstract module *should* help you. If you write your own modules, it is critical that you include abstract modules.

If you haven't done much with parameter entities, you may want to go back to Chapter 6 and review their syntax and usage.

The rules for creating XHTML 1.1's XML DTD modules are presented in Section 5 of the *Building XHTML Modules* draft and demonstrated in Section 6. There are a few additional conventions used in *Modularization of XHTML* that *Building XHTML Modules* doesn't describe, which I cover here as well. They appear useful and help explain some of the syntactical shortcuts (such as the Common attributes) used in abstract modules.

Parameterization just means putting all the contents of declarations into parameter entities. This makes the declarations easier to manage, and at the same time makes it much easier to modify them. While you can modify attribute declarations and parameter entities by making the declaration again, XML prohibits multiple declarations for element types. By putting the contents of those declarations into parameter entities, the creators of XHTML modules can provide a lot more flexibility. To keep track of all the different types of entities, XHTML specifies suffixes for entity names (as shown in Table 15-3).

TABLE 15-3 PARAMETER ENTITY SUFFIXES USED IN XHTML 1.1

Suffix	Use
.content	Used by parameter entities that represent element content models
.class (and .extra)	Used by parameter entities that contain lists of elements in the same class (Class is used fairly loosely in the specification.)
.mix	Used by parameter entities that contain lists of elements from different classes
.attrib	Used by parameter entities representing one or more attribute specifications that can appear within an ATTLIST declaration
.datatype	Used by parameter entities (such as URI.datatype and ContentTypes.datatype) that represent data types that go beyond what XML 1.0 provides
.attlist	Used by parameter entities that control the inclusion or exclusion of attribute content
.element	Used by parameter entities that control the inclusion or exclusion of element declarations
.mod	Used by parameter entities that represent an entire module's worth of content. (Typically these are external parameter entities representing external files, as described next.)
.module	Used by parameter entities that are set to INCLUDE or IGNORE in order to turn on and off the inclusion of module information

Let's look at examples of each of these suffixes taken from the W3C draft DTD, building from the smallest atomic pieces to the largest.

.datatype

The data types in XHTML 1.1 are direct descendants of those in XHTML 1.0, and they are declared in Section B.2.1. Most of the data types are simply more precise names for CDATA, textual content:

```
<!-- a Uniform Resource Identifier, see [URI] -->
<!ENTITY % URI.datatype "CDATA" >
```

These data types are then used in attribute declarations:

```
<!ATTLIST a
                    %Common.attrib;
                    href            %URI.datatype;
#IMPLIED
                    charset         %Charset.datatype;
#IMPLIED
                    type            %ContentType.datatype;
#IMPLIED
                    hreflang        %LanguageCode.datatype;
#IMPLIED
                    rel             %LinkTypes.datatype;
#IMPLIED
                    rev             %LinkTypes.datatype;
#IMPLIED
                    accesskey       %Character.datatype;
#IMPLIED
                    tabindex        %Number.datatype;
#IMPLIED
>
```

All of these data type declarations actually resolve to CDATA when an XML processor reads the DTD, but they make the content that should be stored in these attributes much more identifiable.

TIP   While XML 1.0 processors can't do much to enforce data typing today, schema processors should be capable of accomplishing more with this information in the future. Think of this approach as adding information to the DTD so it's ready for the next version.

These data type names are used in the abstract modules for XHTML 1.1 as well, supplementing the core XML 1.0 set of types.

.attrib

The .attrib suffix is used on parameter entities that represent one or more *attribute specifications* – the part of an attribute list declaration that defines individual attributes, their types, defaults, and possible values. These entities sometimes describe only one attribute, like this one for the id attribute:

```
<!ENTITY % Id.attrib
                "id              ID
```

```
#IMPLIED"
>
```

They may specify multiple attributes, like this one for `xml:lang` and `dir`:

```
<!ENTITY % I18n.attrib
                    "xml:lang         %LanguageCode.datatype;
#IMPLIED
                    dir               ( ltr | rtl )
#IMPLIED"
>
```

These entities also may include other entities with the `.attrib` suffix, as in the ubiquitous `Common.attrib` entity:

```
<!ENTITY % Common.attrib
                    "%Core.attrib;
                    %I18n.attrib;
                    %Events.attrib;"
    >
```

This just includes all of the attribute specifications declared in the `Core.attrib`, `I18n.attrib`, and `Events.attrib` entities, building a large list of common components. The quotes need to be used even though all of the contents of the entity are contained in parameter entities.

.attlist

The `.attlist` suffix (not documented in *Building XHTML Modules*) is used in the XHTML 1.1 DTDs to turn `ATTLIST` declarations on and off. Parameter entities that have the `.attlist` suffix take one of two values: `INCLUDE` or `IGNORE`. These function with a feature of XML 1.0 DTDs not used in XHTML 1.0: *conditional sections*.

 For a much more detailed explanation of conditional sections and their use in other XML contexts, see Chapter 16 of *XML Elements of Style* by Simon St. Laurent (McGraw-Hill, 2000).

Conditional sections may appear in DTDs only; they enable DTD designers to turn sets of declarations on and off. By using parameter entities to determine whether to include or ignore a section, developers make it possible to use portions of a DTD or even choose among different variations on a single DTD.

For example, this DTD fragment includes the attributes for the title element type:

```
<!ENTITY % Title.attlist "INCLUDE" >
<![%Title.attlist;[
             <!ATTLIST title
                    %I18n.attrib;
             >
<!-- end of Title.attlist -->]]>
```

The first line creates a parameter entity named Title.attlist whose value is INCLUDE. In the next line, the entity is substituted with %Title.attlist; to produce these resulting declarations:

```
<![INCLUDE[
             <!ATTLIST title
                    %I18n.attrib;
             >
<!-- end of Title.attlist -->]]>
```

An XML parser strips out the INCLUDE section and the comment, leaving a core of:

```
<!ATTLIST title
  %I18n.attrib;
>
```

Which then becomes:

```
<!ATTLIST title
        xml:lang       %LanguageCode.datatype;   #IMPLIED
        dir              ( ltr | rtl )                    #IMPLIED
>
```

and finally:

```
<!ATTLIST title
        xml:lang       NMTOKEN                          #IMPLIED
        dir              ( ltr | rtl )                    #IMPLIED
>
```

If, on the other hand, another module redeclares the Title.attlist entity to be IGNORE:

```
<!ENTITY % Title.attlist "IGNORE" >
```

then the result is:

```
<![IGNORE[
            <!ATTLIST title
                    %I18n.attrib;
            >
<!-- end of Title.attlist -->]]>
```

which prohibits the parser from processing the declarations at all, leaving `title` with no attributes.

Entities with the `.attlist` suffix surround the attribute list declarations for every element type in the *Modularization of XHTML* draft.

.content

The `.content` suffix functions for parameter entities that describe content models for particular element types. The simplest example, for an `EMPTY` content model, looks like this:

```
<!ENTITY % Input.content   "EMPTY" >
<!ELEMENT input   %Input.content; >
```

When processed, this resolves to:

```
<!ELEMENT input   EMPTY >
```

and defines the input element as having an empty content model. By redeclaring entities with a `.content` suffix, other modules easily can modify the content model of an element.

.class (and .extra)

The `.class` suffix functions for parameter entities that may be used repeatedly in content models for multiple elements, but only when the contents are element type names that all share something in common. In XHTML, this tends to mean that block elements are one class, while inline elements are another class. These entities aren't defined (with one exception, noted next) in the *Modularization of XHTML* draft. They are defined in the customization file, another module, in Appendix C of *XHTML 1.1 - Module-based XHTML*. For example:

```
<!ENTITY % Inlstruct.class "br | span" >
```

Through the abbreviations, you can see that these are structural element types that may appear as inline elements. br is used for line breaks within block elements, while span is an abstract element mostly useful for marking off inline content in ways that aren't reflected by other inline content. This entity and several of its siblings get combined into a larger `Inline.class` entity:

```
<!ENTITY % Inline.class
                "%Inlstruct.class;
                %Inlphras.class;
                %Inlpres.class;
                %I18n.class;
                %Anchor.class;
                %Inlspecial.class;
                %Ruby.class;
                %Inline.extra;"
        >
```

One oddity here is `Inline.extra` — *Building XHTML Modules* describes no "official" convention for `.extra`. `Inline.extra` has this declaration:

```
<!ENTITY % Inline.extra
                "| input | select | textarea | label | button"
>
```

The DTD comments describe how to use this `.extra` suffix:

```
While in some cases this module may need to be rewritten to
accommodate changes to the document model, minor extensions
may be accomplished by redeclaring any of the three *.extra;
parameter entities to contain extension element types as follows:
    %Misc.extra;     whose parent may be any block or
                                           inline element.

    %Inline.extra;   whose parent may be any inline element.

    %Block.extra;    whose parent may be any block element.

If used, these parameter entities must be an OR-separated
list beginning with an OR separator ("|"), eg., "| a | b | c"
```

While `.extra` is undocumented (so far) in *Building XHTML Modules*, it is a critical piece for developers who want to add their own extensions to XHTML 1.1.

The `.class` suffix also functions in at least one place for attributes. The following entity includes all of the input types:

```
<!ENTITY % InputType.class
                "( text | password | checkbox | radio | submit
                | reset | file | hidden | image )"
>
```

This is then used in an attribute declaration:

```
<!ATTLIST input
                    %Common.attrib;
                    type                %InputType.class;
'text'
```

This anomaly probably derives from the input element's unusual use of an attribute to signify its "real" content.

.mix

The .mix suffix creates lists of elements for use in content models in which different classes of items get combined. The Flow.mix entity (also from the customization file of *XHTML 1.1 - Module-based XHTML*) is a good example:

```
<!ENTITY % Flow.mix
                    "%Heading.class;
                    | %List.class;
                    | %Block.class;
                    | %Inline.class;
                    %Misc.class;"
          >
```

Any element that uses Flow.mix within its content model can include just about any element in the XHTML vocabulary. It's definitely a combination.

.mod

Parameter entities that end in .mod assemble complete DTDs out of all of these little parts that comprise XHTML. XHTML 1.1's driver file (included as Appendix B of *XHTML 1.1 - Module-based XHTML*) contains lots of these entities.

```
<!ENTITY % xhtml-form.mod
                    PUBLIC "-//W3C//ELEMENTS XHTML 1.1 Forms
1.0//EN"
                                "xhtml11-form-1.mod" >
%xhtml-form.mod;
```

In this case, the entity is declared using a public identifier and a system part. If the application or parser processing this understands the public identifier, it can use that information to include the DTD. If not, it can use the relative URL that follows to retrieve the file. After the declaration, the contents of the file are immediately included in the DTD.

.module

Parameter entities that end in `.module` turn the entities that end in `.mod` on and off using the same conditional statements (`INCLUDE` and `IGNORE`) that `.attlist` entities use. For example, the XHTML form module normally gets loaded because of this code:

```
<!ENTITY % xhtml-form.module "INCLUDE" >
          <![%xhtml-form.module;[
          <!ENTITY % xhtml-form.mod
                    PUBLIC "-//W3C//ELEMENTS XHTML 1.1 Forms
1.0//EN"
                                 "xhtml11-form-1.mod" >
          %xhtml-form.mod;]]>
```

If you want to keep the form module from loading, all you have to do is define a new `xhtml-form.module` entity before that one, overriding it with a value of `IGNORE`:

```
<!ENTITY % xhtml-form.module "IGNORE" >
...
<!ENTITY % xhtml-form.module "INCLUDE" >
          <![%xhtml-form.module;[
          <!ENTITY % xhtml-form.mod
                    PUBLIC "-//W3C//ELEMENTS XHTML 1.1 Forms
1.0//EN"
                                 "xhtml11-form-1.mod" >
          %xhtml-form.mod;]]>
```

The result is this:

```
<![IGNORE[
          <!ENTITY % xhtml-form.mod
                    PUBLIC "-//W3C//ELEMENTS XHTML 1.1 Forms
1.0//EN"
                                 "xhtml11-form-1.mod" >
          %xhtml-form.mod;
]]>
```

The module doesn't load. Note the naming convention here—both the entities (`.mod` and `.module`) have the same name except for the suffix. This makes the DTDs much more manageable.

Schema Modules

XHTML 1.1 will use XML Schemas when they're ready. The *Modularization of XHTML* draft's Appendix A states, "This appendix will contain implementations of the modules defined in XHTML Abstract Modules via XML Schema [XMLSCHEMA] when the XML Schema becomes a W3C approved recommendation."

The *Building XHTML Modules* draft doesn't specify how to build Schema modules. The current Schema drafts don't use mechanisms that correspond directly to parameter entities, but similar approaches may be possible using general entities (because Schemas are XML documents themselves) and the extension and restriction mechanisms of XML Schemas.

Putting XHTML 1.1 Together

For now, XHTML is assembled using the parameter entities and DTD modules just described. *XHTML 1.1 - Module-based XHTML* includes a driver file and a customization file that handle the formal integration, as well as a set of rules for XHTML 1.1 conformance. Much of the work done in *XHTML 1.1 - Module-based XHTML* builds on the work performed in the other drafts, incorporating them by reference without describing what's happening.

 While *XHTML 1.1 - Module-based XHTML* doesn't describe XHTML in the same kind of detail that HTML 4.01 (or even XHTML 1.0) specifications do, it includes a convenient description of how this flavor of XHTML 1.1 differs from XHTML 1.0 (`http://www.w3.org/TR/xhtml11/changes.html#a_ changes`).

If all you want to do is create XHTML 1.1 documents that conform to the main XHTML 1.1 specification, you just have to use the DOCTYPE declaration listed here and make sure your documents validate:

```
<!DOCTYPE
     html PUBLIC "-//W3C//DTD XHTML 1.1//EN"
     "http://www.w3.org/TR/xhtml11/DTD/xhtml11.dtd">
```

If you work with XHTML 1.0's strict vocabulary, you probably won't have any problems. But note that XHTML 1.1 omits substantial portions of the transitional and frameset vocabularies.

The W3C probably will create additional profiles based on the same XHTML 1.1 modules. The *XHTML Basic* specification, for example (`http://www.w3.org/TR/xhtml-basic`), defines a much smaller profile of XHTML 1.1 and requires that you use a different `DOCTYPE` declaration:

```
<!DOCTYPE
        html PUBLIC "-//W3C//DTD XHTML Basic 1.0//EN"
        "http://www.w3.org/TR/xhtml-basic/xhtml-basic10.dtd">
```

Chapter 18 discusses XHTML Basic in more detail. The specification for XHTML Basic is available at `http://www.w3.org/TR/xhtml-basic/`.

Many users will find these profiles suffice, but developers who build their own modules and need to integrate them with the rest of XHTML must build their own profiles. Following the examples of XHTML 1.1 and XHTML Basic, you should do this through the creation of a driver file and a customization file plus a *Formal Public Identifier (FPI)* that identifies the driver file.

The XHTML profiles provided by the W3C include SGML Open Catalog entries in addition to FPIs, but it isn't clear from the drafts whether Open Catalog entries are required or optional parts of XHTML modularization projects. For more on how to build SGML Open Catalog entries, see `http://www.oasis-open.org/html/a401.htm`.

The Formal Public Identifier is the easiest part to create. FPIs contain four fields, separated by double-slashes (`//`). The first field is always a dash, unless the resource the FPI describes is created by a formal standards organization such as ISO. (If the FPI is created by a standards organization, this field identifies the standard to which it refers.)

The second field contains the name of the organization maintaining the resource. For the XHTML specification, this is `W3C`. For your own FPIs, it should be an identifier for your organization—possibly a domain name. The third field contains a unique name, chosen within your organization, which describes the referenced resource and includes version information as well. The final field should contain a language identifier (from the list in Appendix C). The language identifier describes the language within the resource and doesn't place any limitations on the content of documents using it.

For example, the FPI for XHTML 1.1 is this:

```
-//W3C//DTD XHTML 1.1//EN
```

The first field is a dash (-) because the W3C is technically a vendor consortium, not a standards body proper. The second field contains W3C, the identifier used by the World Wide Web Consortium (W3C). The third field identifies the resource as a Document Type Definition (DTD) for XHTML 1.1. If the DTD changes for version 1.2 or 2.0, the W3C can change the version number within the FPI. Finally, EN identifies that the descriptions used in the DTD are written in English. (If the W3C provides a French translation, it might be FR. But French-language documents can refer to the English DTD without any problem.)

Creating your own FPIs is easy. First (unless you work for ISO), start with a dash. Then identify your organization, followed by your project, followed by the language in which the DTDs are written. For example, if I create a profile that describes "Simon's Markup Language" version 1.0, the FPI might look like this:

```
-//simonstl.com//DTD SimonML 1.0//EN
```

Profile creators also should support a system identifier, typically a URL, where you can retrieve the DTD or other resource. Then the combination of the public and system identifiers is used in the DOCTYPE declaration by documents using the profile:

```
<!DOCTYPE
     simonML PUBLIC "-//simonstl.com//DTD SimonML 1.0//EN"
     "http://www.simonstl.com/xhtml/chap15/simonML.dtd">
```

The system identifier should refer to the driver file for the XHTML profile, just as the identifiers for XHTML 1.1 and XHTML Basic refer to their driver files.

Driver files contain comments describing the module, a few entity declarations, and then an entity declaration that references and includes the customization file. After the customization file is included, the rest of the modules that make up the DTD are included using the .mod and .module parameter entities just described.

Chapter 16 describes creating your own driver and customization files.

It isn't clear quite how the W3C expects these files to fit into Web infrastructure. While XML processors routinely load resources like DTDs from across the Internet, that approach hasn't been used for the most part with HTML processors. Most likely, the W3C expects processors to use the FPI in the `DOCTYPE` declaration to figure out what they have to work with, and then apply logic specific to that document type rather than generic XML validation and processing. Because `DOCTYPE` declarations require a URI in addition to the FPI, however, ordinary XML processors will be capable of processing documents using the information retrieved from that URI. SGML Open Catalog entries (also provided in the XHTML specifications) provide another way for generic XML processors to interpret the FPI and retrieve the needed information.

Chapter 16

Extending XHTML

FRAGMENTING XHTML IS USEFUL if you want to implement portions of XHTML, but many developers need to go the other direction and supplement XHTML's functionality. Fortunately, you can use the exact same set of tools the W3C used to create the XHTML modules to create your own modules. One of the editors of the XHTML drafts, Murray Altheim, has published some tools and templates that may help you get started. It isn't easy, but it's not exactly rocket science either. Of course, defining the markup alone doesn't transform user's Web browsers instantly – you still have to perform a lot of software development (or, at the very least, style sheet development) to make your shiny new vocabularies work.

 You really only need to read this chapter if you plan to build your own extensions to XHTML or you need to understand how new modules from various sources integrate with XHTML. If that isn't your goal right now, skip ahead and come back if you need this material.

Building Your Own Modules

The first part you need to define is the content of your XHTML module. You may be starting from scratch, building your module on the XHTML DTD framework, or converting an existing XML DTD to an XHTML module. In any case, creating an XHTML module involves a good deal more work and tends to produce a much more verbose document description than creating an ordinary XML DTD. You must combine the basic tools described in Chapter 6 with the approach described in Chapter 15, and you should document your work in an abstract module that goes beyond simple DTD creation. While there is definitely extra work involved in creating a formal XHTML module that uses all the parameterization conventions created by the W3C, this approach should produce a more usable result.

You can create modules that work without using the parameter entity and conditional sections approach. After all, modules are just DTDs, and parsers won't care about how many parameter entities or conditional sections you used to create the DTD. On the other hand, developers outside of your project may have a much harder time working with and integrating your vocabulary into their work. Even if you're just prototyping, starting out with and sticking to the XHTML approach makes the management of your modules much easier.

For the most part, building an XHTML module means creating your own vocabulary and laying it out as a set of elements and attributes. It's basically the same as creating an XML vocabulary, with a few extra pieces. I don't cover the ins and outs of creating XML vocabularies here, as that task is well described in (and requires) lots of separate books. Instead, I walk you through a very simple but plausible XHTML module for describing biographical information within XHTML documents.

Lots of books describe how to create your own XML vocabularies. *XML: A Primer* (Simon St. Laurent, IDG Books, 1999) describes XML and provides numerous examples, while *XML Elements of Style* (Simon St. Laurent, McGraw-Hill, 2000) goes into much more detail about the rules and traps of XML. The *XML Bible* (Elliotte Rusty Harold, IDG Books, 1999) runs through a series of baseball-oriented examples in detail. David Megginson's *Structuring XML Documents* (Prentice-Hall, 1998) moves more into SGML, but provides detailed descriptions of various approaches to XML document structure.

If you want to get a head start on your module creation and avoid some of the work described in the next few sections, take a look at *archy* and *instance karma*. Both are from Murray Altheim, one of the editors of XHTML 1.1. archy (available at `http://www.doctypes.org/archy/home.html`) is a framework for building XHTML modules, while instance karma (available at `http://www.doctypes.org/instkrma/home.html`) is an XSLT style sheet that builds a shell DTD from a sample document. If you want to start by creating sample documents, this approach can save you a lot of time.

The XHTML-Biography module you create in this chapter can include and be included in XHTML 1.1 documents, which means that the customization file is especially important. Most of the functionality provided by the module doesn't require extra processing beyond the capabilities of relatively simple cascading style sheets, so you can put the module to work in browsers easily. Non-browser application structures, such as filters that search for information on particular people, can treat the XHTML documents created with this module as XML and seek out the markup vocabulary you create to track down biographical information.

In planning the module, you design for two different kinds of situations and try to accommodate both. The first case is a *formal biography*, a description within an HTML document that provides a complete biography of a person possibly presented in a different way than the rest of an HTML document. These formal biographies use the markup you create here for their basic structures, and a mixture of ordinary HTML and biographical markup for their contents.

The second case enables developers to mark up biographical information within other XHTML documents without the trouble of a full biography. It might point to a formal biography, or it might help automated processors track down documents that contain information about a particular person. This approach is very useful for news sites because it lets them build search engines, for instance, to supplement this module with other modules describing companies and other organizations.

To identify your elements, use this namespace:

```
http://www.simonstl.com/xhtml/xhtml-biography/
```

Within the DTD and abstract modules, use the prefix `biog`. (Using `bio` invites conflicts with biology and changing the prefix can break validation, as described later in this chapter.)

Let's start by creating an abstract module that describes what you're doing here, and then move into the formalities of building a DTD using the XHTML conventions. You need to create elements for identifying biographies when they appear in documents, and these can act as containers for a more formal set of descriptions. Then you create a separate container for identifying people within ordinary XHTML content. Working inside of XHTML documents may require a much more flexible approach while still describing similar information.

These two container elements can hold titles, names, and birth and death dates (as shown in Table 16-1).

TABLE 16-1 THE CONTAINER ELEMENTS OF YOUR XHTML-BIOGRAPHY MODULE

Element Type	Attribute(s)	Minimal Content Model
biog:biography	Common	(biog:title, biog:name, biog:birth, biog:death?, Block)
biog:person	Common, more	(biog:title | biog:name | biog:birth | biog:death | Inline | PCDATA)*

Neither of these elements needs many attributes beyond the Common core. You can use the id and class attributes if needed to identify particular biography information sets within a document. The biog:person element can have a more attribute pointing to a fuller set of information about the person, if appropriate. The content model for biog:biography is much stricter than that for biog:person, but to a sizable extent that is because you plan to have substantially more control over the content and presentation of biog:biography elements. The biog:person element type must demonstrate more flexibility in order to be useful; it should work in situations in which only partial information is available, as well as in a wider variety of sequences.

Next, you need to define the content of the elements you have inside these biographical bits (see Table 16-2).

TABLE 16-2 THE DETAIL ELEMENTS OF YOUR XHTML-BIOGRAPHY MODULE

Element Type	Attribute	Minimal Content Model
biog:title	Common	PCDATA
biog:name	Common	(given | family | middle)*
biog:given	Common	PCDATA
biog:family	Common	PCDATA
biog:middle	Common	PCDATA
biog:birth	Common	date
biog:death	Common	date

Apart from biog:name, all of these elements only contain text. Because names may appear in different orders in different cultures, biog:name has become extremely flexible (perhaps too flexible). You can specify more parts for all of these — the title can refer to the position and the organization or location to which it applies, and the birth and death dates can break down into year, month, and day. For now, let's use date as a placeholder for PCDATA to make its contents more explicit. (This has no effect on parsing.) It's also possible that these items should permit inline HTML elements as well, but let's opt not to do that for now.

This should be all the abstract model you need, so let's move on to building the DTD module and making use of XHTML 1.1's set of naming conventions. Start by declaring the date data type:

```
<!ENTITY % date.datatype "#PCDATA">
```

You don't have any classes or mixes defined in this module, but you use classes defined in XHTML (Block and Inline) to define content models in your element declarations. First you define your elements as suggested in the XHTML specifications, creating a parameter entity that contains the element content model, and then you use that parameter entity in the element type declaration. Do that for all of the elements in Table 16-2, even those with the simplest content models:

```
<!ENTITY % biog:biography.element "INCLUDE" >
<![%biog:biography.element;[
<!ENTITY biog:biography.content "(biog:title, biog:name, biog:birth,
biog:death?, %Block.mix;)"
<!ELEMENT biog:biography %biog:biography.content;>
]]>
<!ENTITY % biog:person.element "INCLUDE" >
<![%biog:person.element;[
<!ENTITY biog:person.content "((biog:title | biog:name | biog:birth
| biog:death | %Inline.mix; | PCDATA)*)"
<!ELEMENT biog:person %biog:person.content;>
]]>
<!ENTITY % biog:title.element "INCLUDE" >
<![%biog:title.element;[
<!ENTITY biog:title.content "(PCDATA)*"
<!ELEMENT biog:title %biog:title.content;>
]]>
<!ENTITY % biog:name.element "INCLUDE" >
<![%biog:name.element;[
<!ENTITY biog:name.content "(given | family | middle)*"
<!ELEMENT biog:name %biog:name.content;>
]]>
<!ENTITY % biog:given.element "INCLUDE" >
<![%biog:given.element;[
<!ENTITY biog:given.content "(PCDATA)*"
<!ELEMENT biog:given %biog:given.content;>
]]>
<!ENTITY % biog:family.element "INCLUDE" >
<![%biog:family.element;[
<!ENTITY biog:family.content "(PCDATA)*"
<!ELEMENT biog:family %biog:family.content;>
]]>
<!ENTITY % biog:middle.element "INCLUDE" >
<![%biog:middle.element;[
<!ENTITY biog:middle.content "(PCDATA)*"
<!ELEMENT biog:middle %biog:middle.content;>
]]>
```

```
<!ENTITY % biog:birth.element "INCLUDE" >
<![%biog:birth.element;[
<!ENTITY biog:birth.content "(%date.datatype;)"
<!ELEMENT biog:birth %biog:birth.content;>
]]>
<!ENTITY % biog:death.element "INCLUDE" >
<![%biog:death.element;[
<!ENTITY biog:death.content "(%date.datatype;)"
<!ELEMENT biog:death %biog:birth.content;>
]]>
```

This code may look more verbose than necessary, but it lets other modules modify the content. Take a similar route with the attributes, using .attrib to create attribute lists for these element types and .attlist to turn them on and off. (Note that you have to add attributes for the namespace prefix — otherwise, the namespaces don't work.)

```
<!ENTITY % biog:biography.attlist "INCLUDE" >
<![%biog:biography.attlist;[
<!ATTLIST biog:biography.attlist
    xmlns:biog    CDATA
    #FIXED "http://www.simonstl.com/xhtml/xhtml-biography/"
    %Common.attrib;>
]]>
<!ENTITY % biog:person.attlist "INCLUDE" >
<![%biog:person.attlist;[
<!ATTLIST biog:person.attlist
    xmlns:biog    CDATA
    #FIXED "http://www.simonstl.com/xhtml/xhtml-biography/"
    %Common.attrib;
    more %URI.datatype; #IMPLIED>
]]>
<!ENTITY % biog:title.attlist "INCLUDE" >
<![%biog:title.attlist;[
<!ATTLIST biog:name.attlist
    %Common.attrib;>
]]>
<!ENTITY % biog:name.attlist "INCLUDE" >
<![%biog:name.attlist;[
<!ATTLIST biog:name.attlist
    %Common.attrib;>
]]>
<!ENTITY % biog:given.attlist "INCLUDE" >
```

```
<![%biog:given.attlist;[
<!ATTLIST biog:given.attlist
    %Common.attrib;>
]]>
<!ENTITY % biog:family.attlist "INCLUDE" >
<![%biog:family.attlist;[
<!ATTLIST biog:family.attlist
    %Common.attrib;>
]]>
<!ENTITY % biog:middle.attlist "INCLUDE" >
<![%biog:middle.attlist;[
<!ATTLIST biog:middle.attlist
    %Common.attrib;>
]]>
<!ENTITY % biog:birth.attlist "INCLUDE" >
<![%biog:birth.attlist;[
<!ATTLIST biog:birth.attlist
    %Common.attrib;>
]]>
<!ENTITY % biog:death.attlist "INCLUDE" >
<![%biog:death.attlist;[
<!ATTLIST biog:death.attlist
    %Common.attrib;>
]]>
```

With these two aspects built, you have an XHTML module. Now you need to integrate with the rest of XHTML.

Building or Modifying Driver Files

Integrating the module with the rest of XHTML requires creating a driver file and a customization file, or overriding and supplementing the entities declared in the existing file. Driver files 'drive' the rest of the DTD processing, setting an initial set of rules and linking everything else into those rules. In some cases – particularly when you want to work with only a small set of XHTML modules – you may find it worth your time to write your own driver file and copy the little pieces you need from the XHTML 1.1 (or XHTML Basic) driver file and customization file. On the other hand, if you're supplementing XHTML 1.1, it probably makes more sense to include the existing XHTML driver and customization file through a parameter entity. It may or may not make sense to create a separate customization file, also.

The XHTML-Biography Module driver has to include the declarations for the module just defined, add its biog:biography element to the Block.mix entity, and then add its `biog:person` element to the `Inline.mix` entity. The quickest way to do this uses a single driver file, referencing the XHTML 1.1 driver file:

```
<!--Quick n' dirty Biography Driver-->

<!--Get the module itself-->
<!ENTITY % xhtml-biog.module "INCLUDE" >
<![%xhtml-biog.module;[
<!ENTITY % xhtml-biog.mod
      PUBLIC "-//SIMONSTLCOM//ELEMENTS Biography 1.0//EN"
      "http://www.simonstl.com/xhtml/code/chap16/xhtml-biog.mod" >
%xhtml-biog.mod;
]]>


<!--Customizations-->
<!--Override the Block.extra entity-->
<!--Note mild risk - a different module could also change this.-->
<!ENTITY % Block.extra
      "| table | form | fieldset | biog:biography" >

<!--Override the Inline.extra entity-->
<!ENTITY % Inline.extra
      "| input | select | textarea | label | button | biog:person" >

<!--Add the biog namespace to the html element-->
<!ATTLIST html
      xmlns:biog      CDATA
      #FIXED "http://www.simonstl.com/xhtml/xhtml-biography/">

<!--Include the rest of XHTML 1.1-->
<!ENTITY xhtml11 PUBLIC "-//W3C//DTD XHTML 1.1//EN"

"http://www.w3.org/TR/xhtml11/DTD/xhtml11.dtd">
%xhtml11;
```

If you want to create a separate customization file (`xhtml-biog-model.mod`), it isn't difficult to pull out the biography customizations:

```
<!--Customizations-->
<!--Override the Block.extra entity-->
<!ENTITY % Block.extra
      "| table | form | fieldset | biog:biography" >
```

```
<!--Override the Inline.extra entity-->
<!ENTITY % Inline.extra
     "| input | select | textarea | label | button | biog:person" >

<!--Add the biog namespace to the html element-->
<!ATTLIST html
     xmlns:biog     CDATA
     #FIXED "http://www.simonstl.com/xhtml/xhtml-biography/">
```

Then you can reference this file from the driver file:

```
<!--More modular Biography Driver-->

<!--Get the module-->
<!ENTITY % xhtml-biog.module "INCLUDE" >
<![%xhtml-biog.module;[
<!ENTITY % xhtml-biog.mod
     PUBLIC "-//SIMONSTLCOM//ELEMENTS Biography 1.0//EN"
     "http://www.simonstl.com/xhtml/code/chap16/xhtml-biog.mod" >
%xhtml-biog.mod;
]]>

<!--Customizations-->
<!ENTITY xhtml-biog-model.mod
     PUBLIC "-//SIMONSTLCOM//ENTITIES Biography 1.0//EN"
     "http://www.simonstl.com/xhtml/code/chap16/xhtml-biog-
model.mod" >

<!--Include the rest of XHTML 1.1-->
<!ENTITY xhtml11 PUBLIC "-//W3C//DTD XHTML 1.1//EN"
     "http://www.w3.org/TR/xhtml11/DTD/xhtml11.dtd">
%xhtml11;
```

With this driver file, you can start creating documents that use this module, in addition to the predefined XHTML 1.1 modules, using the document type definition:

```
<!DOCTYPE
     html PUBLIC "-//SIMONSTLCOM//DTD Biography 1.0//EN"
     "http://www.simonstl.com/xhtml/code/chap16/xhtml-biog.dtd">
```

If processed by an XML parser, this loads the driver file that loads the customization file and the rest of XHTML. It's probably a good idea to make the namespace declaration for the biog prefix explicitly in the html element because non-validating XML parsers may not get the default value for the `xmlns:biog` attribute from the DTD:

```
<html xmlns="http://www.w3.org/1999/xhtml"
      xmlns:biog="http://www.simonstl.com/xhtml/xhtml-biography/"
      xml:lang="en-US" >
```

Requiring this of documents may be impossible—other modules that use the prefix `biog` for their namespace may also exist.

Namespaces, Validation, and Other Complexities

The XHTML 1.1 specification is lucky. It's all assembled within the same namespace. Extensions have a much harder time negotiating a number of implementation issues involving namespaces and different kinds of XML processing. Because XHTML is the dominant vocabulary when `html` is the root element, it's quite clear that XHTML documents should declare the default namespace there. On the other hand, it's difficult both to decide what to do with namespace declarations for extensions and how to sensibly include XHTML within other modules. This is because it may not be wise to always assign XHTML the default namespace.

Namespace problems arise (for now) because XML 1.0 DTDs are not "namespace-aware." Validating parsers don't interpret prefixes as having any meaning other than a simple string of characters in the name. The Namespaces in XML Recommendation makes it clear that you can change the prefix to something else, while referencing the same URL, and still describe the same thing. Because validating parsers don't recognize namespaces, changing the prefix means that documents claiming to be identical under the Namespaces in XML Recommendation aren't recognized as such by XML 1.0—and nothing has been done to resolve this.

XHTML 1.1 doesn't go to the (admittedly extreme) length of parameterizing element names to allow namespace prefix changes—at least as of the 5 January 2000 Last Call drafts. This means that module developers have to watch out for namespace prefix collisions if they plan to use their modules in environments where they might encounter validating XML parsers—an XML document storage system, for instance.

Keeping out of trouble on this issue can be easy, although perhaps not quite perfect. When I chose the prefix for the XHTML-Biography Module, I chose the more verbose (but less common) `biog` over the easier (but more likely to conflict) `bio`. The more specific (or downright weird) the prefix you choose, the less likely it is that others will choose the same one and then want to mix their content with yours. This relatively easy strategy may make sense.

Another option is to parameterize names within your own documents. This might look like the following code:

```
<!ENTITY % biog.nsprefix "biog:">
<!ENTITY % biog.nsuri "http://www.simonstl.com/xhtml/xhtml-
biography/">
<!ENTITY % biog:biography.element "INCLUDE" >
<![%biog:biography.element;[
<!ENTITY biog:biography.content "(biog:title, biog:name, biog:birth,
biog:death?, %Block.mix;)">
<!ENTITY % biog.nsElementName
"%biog.nsprefix;biography%biog:biography.content;">
<!ELEMENT % biog.nsElementName %biog:biography.content;>
]]>
<!ENTITY % biog:biography.attlist "INCLUDE" >
<![%biog:biography.attlist;[
<!ATTLIST biog:biography.attlist
     %biog.nsprefix     CDATA
     #FIXED "%nsuri;"
     %Common.attrib;>
```

Section 4.4.8 of the XML 1.0 Recommendation states: "*When a parameter entity is recognized in the DTD and validated, its replacement text is enlarged by the attachment of one leading and one following space (#x20) character.*" That sounds like your element and attribute names would end up with spaces in them, which is prohibited. However, by creating yet another parameter entity, and combining the namespace prefix with the element name there, you can fall back on section 4.4.5, which avoids adding the space.

The last option, and the one most likely to be honored in practice, is to hope that namespace prefix collisions never occur in a validating XML environment. Most browsers, for instance, are non-validating and don't ever check the names and structures in the document against the DTD. This makes the DTD a formal exercise rather than a binding commitment, a passport into validating environments for some especially conformant documents rather than a set of rules for all the documents of a different type. Non-validating environments may never read the DTD at all, so the #FIXED attribute values used in the preceding code may have no effect there. Always include your namespace declarations within the document as often as necessary to make sure that your elements are identified correctly.

XML Schemas should ease this problem because schema processors are namespace-aware. When Schema modules appear, they may be worth investigating for this feature in particular.

Documenting Extensions

The abstract module and the DTD are a fine start toward building a module, but they're not especially human-friendly. Abstract modules are a definite improvement over DTD modules for casual reading, but they still don't contain explanations of your modules' purpose or their inner workings. They provide a guide to structure, not to usage or processing. To produce a "complete" module, you should provide a few more pieces.

The first piece, unless you plan to be the only one working with your module, is a *user's guide*. The user's guide is basically for authors and readers; it explains the semantics of your document structure. When should you use `biog:given`, and how should it interact with `biog:middle`? What happens when a biography includes 50 other people's names? Should they be marked up? Issues that seem obvious to the creator of a vocabulary are often confusing, invisible, or opaque to the people who use that vocabulary — especially as time passes. The more information you can provide for your users (without putting them to sleep entirely, of course) the better.

The second piece is an explanation for those who need to process your vocabulary. Some information overlaps with the user guide, but there may be a lot more detail about interactions between different elements and also more formal descriptions of things such as style sheet conventions. A reference implementation may be part of this documentation, or it may be left as an exercise for the reader depending on the situation.

There isn't any standard approach for including this kind of material with XHTML modules, but references from the DTD (in comments) and abstract modules should suffice. If not, this material can be part of a larger site explaining how to make the module work.

While there is no universal convention for where to put your documentation, it might be smart to keep it in the same directory as your DTD, and to provide comments in the beginning of your DTD that explain where to find the detailed documentation.

Supporting Your Extensions on the Server

Defining a vocabulary doesn't mean that applications suddenly will understand it or have any idea what to do with it. Some levels of generic XML processing are possible (such as storing XML in databases or modifying it with style sheets), but making good use of many modules requires some custom code. Support on the server is usually much easier than support on the client because you typically have more control over the setup of the server. You can control the hardware, the software, the software versions, and the surrounding environment, and you can code in a language you find most comfortable. Even if you support multiple platforms in a commercial product, the number of server installations is typically much smaller than the number of clients to reduce the probability of odd conflicts.

Some XHTML applications probably will be entirely server-based, converting the XHTML to dynamic HTML or some other interface structure for presentation in a browser. Meanwhile, others (likely including the XHTML-Biography Module) will provide only server-specific functionality for tasks such as search engine assistance. The transformation of XHTML to another format may take place at user request, on the server, or as a consequence of an authoring process that saves both the native XHTML for editing and another format for presentation. Search engine and agent-oriented server tasks may involve customizing code to look for particular vocabularies, but probably will require only the creation of new software for cases in which substantial or complex new vocabularies are introduced.

Server software also may have an important role in mediating the transmission of XHTML documents to a variety of clients that may understand only portions of them as they stand. The CC/PP proposal described in Chapter 14 provides an infrastructure for this kind of work, but older techniques such as browser "sniffing" and an estimation of browser capabilities may be necessary for the next few years of XHTML processing. It isn't clear yet whether browser (and other client) architectures will open enough to support multiple vocabularies, so the role of the server may be critical for a very long time.

Supporting Your Extensions on the Client

Sending XHTML to clients can be very easy or it can be very difficult depending on the needs of your vocabulary for processing and the level of standards compliance of the target browser, should you choose to stay in the browser. Building your own client software gives you incredible freedom, but it means that you have to create a lot more code from the ground up. Conversely, relying on browsers means relying on other people's code — sometimes a good thing, sometimes a bad thing.

Most browsers don't support XHTML 1.0 yet, so expecting compliance with (and understanding of) XHTML 1.1 is too much to ask. Instead, the key tools for using XHTML 1.1 modules in Web browsers are the tools for using its foundations: XML 1.0 and namespaces; the DOM for programmable access to, and modification of, information; and cascading style sheets Level 2 (CSS) and/or Extensible Stylesheet Language (XSL) for presentation.

The easiest way to integrate new XHTML modules into the client is through the use of style sheets. CSS style sheets enable you to deliver your XHTML directly to the client and provide some supplement formatting so that readers can explore your documents. (As CSS develops further, you also may be able to use style sheets to specify behavior — much as is done today with dynamic HTML.) If your module is just designed to present extra information or to annotate information within an XHTML framework, you may not need a style sheet, or you may have an extremely simple style sheet comprised mostly of display:inline property values. More sophisticated modules may need more complex style sheets that include sophisticated semantic rules.

Although Chapter 8 reveals that XSL style sheets probably aren't necessary for most XHTML 1.0 applications, they may become more and more common as new XHTML modules introduce XML vocabularies into what were once HTML documents. XSL style sheets may function on the client to convert these XHTML modules into the HTML that is more easily manipulated in older browsers. In newer browsers that have an understanding of Scalable Vector Graphics (SVG), XSLT may convert XHTML document content into graphs, charts, or pictures — perhaps even using SVG's capabilities to present the entire document layout.

The Document Object Model (DOM) provides similar capabilities and more flexible programmability. The same capabilities that the DOM provides for HTML and XML processing are available for XHTML, without need for modification. (XHTML is just HTML and XML after all!) A client application using an XHTML 1.1 module might just be an HTML and JavaScript wrapper with some extra XML content that gets processed by the script at the whim of the user. These kinds of applications are extremely useful for prototyping, and are sometimes robust enough to be useful in the longer term as well.

Building your own client from scratch requires a lot more investment, as toolkits for doing so aren't readily available. Java applets, ActiveX controls, and browser plug-ins present lightweight solutions that provide a lot of custom code without the need for a large framework. However, building new applications that implement the XHTML vocabulary can be very difficult — even with the structural ambiguities of older HTML removed. In some cases, such as the wireless applications discussed in Chapter 18, this may be the only viable strategy. In others, like those described in the next chapter, the amount of HTML vocabulary used may be small or isolated enough that the other XHTML modules deserve their own program — with the HTML vocabulary given a minimal amount of attention.

Chapter 17

XHTML Inside XML: Using XHTML in an XML Context

WHILE SUPPLEMENTING THE XHTML vocabulary with your own XML modules is a very useful approach for solving a lot of problems, there are also a lot of cases in which XHTML can provide a useful supplement to XML vocabularies. HTML is ubiquitous, well known, and supported by toolkits that make integrating it with some kinds of XML development easier. If XML documents need documentation, if they need a presentation vocabulary, or if they need to act as containers for Web documents, then putting XHTML in XML can be a relatively quick fix for a lot of problems.

Beyond the Browser and Within the Browser

XHTML 1.1 is still designed with an HTML-oriented browser in mind – after all, it's a product of the HTML Working Group at the W3C. Many of the design decisions for XHTML 1.1 – notably its use of the default namespace – make it difficult to use XHTML in something other than a dominant position within the document. Nonetheless, there are plenty of reasons for XML developers to use XHTML within their work. It's possible to make some accommodations with XHTML 1.1 in its current form to produce a workable set of tools.

When XML first appeared, some people considered it an opportunity to throw away the bloated and misused HTML vocabulary and start all over again. To some extent, you can do this using Cascading Style Sheets Level 2 to describe presentation (as described in Chapter 8). But that comes at a rather steep price, especially when features such as hyperlinking for XML still aren't complete. A more practical approach is a middle ground where you can bring the experience of years of HTML work to bear when appropriate. The HTML vocabulary can provide a useful set of basic formatting and linking tools, enabling XML developers who need a bit of human-readable markup in their documents to avoid the extra work of building their own structures and processing tool.

Even before XHTML's emergence, several projects took this approach. John Cowan's Itsy Bitsy Teeny Weeny Simple Hypertext DTD (IBTWSH — at `http://www.ccil.org/~cowan/XML/ibtwsh.dtd`) provided a subset of HTML elements presented as an XML DTD. Other XML DTDs then included IBTWSH by reference, and used its content where needed for basic document markup. IBTWSH also enabled its users to include XML content within its XML element type, making it possible for IBTWSH to both contain XML and be contained by an XML document.

Document Definition Markup Language (*DDML* — at `http://www.w3.org/TR/NOTE-ddml`), a simple schema vocabulary, uses IBTWSH for human-readable documentation of schema components. The DTD fragment includes IBTWSH and employs it for the content model of the DDML:Doc element:

```
<!ENTITY % ibtwsh SYSTEM
"http://www.ccil.org/~cowan/XML/ibtwsh.dtd">
%ibtwsh;
<!ELEMENT DDML:Doc %struct.model;>
<!ATTLIST DDML:Doc
  xmlns CDATA #FIXED ""><!--IBTWSH has no namespace-->
```

The `struct.model` entity is much like the `Block.mix` entity in XHTML; it enables schema designers to add comprehensive comments to their schemas, not just a few sentences.

Although DDML files aren't meant for presentation in a browser — they describe document structures, after all — the use of the HTML vocabulary makes it easy for schema creators to use a familiar vocabulary and familiar tools to describe the structures they create formally with the DDML schema vocabulary. Documentation creators can create transformations that turns the schema "inside out," building an HTML document describing the schema that uses the DDML:Doc elements as a foundation. Even without that extra step, developers may be able to open a DDML file in a browser and get a reasonable amount of information about the schema depending on how (and if) the schema creator uses the DDML:Doc element.

What HTML Has to Offer XML

HTML provides a well-known vocabulary for which an amazing amount of infrastructure is already available. Browsers, widely available for free, are only the most visible aspects of that infrastructure. HTML editors are commodity tools, available in a range of prices and sophistication. Components for viewing HTML in programs are available in environments from Windows (where you can "borrow" Internet Explorer's HTML rendering DLL) to Java (where the Swing library includes a set of components for viewing and editing HTML) to much smaller, text-only environments. HTML has been thoroughly poked, explored, and criticized, leading to the development of best practices that can support information access for the disabled and the integration of complex information structures from a wide variety of sources.

While HTML has its limits, and developers encounter those every day, XHTML seems to lead the path forward to using HTML vocabularies within XML documents, as well as using XML to enrich XML documents. You can work around XHTML's insistence on the default namespace, as you see in the next section. While many XML documents may be capable of getting along just fine without XHTML or the HTML vocabulary, the low cost of using HTML should make it an attractive option for many cases in which it can be useful.

As of this writing, the strengths of HTML are obvious. But the means of integrating that infrastructure with XML are not obvious. The current generation of HTML tools is designed to create HTML documents, not to create XML documents that may include some HTML. As a result, taking advantage of HTML within XML is difficult. However, this approach may be worth the trouble. At the same time, browsers remain very HTML-oriented, and no standard yet exists (XLink may come eventually) that lets XML do tasks that are very simple in HTML (such as the inclusion of images, scripts, and other components). So far, the browser vendors seem content to let XML documents access these facilities through the HTML vocabulary.

Applications for XHTML Islands

While Microsoft is pushing *XML data islands* within HTML documents, let's explore how *XHTML document islands* can fit into an XML framework. We examine both XHTML 1.1-conformant approaches and the more informal set of rules supported by the early XML-aware browsers, trying to find a consistent means of using HTML vocabulary within XML documents that can work over the long run.

 Within this section, you explore the implications of using the XHTML vocabulary within XML documents, not its impact on XML DTDs. The next section discusses the DTD issues for various types of XML development.

Images, scripts, and forms in browsers

HTML provides a rich set of functionality that the XML specifications don't support yet. While any XML document can contain markup describing images, scripts, and forms, there are no standardized tools for notifying applications that this markup should be treated as images, scripts, or forms. Things that seem extremely easy in HTML can be very difficult in XML simply because applications arrive with very few assumptions about XML content. Cascading style sheets, originally built on top of HTML, didn't address these issues because HTML already did. As a result, there's no easy way to include such content in XML documents for display in today's Web browsers — unless you fall back on an HTML vocabulary.

Namespaces ride to the rescue here (although with a few hitches). They enable XML document creators to identify some elements and their attributes as HTML.

Those elements must use the HTML vocabulary — you can't rename an img element type image or picture — but this approach can solve some problems for XML developers targeting Web browsers. At present, the Web browsers (Netscape 6 preview release, Opera 4 beta, and Internet Explorer 5.x) use a namespace-based HTML 4.0 to identify HTML information within an XML document, *not* the namespaces defined in XHTML 1.0. The URI in use is:

```
http://www.w3.org/TR/REC-html40
```

In most of the browsers, you can assign this URI to the default namespace or to a different prefix (typically html or xhtml). However, Microsoft Internet Explorer supports the exclusive use of html as the prefix (and regards all elements prefixed with html as HTML vocabulary even if they are assigned a different namespace).

 TIP For more detailed information on using XML and CSS to create documents for Web browser presentation, see my series of articles at XML.com: http://www.xml.com/pub/au/St._Laurent_Simon.

Let's start with a simple example that you can use for either browser display or machine-to-machine communication that provides some basic information about a book. It uses the HTML img element type to bring in a picture, a for a link, and h1 for a headline:

```
<?xml version="1.0"?>
<?xml-stylesheet type="text/css" href="bookstest.css"?>
<catalog xmlns:html="http://www.w3.org/TR/REC-html40" >
<html:h1>An XML Introduction</html:h1>
<book><cover>
<html:a
href="http://www.amazon.com/exec/obidos/ISBN=076453310X"><html:img
src="http://images.amazon.com/images/P/076453310X.01.MZZZZZZZ.gif"
/></html:a></cover>
<author>Simon St.Laurent</author>
<title> <html:a
href="http://www.amazon.com/exec/obidos/ISBN=076453310X/">XML: A
Primer, 2nd Ed.</html:a></title>
<pubyear>1999</pubyear>
<publisher>IDG Books</publisher>
<isbn>0-7645-3310-X</isbn>
<price>$19.99</price>
</book>
</catalog>
```

You can display this XML document (which has no DTD whatsoever) very easily using the minimalist style sheet shown here:

```
catalog {display:block; }
book {display:block; padding:5px; }
book *{display:block;}
```

You can display the document in Internet Explorer 5.5, Netscape Navigator 6, and Opera 4 (as shown in Figures 17-1 through 17-3). The links and image work across all three browsers.

Figure 17-1: Internet Explorer 5.5 uses the html prefix to determine that the links and image should be interpreted and displayed as pictures and hypertext links.

Figure 17-2: Netscape Navigator 6 uses the namespace URI to determine that the links and image should be interpreted and displayed as pictures and hypertext links.

An XML Introduction

Simon St.Laurent
XML: A Primer. 2nd Ed.
1999
IDG Books
0-7645-3310-X
$19.99

Figure 17–3: Opera 4 uses the namespace URI to determine that the links and image should be interpreted and displayed as pictures and hypertext links.

The current release of Internet Explorer 5.0 for the Macintosh displays the link, but doesn't make it active. (The images work fine.)

The browsers can render the XML portions of the document using the rules provided in the style sheet, and they can render the HTML portion using their built-in understanding of what the HTML vocabulary does. This isn't exactly XHTML — the namespace (and use of the prefix) is different, there is no DOCTYPE declaration, and no modules are included — but it's the likely path toward XHTML within browsers.

Unless XHTML modularization changes to permit namespaces other than the default namespace to represent XHTML, the preceding example will never be valid XHTML. Making it valid requires the creation of a different namespace for the XML and a declaration making the XHTML namespace the default namespace. That will break Internet Explorer's current HTML-in-XML support, which depends on the html: prefix.

Documentation for Human Consumption

DDML provided one demonstration of how you can use an HTML vocabulary to add human-readable information to an XML document, but the need for such notation often goes well beyond the rather formal situation of standards and schema creation. Although XML provides a mechanism for adding notes, which are intended to allow human-readable information in XML documents that will be ignored by the application (comments), the limits of that mechanism give HTML another good area for enriching XML work.

Comments (the ubiquitous <!-- and -->) are very useful in some situations, but they have some distinct disadvantages. Comments may or may not be transmitted to the application from the XML parsing process, and many XML applications will disregard their contents even if they receive the information. XML parsers treat the information stored within comments as plain text and HTML browsers typically ignore it even if it happens to contain HTML.

Developers who want or need to include human-readable documentation within their document structures (as opposed to floating in comments) need to create places where document authors can generate sophisticated human-readable information. While you can create your own format for doing this (or use an XML format such as DocBook), XHTML provides a well known and well supported vocabulary for doing such work. You might need to modify XHTML, as described in the previous chapter, to support the use of your own custom markup within the XHTML. However, XHTML can provide a simple framework for doing such work.

For example, an invoice meant for mostly automated processing might include a Comments section. Rather than develop a formal vocabulary for a relatively freeform area, let users include XHTML in this area. That enables them to handle some critical possibilities such as:

♦ Adding extra emphasis to an order that absolutely must be delivered overnight

♦ Providing tables, charts, and diagrams explaining what the contents of the order will be used for (for cases in which technical assistance may be necessary)

♦ Extra pleading to send the shipment even though the last three payments didn't clear

♦ Requests for extra discounts

♦ Thanks for previous excellent service

Some of these may seem frivolous, but all of them represent exceptional circumstances that happen fairly frequently in the real world. None of them are easily captured by the formal structures most document designers use to capture the "core" information on an invoice, such as shipping addresses and mechanisms, billing information, and the requested materials. Automated ordering systems are similarly poor at handling this kind of information. On the other hand, these are all circumstances that happen on a fairly regular basis when paper forms are used – people are very good at scribbling such things in the margins or on the invoice, expecting other people to read and act on them.

Because the information is really meant to represent human-to-human contact, it's a very good candidate for XHTML. XHTML provides the structures people need to communicate this kind of information, supplying tables, pictures, and emphasis. Programs meant to support human creation of these forms can use an XHTML editor component to write the XHTML, while the recipient end can show the comment contents on paper or onscreen using HTML or XHTML browser components. While some of it may be machine-interpreted, much of it probably represents situations that demand some level of human intervention.

Document containers

XML can be very useful as a container format, enabling developers to package and distribute sets of information. In this case, XHTML provides a format for the "real" content of the documents — its XML structures allow it to get through the XML processing infrastructure and be a part of the package; but its HTML vocabulary is only relevant to its final recipient, not to processing along the way. Document sets can be assembled as a single, large XML document, complete with headers describing the set and the individual documents they contain. You can use this for simple projects like snapshots of Web sites, or more complex projects like selling and trading documents among sites.

 The use of binary formats for images and other Web site content does limit the usefulness of this technique to some extent, but it may be appropriate for situations in which the text is central or graphics are represented using textual formats such as Scalable Vector Graphics (SVG).

The container document can use a prefix for its own elements and leave the default namespace undeclared, letting all of the contained documents declare it for themselves. This provides maximum flexibility while making clear the distinction between the XML elements that are part of the container and the (XHTML or other) documents being contained. For example, a simple container might look like this:

```
<?xml version="1.0"?>
<docpac:documents
xmlns:docpac="http://www.simonstl.com/xhtml/code/chap17/docpac">
<docpac:info>
<docpac:docsetname>Discarded Files</docpac:docsetname>
<docpac:owner>Simon St.Laurent</docpac:owner>
</docpac:info>
<docpac:document>
<docpac:author>Simon St.Laurent</docpac:author>
<docpac:name>Revolutionary Traditions</docpac:name>
<docpac:daterevised>04202000</docpac:daterevised>
<docpac:content>
<html xmlns="http://www.w3.org/1999/xhtml" lang="en-US"
```

```
xml:lang="en-US">
document content
</html>
</docpac:content>
</docpac:document>
<docpac:document>
<docpac:author>Spring the Friendly Dog</docpac:author>
<docpac:name>Kibble Revisited</docpac:name>
<docpac:daterevised>04202000</docpac:daterevised>
<docpac:content>
<html xmlns="http://www.w3.org/1999/xhtml" lang="en-US"
xml:lang="en-US">
document content
</html>
</docpac:content>
</docpac:document>
<docpac:document>
<docpac:author>Simon St.Laurent</docpac:author>
<docpac:name>Traditional Revolutions</docpac:name>
<docpac:daterevised>04202000</docpac:daterevised>
<docpac:content>
<html xmlns="http://www.w3.org/1999/xhtml" lang="en-US"
xml:lang="en-US">
document content
</html>
</docpac:content>
</docpac:document>
</docpac:documents>
```

Commercial document packaging systems provide more sophisticated metadata and content management, but the basic structure likely is similar.

One sizable problem arises with this approach, however. DOCTYPE declarations can only appear at the top of an XML document, not in the middle, so you can't transmit fully conforming XHTML documents this way. A lightweight transformation that converts the DOCTYPE declaration into elements and then back to a DOCTYPE declaration might be capable of fixing this, but for now it's a complicating factor.

TIP

XML Schemas don't use DOCTYPE declarations. When they appear, Schemas may be a way around this issue because XHTML documents that are fully conformant to the set of XML Schema modules may not have to use DOCTYPE declarations. The XHTML specification may require them, however — it's too early to know.

Inline and mixed-up markup

Sometimes you may want to mix the HTML vocabulary with your own vocabulary at a very low level. A number of XML DTDs include the ubiquitous b and i element types for bold and italic; more use of HTML vocabulary types may make sense in your own markup. While this does not produce documents intended for a Web browser necessarily (unless you produce style sheets that make your XML readily presentable), it can make it easier to create document types without reinventing the wheel entirely.

You can use HTML element names in your own XML without creating any (official) conflict with XHTML, provided that you don't use an HTML or XHTML namespace to identify your elements. While your document structures may look like familiar XHTML to you, applications identify the information as belonging to your vocabulary rather than the XHTML vocabulary and rely on style sheets that you create for formatting or processing. There are some limits to this – as previously noted, images and scripts are especially difficult to process without using the functionality that browsers support for HTML. Still, if you only need to include a small fragment of familiar markup, this may be an appropriate route.

If you want to stick to identifying XHTML as XHTML, you can – although you probably need to use namespace prefixes (and the default namespace, no prefix) to distinguish between your own vocabulary and the XHTML vocabulary. While it might seem obvious to you (or to document authors), it isn't so obvious to the programs processing your documents.

Is Formal XHTML Module Inclusion Worth the Trouble?

The W3C has put forth a number of specifications that offer different approaches to mixing XML and XHTML, and the browser vendors (as previously noted) have focused on only one of those approaches – using namespaces to separate XML from HTML vocabulary. This approach doesn't require any DOCTYPE magic, nor do you have to create and manipulate parameterized XHTML DTDs. At the same time, however, you definitely lose something by skipping out on the DTD creation process described in the last chapter.

 As of this writing, none of the available browsers actually support the XHTML namespace (http://www.w3.org/1999/xhtml) as an identifier for HTML vocabularies. Using the namespace they do support (http://www.w3.org/TR/REC-html40) means that your documents don't conform to even the namespace end of XHTML, despite conforming otherwise. While it may be useful as a stopgap measure, be prepared for a massive search and replace when (and if) XHTML becomes the standard.

XML 1.0 made a deliberate point of not requiring a DTD or even a DOCTYPE declaration for documents – although this lack of a DTD bars these documents from being used with a certain class of parsers, called *validating parsers*. Most browsers use non-validating parsers for processing XML and HTML. (Microsoft's built-in parser can be told to validate, but it doesn't normally validate when loading documents for display.) As a result, these tools don't check documents for conformance to an XHTML DTD. They also don't check the modules you create in addition to the XHTML DTD.

However, many other kinds of processors may check your documents against the DTD your documents specify, and they may reject documents that don't specify a DTD for such examination. If your documents have to deal with such parsers – which is likely if you exchange business information within your documents – the extra work of building XHTML DTD modules is worth the cost. (You need to create a DTD for your extensions anyway.) The modular and parameterized approach taken by XHTML 1.1 can help you manage and eventually extend the vocabulary and structures you create.

Even if you don't know in advance that your documents will be subject to such inspection, you may find it useful to build an XHTML DTD module that provides a formal description of what you're doing. To a certain extent, it's a documentation process that codifies the work you do, while making it easier to share with others. This module also provides insurance against a future in which your documents may have to be fed into validating XML parsers, avoiding a major crunch. By creating constraints early, you can avoid producing a monstrous number of variations on your structures and make them more manageable. Having a DTD enables you to use a wider set of tools, as valid documents that conform to a specified DTD can be parsed by both validating and non-validating parsers and used in the applications built on those parsers.

While it may not be necessary in every case to build a formal description of what your extensions to XHTML are and how they integrate with the XHTML vocabulary, you definitely should consider the process as your documents move from prototypes and experiments to full-scale production. It's more than insurance against a changing future – it's an opportunity to learn about how you structure information and how to make necessary corrections early.

Part V

XHTML and XML Futures

CHAPTER 18
A Case Study: WAP and the Wireless
Markup Language

CHAPTER 19A
A Case Study: Mozquito Factory and FML

CHAPTER 20
XML and the Next Generation of the Web

Chapter 18

A Case Study: WAP and the Wireless Markup Language

As THE WEB HAS BECOME more ubiquitous, developers have started looking at other devices to use for Web access. In the last few years, handheld and wireless devices such as pagers, cell phones, and PDAs have become an integral part of our technological society. It makes perfect sense then, to Web-enable these devices. That's where WAP comes in.

The Wireless Application Protocol (WAP) started out as a proposal to the W3C — called the *Handheld Device Markup Language (HDML)* — in May of 1997 by a company named Unwired Planet. Almost a month later, HDML was subsumed by the Wireless Application Protocol which drew from elements of both HDML and the Handheld Device Transport Protocol (HDTP) — creations of Unwired Planet. The group of companies working with the newly proposed WAP (including Ericsson, Motorola, and Nokia, alongside Phone.com [formerly Unwired Planet]), felt it should be telephony-based and so they created the WAP Forum. The elusive HDML reappeared in WAP as the Wireless Markup Language (WML), which is what I primarily discuss in this chapter.

 WML seems to be an interim approach that will be replaced in the longer term by some form of integration with XHTML, as discussed at the end of this chapter. WML remains important as an HTML-like XML vocabulary, and probably will be one of the more common transformation targets as XHTML information from the Web gets converted into WML for final delivery to a cell phone. Interim approaches do have a way of sticking around.

Choosing Your Emulator

Before you get started in programming an example WML document, you need to find something to enable you to see what it looks like. There are several WAP emulators out there, but it's important to make sure you choose the right one.

WAP emulators

♦ **Gelon.Net's Wapalizer** (`http://gelon.net/`). This is the easiest of the three emulators on this list to use. All you have to do is reference a URL to your WML file in the input box and click "Wapalize." Unfortunately, the current version has issues — including problems with card titles beyond the first card, and difficulties parsing variables (see Figure 18-1).

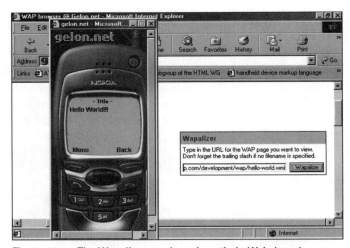

Figure 18-1: The Wapalizer emulator is entirely Web-based.

♦ **Ericsson R380 WAP emulator** (`http://www.symbian.com/epoc/r380wapemulator.html`). This emulator is an 8MB download and requires a Java Runtime Environment in order to run. It has many complex features and is difficult to configure. It tells you when your WML files aren't valid, but it doesn't give any assistance beyond that (see Figure 18-2).

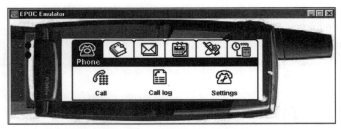

Figure 18-2: The Ericsson emulator is quite confusing and more complex than what you need here.

◆ **Nokia WAP Emulator** — part of the Nokia WAP Toolkit (http://www.forum.nokia.com/). If you haven't guessed, this is my emulator of choice. It's large — a 10MB download — and not only does it have a fully functioning WAP browser, it features a WML Validator and a WBMP converter. This is an all-in-one package that enables you to bypass multiple programs (see Figure 18-3).

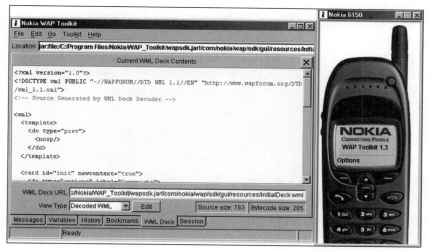

Figure 18-3: The Nokia WAP Toolkit is the best package for working on this chapter.

Downloading the Nokia WAP Toolkit

To download the Nokia WAP Toolkit (version 1.3 beta or higher), go to the Nokia Forum page (http://www.forum.nokia.com). Click WAP Developers and choose the Registration Form option. Sign up for forum access and select Nokia WAP Developer Forum. Follow the links for the Nokia WAP Toolkit and download it. If you need a Java Runtime Environment, install that as well.

Feel free to use the Wapalizer for your WML examples if you're concerned about the size of the Nokia download or having to sign up for the developer forum. Just remember that as of this writing, there are several problems with the Wapalizer.

Adding MIME Types to Your Web Server

In order for me to be able to "host" WAP-related documents, I have to modify the file on my server that tells the Web server that it is allowed to serve the WAP files as they were intended instead of unrecognizable text files. You will need to do the same to view WAP-related documents. You need to find a file called `mime.types` on your server and add the following lines:

Content	MIME Type	Extension
WML source	`text/vnd.wap.wml`	`wml`
Compiled WML	`application/vnd.wap.wmlc`	`wmlc`
WMLScript	`sourcetext/vnd.wap.wmlscript`	`wmls`
Compiled WMLScript	`application/vnd.wap.wmlscriptc`	`wmlsc`
Wireless bitmap	`image/vnd.wap.wbmp`	`wbmp`

Then save your file and, if you need to, restart your server.

Using the Nokia WAP Toolkit

When you first open up the toolkit, you see two pop-up windows. The first is the editor/compiler window and the second is the WAP browser emulator (see Figure 18-3). The editor/compiler window has six tabs, which enable you to perform the following tasks:

WML Deck   The default tab. This is where you edit, validate, and compile your WML documents. To make these modifications, click Edit to bring up the Editor1 window. To create additional documents, select File → New.

Messages   Contains a pull-down menu of six options where you can find a history of compile errors and warnings.

Variables   Adds, sets, modifies, and manages variables for WML documents.

History   Provides you with a running total of everything the browser emulator does.

Bookmarks   Contains links to your "most used" WML documents.

Session   Tells you what has gone through the browser emulator in its current session.

Before you get started, go to your Bookmark tab and add the bookmarks listed in Table 18-1 (see Figure 18-4). These are links to the examples you use throughout this chapter.

TABLE 18-1 EXAMPLE BOOKMARKS

Name	Location
Hello World	Http://www.zotgroup.com/development/wap/hello-world.wml
Multiple Card Interaction	Http://www.zotgroup.com/development/wap/two-cards.wml
Timed Automation	Http://www.zotgroup.com/development/wap/timer.wml
Inputting Form Data	Http://www.zotgroup.com/development/wap/form-input.wml
Submitting a Form	Http://www.zotgroup.com/development/wap/form-submit.wml
Inserting an Image	Http://www.zotgroup.com/development/wap/image.wml
Image Conversion	Http://www.zotgroup.com/development/wap/window.wml

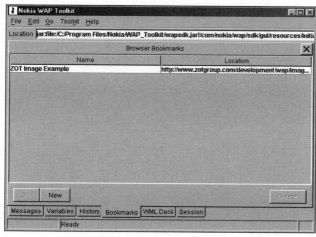

Figure 18-4: Enter your bookmarks into this window so you can reference them as you practice the examples.

A bookmark isn't considered added until you exit each cell. After you type in your location URL, tab back to the Name cell to complete the addition.

Authoring a WML Document

To start your first WML document, click File → New → WML Deck. The document that opens along with the window is the basic template for any WML document. The first two elements are the XML and DOCTYPE declarations. A valid WML document is a valid XML document. Therefore, both the XML and DOCTYPE declarations are required for any WML document. This section of your WML document is known as the *prolog* and it is considered an error to omit this section from your document:

```
<?xml version="1.0"?>
<!DOCTYPE wml PUBLIC "-//WAPFORUM//DTD WML 1.1//EN"
"http://www.wapforum.org/DTD/wml_1.1.xml">
```

A deck of cards

The structure of your WML document revolves around a "deck of cards" analogy. Each singular WML document is a deck, and each card within that deck contains the document's content and navigation information. Think of a card as a DHTML layer or, if you ever used Apple's HyperCard, think of it as a card in a HyperCard stack. What layer is displayed at any given time depends on where the user chooses to click. The next element after the prolog is the <wml> element. This tag defines a WML "deck" and encloses all the "cards" contained within the document.

A card is specified using the <card> element. Each card has an id and title attribute. While the id is mostly for internal document use, the title attribute value shows up almost like the HTML <title> element.

Hello World

The first program everyone learns when delving into any new computer-based language is Hello World. WML should be no different. You may have noticed that the Nokia template does this for you:

```
<?xml version="1.0"?>
<!DOCTYPE wml PUBLIC "-//WAPFORUM//DTD WML 1.1//EN"
"http://www.wapforum.org/DTD/wml_1.1.xml">
```

```
<wml>

    <card id="card1" title="Title">
        <p>
            <!-- Write your card implementation here. -->
            Hello World!!!
        </p>
    </card>

</wml>
```

You now have your first WML document sitting right in front of you. Click Compile to make sure it works; it then prompts you to save it. Choose a directory in which to place all of your future WML documents and name this one `hello-world.wml`. Then click Show to view it in the Nokia Browser Emulator included in the Nokia WAP Toolkit. (see Figure 18-5).

Figure 18-5: This is your first WML
document. Hello World!!!

To see what happens when your document does not compile correctly, remove the `<wml>` element and click Compile. The error tells you the name of the document with the error, the problem, and the line and column number where the error is located (see Figure 18-6).

Figure 18-6: If you see an error like this, then your
document most likely is not valid.

Notice that in your first document, you have a `<p>` element. This, like in HTML 4.01, designates a paragraph. Every card is required to have at least one paragraph.

Navigation

One of the primary features of the Web is to enable users to navigate through different pages utilizing links. To get to a new page, you click the link. WML employs links to get from card to card. But instead of using the non-specific <a> element, it uses <do> and <go>. These elements give a little more context than their HTML counterpart.

```
<card id="mycard" title="Welcome to my World">
<do type="accept" label="Forward">
<go href="#mycard2"/>
</do>
<p>
Click "forward" to go to the next card.
</p>
</card>
```

The <do> element tells the browser to "do" whatever actions are specified within it. In this case, it says to "go" to the hypertext reference of mycard2 due to the value of the <go> element. The browser screen shows the title of the <do> element and says to Click forward to go to the next card.

Add it all together and here's what your WML document looks like:

```
<?xml version="1.0"?>
    <!DOCTYPE wml PUBLIC "-//WAPFORUM//DTD WML 1.1//EN"
"http://www.wapforum.org/DTD/wml_1.1.xml">
    <wml>
    <card id="mycard" title="My World">
    <do type="accept" label="Forward">
    <go href="#mycard2"/>
    </do>
    <p>
    Click "forward" to go to the next card.
    </p>
    </card>
    <card id="mycard2" title="Card 2">
    <p>
    Welcome to Card number 2.
    </p>
    </card>
    </wml>
```

Do a File → Save As and save your document with the name **two-cards.wml**. Compile and view it in the browser. On your browser, click the button just under Options to see where the label attribute value Forward shows up (refer to

Figure 18-7). Make sure it's highlighted and click the same button again to complete the <do> element. You now should be at Card 2 (see Figure 18-8).

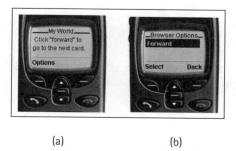

(a)   (b)

Figure 18-7: Card 1 contains (a) navigation information.
Choose (b) Forward to move to the next card.

Figure 18-8: Card 2 is the result of navigating from Card 1.

The <do> element has other types besides accept. You can also use help to get some assistance on what you're doing, reset to reset all values, options to give you a set of possible options to choose from, and prev to navigate in reverse.

actually has a few different attributes and values. You've already used href, which can refer to a card within the current deck or a URL that points to a different deck altogether. You can actually specify whether or not you want the user's browser to send an HREF referrer URL to the server specified in the href attribute by using the sendreferrer attribute and setting it to TRUE. If you deal with forms (discussed later in this chapter), you can specify Get or Post as the value for the method attribute that deals with the corresponding href attribute.

Time-based automation

If a developer wants to have a *splash page* that automatically forwards the user to the main Web page of a site, he or she uses the HTML 4.01 <meta> element with an http-equiv value of refresh. In addition, the developer use a content value that contains the amount of seconds to wait before it forwards the browser to a URL, which is also designated in the content value.

You can still use this method in WML, but the editors of the specification have created the <timer> element to allow timed automation between each card in a deck.

```
<card id="mycard" ontimer="#mycard2" title="My World">
<timer value="150" />
```

The preceding code says that after the amount of time specified in the <timer> element (15 seconds entered in tenths), the browser should forward from the current screen to the card whose id value is specified in the ontimer intrinsic event.

Let's see how it works:

```
<?xml version="1.0"?>
    <!DOCTYPE wml PUBLIC "-//WAPFORUM//DTD WML 1.1//EN"
"http://www.wapforum.org/DTD/wml_1.1.xml">
    <wml>
    <card id="mycard" ontimer="#mycard2" title="My World">
    <timer value="150" />
    <p>
    In 15 seconds, we will automatically forward you to our main
page or
        <a href="#mycard2"> go to it yourself</a> if you don't want
to wait

    </p>
    </card>
    <card id="mycard2" title="Welcome to my World">
     <p>
    Welcome to the main page of "My World."
    </p>
    </card>
    </wml>
```

Notice that you also add an <a> element. This is exactly like the <a> element used in HTML 4.01 to create a link within a Web page.

Save this document as **timer.wml**, then compile and view it in your browser (see Figure 18-9). You can wait the 15 seconds or notice that between the two top buttons on the left and right there is a set of two arrows – one pointing up and one down. Use the down arrow to scroll toward the bottom of the text and find the highlighted link. Once again, click the button under Options and choose Follow Link. You should be at Card 2 now!

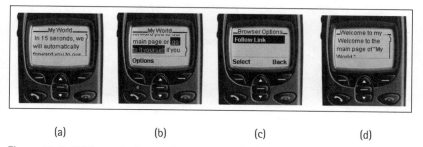

(a)   (b)   (c)   (d)

Figure 18-9: With any luck, your browser automatically should forward from Card 1 (a) to Card 2 (d) in 15 seconds. If you don't have the patience, feel free to (b) find the link and (c) follow it yourself.

User input and forms

Everything you've seen so far with WML is basic, run-of-the-mill Web stuff — not the interactivity that phone companies keep claiming in flamboyant commercials.

Let's now try to solicit some information from a user. Use of user input WML forms definitely increases the capability for wireless navigators to make choices rather than deal with the content that is thrust at them.

Let's start with a simple, text-based input box. This element is based on its HTML 4.01 counterpart:

```
First Name:<br />
<input type="text" name="firstname" /><br />
Last Name:<br />
<input type="text" name="lastname" />
```

To insert the values of the input elements into a future card, you use $(first-name) and $(lastname).

```
Welcome $(firstname) $(lastname). Please click Back to return to the
previous page.
```

With the addition of a few more elements — including <do>, <go />, and <prev /> — you have a fully interactive experience:

```
<?xml version="1.0"?>
    <!DOCTYPE wml PUBLIC "-//WAPFORUM//DTD WML 1.1//EN"
"http://www.wapforum.org/DTD/wml_1.1.xml">
    <wml>    <card id="mycard" title="Welcome to my World">
```

```
<do type="accept" label="Forward">
<go href="#mycard2"/>
</do>
<p>
First Name:<br />
<input type="text" name="firstname" /><br />
Last Name:<br />
<input type="text" name="lastname" />
</p>
</card>
<card id="mycard2" title="My World">
<do type="prev" label="Back">
<prev />
</do>
<p>
Welcome, $(firstname) $(lastname). Please click "Back" to
return to the previous page.
</p>
</card>
</wml>
```

Save this file as **form-input.wml**, compile it, and send it to your browser (see Figure 18-10).

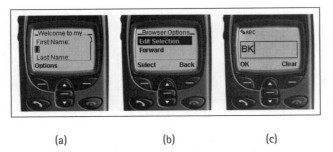

(a)   (b)   (c)

Figure 18-10: Input your information into the (a) form fields by using the (b) Edit Selection feature via the (c) text input box.

When you first load this file, you should see two input boxes. One is labeled First Name and the other Last Name (Figure 18-11). To fill them both out, click the Options button and choose Edit Selection. An edit field appears where you can type your name. Notice that the Options button currently is marked OK. Click it and do the same with the next field.

     (a)   (b)

Figure 18-11: To move from the (a) form fields, select Forward from the menu to (b) see your results.

After clicking OK the second time, select the Options button again and choose Forward. Now you should see a card titled "My World" that says, "Welcome, first-name lastname. Please click 'Back' to return to the previous page."

This time you also add the <prev /> element, which creates a function for you to return to the previous page by clicking the button marked Back.

Submitting a form

Now that you've determined how to input data into form fields, you must figure out how to get it to your server for processing. The easiest way to do this is by introducing a new element called <postfield>. Also modify your go so it's set up to post to a CGI script.

```
<?xml version="1.0"?>
    <!DOCTYPE wml PUBLIC "-//WAPFORUM//DTD WML 1.1//EN"
"http://www.wapforum.org/DTD/wml_1.1.xml">
    <wml>
    <card id="mycard" title="Welcome to my World"> <do
type="accept" label="Forward">
        <go method="post" href="www.example.com/form.pl">
    <postfield name="name" value="$(firstname)"/>
    <postfield name="age" value="20"/>
    </go>
    </do>
    <p>
    First Name:<br />
<input type="text" name="firstname" /><br />
Last Name:<br />
<input type="text" name="lastname" />
    </p>
    </card>
    </wml>
```

There's no easy way to show you the results. If you have the ability to create an echo CGI script that shows you the values submitted in WML, then go ahead and give it a try. Otherwise, this WML document looks exactly like **form-input.wml**.

Images in WML

Adding images to your WML is no different from doing it in HTML 4.01, with the exception that the files are in a different format. Instead of using JPG, GIF, or PNG, you use a WAP-only format of WBMP or WAP Bitmap. (See the following section, "Creating WBMP images.")

```
<img src="http://www.zotgroup.com/development/wap/images/sunny.wbmp"
alt="The Sun" />
```

Create a new card and input this line:

```
<?xml version="1.0"?>
    <!DOCTYPE wml PUBLIC "-//WAPFORUM//DTD WML 1.1//EN"
"http://www.wapforum.org/DTD/wml_1.1.xml">
    <wml>
    <card id="mycard" title="My World">
       <p>
        <img src="http://www.zotgroup.com/development/wap/images/
sunny.wbmp" alt="The Sun" /> is sunny.</p> <p align="center"> How
about yours?
       </p>
    </card>
    </wml>
```

Save it as **image.wml**, compile it, and show it in your browser (Figure 18-12)

Figure 18-12: It's a sun-shiny day in "My World."

Along with the `alt` attribute, you also can use `height` and `width` attributes. Keep in mind the sizes of the device screens (for example, the Nokia 7110 is 48×96 pixels).

Creating WBMP images

Currently, the only image format supported in WAP is the proprietary *WBMP* or *WAP Bitmap.* These images must be small in both file size and height/width and be black and white. The best way to create a WBMP is to open up a GIF or JPG file in your favorite graphics program, make sure the pixel size corresponds with that of the traditional WAP device screen, and save it. Then open it up in the Nokia WAP Toolkit — there is an option to open "Images for import to WBMP (`.gif`, `.jpg`), which strips out the colors. Finally, save it as a WBMP. Let's look at an example of this process.

Grab the GIF at `http://www.zotgroup.com/development/wap/images/window.gif`. Open it in your graphics program; make sure the pixel size is at least 49×42 and it's non-interlaced when you resave it. Open it up in the Nokia WAP Toolkit and resave it as a WBMP. Now add it to the following code. (I include a link to an example so you can see what it should look like.)

```
<?xml version="1.0"?>
    <!DOCTYPE wml PUBLIC "-//WAPFORUM//DTD WML 1.1//EN" "http://
www.wapforum.org/DTD/wml_1.1.xml">
        <wml>
      <card id="mycard" title="WinLove">
       <p>
        <img src="http://www.zotgroup.com/development/wap/images/
window.wbmp" alt="Windows" />
       </p>
      </card>
     </wml>
```

You may have to play around with your GIF or JPG a bit so it displays in the browser correctly, but all in all it's not bad for such a tiny screen (see Figure 18-13).

Figure 18-13: Your first WBMP

Integrating WML and XHTML

On October 30, 1998 the WAP Forum, the creators of WML, and the W3C published a document detailing their intent to cooperate on future standards efforts. So far, the WAP Forum has contributed the following three Notes to the W3C:

- ◆ *Composite Capability/Preference Profiles (CC/PP): A User Side Framework for Content Negotiation* (http://www.w3.org/TR/NOTE-CCPP)

- ◆ *CC/PP Exchange Protocol Based on HTTP Extension Framework* (http://www.w3.org/TR/NOTE-CCPPexchange)

- ◆ *WAP Binary XML Content Format* (http://www.w3.org/TR/wbxml)

These documents are the first steps toward the eventual reconciliation and integration of the WAP/WML approach with the W3C/XHTML approach, and members of the WAP Forum have been active in various W3C activities (notably XHTML Basic). Bits and pieces of WAP documents are included in the *Modularization for XHTML* working draft as a "content negotiation" section, and they are included as references as well.

Although it isn't clear how smooth the project will be, or how long it will take these new developments to reach maturity within the cellular architectures that WAP currently dominates, this work may bring cellular technology to XHTML and vice versa. (A few of WAP's competitors already use vocabularies similar to XHTML Basic.) The integration of Internet Engineering Task Force (IETF) work on content negotiation may add yet a few more bumps to the mix.

Until such reconciliation takes place at the standards level, developers can take some comfort in using XHTML's cleaner structures to maintain an easier transformation path to WML documents. Standard XML tools, including the XSLT style sheets described in Chapter 12, can manage the relatively mild transition from XHTML to WML. This makes it easier to create one document and let programs create the derivatives.

Chapter 19

A Case Study: Mozquito Factory and FML

THE REALITY FOR WEB programmers today is that browser manufacturers have made it nearly impossible to develop highly interactive Web sites that also make use of the latest and greatest in Web technologies. For instance, in order to create a dynamic form that enables users to toggle between screens, edit pull-down menus, and calculate values on the fly, a programmer must first code the application using several JavaScript functions. Then that programmer has to go back through the program and debug it until it works on all DHTML-supporting versions of Netscape and Internet Explorer. Next, a second-round of tests must ensure the program runs on all Macintosh and Windows versions of both browsers. Once the application is complete, the programmer must create a backend CGI script that confirms the user has filled in all the mandatory data fields when the form is submitted.

This is not a pretty picture – especially for Web authors who haven't had time to learn basic JavaScript, let alone how to make sure what they produce doesn't shut out half their user base. This is where Mozquito.com's Mozquito Factory comes in. Developers can design and create dynamic forms using an extension of XHTML 1.0 called *Forms Markup Language (FML).*

The Mozquito Factory Approach

Sounds a little too simple doesn't it? You may wonder how an extension to a relatively new standard would work in existing browsers if none of them even correctly support XML or XHTML. When developing your page in the easy-to-use FML, simply clicking a button in Mozquito Factory converts the FML into DHTML that any browser supporting JavaScript 1.2 understands. In the meantime, this solution enables you to use a soon-to-be standard now and – once browsers have the full support necessary to handle this iteration of XHTML – you can use your FML documents as they are.

One of the issues with HTML forms is that they haven't been modified since HTML 2.0 was released in 1995. Everything done with forms since then has been the result of creative Web developers utilizing DHTML, JavaScript, PHP, and CGI scripts, among other tools. With Mozquito, working with forms using a markup language gets a kick-start. While it was created first, FML is in compliance with the W3C XForms standard currently under development. As XForms matures, so does Mozquito's handling of it. FML fulfills many of the current requirements for XForms, including those found in the W3C Working Draft, "XForms Requirements." When XForms reaches full-fledged standard status, FML 2.0 will be 100 percent compliant.

What I hope to cover in this chapter includes an introduction on how to use Mozquito Factory and an in-depth look at FML, including content validation, input reuse, on-the-fly calculation, and editable select lists. I do all this using an example of an online order form similar to what you might find on any e-commerce site today.

Using Mozquito Factory

Before you dive into FML and start making your first form, work on getting a grasp on Mozquito Factory and how to use its various features. This will be important later when you use it as your FML authoring tool.

When you think of Mozquito Factory, picture it as having three separate functions:

1. **The XHTML Validator.** As discussed in Chapter 5, XHTML (like XML) needs to be both well formed and valid. This portion of Mozquito Factory checks to make sure the markup you author is both. If not, it lets you know it.

2. **The Mozquito Engine.** This segment takes the XHTML-FML you author and converts it into an HTML document with a JavaScript application. Be sure to take a look at one of the HTML sources of the resulting document throughout the authoring process. It gives you a good idea of the amount of JavaScript you would have to learn in order to accomplish what the FML does.

3. **The Editor.** This is a simple Java-based application in which you type in your XHTML-FML and it brings the Validator and Engine together, enabling you to use all three functions.

Keep in mind that if you're more comfortable using your preferred HTML editor to author your HTML, convert it to XHTML, and add in your FML, then by all means take that route. You still need to use Mozquito to validate your XHTML-FML before you run the conversion process. Conceivably, Mozquito may show up in your favorite authoring tool in the form of a plug-in or bundled as a separate application. If you choose this route, you can open up the template discussed next in your own editor. It appears in the "templates" subdirectory in whatever directory Mozquito is installed. The file you want to open is **template1.xhtml**.

When to use Mozquito in your Web development

Don't use XHTML-FML for every page on your Web site. Its primary purpose is to add more interactivity to forms whether they are a simple feedback form, a questionnaire, a registration form for an event, or a standard "shopping cart" form. If you already use JavaScript in some of your projects, you may also discover (through the following example) that you can also substitute XHTML-FML for DHTML layers.

When Mozquito Factory converts the XHTML-FML to JavaScript, only users with certain browsers will be able to view your dynamic content. People using older browsers or with disabilities won't be able to make use of what you produce. With Web accessibility becoming more of an issue for Web developers, it will be important to tweak the resulting Mozquito HTML. Be sure to read the section at the end of this chapter on Web accessibility to find out how, within the same HTML file that your Mozquito-produced JavaScript is, you can create a duplicate version of your FML form in universally accessible HTML.

Downloading and installing Mozquito

Before you can actually use Mozquito Factory, you have to download and install it. Go to the Mozquito Web site at `http://www.mozquito.com`, click Download, and make sure you follow the instructions for the "30-day trial version." If you find out you like the Mozquito Factory authoring environment after working with the demo, you can always go back to the Web site and purchase it.

Because Mozquito Factory is Java-based software, you also need to download a *Java Runtime Environment (JRE)* or a software program that will allow you to run Java applications. For Windows 95, 98, 2000, and NT, a JRE is automatically downloaded as part of the Internet Explorer 5.0 browser package. However, the folks at Mozquito.com recommend using the JRE 1.1.7 or higher from either IBM (`http://www6.software.ibm.com/dl/dkw/dkre-p`) or Sun Microsystems (`http://java.sun.com/products/jdk/1.1/jre/download-jre-windows.html`).

To run Mozquito on a Macintosh system, you need to download and install the *MacOS Runtime for Java (MRJ)*. Be sure you get at least version 2.1.4 or newer to prevent any problems when running Mozquito. Your system should be running MRJ already. If it isn't, you can find a copy at Apple's Java Web site (`http://www.apple.com/java`).

Learning Forms Markup Language 1.0 (FML)

If you install both the JRE and Mozquito Factory correctly, you should see a Getting started window with six different steps that give a quick overview of Mozquito Factory and FML (see Figure 19-1).

Figure 19-1: Mozquito Factory's Getting started window

Feel free to explore this mini-tutorial if you want, although I cover everything in it step-by-step throughout this chapter. When you're ready to get started, click OK and continue reading the chapter.

Let's get to know a little bit about using Mozquito so you can get started on the example. Create your first "new" document by clicking the File menu and choosing New (or File → New). Notice you now have the choice of several documents including XHTML-FML and the three XHTML 1.0 DTDs: strict, transitional, and frameset (discussed in Chapter 7). In order to work with FML, you must choose the XHTML-FML selection for your first document. After you make your selection, the structure for a basic XHTML-FML document appears in the Mozquito Editor window.

Notice the DOCTYPE declaration contains information for an XHTML-FML 1.0 document as shown here:

```
<!DOCTYPE html PUBLIC "-//OVERFLOW//DTD XHTML-FML 1.0//EN"
"http://www.mozquito.org/dtd/xhtml-fml1.dtd">
```

In addition to the XHTML namespace, the HTML element contains a reference to the FML namespace:

```
xmlns:x="http://www.mozquito.org/xhtml-fml"
```

This means that the Forms Markup Language namespace is now available for use in the document using the prefix x: for each element.

Error-checking your XHTML-FML

Even though you barely have a shell of a document, you can still check for its well-formedness and validity. Look at the taskbar above your document. Included in the taskbar are two checkmark buttons that enable you to validate your document (refer to Figure 19-2). Click the left-hand checkmark to verify your well-formedness.

Figure 19-2: The checkmark on the left verifies a document's well-formedness, while the one on the right checks for validity.

To make sure your document is valid, click the right-hand checkmark. Provided you haven't changed anything in your document shell, everything should check out fine (see Figure 19-3).

Figure 19-3: Mozquito confirms your XHTML-FML file to be well formed and valid.

Mozquito documents must check out as both well formed and valid. To see what happens when things aren't correct, delete the </title> element and recheck your document. Notice that you get the "</title> element expected" error message (see Figure 19-4), which is certainly nice. It tells you the nature of the XHTML error; if you highlight it, it tells you where it expects the </title> element to be. This "showing you where the error is" function isn't 100 percent accurate, so don't worry if you get confused while trying to follow it. You're not crazy.

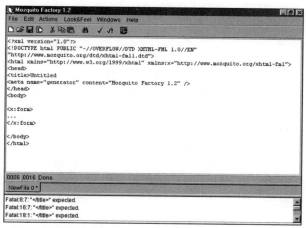

Figure 19-4: Mozquito Factory tells you when your document is not valid or well formed. Check for error messages in the status window in the bottom-half of your Mozquito document.

Don't forget to replace the `</title>` element before moving on to the next section.

Pushing your FML through to a browser

In its current state, pushing the FML shell through a browser results in a blank page in the browser window. In order to test the Mozquito "Display in Default Browser" function, you need to add in some XHTML:

```
<body>
<h1>My first test page for using FML in Mozquito Factory</h1>

<p>This is a test..a test of the Emergency XHTML Broadcast
system.<br />
        If this were a real emergency, your browser would explode and
chaos would ensue.</p>
<hr />
```

Now do a File → Save As and name your document **first-test.xhtml**. Then click the button in the taskbar that resembles half the Netscape Navigator logo fitted with half the MS Internet Explorer logo and wait (see Figure 19-5). Your XHTML-FML document should show up in whatever browser the default application is using for viewing HTML files. It should be set to one of the browsers mentioned in the Mozquito browser compatibility sidebar.

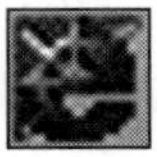

Figure 19-5: Clicking the Browser button pushes your FML document through to a browser for testing.

 Make sure your document is both well formed and valid before you push it through to the browser. Otherwise, Mozquito Factory adds an error message to your JavaScript that is the only thing to display when your document appears in the browser. If you want to have Mozquito double check this before any exporting of your XHTML-FML, you can set this in the Edit → Options window under the Settings tab. Make sure "Check validity on export" is checked before you click OK.

If at any point you'd rather not preview your XHTML-FML in a browser but would like to just convert it to the HTML file for later use, go to File → Export, name your file with an `.html` extension, and click Export.

Mozquito-Supported Browsers:

Mozquito.com currently claims that the JavaScript Mozquito Factory produces works in any browser that supports JavaScript 1.2. These include:

- **Windows 95/98/NT/2000**
  - MS Internet Explorer 4+
  - NS Navigator 4+
- **MacOS**
  - MS Internet Explorer 5+
  - NS Navigator 4+

According to Mozquito.com, other browsers may be able to display the Mozquito-produced JavaScript. MacIE 4.x has some difficulties due to the limitations of its DOM implementation. The Mozquito team is currently working on support for the Opera family of browsers.

You can also automatically validate and convert your XHTML-FML files without the Mozquito Factory Editor even running. When Mozquito Factory originally installs on Windows machines, it automatically associates itself with any `.xhtml` file on your system. Provided you haven't modified that association, double-clicking any `.xhtml` file pushes it through the Mozquito Engine, verifies its well-formedness and validity, converts it to HTML and JavaScript, displays it in your browser, and places a copy of the HTML file in the same directory as your XHTML-FML document.

NOTE Mozquito.com also has a server-side solution called *Chameleon* that does the validation and conversion process on the fly. If all you want to do in your authoring process is create XHTML-FML files, run Chameleon on your server instead of manually converting your documents every time you make a change.

The E-Commerce Order Form

Now that you've got a good handle on how to use the various basic features of Mozquito Factory, you learn how to harness the power of FML. Close your **first-test. xhtml** file and open up a new XHTML-FML document (as shown in Figure 19-6).

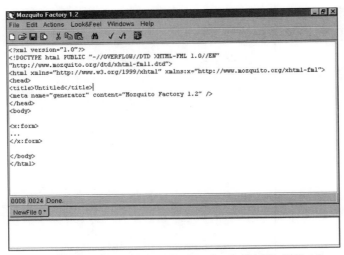

Figure 19-6: This is a standard template for an XHTML-FML 1.0
document.

Here's the code you should see:

```
<?xml version="1.0"?>
<!DOCTYPE html PUBLIC "-//OVERFLOW//DTD XHTML-FML 1.0//EN"
   "http://www.mozquito.org/dtd/xhtml-fml1.dtd">
<html xmlns="http://www.w3.org/1999/xhtml"
   xmlns:x="http://www.mozquito.org/xhtml-fml">
<head>
<title>Untitled</title>
<meta name="generator" content="Mozquito Factory 1.2" />
</head>
<body>
<x:form>
...
</x:form>
</body>
</html>
```

Remember from earlier in the chapter the discussion on the use of the FML DTD
in the DOCTYPE declaration and the FML namespace. Notice that your first FML element <x:form> makes use of this namespace.

This eventually becomes your order form with two parts. First, I guide you through the basics of FML by creating the contact information form. Then you move on to some of the more complex features of FML by authoring the shopping cart segment of the form.

A simple contact information form

The FML element you need to learn first (`<x:form>`) is already in place. Notice that the FML form container almost identically matches its HTML 4.01 counterpart, with the exception that it utilizes the FML namespace prefix. Also notice that most of the form components for FML are very similar to HTML 4.01, which enables you to learn this markup language quickly.

The next FML element you use is the text input box, or `<x:textinput>`. If you were doing this in HTML, it would read `<input type="text">`. As you go through this example and learn the basic FML elements, remember their HTML counterparts. You need them when you get to the section about Web accessibility.

Now let's give it an ID of `name`. This labels the text-input box; if it gets called by other parts of the form, it knows which text box the form wants.

```
<x:form>
Name:
<x:textinput id="name" /><br />
</x:form>
```

Save this file as **contact-orderform.xhtml** and then click the Push to browser button. Your screen should resemble that shown in Figure 19-7.

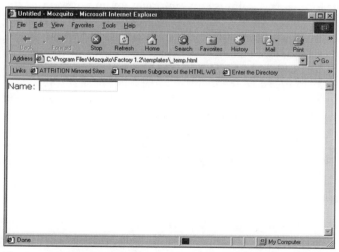

Figure 19-7: This is what your `<x:textinput>` element should look like in a browser.

You will have several different iterations of this form, so you may want to split it into separate files and bring them together at the end. One file will contain the contact information and the other will have the catalog.

Let's add the `size` attribute with a value of 30. As in HTML, the `size` attribute determines the approximate size of the input box. Next, let's add a second `<x:textinput>` element with an ID of `email`.

```
<x:form>
Name:
<x:textinput id="name" size="30" /><br />
E-Mail:
<x:textinput id="email" size="30" /><br />
</x:form>
```

 In most browsers, the number of characters that can fit in a text input box is based on the fixed-width Courier font. If you define a different font, either with a style sheet or by other means, you may not be able to fit the same number of characters as defined by the `size` attribute.

Input validation

All you can do with your form at this point is enter information into the text boxes. This is an ideal point to have some sort of mechanism for verifying the format of the typed information. Normally this is done with complex JavaScripting. You also can accomplish this with the CGI script that handles form post-processing after you click the Submit button. With the flexibility of FML, you can do this with two attributes in the `<x:textinput>` element called `ctype` (content type) and `validation`.

Mozquito Factory currently uses the eight predefined content type values in Table 19-1. Conceivably, more will be added in the future.

TABLE 19-1 MOZQUITO FACTORY'S PREDEFINED CONTENT TYPE VALUES

Content Type	Function
Creditcard	For the 15 or 16 digits of a credit card number

Content Type	Function
Date	For verifying the following date formats: (U.S.) MM.DD.YY MM.DD.YYYY MM/DD/YY MM/DD/YYYY (European) DD.MM.YY DD.MM.YYYY DD/MM/YY DD/MM/YYYY
Email	For determining the validity of an e-mail address (for example, fml-dev@zotgroup.com)
Expiredate	For verifying the expiration date of a credit card: MM/YY
Num	For verifying numerical-only fields
Text	For alphanumeric characters
url	For verifying URL formats (for example, <http://www.zotgroup.com> or http://www.attrition.org/mirror/attrition)
www	For verifying domains (for example, www.zotgroup.com)

All content type elements function in `<x:textinput>` as follows:

```
<x:textinput id="email" size="30" ctype="email"> :
```

The `validation` attribute enables you to choose between two types of validation: *strict* or *loose*. If you choose strict, then whatever the user typed previously into the field is deleted and the user either has to type it correctly or leave the field blank.

Choosing loose validation leaves whatever data was in the box and sends a "friendly warning" to the user, enabling him or her to proceed without having to fix the format of the input.

Let's add input validation to the e-mail input box:

```
<x:form>

Name:
<x:textinput id="name" size="30" /><br />
```

```
E-Mail:
<x:textinput id="email" size="30" ctype="email" validation="strict"
/><br />

</x:form>
```

Now push this through to your browser so you can test what happens. Once the modified form is opened in your browser, fill out the `email` field with text that doesn't resemble an e-mail address at all. Then try to click the `name` field or press your Tab key to tab out of the box. You should see the error message shown in figure 19-8.

Figure 19-8: This alert box appears when you do not enter a valid e-mail address.

Close the error box by clicking OK. Notice that whatever you typed into the e-mail box has disappeared. The cursor should be blinking in the e-mail box, awaiting you to reenter something correct.

The ctype `email` looks for the following required features when verifying a correct e-mail address:

◆ An @ sign

◆ One or more alphanumeric characters before the @ sign

◆ One or more alphanumeric characters after the @ sign

◆ A dot: "."

◆ After the dot, two or more alphabetic characters

While it is possible to verify the format of an e-mail address, it is difficult to verify whether the e-mail actually exists. Normally, you could do this by sending a `vrfy` query to the SMTP server set up to handle that particular e-mail address. However the `vrfy` command is also seen as a way for spammers to verify, obtain, and catalogue e-mail addresses using a preprogrammed dictionary. In effect, it is often disabled.

Submitting forms

Now you run a test to see how functional your form is and add the FML tags that enable the user to submit your form after they've filled it out. There are four things you currently need to add to your markup to enable you to send the form. First, you need to give the form itself an ID. Do this by adding the `id` attribute with a value of `contactform` to the `<x:form>` element:

```
<x:form id="contactform">
```

Next you need to give the form a location to which it can send its data. This means you need to add the `action` attribute to your `<x:form>` element. You have not learned yet how to write a script to parse the form values that a Mozquito Factory form produces, so use an *echo script* located at Mozquito.com for the value of the `action` attribute. This preexisting script echoes the input from the various form fields to tell you that the form was submitted correctly.

```
<x:form id="contactform" action="
http://www.mozquito.org/servlets/Echo">
```

The next step in preparing your form for submission is to add another attribute to each of your `<x:textinput>` elements. The `send` attribute tells Mozquito whether the input in that particular box should be sent when the form is submitted. Input is not automatically sent by default. You need to add the `send` attribute with a value of `yes` if you want a particular field's data sent.

The reasoning behind having to designate what data is sent and what is not lies in the fact that many of the features in an FML form may be used for navigational purposes only. In this case, there is no reason to submit such data along with the form. Consequently, it is important for you to indicate which input box's data to send.

In order to submit your form, you need to create a button for users to click that sends the form off to wherever the `action` attribute points. So add the `<x:button>` element:

```
<x:button value="Submit Form">
```

The `value` attribute of the `button` element contains the text that appears on the button when the FML pops up in the browser. This element is similar to the HTML 4.01 counterparts of `<button>` and `<input type="button">`.

Using the event handler attribute `onclick`, tell Mozquito what you want to happen when the button is clicked. Set the value of `onclick` to `submit:contactform`. This tells Mozquito that when the button is clicked, it should do whatever the action the form element with the ID of `contactform` says to do.

```
<x:button value="Submit Form" onclick="submit:contactform">
```

This becomes very useful when you have a document with multiple forms as choices. Once the user selects a form, you can set up the rest of the document so only that particular form is submitted.

 In HTML, it is commonplace to use the event handler "onClick" instead of "onclick." Make sure all tags and attributes are lowercase including JavaScript handlers like onclick.

Here's what your form looks like in its full FML glory:

```
<x:form id="contactform"
action="http://www.mozquito.org/servlets/Echo">

Name:
<x:textinput id="name" size="30" send="yes" /><br />

E-Mail:
<x:textinput id="email" size="30" ctype="email" validation="strict"
send="yes" /><br />

<x:button value="Submit" onclick="submit:contactform" />

</x:form>
```

Now is a good time to double check its validity and well-formedness. Also, push it through to the browser to see what it looks like (refer to Figure 19-9).

Go through the motions of filling out the form. Then click Submit. If you currently have an Internet connection, the form should be submitted to Mozquito. com's echo script and you should see the results shown in Figure 19-10.

Mandatory field requirements

Now that you know how to enable users to submit forms, you can learn how to require that certain fields be filled out. One of the biggest problems with having forms on a Web site is that people never fill out all the information you want them to. This next feature of FML designates the required fields, which combined with the input validation discussed earlier, is designed to ensure you get the most accurate data possible short of reading and verifying it yourself.

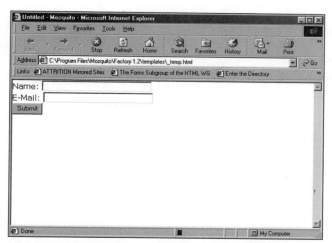

Figure 19-9: This is what your form looks like when rendered in a browser.

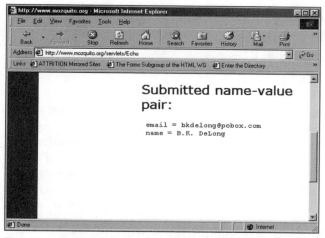

Figure 19-10: When you click the Submit button, the Mozquito.com echo script returns the values of your fields.

With your form, you want shoppers to supply a valid name and e-mail address so you have a place to both ship the merchandise and an e-mail to which you can send the receipt. Using the attribute `mandatory` with a value of `yes`, you can set each field to require that the user fill it out with data. Here's what your FML now looks like with the mandatory requirements:

```
<x:form id="contactform"
action="http://www.mozquito.org/servlets/Echo">
```

```
Name:
<x:textinput id="name" size="30" send="yes" mandatory="yes" /><br />

E-Mail:
<x:textinput id="email" size="30" ctype="email" validation="strict"
send="yes" mandatory="yes" /><br />

<x:button value="Submit" onclick="submit:contactform" />

</x:form>
```

Save your file and push it through to the browser. Try clicking the Submit button without filling in the form. What happens? You should see the same message shown in Figure 19-11.

Figure 19-11: The alert box you should see if you click
Submit without entering data into the mandatory fields.

You cannot submit the form until all the required fields have been filled out. In the case of the email field, the required data would be a valid e-mail address.

Sometimes showing the ID for a field in the error alert can be confusing to a user, especially if you have lots of fields and lots of different forms. The field names may not even correspond with the text that appears next to it. In order to make mandatory field errors a little more understandable, you need to define the adjacent text as the field's *labels*. This results in the labels, rather than the field names, appearing in the error message so they are more specific and a little clearer. Use of the element <x:label> is identical to that of its HTML 4.01 brother, <label> . The for attribute of the label element contains the value of the name attribute for the field with which it is associated.

```
<x:label for="name">Name</x:label>:
<x:textinput id="name" size="30" send="yes" mandatory="yes" />
```

Here's what the new FML code should look like:

```
<x:form id="contactform"
action="http://www.mozquito.org/servlets/Echo">
```

```
<x:label for="name">Name</x:label>:
<x:textinput id="name" size="30" send="yes" mandatory="yes" /><br />

<x:label for="email">E-Mail</x:label>:
<x:textinput id="email" size="30" ctype="email" validation="strict"
send="yes" mandatory="yes" /><br />

<x:button value="Submit" onclick="submit:contactform" />

</x:form>
```

Save your file and push it through to the browser. This time, try to submit the form without filling in anything. See the difference? The error message shows the name of the field's label instead of the field name itself, as shown in Figure 19-12.

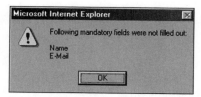

Figure 19-12: This is how the same alert box from Figure 19-11 looks with the use of labels.

Now that you have a pretty thorough form structure, add the rest of the fields, including address, city, state, country, postal code, and phone number. After adding these fields, and requiring all of them to be mandatory, you should now have the following (expanded) FML document:

```
<x:form id="contactform"
action="http://www.mozquito.org/servlets/Echo">

<x:label for="name">Name</x:label>:
<x:textinput id="name" size="30" send="yes" mandatory="yes" /><br />

<p><x:label for="address1">Address</x:label>:
<x:textinput id="address1" size="30" send="yes" mandatory="yes"
/><br />

<x:label for="address2">Address 2</x:label>:
<x:textinput id="address2" size="30" send="yes" mandatory="yes"
/><br />
```

```
<x:label for="city">City</x:label>:
<x:textinput id="city" size="30" send="yes" mandatory="yes" /><br />
<x:label for="state">State</x:label>:
<x:textinput id="state" size="2" send="yes" mandatory="yes" /><br />
<x:label for="postal">Postal Code</x:label>:
<x:textinput id="postal" size="10" send="yes" mandatory="yes" /><br
/>
<x:label for="country">Country</x:label>:
<x:textinput id="country" size="30" send="yes" mandatory="yes" /><br
/>
</p>

<p>
<x:label for="phone">Phone Number</x:label>:
<x:textinput id="phone" size="30" send="yes" mandatory="yes" />
</p>

<x:label for="email">E-Mail</x:label>:
<x:textinput id="email" size="30" ctype="email" validation="strict"
send="yes" mandatory="yes" /><br />

<x:button value="Submit" onclick="submit:contactform" />

</x:form>
```

Check that your form is well formed and valid, then save it and push it through to your browser. It's not the prettiest looking thing in the world, but you can fix that later in the chapter. Functionality is your primary goal at the moment.

Speaking of functionality, it is time to make some of those fields more useful. After a while, your users will tire of filling out all that information. You can help them by turning some of the "common-knowledge" fields like Country or State into pull-down lists.

Editable lists

One of the great things about the versatility of FML is that it allows you to employ lists to which the user can add. For instance, let's say you want to turn the Country list into a pull-down. We wouldn't want 100 options from which to choose. That would bulk out your final page with more data than you need. Why not start with the so-called "Global Eight" nations?

Here's an example of an FML pull-down menu. Instead of the <select> element as used in HTML 4.01, FML uses <x:pulldown> for a more logical approach:

```
<x:label for="countries">Country</x:label>:
<x:pulldown id="countries" send="yes" mandatory="yes">
```

```
<x:option>Make your choice:</x:option>
<x:option value="Canada">Canada</x:option>
<x:option value="France">France</x:option>
<x:option value="Germany">Germany</x:option>
<x:option value="Italy">Italy</x:option>
<x:option value="Japan">Japan</x:option>
<x:option value="Russia">Russia</x:option>
<x:option value="United Kingdom">United Kingdom</x:option>
<x:option value="United States">United States</x:option>
</x:pulldown>
```

Notice that the content between the `<x:option>` and `</x:option>` elements shows up in the browser. The content in the `value` attribute is what actually gets sent. The `<x:pulldown>` element only allows for a single selection. If you want your users to be able to select more than one option, change `<x:pulldown>` to `<x:listbox>`. The `<x:listbox>` element also has an extra attribute of `rows`. If you want your users to see a scroll bar, be sure to set the value of the `rows` attribute to less than the amount of `<x:option>` elements. If you do not want to see a scroll bar at all, then set the value of `rows` to the exact number of `<x:option>` elements.

What happens if your user selects the "Make your choice" option? Nothing, actually. The only thing sent back to the server is content within the `value` attribute, so this option sends no information because it lacks the `value` attribute.

Let's say you want to solicit further information from the user. While this may not be mandatory information for processing an order, it never hurts to get some extra data from your customers. Add a question asking the gender of the person filling out the form. But instead of a pull-down menu, which is inappropriate for this type of information, use radio buttons.

Radio buttons are done very similar to a pull-down menu except you use `<x:item>` in place of the `<x:option>`.

```
What is your <x:label for="gender">gender</x:label>:<br />
<x:radio id="gender" send="yes">
<x:item value="Male">Male</x:item>
<x:item value="Female">Female</x:item>
</x:radio>
```

The element `<x:checkbox>` also utilizes the `<x:item>` element.

Save your document and push it through to the browser. You should see the screen shown in Figure 19-13.

Now you're ready for the final piece of your contact form: the comments section. For user comments, you need to place the `<x:textarea>` element. Almost exactly as you do with the HTML 4.01 version of this element, determine the size of the content area with the `rows` and `cols` attributes.

```
<x:textarea id="comments" rows="5" cols="25" send="yes"
mandatory="yes" />
```

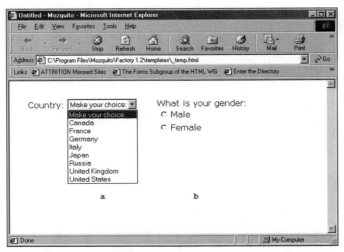

Figure 19-13: When rendered, this is how your (a) pull-down menu looks as well as your (b) radio button list.

Creating an open-ended pull-down menu

Remember when I said at the beginning of the chapter that these lists were editable? To do this, use FML's `<x:toggle>` element, which enables people to select "Other" from the pull-down list and then input their selection manually. Let's try it out.

First you need to add another option to your pull-down menu. Give this option a value of `other` and include the `onclick` event handler with a value of `toggle:` `openlist`.

```
<x:option value="Other: " onclick="toggle:editlist">Other</x:option>
```

After the `</x:pulldown>` element, add a new `<x:textinput>` element with an attribute size value of 15, an `id` attribute value of `other`, and the event handler `onchange` with a value of `toggle:editlist`.

```
<x:textinput size="15" id="other" onchange="toggle:editlist" />
```

Finally, you need to have an `<x:toggle>` element wrapping the pull-down menu. To do this, give it an `id` attribute with the value `editlist` and a new attribute `shared` with a value of `yes`.

When completed, click Other in the pull-down menu and the `onclick` event handler looks for the element with an `id` value of `editlist`. Once it finds this element and realizes it's a toggle, it keeps the pull-down menu in an editable state while it goes to the next line after the menu — which is the new `<x:textinput>` element. After you fill out your Other country in the input box, the state of the field changes. The `onchange` event handler now adds the new country entry into the pull-down menu for the user to select.

The `shared` attribute of `<x:toggle>` means that any element within the toggle shares the same `id` value. Therefore, any new value you enter into the input box that pops up becomes part of the pull-down and shares the new `id` value.

Here is what the FML for this section looks like:

```
<x:toggle id="editlist" shared="yes">
<x:pulldown id="countries" send="yes" mandatory="yes">
  <x:option>Make Your choice:</x:option>
  <x:option value="Canada">Canada</x:option>
  <x:option value="France">France</x:option>
  <x:option value="Germany">Germany</x:option>
  <x:option value="Italy">Italy</x:option>
  <x:option value="Japan">Japan</x:option>
  <x:option value="Russia">Russia</x:option>
  <x:option value="United Kingdom">United Kingdom</x:option>
  <x:option value="United States">United States</x:option>
<x:option value="Other: " onclick="toggle:editlist">Other</x:option>
</x:pulldown>
<x:textinput id="another" size="15" onchange="toggle:editlist" />
</x:toggle>
```

After you save your document with the new FML and push it through to your browser, follow the steps of selecting the Other option from the pull-down menu and add your own country. The process should match that shown in Figure 19-14.

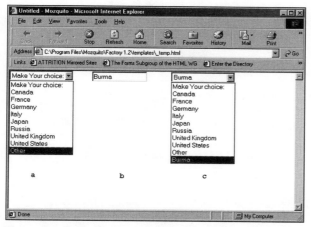

Figure 19-14: When you select the (a) Other option in the pull-down menu, you get (b) an input box for you to add your own country. When completed (c), your new entry becomes part of the selection.

The finished form

Now that you've completed your contact form, clean it up a bit. You can add some CSS to improve the content style and some tables to fix the layout. Here is my version of the completed contact information form FML:

```
<?xml version="1.0"?>
<!DOCTYPE html PUBLIC "-//OVERFLOW//DTD XHTML-FML 1.0//EN"
"http://www.mozquito.org/dtd/xhtml-fml1.dtd">
<html xmlns="http://www.w3.org/1999/xhtml"
xmlns:x="http://www.mozquito.org/xhtml-fml">
<head>
<title>Contact Information</title>
<meta name="generator" content="Mozquito Factory 1.2" />
<link rel="stylesheet" type="text/css"
href="http://www.w3.org/StyleSheets/Core/Modernist" />
</head>
<body>

<h1 align="center">Contact Information</h1>

<x:form id="contactform"
action="http://www.mozquito.org/servlets/Echo">
<table border="0" align="center" cellpadding="7">
<tr><td colspan="3"> </td></tr>
<tr>
<td colspan="3"><x:textinput id="name" size="30" send="yes"
mandatory="yes" /><br />
<div align="left"><x:label for="name">Name</x:label></div>
</td>
</tr>
<tr>
<td colspan="3">
<x:textinput id="address1" size="30" send="yes" mandatory="yes"
/><br />
<x:label for="address1">Address</x:label>
</td>
</tr>
<tr>
<td colspan="3">
<x:textinput id="address2" size="30" send="yes" mandatory="yes"
/><br />
<x:label for="address2">Address 2</x:label>
```

```
</td>
</tr>
<tr>
<td>
<x:textinput id="city" size="30" send="yes" mandatory="yes" /><br />
<x:label for="city">City</x:label>
</td>
<td>
<x:textinput id="state" size="2" send="yes" mandatory="yes" />, <br
/>
<x:label for="state">State</x:label>
</td>
<td>
<x:textinput id="postal" size="10" send="yes" mandatory="yes" /><br
/>
<x:label for="postal">Postal Code</x:label>
</td>
</tr>
<tr>
<td colspan="3">
<x:toggle id="editlist" shared="yes">
<x:pulldown id="countries" send="yes" mandatory="yes">
  <x:option>Make your choice:</x:option>
  <x:option value="Canada">Canada</x:option>
  <x:option value="France">France</x:option>
  <x:option value="Germany">Germany</x:option>
  <x:option value="Italy">Italy</x:option>
  <x:option value="Japan">Japan</x:option>
  <x:option value="Russia">Russia</x:option>
  <x:option value="United Kingdom">United Kingdom</x:option>
  <x:option value="United States">United States</x:option>
<x:option value="Other: " onclick="toggle:editlist">Other</x:option>
</x:pulldown>
<x:textinput id="another" size="15" onchange="toggle:editlist" />
</x:toggle><br />
<x:label for="countries">Country</x:label>
</td>
</tr>
<tr><td colspan="3"> </td></tr>
<tr>
<td>
<x:textinput id="phone" size="30" send="yes" mandatory="yes" /><br
/>
```

```
<x:label for="phone">Phone Number</x:label>
</td>
</tr>
<tr>
<td>
<x:textinput id="email" size="30" ctype="email" validation="strict"
send="yes" mandatory="yes" /><br />
<x:label for="email">E-Mail</x:label>
</td>
</tr>
<tr><td colspan="3"> </td></tr>
<tr>
<td colspan="3">
<p><strong>What is your <x:label
for="gender">gender</x:label>:</strong><br />
<x:radio id="gender" send="yes">
<x:item value="Male">Male</x:item>
<x:item value="Female">Female</x:item>
<x:item value="Other">Other</x:item>
</x:radio>
</p>
</td>
</tr>
<tr>
<td colspan="3">
<x:label for="comments">Comments</x:label>:<br />
<x:textarea id="comments" rows="5" cols="25" send="yes"
mandatory="no" />
<p><x:button value="Submit" onclick="submit:contactform" /></p>
</td>
</tr>
</table>

</x:form>

</body>
</html>
```

When the completed form is pushed through to the browser, it should appear like the screen shown in Figure 19-15.

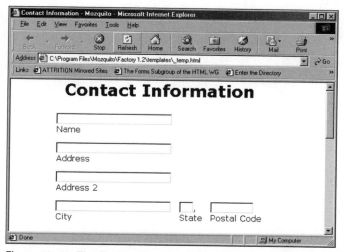

Figure 19-15: The final rendered version of the contact information form

The Shopping Cart Form

You now know enough of XHTML-FML to create a contact information form, so it's time to move to more complex markup. You can take some of what you've learned so far to create an interactive, generic shopping cart complete with on-the-fly calculations, images, and cross-layer navigation — all with FML.

Start with a single product

You're about to start a completely new segment of your e-commerce order form so you should save your contact information form (**contactform.xhtml**) and open a new file. Save this new file and call it **shoppingcart.xhtml**.

The first step is to set up a toggled <x:pulldown> menu with several <x:option> elements having numerical values of 0–6. The eighth <x:option> element should utilize the same `onclick` event handler as the preceding editable list used `more` as the option content (not value). The <x:textinput> element should strictly validate for a numerical value and should utilize the same `onchange` event handler as the previous editable list. Finally, you need to add the item the person is purchasing along with a brief description about it.

This is your initial source code inside the body of a new XHTML-FML document:

```
<x:form>
```

```
<p> </p>
```

```
<table bgcolor="lightblue" style="border-color:blue" border="2">
```

```
<tr>
<td colspan="2" align="center">Key</td>
</tr>
<tr>
<th>Dollars</th><th>Coins</th>
</tr>
<tr>
<td>$.10</td><td>Copper Pieces (CP)</td>
</tr>
<tr>
<td>$1</td><td>Silver Pieces (SP)</td>
</tr>
<tr>
<td>$10</td><td>Gold Pieces (GP)</td>
</tr>
<tr>
<td>$100</td><td>Platinum Pieces (PP)</td>
</tr>
</table>

<p> </p>
<table style="border-color:blue" border="2" bgcolor="lightblue"
cellpadding="10" width="85%" align="center">
<tr>

<td>
Fiery Avenger
</td>
<td>
A powerful magic sword, <br /> the blade is a red-hot flame
</td>
<td>
<x:toggle id="editamount" shared="yes">
<x:pulldown id="amount" send="yes">
<x:option value="0">0</x:option>
<x:option value="1">1</x:option>
<x:option value="2">2</x:option>
<x:option value="3">3</x:option>
<x:option value="4">4</x:option>
<x:option value="5">5</x:option>
<x:option value="6" onclick="toggle:editamount">More</x:option>
</x:pulldown>
<x:textinput size="5" id="more" onchange="toggle:editamount"
ctype="num" validation="strict" />
</x:toggle>
```

```
</td>

</tr>
</table>

</x:form>
```

Figure 19-16 shows how the preceding form looks in a browser window.

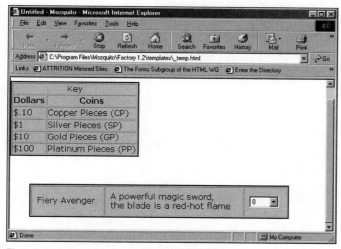

Figure 19-16: What your initial form looks like

Now that you have your product and the ability to choose an amount, you need to set a price and something to calculate a total. Enter two new elements: `<x:textoutput>` and `<x:calc>`. You use `<x:textoutput>` to set the price. It's a static amount, so there is no need for a user to modify it. Next you insert the `<x:calc>` element to add up the sum of the price and the amount. Note that `<x:calc>` does not actually output anything directly to the browser per se. The second `<x:textoutput>` wrapped by the `<x:calc>` inherits the value of total and prints it.

```
<td>
<x:textoutput id="price" value="10000" send="yes" /> PP
</td>
<td>
<x:calc id="total" term="amount * price" send="yes">
<x:textoutput />
</x:calc> PP
</td>
```

I added a key to explain the monetary values for this fictional shop. Note that I placed the currency designation outside of the actual price value. The currency designation remains the same if the amount is in deutsche marks or dollars. The currency symbol has little to do with the actual amount and interferes with the calculation if it becomes part of the value. Take a look at your form so far (see Figure 19-17).

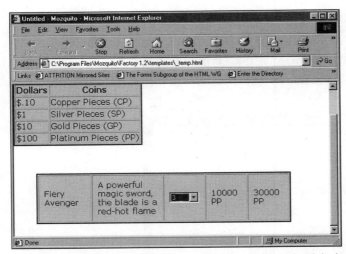

Figure 19-17: When you select an amount, the total on the right increases.

Let's add a new item with a different price appearance:

```
<tr>
<td>
Honey Mead
</td>
<td>
Made with the best Royal Jelly<br />
(Wasp Honey)
</td>
<td>
<x:toggle id="edit2amount" shared="yes">
<x:pulldown id="amount2" send="yes">
<x:option value="0">0</x:option>
<x:option value="1">1</x:option>
<x:option value="2">2</x:option>
<x:option value="3">3</x:option>
<x:option value="4">4</x:option>
<x:option value="5">5</x:option>
<x:option value="more" onclick="toggle:edit2amount">More</x:option>
```

```
</x:pulldown>
<x:textinput size="5" id="more2" onchange="toggle:edit2amount"
ctype="num" validation="strict" />
</x:toggle>
</td>
<td>
<x:textoutput id="price2" value="1.60" send="yes" /> SP
</td>
<td>
<x:calc id="total2" term="amount2 * price2" send="yes">
<x:textoutput />
</x:calc> SP
</td>

</tr>
```

Notice how even though this mead costs 1 Silver Piece and 6 Copper Pieces, it keeps rounding up to a whole number. You easily can fix this problem by adding the digits element to the <x:calc> element.

```
<x:calc id="total2" term="amount2 * price2" send="yes" digits="2">
```

Giving a value of 2 to the digits element tells Mozquito to round up based on the first two digits after the decimal point.

In order to show the example of decimal point rounding, you add a second product. You may not have noticed that the source code has nearly doubled in length from 80 to 112 lines. If you cut-and-paste, you may also miss the fact that not only do you have to change most of the values, but each id must be different as well.

Annoying, isn't it? Think of how tedious it is if you have to add 100 items or more. Thankfully, there's a new element to come to the rescue called <x:template>. You simply define the entire table row as part of a template and then use the <x:insert> element any time you want to make use of your template—a much easier process than the original solution.

First, you need to remove the table from the <x:form> element, place it inside <x:template>, and give the template element an id value of item. (Don't forget to add the </x:template> after the table closes.)

```
<x:template id="item">
(Item Table)
</x:template>
```

Next, back in the <x:form> element, you add the <x:insert> . Each instance of this element gets its own id value and references the template with an attribute:

```
<x:form>
(Monetary Key Table)
```

```
<x:insert id="eq1" template="item">
<x:insert id="eq2" template="item">
</x:form>
```

Here's what your FML looks like with it all put together. Note that you've temporarily removed the second item table altogether.

```
<?xml version="1.0"?>
<!DOCTYPE html PUBLIC "-//OVERFLOW//DTD XHTML-FML 1.0//EN"
"http://www.mozquito.org/dtd/xhtml-fml1.dtd">
<html xmlns="http://www.w3.org/1999/xhtml"
xmlns:x="http://www.mozquito.org/xhtml-fml">
<head>
<title>Untitled</title>
<meta name="generator" content="Mozquito Factory 1.2" />
</head>
<body>

<x:template id="item">
<table style="border-color:blue" border="2" bgcolor="lightblue"
cellpadding="10" width="85%" align="center">
<tr>

<td>
Fiery Avenger
</td>
<td>
A powerful magic sword, <br /> the blade is a red-hot flame
</td>
<td>
<x:toggle id="editamount" shared="yes">
<x:pulldown id="amount" send="yes">
<x:option value="0">0</x:option>
<x:option value="1">1</x:option>
<x:option value="2">2</x:option>
<x:option value="3">3</x:option>
<x:option value="4">4</x:option>
<x:option value="5">5</x:option>
<x:option value="6" onclick="toggle:editamount">More</x:option>
</x:pulldown>
<x:textinput size="5" id="more" onchange="toggle:editamount"
ctype="num" validation="strict" />
</x:toggle>
</td>
<td>
```

```
<x:textoutput id="price" value="10000" send="yes" /> PP
</td>
<td>
<x:calc id="total" term="amount * price" send="yes">
<x:textoutput />
</x:calc> PP
</td>
</tr>
</table>
</x:template>

<x:form>

<p> </p>

<table bgcolor="lightblue" style="border-color:blue" border="2">
<tr>
<td colspan="2" align="center">Key</td>
</tr>
<tr>
<th>Dollars</th><th>Coins</th>
</tr>
<tr>
<td>$1</td><td>Copper Pieces (CP)</td>
</tr>
<tr>
<td>$10</td><td>Silver Pieces (SP)</td>
</tr>
<tr>
<td>$100</td><td>Gold Pieces (GP)</td>
</tr>
<tr>
<td>$1000</td><td>Platinum Pieces (PP)</td>
</tr>
</table>

<p> </p>

<x:insert id="eq1" template="item" />
<x:insert id="eq2" template="item" />

</x:form>

</body>
</html>
```

Figure 19-18 shows how this new form appears in a browser window.

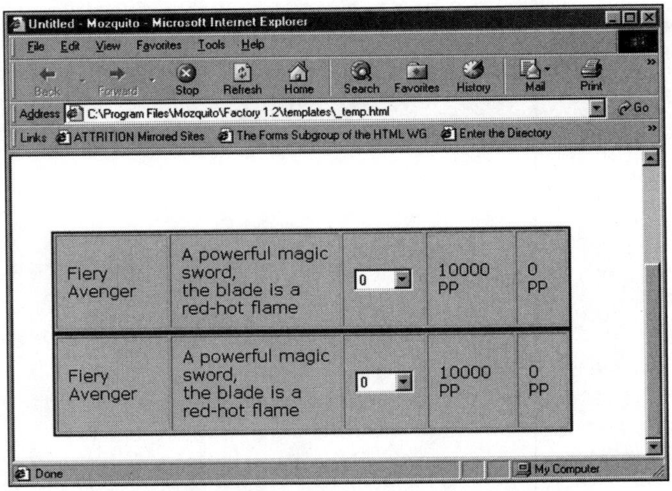

Figure 19-18: The current form as it appears in your browser

This is great because instead of duplicating the huge table, you add only four new lines of code. But something's still missing. In order to make use of the template, you have to dump the table containing the Honey Mead item. How can you get that back in there while still making use of the code-reducing template element?

Simple. You use the `<x:prop>` element. Every time you use the `<x:insert>` element, you can have a series of `<x:prop>` elements that feed the template the different data for each new item. In the template, replace the item property mentions with `id` values surrounded by pipe symbols (|). For example:

```
<x:textoutput id="price" value="10000" send="yes" /> PP
```

changes to

```
<x:textoutput id="price" value="|cost|" send="yes" /> PP
```

Under the `<x:insert>` element, add the price variables:

```
<x:insert id="eq1" template="item">
<x:prop name="cost">10000</x:prop>
</x:insert>
<x:insert id="eq2" template="item">
<x:prop name="cost">1.60</x:prop>
</x:insert>
```

Once you add in all the other fields and data, here's what the full FML form looks like:

```
<x:template id="item">
<table style="border-color:blue" border="2" bgcolor="lightblue"
cellpadding="10" width="85%" align="center">
<tr>

<td>
|item|
</td>
<td>
|description|
</td>
<td>
<x:toggle id="editamount" shared="yes">
<x:pulldown id="amount" send="yes">
<x:option value="0">0</x:option>
<x:option value="1">1</x:option>
<x:option value="2">2</x:option>
<x:option value="3">3</x:option>
<x:option value="4">4</x:option>
<x:option value="5">5</x:option>
<x:option value="6" onclick="toggle:editamount">More</x:option>
</x:pulldown>
<x:textinput size="5" id="more" onchange="toggle:editamount"
ctype="num" validation="strict" />
</x:toggle>
</td>
<td>
<x:textoutput id="price" value="|cost|" send="yes" /> PP
</td>
<td>
<x:calc id="total" term="amount * price" send="yes" digits="2">
<x:textoutput />
</x:calc> PP
</td>
</tr>
</table>
</x:template>

<x:form>

<p> </p>
```

```
<table bgcolor="lightblue" style="border-color:blue" border="2">
<tr>
<td colspan="2" align="center">Key</td>
</tr>
<tr>
<th>Dollars</th><th>Coins</th>
</tr>
<tr>
<td>$1</td><td>Copper Pieces (CP)</td>
</tr>
<tr>
<td>$10</td><td>Silver Pieces (SP)</td>
</tr>
<tr>
<td>$100</td><td>Gold Pieces (GP)</td>
</tr>
<tr>
<td>$1000</td><td>Platinum Pieces (PP)</td>
</tr>
</table>

<p> </p>

<x:insert id="eq1" template="item">
<x:prop name="cost">10000.00</x:prop>
<x:prop name="item">Fiery Avenger</x:prop>
<x:prop name="description">A powerful magic sword with a burning
flame for a blade</x:prop>
</x:insert>

<x:insert id="eq2" template="item">
<x:prop name="cost">1.60</x:prop>
<x:prop name="item">Honey Mead</x:prop>
<x:prop name="description">Made with the best Royal Jelly (Wasp
Honey)</x:prop>
</x:insert>

</x:form>
```

Now take a look at it in your browser (see Figure 19-19).

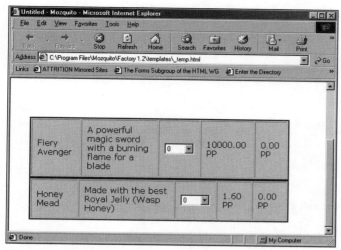

Figure 19-19: Using templates, your form doesn't look much different — but it uses much less code and markup.

This is great, but it's still missing something. It would be convenient if you could also set up a running grand total of what you've purchased so far. This is quite simple.

After the group of <x:insert> elements, set up another <x:calc> equation. This time, add the values of the total for each <x:insert> element:

```
Total:
<x:calc id="grandtotal" term="eq1.total + eq2.total" digits="2">
<x:textoutput />
</x:calc>
```

Be sure to wrap your table around it:

```
<table style="border-color:blue" border="2" bgcolor="lightblue"
cellpadding="10" width="85%" align="center">
<tr>
<td colspan="5">
<strong>Total:
<x:calc id="grandtotal" term="eq1.total + eq2.total" digits="2">
<x:textoutput />
</x:calc>
</strong>
</td>
</tr>
</table>
```

Add the preceding code between your last `<x:insert>` set and your `</x:form>` element, save your file, and push it through to your browser (see Figure 19-20).

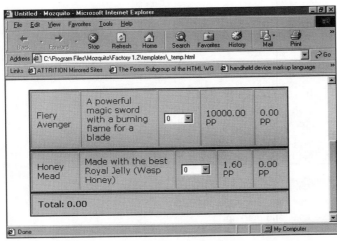

Figure 19-20: The current form as it appears in your browser

Note that the grand total of your entire order is calculated as soon as you change values (see Figure 19-21).

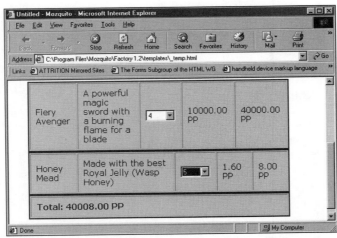

Figure 19-21: The grand total is calculated when the values are changed.

Layers

Earlier I mentioned the convenience of templates, inserts, and props if you have a huge database of items that you want to add to your form. Even if you have only a few, it's still a convenient way to get the job done. Along the same lines, why list all your items on one page? You can take advantage of the <x:toggle> element that you've already used for editable lists to create multiple pages within one FML document.

To do this, place an <x:toggle> element with an id attribute value of navigate just above your first <x:insert> element and below the <x:form> element. Place the corresponding </x:toggle> under the last </x:insert> element.

```
<x:toggle id="navigate">
<x:insert id="eq1" template="item">
<x:prop name="item">Fiery Avenger</x:prop>
<x:prop name="description">A powerful magic sword with a burning
flame for a blade</x:prop>
<x:prop name="cost">10000.00</x:prop>
</x:insert>

<x:insert id="eq2" template="item">
<x:prop name="item">Honey Mead</x:prop>
<x:prop name="description">Made with the best Royal Jelly (Wasp
Honey)</x:prop>
<x:prop name="cost">1.60</x:prop>
</x:insert>
</x:toggle>
```

Underneath the "grand total" table, place two <x:button> elements using the event handler onclick as follows:

```
<x:button value="Back" onclick="toggle:navigate,-" />
<x:button value="Forward" onclick="toggle:navigate,+" />
```

After you make these changes and additions, save your file and push it through to your browser. While you don't change much, note that you can navigate the two items separated by two different layers by using the Forward and Back buttons (see Figure 19-22 and Figure 19-23).

When you click the Forward button, you can move between layers in one direction; clicking Back takes you in the reverse direction.

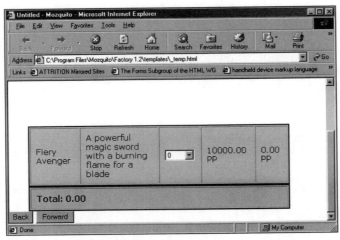

Figure 19-22: This is your first layer.

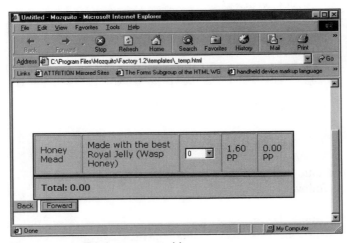

Figure 19-23: This is your second layer.

Cleaning up

Now that you've covered most of FML, you can finalize the shopping cart portion of your e-commerce order form by adding some images. Using the `<x:prop>` element, you can preload images for each item.

As an example, modify the location of the |item| variable and add a new element <x:img>:

```
<td>
|item|
</td>
```

to

```
<td>
|item|  <br /><x:img src="|image|" alt="|item|" width="50"
height="50" preload="yes" />
</td>
```

Note the reuse of the |item| variable for the value of the alt attribute. Also, for <x:img> elements, it is a requirement to set the width and height. In order to prevent long load times as you move from item to item, add an attribute preload set to the value of yes. This loads all the <x:prop>-set images at once.

Don't forget to add a <x:prop> element for |image|:

```
<x:toggle id="navigate">
<x:insert id="eq1" template="item">
<x:prop name="cost">10000.00</x:prop>
<x:prop name="item">Fiery Avenger</x:prop>
<x:prop name="description">A powerful magic sword with a burning
flame for a blade</x:prop>
<x:prop
name="image">http://www.eqmaps.com/itemicons/2hslash003.jpg</x:prop>
</x:insert>

<x:insert id="eq2" template="item">
<x:prop name="cost">1.60</x:prop>
<x:prop name="item">Honey Mead</x:prop>
<x:prop name="description">Made with the best Royal Jelly (Wasp
Honey)</x:prop>
<x:prop
name="image">http://www.eqmaps.com/itemicons/potion001.jpg</x:prop>
</x:insert>
</x:toggle>
```

You've finally done it. Save your **shoppingcart.xhtml** file one last time and push it through to your browser. You should be proud. Take a look at what you've accomplished (see Figure 19-24 and Figure 19-25).

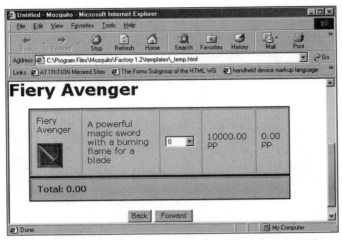

Figure 19-24: Your shopping cart form complete with images for the Fiery Avenger

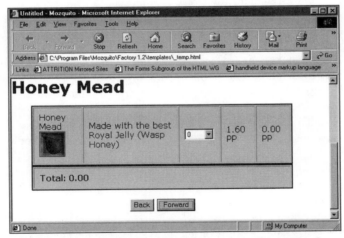

Figure 19-25: Your shopping cart form complete with images for Honey Mead

Adding in the Contact Information Form

But wait...you're not quite finished with your full order form. You still need to add in your contact information form to make sure users get the items they've purchased. After the final `</x:insert>`, but before the `</x:toggle>`, you need to add a `<x:tg>` (toggle group) element. Then open up **contactform.xhtml** and paste it under the new `<x:tg>` element. Add a `</x:tg>` element at the end and check its well-formedness and validity.

 Paste only the FML between the `<x:form>` and `</x:form>` elements. Make sure you do not paste the `<x:form>` element itself. Take the id and action attributes from the contact information form `<x:form>` element and add them to the `<x:form>` element in the shopping cart FML page.

When all is said and done, you should have a page that looks something like this:

```
<?xml version="1.0"?>
<!DOCTYPE html PUBLIC "-//OVERFLOW//DTD XHTML-FML 1.0//EN"
"http://www.mozquito.org/dtd/xhtml-fml1.dtd">
<html xmlns="http://www.w3.org/1999/xhtml"
xmlns:x="http://www.mozquito.org/xhtml-fml">
<head>
<title>Untitled</title>
<meta name="generator" content="Mozquito Factory 1.2" />
</head>
<body>

<x:template id="item">
<h1>|item|</h1>
<table style="border-color:blue" border="2" bgcolor="lightblue"
cellpadding="10" width="85%" align="center">
<tr>

<td>
|item|  <br /><x:img src="|image|" alt="|item|" width="50"
height="50" preload="yes" />
</td>
<td>
|description|
</td>
<td>
<x:toggle id="editamount" shared="yes">
<x:pulldown id="amount" send="yes">
<x:option value="0">0</x:option>
<x:option value="1">1</x:option>
<x:option value="2">2</x:option>
<x:option value="3">3</x:option>
<x:option value="4">4</x:option>
```

```
<x:option value="5">5</x:option>
<x:option value="6" onclick="toggle:editamount">More</x:option>
</x:pulldown>
<x:textinput size="5" id="more" onchange="toggle:editamount"
ctype="num" validation="strict" />
</x:toggle>
</td>
<td>
<x:textoutput id="price" value="|cost|" send="yes" /> PP
</td>
<td>
<x:calc id="total" term="amount * price" send="yes" digits="2">
<x:textoutput />
</x:calc> PP
</td>
</tr>
</table>
</x:template>

<x:form id="contactform"
action="http://www.mozquito.org/servlets/Echo">

<p> </p>

<table bgcolor="lightblue" style="border-color:blue" border="2">
<tr>
<td colspan="2" align="center">Key</td>
</tr>
<tr>
<th>Dollars</th><th>Coins</th>
</tr>
<tr>
<td>$1</td><td>Copper Pieces (CP)</td>
</tr>
<tr>
<td>$10</td><td>Silver Pieces (SP)</td>
</tr>
<tr>
<td>$100</td><td>Gold Pieces (GP)</td>
</tr>
<tr>
<td>$1000</td><td>Platinum Pieces (PP)</td>
</tr>
</table>
```

```
<p> </p>

<x:toggle id="navigate">
<x:insert id="eq1" template="item">
<x:prop name="cost">10000.00</x:prop>
<x:prop name="item">Fiery Avenger</x:prop>
<x:prop name="description">A powerful magic sword with a burning
flame for a blade</x:prop>
<x:prop
name="image">http://www.eqmaps.com/itemicons/2hslash003.jpg</x:prop>
</x:insert>

<x:insert id="eq2" template="item">
<x:prop name="cost">1.60</x:prop>
<x:prop name="item">Honey Mead</x:prop>
<x:prop name="description">Made with the best Royal Jelly (Wasp
Honey)</x:prop>
<x:prop
name="image">http://www.eqmaps.com/itemicons/potion001.jpg</x:prop>
</x:insert>
<x:tg>
<h1 align="center">Contact Information</h1>

<table border="0" align="center" cellpadding="7">
<tr><td colspan="3"> </td></tr>
<tr>
<td colspan="3"><x:textinput id="name" size="30" send="yes"
mandatory="yes" /><br />
<div align="left"><x:label for="name">Name</x:label></div>
</td>
</tr>
<tr>
<td colspan="3">
<x:textinput id="address1" size="30" send="yes" mandatory="yes"
/><br />
<x:label for="address1">Address</x:label>
</td>
</tr>
<tr>
<td colspan="3">
<x:textinput id="address2" size="30" send="yes" mandatory="yes"
/><br />
<x:label for="address2">Address 2</x:label>
</td>
```

```
</tr>
<tr>
<td>
<x:textinput id="city" size="30" send="yes" mandatory="yes" /><br />
<x:label for="city">City</x:label>
</td>
<td>
<x:textinput id="state" size="2" send="yes" mandatory="yes" />, <br
/>
<x:label for="state">State</x:label>
</td>
<td>
<x:textinput id="postal" size="10" send="yes" mandatory="yes" /><br
/>
<x:label for="postal">Postal Code</x:label>
</td>
</tr>
<tr>
<td colspan="3">
<x:toggle id="editlist" shared="yes">
<x:pulldown id="countries" send="yes" mandatory="yes">
  <x:option>Make your choice:</x:option>
  <x:option value="Canada">Canada</x:option>
  <x:option value="France">France</x:option>
  <x:option value="Germany">Germany</x:option>
  <x:option value="Italy">Italy</x:option>
  <x:option value="Japan">Japan</x:option>
  <x:option value="Russia">Russia</x:option>
  <x:option value="United Kingdom">United Kingdom</x:option>
  <x:option value="United States">United States</x:option>
<x:option value="Other: " onclick="toggle:editlist">Other</x:option>
</x:pulldown>
<x:textinput id="another" size="15" onchange="toggle:editlist" />
</x:toggle><br />
<x:label for="countries">Country</x:label>
</td>
</tr>
<tr><td colspan="3"> </td></tr>
<tr>
<td>
<x:textinput id="phone" size="30" send="yes" mandatory="yes" /><br
/>
<x:label for="phone">Phone Number</x:label>
</td>
```

```
</tr>
<tr>
<td>
<x:textinput id="email" size="30" ctype="email" validation="strict"
send="yes" mandatory="yes" /><br />
<x:label for="email">E-Mail</x:label>
</td>
</tr>
<tr><td colspan="3"> </td></tr>
<tr>
<td colspan="3">
<p><strong>What is your <x:label
for="gender">gender</x:label>:</strong><br />
<x:radio id="gender" send="yes">
<x:item value="Male">Male</x:item>
<x:item value="Female">Female</x:item>
<x:item value="Other">Other</x:item>
</x:radio>
</p>
</td>
</tr>
<tr>
<td colspan="3">
<x:label for="comments">Comments</x:label>:<br />
<x:textarea id="comments" rows="5" cols="25" send="yes"
mandatory="no" />
<p><x:button value="Submit" onclick="submit:contactform" /></p>
</td>
</tr>
</table>
</x:tg>


</x:toggle>

<table style="border-color:blue" border="2" bgcolor="lightblue"
cellpadding="10" width="85%" align="center">
<tr>
<td colspan="5">
<strong>Total:
<x:calc id="grandtotal" term="eq1.total + eq2.total" digits="2">
<x:textoutput />
</x:calc>
</strong>
</td>
```

```
</tr>
</table>

<p align="center">
<x:button value="Back" onclick="toggle:navigate,-" />
<x:button value="Forward" onclick="toggle:navigate,+" />
</p>

</x:form>

</body>
</html>
```

And that...as they say...is a wrap.

Making your Mozquito HTML/ JavaScript Accessible

While Mozquito Factory produces HTML and JavaScript that functions on any browser supporting JavaScript 1.2, you need to exert some extra effort to make your documents as accessible as possible. Unfortunately, many Web developers think Web accessibility is limited only for people with disabilities. Keep in mind that people with older versions of browsers, text-based browsers, and browsers on new devices such as cell phones and PDAs will have great difficulty with Mozquito-produced content.

Open up a Mozquito-produced HTML file in Notepad, WordPad, or any other text editor. Scroll down to the very bottom of the document and you can see their use of the <NOSCRIPT> element:

```
<noscript>
<center>
Sorry, your browser doesn't support JavaScript, or you have turned off
JavaScript in your browser.<p>
<b>Please activate JavaScript or get the latest
<a href="http://home.netscape.com">Netscape Navigator</a> or
<a href="http://www.microsoft.com/windows/ie/default.htm">Internet Explorer</a>
to view this page properly!</b><p>
</center>
</noscript>
```

As I mentioned several times in this chapter, FML closely resembles the HTML 4.01 version of forms. Strip out the preloading images, editable lists, and layers, and you can duplicate your entire FML form in HTML 4.01. Table 19-2 shows you a comparison of which HTML tags correspond to which FML tags. If you have time to spare after you complete your FML document, make the edits in a separate HTML file and copy them over to your Mozquito HTML document. (Keep in mind that each time you export from your FML document to the Mozquito HTML document you lose your code.) That's why it's important to save it in a separate HTML file and add it to your Mozquito HTML just before you post it on your Web server.

TABLE 19-2 COMPARING FML 1.0 AND HTML 4.01

FML 1.0	HTML 4.01
`<x:textinput />`	`<input type="text>`
`<x:textarea> </x:textarea>`	`<textarea> </textarea>`
`<x:label> </x:label>`	`<label> </label>`
`<x:button />`	`<button>` or `<input type="button>`
`<x:radio> </x:radio>`	`<input text="radio">`
`<x:checkbox> </x:checkbox>`	`<input type="checkbox">`
`<x:pulldown> </x:pulldown>`	`<select> </select>`
`<x:option> </x:option>`	`<option> </option>`
`<x:img />`	`<img>`

For more information on making your JavaScript and forms more accessible, take a look at the W3C Web Content Accessibility Guidelines (`<http://www.w3.org/TR/WAI-WEBCONTENT>`).

Chapter 20

XML and the Next Generation of the Web

You've looked at XHTML from all different angles, from the new capabilities it introduces to the new costs it imposes, and pondered its use in devices from cell phones to Web browsers on PCs to Web servers and even larger-scale devices. Now that you've waded through all of that, it's time to consider the long-term payoff — the overall impact on the once familiar World Wide Web.

Person to Person and Machine to Machine

So far, the Web has mostly been a tool for person-to-person and person-to-machine connections. While simple advertising-oriented *brochureware* Web sites and most information content of the Web is intended for human consumption, much of the driving force (read: investment opportunities) behind the Web has come from projects that make it easier for humans to connect to machines. Humans connect to machines to enter orders for goods, for instance, setting off a whole series of events that is largely managed by the computers while involving many people along the way.

For the most part, humans have maintained a "don't call me, I'll call you" attitude toward computers. Commercial automated e-mail, commonly known as *spam* when it is unsolicited, is seen as a bane of the Internet and not one of its attractions. While machine-to-person communications got a small boost in the brief period when *push* seemed popular, bandwidth concerns and the growing ease with which people could retrieve information themselves left push without many customers. Similarly, people don't seem excited over the prospect of computer monitoring of their Web surfing that results in suggestions about buying products seemingly appropriate to their interests.

XHTML enters this framework — in which markup has provided human-readable information and form responses have provided machine-readable information — and it opens some new doors. Markup still presents information to people, but it also carries information from machine to machine. XHTML modularization and the extensibility it can provide, specifically for forms, promises sizable improvements in the kinds of information people can send to machines. And while nothing in

XHTML makes spam any more interesting, XHTML at least opens the possibility of machine-to-person transmissions that carry useful information for your computer that you don't need to read. A teacher can read a neatly formatted message that three new students have been added to her class, sent automatically by the school's computer. Meanwhile, her computer has already extracted their names and added them to the grade book.

Automating – and Fragmenting – the Web

The preceding example exemplifies a tiny piece of what XHTML makes possible. By enabling developers to create application-specific vocabularies and use them in combination with the more generic HTML vocabulary, XHTML lets documents carry multiple layers of information. These layers may be aimed at different "customers" of the document, with one layer (likely using the HTML vocabulary) presenting the message as a document for human consumption and the other layers containing information for use in automated processing tools.

Although HTML may look fragmented and riddled with incompatibilities if you're a Web developer trying to perform complex tasks across browsers from multiple vendors, the overall similarities of those implementations generally outweigh their differences. The expectation of similarity that simple HTML creates often makes it more frustrating when the differences begin to appear. XHTML to some extent – and XML to a much greater extent – has frightened lots of people with the prospect of wildly different vocabularies shattering the shared understanding that has kept the Web (mostly) unified up to this point.

As the Web grows, however, demand for such customized vocabularies rises. The value of more specific descriptions becomes more obvious as developers of Web applications try to build in additional functionality. Many intranet sites already include bastardized HTML, containing markup that isn't HTML. The generic `div` and `span` elements have become placeholders for this kind of information for developers who want to stay within the HTML framework. They can use the `class` attribute to indicate what the information really is. (This attribute offers limited extensibility.) Microsoft provides XML *data islands* within HTML documents that give developers a more formal set of tools for working with this information, although that set only works within Microsoft's own software frameworks.

The primary benefit of this additional vocabulary is increased customizability, which enables developers to build all kinds of application hooks into documents that let scripts or programs process them efficiently and reliably. The costs are a bit more complex, but they mostly stem from the fact that not all of the potential recipients of a document have the tools needed to process that document completely. Web developers who rely on plug-in capabilities already face this problem, but extending the HTML vocabulary threatens to make it worse, at least in the short run. Developers can either ship all the information, whether the recipient can use it or not, or spend processing cycles negotiating which information the recipient can process.

The shape of these negotiating and processing frameworks isn't clear yet. While it's reasonable to assume that it will be built on the structures already used for content negotiation (such as HTTP headers and MIME content types) and markup processing (such as the Document Object Model and XSLT), lots of missing pieces remain. Using XHTML to extend the HTML vocabulary will be a risky process, and at least will involve some serious inefficiencies at first. Negotiation can consume resources, while skipping negotiation and just shipping information may mean users get information for which they don't have tools. Unlike the information sent for use with plug-ins today, XHTML doesn't provide an extra built-in step that gives the user a chance to say, "No, I don't want that content or the software to display it."

Using XHTML (as a foundation) and additional XML (incorporated as XHTML modules) to extend that foundation should ensure a basic level of understanding for users, even if their tools can't process the entire document. As the level of XML content rises, however, it may become more difficult for users to handle documents appropriately without the right tools. Infrastructure for dealing with these cases and for helping users find the right tools is just getting started. For now, extending XHTML is a fairly risky task that may cause more trouble than it's worth.

Automation of the kind just described may incur security risks. Building programs that respond to content in messages makes those messages the bearers of potentially damaging information. If you write these kinds of applications, make certain to build them within a secure framework that includes authentication and provides safeguards against corrupted or lost information. It's also worthwhile to set boundaries that require human intervention, as many workflow applications have found.

Information Leaks

As XHTML documents come to include more and more "real" information, the risks of unplanned information distribution increase. HTML documents can, of course, contain confidential or other sensitive information. However, HTML has a more comforting "all the information is on the surface" style. As developers start to include multiple layers of information in documents, some of those layers may not be visible to users directly.

To take an extreme case, imagine a corporate annual report prepared for public consumption. Underneath the calculated public numbers and pretty pie charts lie an enormous number of confidential details about the company's operations, along with auditing information and production notes. All of this information is removed from the *final HTML version*, which fits the preceding description – all the information is on the surface.

Suppose, however, that someone decides that the annual report might be very useful to certain parts of the company – say top management or the board of directors – as an interface to the more concrete details. Unlike the *flat HTML version*, this enhanced XHTML version would enable its users to click through tables and charts to reach the underlying information, rearranging it if needed for different viewpoints. When opened, the interface is very familiar; the annual report looks just like it did before, in HTML. The extra features and information require user interaction to set them off.

If this thoroughly enhanced XHTML document is mistaken for its flatter cousin and it reaches the outside world, maybe an analyst, the consequences could be dire. The problem doesn't involve crackers breaking into systems; it involves human error and a lack of infrastructure for managing such information. While this is pretty much a worst-case scenario, it warns of things that are newly possible when sophisticated representations of private information are used in the same framework as their public versions. XHTML opens new possibilities, but it brings with it new responsibilities. The security infrastructure isn't there yet, and markup provides no security on its own.

Reviving the Agent Dream

While information leakage may be harmful in some contexts, it reopens the door to a whole range of applications that weren't possible in the HTML Web. *Agents*, software designed to automatically find and process information to meet user needs, may have another chance. While agents originally promised to give users customized tools for finding the information they wanted (sale prices on tuxedos, for instance), they were often stymied by the difficulty of sorting out HTML markup and the imprecise nature of the human languages surrounding the information.

XHTML isn't a magic cure-all for these problems. Human language remains an important part of the content that agents must deal with for many kinds of searches, and the core of XHTML itself remains fairly difficult for agents to interpret. If prices, for instance, are rendered as red and bold using cascading style sheets, that information might not even appear within the document. Agents need to figure out something else (the `class` attribute?) to latch on to, if they hope to reliably extract information that users want.

On the other hand, XHTML's extensibility may give agents some real information to work with in the form of embedded XML content. If, for instance, a common module for marking up sales information was widely used – or even if multiple modules came into use – agents would have meaningful pointers to the information they wanted. While companies may be concerned about enabling comparison shopping by providing such information, they may find that it brings them new customers as well.

Will XHTML Survive?

Right now, the question is whether XHTML will take off; Chapter 5 demonstrates that the transition may not be smooth. In the longer term, however, it isn't entirely clear that XHTML will be capable of competing with its more versatile cousin XML. Is XHTML merely a temporary gateway to XML, or is it viable for the foreseeable future? There are lots of possible forecasts.

Some early critics of HTML have waited a long while for a replacement to come along. From their perspectives, XML offers a much more versatile set of tools with a minimal learning curve and it can fit into the same infrastructures (browsers, HTTP, and Web servers) that HTML does today. Tools such as XLink can give XML hyperlinking capabilities that go far beyond the simple mechanisms provided in HTML, and XSL style sheets promise formatting power that similarly surpasses the wildest dreams of HTML-based Web developers. XML makes it possible to create vocabularies, such as Structured Vector Graphics (SVG) and Synchronized Multimedia Integration Language (SMIL), which can present graphics and multimedia far better than the more general purpose document-oriented HTML. Seen from this perspective, HTML is past its prime – a weak tool whose replacement is only forestalled by the existence of many millions of *legacy* browsers.

A friendlier perspective finds the HTML vocabulary more valuable. Even apart from the millions of browsers already distributed, or the large community of developers who already have a solid understanding of how it works, HTML still works well for many of the reasons that catapulted it to prominence in the first place. It's not difficult to create HTML documents, and even while XHTML imposes a few more rules on structure, those rules can actually help keep beginners out of trouble. The fixed HTML vocabulary provides a set of boundaries that keeps projects from aiming at impossible goals, while giving document creators the power they need to build usable interfaces. HTML has already proven capable of accommodating extensions, from scripting to style sheets to applets and objects. You can argue that much of the world gets along just fine without XML and won't gain that much by using it.

It seems likely that Web development will follow a more moderate course than these two proposals. The HTML vocabulary is too well known and too well supported to disappear quickly, and it will probably always provide a kind of baseline vocabulary for many types of markup. As Chapter 16 demonstrates, XHTML makes it easy to use the HTML vocabulary inside of XML documents for tasks like annotation and commentary that may not be worth the trouble of inventing entirely new vocabularies. Similarly, although XSL formatting objects may describe presentation much more comprehensively than HTML can, it's not clear whether every developer will find it worth the learning curve to deal with the extra verbosity and complexity of XSL-FOs.

The HTML vocabulary contains some other features that will be a long time coming in XML, providing semantics for information that isn't just formatting. HTML forms are one area in which HTML has a distinct advantage, but HTML includes a lot of other features for describing content that have yet to be implemented in any widely used manner in XML. XML provides no general tool for including scripts in documents and it lacks a general way of including style sheet information within a document. Ad hoc solutions to all of these problems can be developed on a vocabulary-by-vocabulary basis, but XHTML already has ready-made solutions to these problems and a large community of developers who know how to use them.

XHTML's development promises to eradicate the largest problem facing HTML: its brittleness brought on by its lack of extensibility. At the same time, XHTML may solve some of the problems XML developers face as they bring XML into the Web environment by providing reusable solutions to real-world problems. While XHTML documents may eventually look very little like their HTML forbearers, it seems probable that many of HTML's features will last beyond the transition period (perhaps with some remodeling). Making the leap directly to XML will remain difficult unless more tools for integrating it with other Web tools appear, and XHTML already holds much of that needed toolkit.

Efficient, Friendly, Invisible

XHTML is probably the biggest change to the underlying architecture of the World Wide Web since it first appeared. HTTP 1.1 refined the protocol for transferring information, but XHTML remodels HTML in a way that may eventually make it unrecognizable. Instead of battling *tag soup,* the ever-growing and uncontrolled additions to HTML made by vendors, the W3C has changed its tune and thrown the doors open to new vocabularies. New vocabularies should come properly attired in namespaces and XHTML modules, but the possibilities are there.

XHTML promises to change the Web from a medium that people use to communicate with other people to a medium that people and computers use to communicate with other people and computers. This transition will incur some costs and produce some problems along the way, but the end result may be a Web that saves people time and effort. The Web has already demonstrated that large networks can create new opportunities, but its current form means that many opportunities have been ignored or wasted. These problems don't involve the more obvious bandwidth issues, although those remain important, but what we can do with that bandwidth.

Perhaps the most important aspect of this change is how small it is, at least at first. As you've seen, XHTML 1.0 starts the transition with as little disruption as possible (although some disruption is unavoidable). While the transition through XHTML 1.1 to the future XHTML 2.0 is likely to involve more bumps, these new structures are being built on the same familiar infrastructure that has supported HTML for years. XHTML isn't starting afresh with a brand-new Web; it's adding new potential to the existing Web. Users and developers, building on familiar tools, hopefully will find that the XHTML tune-up gives them a more useful Web without requiring them to understand the underpinnings.

TIP Still want to know more about XHTML, or discuss its working? Try the XHTML-L list. Details are available at `http://www.egroups.com/group/XHTML-L`.

Appendix A

XHTML Elements, by DTD

THE FOLLOWING TABLE LISTS all of the elements in XHTML 1.0, along with a list of their attributes and a description of their content models. Not all of the options listed here are available in every XHTML 1.0 DTD or in XHTML 1.1.

- Structures in plain text are available in all three XHTML DTDs.

- Structures in **bold** but not *italic* are only available in the XHTML transitional DTD.

- Structures in *italic* but not **bold** are only available in the XHTML frameset DTD.

- Structures in ***bold italic*** are available in both the transitional and frameset DTDs.

- Structures in `strikeout` text are available in the strict and transitional DTDs, but not the frameset DTD.

Structures that are underlined will be dropped from XHTML 1.1, according to the 5 January 2000 draft of XHTML 1.1 – Module-based XHTML.

Element Name	Attributes	Minimal Content Model
a	id, class, style, title, <u>lang</u>, xml:lang, dir, onclick, ondblclick, onmousedown, onmouseup, onmouseover, onmousemove, onmouseout, onkeypress, onkeydown, onkeyup, charset, type, <u>name</u>, href, hreflang, rel, rev, <u>accesskey</u>, shape (rect|circle|poly|default), coords, <u>tabindex</u>, onfocus, onblur, *target*	(#PCDATA | br | span | bdo | <u>object</u> | *applet* | img | map | *iframe* | tt | i | b | big | small | <u>*u*</u> | <u>*s*</u> | <u>*strike*</u> |<u>*font*</u> | <u>*basefont*</u> | em | strong | dfn | code | q | sub | sup | samp | kbd | var | cite | abbr | acronym | input | select | textarea | label | button | ins | del | script | noscript)*

Continued

Element Name	Attributes	Minimal Content Model
abbr	id, class, style, title, lang, xml:lang, dir, onclick, ondblclick, onmousedown, onmouseup, onmouseover, onmousemove, onmouseout, onkeypress, onkeydown, onkeyup	(#PCDATA | a | br | span | bdo | object | applet | img | map | iframe | tt | i | b | big | small | u | s | strike | font | basefont | em | strong | dfn | code | q | sub | sup | samp | kbd | var | cite | abbr | acronym | input | select | textarea | label | button | ins | del | script | noscript)*
acronym	id, class, style, title, lang, xml:lang, dir, onclick, ondblclick, onmousedown, onmouseup, onmouseover, onmousemove, onmouseout, onkeypress, onkeydown, onkeyup	(#PCDATA | a | br | span | bdo | object | applet | img | map | iframe | tt | i | b | big | small | u | s | strike | font | basefont | em | strong | dfn | code | q | sub | sup | samp | kbd | var | cite | abbr | acronym | input | select | textarea | label | button | ins | del | script | noscript)*
address	id, class, style, title, lang, xml:lang, dir, onclick, ondblclick, onmousedown, onmouseup, onmouseover, onmousemove, onmouseout, onkeypress, onkeydown, onkeyup	(#PCDATA | a | br | span | bdo | object | applet | img | map | iframe | tt | i | b | big | small | u | s | strike | font | basefont | em | strong | dfn | code | q | sub | sup | samp | kbd | var | cite | abbr | acronym | input | select | textarea | label | button | ins | del | script | noscript)*

Element Name	Attributes	Minimal Content Model
applet	id, class, style, title, codebase, archive, code, _object_, alt, name, width, height, align (top|middle|bottom|left|right), hspace, vspace	(#PCDATA | param | p | h1|h2|h3|h4|h5|h6 | div | ul | ol | dl | _menu_ | dir | pre | hr | blockquote | address center | _noframes_ | _isindex_ | fieldset | table | form | a | br | span | bdo |_object_ | applet | img | map | _iframe_ | tt | i | b | big | small | _u_ | _s_ | _strike_ | _font_ | _basefont_ | em | strong | dfn | code | q | sub | sup | samp | kbd | var | cite | abbr | acronym | input | select | textarea | label | button | ins | del | script | noscript)*
area	id, class, style, title, _lang_, xml:lang, dir, onclick, ondblclick, onmousedown, onmouseup, onmouseover, onmousemove, onmouseout, onkeypress, onkeydown, onkeyup, shape (rect|circle|poly|default), coords, href, nohref (nohref), alt, tabindex, accesskey, onfocus, onblur, _target_	EMPTY
b	id, class, style, title, _lang_, xml:lang, dir, onclick, ondblclick, onmousedown, onmouseup, onmouseover, onmousemove, onmouseout, onkeypress, onkeydown, onkeyup	(#PCDATA | a | br | span | bdo |_object_ | _applet_ | img | map | _iframe_ | tt | i | b | big | small | _u_ | _s_ | _strike_ |_font_ | _basefont_ | em | strong | dfn | code | q | sub | sup | samp | kbd | var | cite | abbr | acronym | input | select | textarea | label | button | ins | del | script | noscript)*

Continued

Element Name	Attributes	Minimal Content Model
base	href, *target*	EMPTY
basefont	*id, size, color, face*	*EMPTY*
bdo	Onclick, ondblclick, onmousedown, onmouseup, onmouseover, onmousemove, onmouseout, onkeypress, onkeydown, onkeyup, lang, xml:lang, dir (ltr|rtl)	(#PCDATA | a | br | span | bdo |object| *applet* | img | map | *iframe* | tt | i | b | big | small | *u* | *s* | *strike* | *font* | *basefont* | em | strong | dfn | code | q | sub | sup | samp | kbd | var | cite | abbr | acronym | input | select | textarea | label | button | ins | del | script | noscript)*
big	id, class, style, title, lang, xml:lang, dir, onclick, ondblclick, onmousedown, onmouseup, onmouseover, onmousemove, onmouseout, onkeypress, onkeydown, onkeyup	(#PCDATA | a | br | span | bdo |object| *applet* | img | map | *iframe* | tt | i | b | big | small | *u* | *s* | *strike* | *font* | *basefont* | em | strong | dfn | code | q | sub | sup | samp | kbd | var | cite | abbr | acronym | input | select | textarea | label | button | ins | del | script | noscript)*
blockquote	id, class, style, title, lang, xml:lang, dir, onclick, ondblclick, onmousedown, onmouseup, onmouseover, onmousemove, onmouseout, onkeypress, onkeydown, onkeyup, cite	(*#PCDATA*| p | h1|h2|h3|h4| h5|h6 | div | ul | ol | dl | *menu* | *dir* | pre | hr | blockquote | address | *center* | **noframes** | *isindex* | fieldset | table | form | a | br | span | bdo |object| *applet* | img | map | *iframe* | tt | i | b | big | small | *u* | *s* | *strike* |*font* | *basefont* | em | strong | dfn | code | q | sub | sup | samp | kbd | var | cite | abbr | acronym | input | select | textarea | label | button | ins | del | script | noscript)*

Element Name	Attributes	Minimal Content Model
body	id, class, style, title, _lang_, xml:lang, dir, onclick, ondblclick, onmousedown, onmouseup, onmouseover, onmousemove, onmouseout, onkeypress, onkeydown, onkeyup, onload, onunload, _background, bgcolor, text, link, vlink, alink_	(_#PCDATA_| p | h1|h2|h3|h4| h5|h6 | div | ul | ol | dl | _menu_ | _dir_ | pre | hr | blockquote | address | _center_ | **noframes** | _isindex_ | fieldset | table | form | a | br | span | bdo |object| applet | img | map | _iframe_ | tt | i | b | big | small | _u_ |_s_| _strike_ |_font_ | _basefont_ | em | strong | dfn | code | q | sub | sup | samp | kbd | var | cite | abbr | acronym | input | select | textarea | label | button | ins | del | script | noscript)* **[In the strict DTD, body has the same content model as blockquote]**
br	id, class, style, title, _clear (left|all|right|none)_	EMPTY
button	id, class, style, title, _lang_, xml:lang, dir, onclick, ondblclick, onmousedown, onmouseup, onmouseover, onmousemove, onmouseout, onkeypress, onkeydown, onkeyup, name, value, type (button|submit|reset) submit, disabled (disabled), tabindex, accesskey, onfocus, onblur	(#PCDATA | p | h1|h2|h3|h4|h5|h6 | div | ul | ol | dl | _menu_ | _dir_ | pre | hr | blockquote | address | _center_ |**noframes** | table | br | span | bdo | object | _applet_ | img | map | tt | i | b | big | small | _u_ | _s_ | _strike_ |_font_ | _basefont_ | em | strong | dfn | code | q | sub | sup | samp | kbd | var | cite | abbr | acronym | ins | del | script | noscript)*

Continued

Element Name	Attributes	Minimal Content Model
caption	id, class, style, title, <u>lang</u>, xml:lang, dir, onclick, ondblclick, onmousedown, onmouseup, onmouseover, onmousemove, onmouseout, onkeypress, onkeydown, onkeyup, <u>*align (top|bottom|left|right)*</u>	(#PCDATA | a | br | span | bdo |<u>object</u> | *applet* | img | map | <u>*iframe*</u> | tt | i | b | big | small | <u>u</u> | <u>s</u> | <u>*strike*</u> | <u>*font*</u> | <u>*basefont*</u> | em | strong | dfn | code | q | sub | sup | samp | kbd | var | cite | abbr | acronym | input | select | textarea | label | button | ins | del | script | noscript)*
<u>*center*</u>	*id, class, style, title, <u>lang</u>, xml:lang, dir, onclick, ondblclick, onmousedown, onmouseup, onmouseover, onmousemove, onmouseout, onkeypress, onkeydown, onkeyup*	*(#PCDATA | p | h1|h2|h3| h4|h5|h6 | div | ul | ol | dl | <u>menu</u> | dir | pre | hr | blockquote | address | <u>**noframes**</u> | <u>isindex</u> | fieldset | table | form | a | br | span | bdo |<u>object</u> | applet | img | map | <u>iframe</u> | tt | i | b | big | small | <u>u</u> | <u>s</u> | <u>strike</u> |<u>font</u> | <u>basefont</u> | em | strong | dfn | code | q | sub | sup | samp | kbd | var | cite | abbr | acronym | input | select | textarea | label | button | ins | del | script | noscript)**
cite	id, class, style, title, <u>lang</u>, xml:lang, dir, onclick, ondblclick, onmousedown, onmouseup, onmouseover, onmousemove, onmouseout, onkeypress, onkeydown, onkeyup	(#PCDATA | a | br | span | bdo |<u>object</u> | *applet* | img | map | <u>*iframe*</u> | tt | i | b | big | small | <u>u</u> | <u>s</u> | <u>*strike*</u> |<u>*font*</u> | <u>*basefont*</u> | em | strong | dfn | code | q | sub | sup | samp | kbd | var | cite | abbr | acronym | input | select | textarea | label | button | ins | del | script | noscript)*

Element Name	Attributes	Minimal Content Model
code	id, class, style, title, <u>lang</u>, xml:lang, dir, onclick, ondblclick, onmousedown, onmouseup, onmouseover, onmousemove, onmouseout, onkeypress, onkeydown, onkeyup	(#PCDATA | a | br | span | bdo |<u>object</u> | *applet* | img | map | <u>*iframe*</u> | tt | i | b | big | small | <u>u</u> | <u>s</u> | <u>*strike*</u> | <u>*font*</u> | <u>*basefont*</u> | em | strong | dfn | code | q | sub | sup | samp | kbd | var | cite | abbr | acronym | input | select | textarea | label | button | ins | del | script | noscript)*
col	id, class, style, title, <u>lang</u>, xml:lang, dir, onclick, ondblclick, onmousedown, onmouseup, onmouseover, onmousemove, onmouseout, onkeypress, onkeydown, onkeyup, span, width , align (left|center|right|justify|char), char, charoff, valign (top|middle|bottom|baseline)	EMPTY
colgroup	id, class, style, title, <u>lang</u>, xml:lang, dir, onclick, ondblclick, onmousedown, onmouseup, onmouseover, onmousemove, onmouseout, onkeypress, onkeydown, onkeyup, span, width , align (left|center|right|justify|char), char, charoff, valign (top| middle|bottom|baseline)	col*

Continued

Element Name	Attributes	Minimal Content Model
dd	id, class, style, title, _lang_, xml:lang, dir, onclick, ondblclick, onmousedown, onmouseup, onmouseover, onmousemove, onmouseout, onkeypress, onkeydown, onkeyup	#PCDATA | p | h1|h2|h3| h4|h5|h6 | div | ul | ol | dl | _menu_ | _dir_ | pre | hr | blockquote | address | _center_ | **_noframes_** | _isindex_ | fieldset | table | form | a | br | span | bdo |_object_ | _applet_ | img | map | _iframe_ | tt | i | b | big | small | _u_ |_s_ | _strike_ |_font_ | _basefont_ | em | strong | dfn | code | q | sub | sup | samp | kbd | var | cite | abbr | acronym | input | select | textarea | label | button | ins | del | script | noscript)*
del	id, class, style, title, _lang_, xml:lang, dir, onclick, ondblclick, onmousedown, onmouseup, onmouseover, onmousemove, onmouseout, onkeypress, onkeydown, onkeyup, cite, datetime	(#PCDATA | p | h1|h2|h3| h4|h5|h6 | div | ul | ol | dl | _menu_ | _dir_ | pre | hr | blockquote | address | _center_ | **_noframes_** | _isindex_ | fieldset | table | form | a | br | span | bdo |_object_ | _applet_ | img | map | _iframe_ | tt | i | b | big | small | _u_ |_s_ | _strike_ |_font_ | _basefont_ | em | strong | dfn | code | q | sub | sup | samp | kbd | var | cite | abbr | acronym | input | select | textarea | label | button | ins | del | script | noscript)*

Element Name	Attributes	Minimal Content Model
dfn	id, class, style, title, <u>lang</u>, xml:lang, dir, onclick, ondblclick, onmousedown, onmouseup, onmouseover, onmousemove, onmouseout, onkeypress, onkeydown, onkeyup	(#PCDATA | a | br | span | bdo |<u>object</u>| <i>applet</i>| img | map | <i><u>iframe</u></i> | tt | i | b | big | small | <u>u</u> | <u>s</u> | <i><u>strike</u></i> | <i><u>font</u></i> | <i><u>basefont</u></i> | em | strong | dfn | code | q | sub | sup | samp | kbd | var | cite | abbr | acronym | input | select | textarea | label | button | ins | del | script | noscript)*
dir	id, class, style, title, <u>lang</u>, xml:lang, dir, onclick, ondblclick, onmousedown, onmouseup, onmouseover, onmousemove, onmouseout, onkeypress, onkeydown, onkeyup, <i>compact (compact)</i>	li+
div	id, class, style, title, <u>lang</u>, xml:lang, dir, onclick, ondblclick, onmousedown, onmouseup, onmouseover, onmousemove, onmouseout, onkeypress, onkeydown, onkeyup, <i><u>align</u></i>	(#PCDATA | p | h1|h2|h3|h4| h5|h6 | div | ul | ol | dl | <i><u>menu</u></i> | <i>dir</i> | pre | hr | blockquote | address | <i>center</i> | <u>noframes</u> | <i><u>isindex</u></i> | fieldset | table | form | a | br | span | bdo | <u>object</u> | <i>applet</i> | img | map | <i><u>iframe</u></i> | tt | i | b | big | small | <u>u</u> | <u>s</u> | <i><u>strike</u></i> |<i><u>font</u></i> | <i><u>basefont</u></i> | em | strong | dfn | code | q | sub | sup | samp | kbd | var | cite | abbr | acronym | input | select | textarea | label | button | ins | del | script | noscript)*

Continued

Element Name	Attributes	Minimal Content Model
dl	id, class, style, title, _lang_, xml:lang, dir, onclick, ondblclick, onmousedown, onmouseup, onmouseover, onmousemove, onmouseout, onkeypress, onkeydown, onkeyup, _compact (compact)_	(dt|dd)+
dt	id, class, style, title, _lang_, xml:lang, dir, onclick, ondblclick, onmousedown, onmouseup, onmouseover, onmousemove, onmouseout, onkeypress, onkeydown, onkeyup	(#PCDATA | a | br | span | bdo |object | _applet_ | img | map | _iframe_ | tt | i | b | big | small | _u_ | _s_ | _strike_ | _font_ | _basefont_ | em | strong | dfn | code | q | sub | sup | samp | kbd | var | cite | abbr | acronym | input | select | textarea | label | button | ins | del | script | noscript)*
em	id, class, style, title, _lang_, xml:lang, dir, onclick, ondblclick, onmousedown, onmouseup, onmouseover, onmousemove, onmouseout, onkeypress, onkeydown, onkeyup	(#PCDATA | a | br | span | bdo |object | _applet_ | img | map | _iframe_ | tt | i | b | big | small | _u_| _s_ | _strike_ | _font_ | _basefont_ | em | strong | dfn | code | q | sub | sup | samp | kbd | var | cite | abbr | acronym | input | select | textarea | label | button | ins | del | script | noscript)*

Element Name	Attributes	Minimal Content Model
fieldset	id, class, style, title, <u>lang</u>, xml:lang, dir, onclick, ondblclick, onmousedown, onmouseup, onmouseover, onmousemove, onmouseout, onkeypress, onkeydown, onkeyup	(#PCDATA | legend | p | h1|h2|h3|h4|h5|h6 | div | ul | ol | dl | <u>*menu*</u> | *dir* | pre | hr | blockquote | address | <u>*center*</u> | <u>**noframes**</u> | <u>*isindex*</u> | fieldset | table | form | a | br | span | bdo |<u>object</u> | applet | img | map | <u>*iframe*</u> | tt | i | b | big | small | <u>*u*</u> | <u>*s*</u> | <u>*strike*</u> |<u>*font*</u> | <u>*basefont*</u> | em | strong | dfn | code | q | sub | sup | samp | kbd | var | cite | abbr | acronym | input | select | textarea | label | button | ins | del | script | noscript)*
<u>font</u>	*id, class, style, title, <u>lang</u>, xml:lang, dir, size, color, face*	*(#PCDATA | a | br | span | bdo | <u>object</u> | applet | img | map | <u>iframe</u> | tt | i | b | big | small | <u>u</u> | <u>s</u> | <u>strike</u> |<u>font</u> | <u>basefont</u> | em | strong | dfn | code | q | sub | sup | samp | kbd | var | cite | abbr | acronym | input | select | textarea | label | button | ins | del | script | noscript)**

Continued

Element Name	Attributes	Minimal Content Model
form	id, class, style, title, lang, xml:lang, dir, onclick, ondblclick, onmousedown, onmouseup, onmouseover, onmousemove, onmouseout, onkeypress, onkeydown, onkeyup, action, method (get|post), name, enctype, onsubmit, onreset, accept, accept-charset, *target*	(*#PCDATA* | p | h1|h2|h3| h4|h5|h6 | div | ul | ol | dl | *menu* | *dir* | pre | hr | blockquote | address | *center* | **noframes** | *ISINDEX* | fieldset | table | *a* | *br* | *span* | *bdo* |*object* | *applet* | *img* | *map* | *iframe* | *tt* | *i* | *b* | *big* | *small* | *u* | *s* | *strike* |*font* | *basefont* | *em* | *strong* | *dfn* | *code* | *q* | *sub* | *sup* | *samp* | *kbd* | *var* | *cite* | *abbr* | *acronym* | *input* | elect | *textarea* | *label* | *button* | ins | del | script | noscript)*
frame	*id, class, style, title, longdesc, name, src, frameborder (1|0), marginwidth, marginheight, noresize (noresize), scrolling (yes|no|auto)*	*EMPTY*
frameset	*id, class, style, title, rows, cols, onload, onunload*	*(frameset|frame|noframes)**
h1	id, class, style, title, lang, xml:lang, dir, onclick, ondblclick, onmousedown, onmouseup, onmouseover, onmousemove, onmouseout, onkeypress, onkeydown, onkeyup, *align*	(#PCDATA | a | br | span | bdo |*object* | *applet* | img | map | *iframe* | tt | i | b | big | small | *u*| *s* | *strike* |*font* | *basefont* | em | strong | dfn | code | q | sub | sup | samp | kbd | var | cite | abbr | acronym | input | select | textarea | label | button | ins | del | script | noscript)*

Element Name	Attributes	Minimal Content Model
h2	id, class, style, title, _lang_, xml:lang, dir, onclick, ondblclick, onmousedown, onmouseup, onmouseover, onmousemove, onmouseout, onkeypress, onkeydown, onkeyup, _align_	(#PCDATA | a | br | span | bdo |object| _applet_ | img | map | _iframe_ | tt | i | b | big | small | _u_ | _s_ | _strike_ |_font_| _basefont_ | em | strong | dfn | code | q | sub | sup | samp | kbd | var | cite | abbr | acronym | input | select | textarea | label | button | ins | del | script | noscript)*
h3	id, class, style, title, _lang_, xml:lang, dir, onclick, ondblclick, onmousedown, onmouseup, onmouseover, onmousemove, onmouseout, onkeypress, onkeydown, onkeyup, _align_	(#PCDATA | a | br | span | bdo |object| _applet_ | img | map | _iframe_ | tt | i | b | big | small | _u_ | _s_ | _strike_ | _font_ | _basefont_ | em | strong | dfn | code | q | sub | sup | samp | kbd | var | cite | abbr | acronym | input | select | textarea | label | button | ins | del | script | noscript)*
h4	id, class, style, title, _lang_, xml:lang, dir, onclick, ondblclick, onmousedown, onmouseup, onmouseover, onmousemove, onmouseout, onkeypress, onkeydown, onkeyup, _align_	(#PCDATA | a | br | span | bdo |object| _applet_ | img | map | _iframe_ | tt | i | b | big | small | _u_ | _s_ | _strike_ | _font_ | _basefont_ | em | strong | dfn | code | q | sub | sup | samp | kbd | var | cite | abbr | acronym | input | select | textarea | label | button | ins | del | script | noscript)*

Continued

Element Name	Attributes	Minimal Content Model
h5	id, class, style, title, _lang_, xml:lang, dir, onclick, ondblclick, onmousedown, onmouseup, onmouseover, onmousemove, onmouseout, onkeypress, onkeydown, onkeyup, _align_	(#PCDATA | a | br | span | bdo |object | _applet_ | img | map | _iframe_ | tt | i | b | big | small | _u_ | _s_ | _strike_ | _font_ | _basefont_ | em | strong | dfn | code | q | sub | sup | samp | kbd | var | cite | abbr | acronym | input | select | textarea | label | button | ins | del | script | noscript)*
h6	id, class, style, title, _lang_, xml:lang, dir, onclick, ondblclick, onmousedown, onmouseup, onmouseover, onmousemove, onmouseout, onkeypress, onkeydown, onkeyup, _align_	(#PCDATA | a | br | span | bdo |object | _applet_ | img | map | _iframe_ | tt | i | b | big | small | _u_ | _s_ | _strike_ | _font_ | _basefont_ | em | strong | dfn | code | q | sub | sup | samp | kbd | var | cite | abbr | acronym | input | select | textarea | label | button | ins | del | script | noscript)*
head	_lang_, xml:lang, dir, profile	title (required) | base | script | style | meta | link | object | _isindex_
hr	id, class, style, title, _lang_, xml:lang, dir, onclick, ondblclick, onmousedown, onmouseup, onmouseover, onmousemove, onmouseout, onkeypress, onkeydown, onkeyup, _align (left|center| right), noshade (noshade), size, width_	EMPTY
html	_lang_, xml:lang, dir, xmlns (fixed: 'http://www.w3.org/ 1999/xhtml')	(head, body, _frameset_)(body not in frameset)

Element Name	Attributes	Minimal Content Model
i	id, class, style, title, lang, xml:lang, dir, onclick, ondblclick, onmousedown, onmouseup, onmouseover, onmousemove, onmouseout, onkeypress, onkeydown, onkeyup	(#PCDATA | a | br | span | bdo |object | applet | img | map | iframe | tt | i | b | big | small | u| s | strike | font | basefont | em | strong | dfn | code | q | sub | sup | samp | kbd | var | cite | abbr | acronym | input | select | textarea | label | button | ins | del | script | noscript)*
iframe	id, class, style, title, longdesc, name, src, frameborder (1|0), marginwidth, marginheight, scrolling (yes|no|auto), align (top|middle|bottom|left| right), height, width	(#PCDATA | p | h1|h2|h3|h4| h5|h6 | div | ul | ol | dl | dir | pre | hr | blockquote | address | menu | noframes | isindex | fieldset | table | form | a | br | span | bdo |object | applet | img | map | iframe | tt | i | b | big | small | u| s | strike |font | basefont | em | strong | dfn | code | q | sub | sup | samp | kbd | var | cite | abbr | acronym | input | select | textarea | label | button | ins | del | script | noscript)*
img	id, class, style, title, lang, xml:lang, dir, onclick, ondblclick, onmousedown, onmouseup, onmouseover, onmousemove, onmouseout, onkeypress, onkeydown, onkeyup, src, alt, name, longdesc, height, width, usemap, ismap (ismap), align (top|middle|bottom| left|right), border, hspace, vspace	EMPTY

Continued

Element Name	Attributes	Minimal Content Model
input	id, class, style, title, <u>lang</u>, xml:lang, dir, onclick, ondblclick, onmousedown, onmouseup, onmouseover, onmousemove, onmouseout, onkeypress, onkeydown, onkeyup, type (text | password | checkbox | radio | submit | reset | file | hidden | image | button), name, value, checked (checked), disabled (disabled), readonly (readonly), size, maxlength, src, alt, usemap, tabindex, accesskey, onfocus, onblur, onselect, onchange, accept, *align (top|middle|bottom| left|right)*	EMPTY
ins	id, class, style, title, <u>lang</u>, xml:lang, dir, onclick, ondblclick, onmousedown, onmouseup, onmouseover, onmousemove, onmouseout, onkeypress, onkeydown, onkeyup, cite, datetime	(#PCDATA | p | h1|h2|h3|h4| h5|h6 | div | ul | ol | dl | *menu* | *dir* | pre | hr | blockquote | address | *center* | **noframes** | *<u>isindex</u>* | fieldset | table | form | a | br | span | bdo |<u>object</u> | *applet* | img | map | *<u>iframe</u>* | tt | i | b | big | small | *<u>u</u>|<u>s</u>* | *<u>strike</u>* |*<u>font</u>* | *<u>basefont</u>* | em | strong | dfn | code | q | sub | sup | samp | kbd | var | cite | abbr | acronym | input | select | textarea | label | button | ins | del | script | noscript)*
<u>isindex</u>	*id, class, style, title, <u>lang</u>, xml:lang, dir, prompt*	*EMPTY*

Element Name	Attributes	Minimal Content Model
kbd	id, class, style, title, _lang_, xml:lang, dir, onclick, ondblclick, onmousedown, onmouseup, onmouseover, onmousemove, onmouseout, onkeypress, onkeydown, onkeyup	(#PCDATA | a | br | span | bdo |_object_ | _applet_ | img | map | _iframe_ | tt | i | b | big | small | _u_| _s_ | _strike_ | _font_ | _basefont_ | em | strong | dfn | code | q | sub | sup | samp | kbd | var | cite | abbr | acronym | input | select | textarea | label | button | ins | del | script | noscript)*
label	id, class, style, title, _lang_, xml:lang, dir, onclick, ondblclick, onmousedown, onmouseup, onmouseover, onmousemove, onmouseout, onkeypress, onkeydown, onkeyup, accesskey, onfocus, onblur	(#PCDATA | a | br | span | bdo |_object_ | _applet_ | img | map | _iframe_ | tt | i | b | big | small | _u_ | _s_ | _strike_ | _font_ | _basefont_ | em | strong | dfn | code | q | sub | sup | samp | kbd | var | cite | abbr | acronym | input | select | textarea | label | button | ins | del | script | noscript)*
legend	id, class, style, title, _lang_, xml:lang, dir, onclick, ondblclick, onmousedown, onmouseup, onmouseover, onmousemove, onmouseout, onkeypress, onkeydown, onkeyup, accesskey, _align (top|bottom|left|right)_	(#PCDATA | a | br | span | bdo |_object_ | _applet_ | img | map | _iframe_ | tt | i | b | big | small | _u_ | _s_ | _strike_ | _font_ | _basefont_ | em | strong | dfn | code | q | sub | sup | samp | kbd | var | cite | abbr | acronym | input | select | textarea | label | button | ins | del | script | noscript)*

Continued

Element Name	Attributes	Minimal Content Model
li	id, class, style, title, <u>lang</u>, xml:lang, dir, onclick, ondblclick, onmousedown, onmouseup, onmouseover, onmousemove, onmouseout, onkeypress, onkeydown, onkeyup, _type, value_	(#PCDATA | p | h1|h2|h3|h4| h5|h6 | div | ul | ol | dl | _menu_ | _dir_ | pre | hr | blockquote | address | _center_ | **noframes** | _isindex_ | fieldset | table | form | a | br | span | bdo |object| _applet_ | img | map | _iframe_ | tt | i | b | big | small | _u_ | _s_ | _strike_ |_font_ | _basefont_ | em | strong | dfn | code | q | sub | sup | samp | kbd | var | cite | abbr | acronym | input | select | textarea | label | button | ins | del | script | noscript)*
link	id, class, style, title, <u>lang</u>, xml:lang, dir, onclick, ondblclick, onmousedown, onmouseup, onmouseover, onmousemove, onmouseout, onkeypress, onkeydown, onkeyup, charset, href, hreflang, type, rel, rev, media, _target_	EMPTY
map	lang, xml:lang, dir, onclick, ondblclick, onmousedown, onmouseup, onmouseover, onmousemove, onmouseout, onkeypress, onkeydown, onkeyup, id, class, style, title, <u>name</u>	((p | h1|h2|h3|h4|h5|h6 | div | ul | ol | dl | _menu_ | _dir_ | pre | hr | blockquote | address | _center_ | **noframes** | _isindex_ | fieldset | table | form | ins | del | script | noscript)+ | area+)
menu	_id, class, style, title, <u>lang</u>, xml:lang, dir, onclick, ondblclick, onmousedown, onmouseup, onmouseover, onmousemove, onmouseout, onkeypress, onkeydown, onkeyup, compact (compact)_	_li+_

Element Name	Attributes	Minimal Content Model
meta	lang, xml:lang, dir, http-equiv, name, content, scheme	EMPTY
noframes	_id, class, style, title, <u>lang</u>, xml:lang, dir, onclick, ondblclick, onmousedown, onmouseup, onmouseover, onmousemove, onmouseout, onkeypress, onkeydown, onkeyup_	_Body_
noscript	id, class, style, title, <u>lang</u>, xml:lang, dir, onclick, ondblclick, onmousedown, onmouseup, onmouseover, onmousemove, onmouseout, onkeypress, onkeydown, onkeyup	_#PCDATA_ | p | h1|h2|h3|h4|h5|h6 | div | ul | ol | dl | _menu_ | _dir_ | pre | hr | blockquote | address | _center_ | **_noframes_** | _isindex_ | fieldset | table | form | a | br | span | bdo |<u>object</u> | _applet_ | img | map | _<u>iframe</u>_ | tt | i | b | big | small | <u>_u_</u> |<u>_s_</u> | _strike_ |<u>_font_</u> | <u>_basefont_</u> | em | strong | dfn | code | q | sub | sup | samp | kbd | var | cite | abbr | acronym | input | select | textarea | label | button | ins | del | script | noscript)*

Continued

Element Name	Attributes	Minimal Content Model
object	id, class, style, title, lang, xml:lang, dir, onclick, ondblclick, onmousedown, onmouseup, onmouseover, onmousemove, onmouseout, onkeypress, onkeydown, onkeyup, declare (declare), classid, codebase, data, type, codetype, archive, standby, height, width, usemap, name, tabindex, align (top|middle|bottom|left|right), border, hspace, vspace	(#PCDATA | param | p | h1|h2|h3|h4|h5|h6 | div | ul | ol | dl | menu | dir | pre | hr | blockquote | address | center | noframes | isindex | fieldset | table | form |a | br | span | bdo |object | applet | img | map | iframe | tt | i | b | big | small | u| s | strike | font | basefont | em | strong | dfn | code | q | sub | sup | samp | kbd | var | cite | abbr | acronym | input | select | textarea | label | button | ins | del | script | noscript)*
ol	id, class, style, title, lang, xml:lang, dir, onclick, ondblclick, onmousedown, onmouseup, onmouseover, onmousemove, onmouseout, onkeypress, onkeydown, onkeyup, type, compact (compact), start	li+
optgroup	id, class, style, title, lang, xml:lang, dir, onclick, ondblclick, onmousedown, onmouseup, onmouseover, onmousemove, onmouseout, onkeypress, onkeydown, onkeyup, disabled (disabled), label	option+
option	id, class, style, title, lang, xml:lang, dir, onclick, ondblclick, onmousedown, onmouseup, onmouseover, onmousemove, onmouseout, onkeypress, onkeydown, onkeyup, selected (selected), disabled (disabled), label, value	PCDATA

Element Name	Attributes	Minimal Content Model
p	id, class, style, title, <u>lang</u>, xml:lang, dir, onclick, ondblclick, onmousedown, onmouseup, onmouseover, onmousemove, onmouseout, onkeypress, onkeydown, onkeyup, <u>*align*</u>	(#PCDATA | a | br | span | bdo |<u>object</u> | *applet* | img | map | *<u>iframe</u>* | tt | i | b | big | small | <u>*u*</u> | <u>*s*</u> | *<u>strike</u>* |<u>*font*</u> | <u>*basefont*</u> | em | strong | dfn | code | q | sub | sup | samp | kbd | var | cite | abbr | acronym | input | select | textarea | label | button | ins | del | script | noscript)*
param	id, name, value, valuetype (data|ref|object), type	EMPTY
pre	id, class, style, title, <u>lang</u>, xml:lang, dir, onclick, ondblclick, onmousedown, onmouseup, onmouseover, onmousemove, onmouseout, onkeypress, onkeydown, onkeyup, <u>*width*</u>, xml:space (preserve)	(#PCDATA | a | br | span | bdo | map | tt | i | b | <u>*u*</u> | <u>*s*</u>| em | strong | dfn | code | q | sub | sup | samp | kbd | var | cite | abbr | acronym | input | select | textarea | label | button)*
q	id, class, style, title, <u>lang</u>, xml:lang, dir, onclick, ondblclick, onmousedown, onmouseup, onmouseover, onmousemove, onmouseout, onkeypress, onkeydown, onkeyup	(#PCDATA | a | br | span | bdo |<u>object</u> | *applet* | img | map | *<u>iframe</u>* | tt | i | b | big | small | <u>*u*</u> | <u>*s*</u> | *<u>strike</u>* | *<u>font</u>* | <u>*basefont*</u> | em | strong | dfn | code | q | sub | sup | samp | kbd | var | cite | abbr | acronym | input | select | textarea | label | button | ins | del | script | noscript)*

Continued

Element Name	Attributes	Minimal Content Model
_s_	id, class, style, title, _lang_, xml:lang, dir, onclick, ondblclick, onmousedown, onmouseup, onmouseover, onmousemove, onmouseout, onkeypress, onkeydown, onkeyup	(#PCDATA | a | br | span | bdo |object | applet | img | map | iframe | tt | i | b | big | small | u | s | strike |font | basefont | em | strong | dfn | code | q | sub | sup | samp | kbd | var | cite | abbr | acronym | input | select | textarea | label | button | ins | del | script | noscript)*
samp	id, class, style, title, lang, xml:lang, dir, onclick, ondblclick, onmousedown, onmouseup, onmouseover, onmousemove, onmouseout, onkeypress, onkeydown, onkeyup	(#PCDATA | a | br | span | bdo |object | applet | img | map | iframe | tt | i | b | big | small | u | s | strike |font | basefont | em | strong | dfn | code | q | sub | sup | samp | kbd | var | cite | abbr | acronym | input | select | textarea | label | button | ins | del | script | noscript)*
script	Charset, type, language, src, defer (defer), xml:space (preserve)	#PCDATA (likely within CDATA sections)
select	id, class, style, title, lang, xml:lang, dir, onclick, ondblclick, onmousedown, onmouseup, onmouseover, onmousemove, onmouseout, onkeypress, onkeydown, onkeyup, name, size, multiple (multiple), disabled (disabled), tabindex, onfocus, onblur, onchange	(optgroup|option)+

Element Name	Attributes	Minimal Content Model
small	id, class, style, title, <u>lang</u>, xml:lang, dir, onclick, ondblclick, onmousedown, onmouseup, onmouseover, onmousemove, onmouseout, onkeypress, onkeydown, onkeyup	(#PCDATA | a | br | span | bdo |<u>object</u> | *applet* | img | map | *<u>iframe</u>* | tt | i | b | big | small | *<u>u</u>* | *<u>s</u>* | *<u>strike</u>* |<u>*font*</u> | *<u>basefont</u>* | em | strong | dfn | code | q | sub | sup | samp | kbd | var | cite | abbr | acronym | input | select | textarea | label | button | ins | del | script | noscript)*
span	id, class, style, title, <u>lang</u>, xml:lang, dir, onclick, ondblclick, onmousedown, onmouseup, onmouseover, onmousemove, onmouseout, onkeypress, onkeydown, onkeyup	(#PCDATA | a | br | span | bdo |<u>object</u> | *applet* | img | map | *<u>iframe</u>* | tt | i | b | big | small | *<u>u</u>* | *<u>s</u>* | *<u>strike</u>* |<u>*font*</u> | *<u>basefont</u>* | em | strong | dfn | code | q | sub | sup | samp | kbd | var | cite | abbr | acronym | input | select | textarea | label | button | ins | del | script | noscript)*
<u>strike</u>	*id, class, style, title, <u>lang</u>, xml:lang, dir, onclick, ondblclick, onmousedown, onmouseup, onmouseover, onmousemove, onmouseout, onkeypress, onkeydown, onkeyup*	*(#PCDATA | a | br | span | bdo |<u>object</u> | applet | img | map | <u>iframe</u> | tt | i | b | big | small | <u>u</u> | <u>s</u> | <u>strike</u> |<u>font</u> | <u>basefont</u> | em | strong | dfn | code | q | sub | sup | samp | kbd | var | cite | abbr | acronym | input | select | textarea | label | button | ins | del | script | noscript)**
strong	id, class, style, title, <u>lang</u>, xml:lang, dir, onclick, ondblclick, onmousedown, onmouseup, onmouseover, onmousemove, onmouseout, onkeypress, onkeydown, onkeyup	(#PCDATA | a | br | span | bdo |<u>object</u> | *applet* | img | map | *<u>iframe</u>* | tt | i | b | big | small | *<u>u</u>* | *<u>s</u>* | *<u>strike</u>* |<u>*font*</u> | *<u>basefont</u>* | em | strong | dfn | code | q | sub | sup | samp | kbd | var | cite | abbr | acronym | input | select | textarea | label | button | ins | del | script | noscript)*

Continued

Element Name	Attributes	Minimal Content Model
style	lang, xml:lang, dir, type, media, title, xml:space (preserve)	#PCDATA (likely within CDATA sections)
sub	id, class, style, title, lang, xml:lang, dir, onclick, ondblclick, onmousedown, onmouseup, onmouseover, onmousemove, onmouseout, onkeypress, onkeydown, onkeyup	(#PCDATA | a | br | span | bdo |object | applet | img | map | iframe | tt | i | b | big | small | u | s | strike |font | basefont | em | strong | dfn | code | q | sub | sup | samp | kbd | var | cite | abbr | acronym | input | select | textarea | label | button | ins | del | script | noscript)*
sup	id, class, style, title, lang, xml:lang, dir, onclick, ondblclick, onmousedown, onmouseup, onmouseover, onmousemove, onmouseout, onkeypress, onkeydown, onkeyup	(#PCDATA | a | br | span | bdo |object | applet | img | map | iframe | tt | i | b | big | small | u | s | strike |font | basefont | em | strong | dfn | code | q | sub | sup | samp | kbd | var | cite | abbr | acronym | input | select | textarea | label | button | ins | del | script | noscript)*
table	id, class, style, title, lang, xml:lang, dir, onclick, ondblclick, onmousedown, onmouseup, onmouseover, onmousemove, onmouseout, onkeypress, onkeydown, onkeyup, summary, width, border, frame (void|above| below|hsides|lhs|rhs|vsides| box|border), rules (none | groups | rows | cols | all), cellspacing, cellpadding, align (left|center|right), bgcolor	(caption?, (col*|colgroup*), thead?, tfoot?, (tbody+|tr+))

Element Name	Attributes	Minimal Content Model
tbody	id, class, style, title, <u>lang</u>, xml:lang, dir, onclick, ondblclick, onmousedown, onmouseup, onmouseover, onmousemove, onmouseout, onkeypress, onkeydown, onkeyup, align (left|center| right|justify|char), char, charoff, valign (top|middle| bottom|baseline)	(tr)+
td	id, class, style, title, <u>lang</u>, xml:lang, dir, onclick, ondblclick, onmousedown, onmouseup, onmouseover, onmousemove, onmouseout, onkeypress, onkeydown, onkeyup, abbr, axis, headers, scope (row|col|rowgroup| colgroup), rowspan, colspan, align (left|center|right| justify|char), char, charoff, valign (top|middle|bottom| baseline), <u>*nowrap (nowrap)*</u>, <u>*bgcolor*</u>, <u>*width*</u>, <u>*height*</u>	#PCDATA | p | h1|h2|h3|h4| h5|h6 | div | ul | ol | dl | <u>*menu*</u> | *dir* | pre | hr | blockquote | address | <u>*center*</u> | **<u>noframes</u>** | <u>*isindex*</u> | fieldset | table | form | a | br | span | bdo |<u>object</u> | *applet* | img | map | <u>*iframe*</u> | tt | i | b | big | small | <u>*u*</u> |<u>*s*</u>| <u>*strike*</u> |<u>*font*</u> | <u>*basefont*</u> | em | strong | dfn | code | q | sub | sup | samp | kbd | var | cite | abbr | acronym | input | select | textarea | label | button | ins | del | script | noscript)*
textarea	id, class, style, title, <u>lang</u>, xml:lang, dir, onclick, ondblclick, onmousedown, onmouseup, onmouseover, onmousemove, onmouseout, onkeypress, onkeydown, onkeyup, name, rows, cols, disabled (disabled), readonly (readonly), tabindex, accesskey, onfocus, onblur, onselect, onchange	PCDATA

Continued

Element Name	Attributes	Minimal Content Model
tfoot	id, class, style, title, _lang_, xml:lang, dir, onclick, ondblclick, onmousedown, onmouseup, onmouseover, onmousemove, onmouseout, onkeypress, onkeydown, onkeyup, align (left|center|right|justify|char), char, charoff, valign (top|middle|bottom|baseline)	(tr)+
th	id, class, style, title, _lang_, xml:lang, dir, onclick, ondblclick, onmousedown, onmouseup, onmouseover, onmousemove, onmouseout, onkeypress, onkeydown, onkeyup, abbr, axis, headers REFS, scope (row|col|rowgroup|colgroup), rowspan, colspan, align (left|center|right|justify|char), char, charoff, valign (top|middle|bottom|baseline), _nowrap (nowrap)_, _bgcolor_, _width_, _height_	(#PCDATA | p | h1|h2|h3|h4|h5|h6 | div | ul | ol | dl | _menu_ | _dir_ | pre | hr | blockquote | address | _center_ | **noframes** | _isindex_ | fieldset | table | form | a | br | span | bdo |_object_ | _applet_ | img | map | _iframe_ | tt | i | b | big | small | _u_ |_s_ | _strike_ |_font_ | _basefont_ | em | strong | dfn | code | q | sub | sup | samp | kbd | var | cite | abbr | acronym | input | select | textarea | label | button | ins | del | script | noscript)*
thead	id, class, style, title, _lang_, xml:lang, dir, onclick, ondblclick, onmousedown, onmouseup, onmouseover, onmousemove, onmouseout, onkeypress, onkeydown, onkeyup, align (left|center|right|justify|char), char, charoff, valign (top|middle|bottom|baseline)	(tr)+
title	_lang_, xml:lang, dir	PCDATA

Element Name	Attributes	Minimal Content Model
tr	id, class, style, title, <u>lang</u>, xml:lang, dir, onclick, ondblclick, onmousedown, onmouseup, onmouseover, onmousemove, onmouseout, onkeypress, onkeydown, onkeyup, align (left|center| right|justify|char), char, charoff, valign (top|middle| bottom|baseline), <u>bgcolor</u>	(th | td)+
tt	id, class, style, title, <u>lang</u>, xml:lang, dir, onclick, ondblclick, onmousedown, onmouseup, onmouseover, onmousemove, onmouseout, onkeypress, onkeydown, onkeyup	(#PCDATA | a | br | span | bdo |<u>object</u> | *applet* | img | map | *iframe* | tt | i | b | big | small | <u>*u*</u> | <u>*s*</u> | <u>*strike*</u> |<u>*font*</u> | <u>*basefont*</u> | em | strong | dfn | code | q | sub | sup | samp | kbd | var | cite | abbr | acronym | input | select | textarea | label | button | ins | del | script | noscript)*
u	*id, class, style, title, <u>lang</u>, xml:lang, dir, onclick, ondblclick, onmousedown, onmouseup, onmouseover, onmousemove, onmouseout, onkeypress, onkeydown, onkeyup*	*(#PCDATA | a | br | span | bdo |<u>object</u> | applet | img | map | iframe | tt | i | b | big | small | <u>u</u> | <u>s</u> | <u>strike</u> |<u>font</u> | <u>basefont</u> | em | strong | dfn | code | q | sub | sup | samp | kbd | var | cite | abbr | acronym | input | select | textarea | label | button | ins | del | script | noscript)**
ul	id, class, style, title, <u>lang</u>, xml:lang, dir, onclick, ondblclick, onmousedown, onmouseup, onmouseover, onmousemove, onmouseout, onkeypress, onkeydown, onkeyup, <u>*type (disc|square| circle)*</u>, <u>*compact (compact)*</u>	li+

Continued

Element Name	Attributes	Minimal Content Model
var	id, class, style, title, <u>lang</u>, xml:lang, dir, onclick, ondblclick, onmousedown, onmouseup, onmouseover, onmousemove, onmouseout, onkeypress, onkeydown, onkeyup	(#PCDATA | a | br | span | bdo |<u>object</u> | *applet* | img | map | *<u>iframe</u>* | tt | i | b | big | small | *<u>u</u>* | *<u>s</u>* | *<u>strike</u>* |*<u>font</u>* | *<u>basefont</u>* | em | strong | dfn | code | q | sub | sup | samp | kbd | var | cite | abbr | acronym | input | select | textarea | label | button | ins | del | script | noscript)*

Appendix B

Commonly Used Encodings

Encoding	Bits Per Character	Usage
UTF-8	8	UCS Transformation Format - 8 bits (Very commonly used for Latin-based languages, while supporting characters from other regions)
UTF-16	16	UCS Transformation Format - 16 bits (Provides access to 32-bit characters and is more efficient than UTF-8 for non-Western languages)
UTF-7	7	UCS Transformation Format - 7 bits (Used for mail and news; relatively uncommon)
UCS-2	16	Universal Character System - 2 bytes (Pretty much the core of Unicode and ISO 10646.)
UCS-4	32	Universal Character System - 4 bytes
ISO-8859-1	8	Latin alphabets No. 1 (Western Europe, Latin America)
ISO-8859-2	8	Latin alphabets No. 2 (Central and Eastern Europe)
ISO-8859-3	8	Latin alphabets No. 3 (Southeastern Europe, Miscellaneous, Esperanto and Maltese)
ISO-8859-4	8	Latin alphabets No. 4 (Western Europe, Latin America)
ISO-8859-5	8	Latin, Cyrillic
ISO-8859-6	8	Latin, Arabic
ISO-8859-7	8	Latin, Greek
ISO-8859-8	8	Latin, Hebrew
ISO-8859-9	8	Latin, Turkish
ISO-8859-10	8	Latin, Lappish, Nordic, and Eskimo
EUC-JP	8	Japanese (Using multibyte encoding)

Continued

Encoding	Bits Per Character	Usage
Shift_JIS	16	Japanese (Using multibyte encoding)
ISO-2022-JP	7	Japanese (Using multibyte encoding; for mail and news)
US-ASCII	7	Early standard used for American English
EBCDIC	7	IBM standard used for English
Big5	16	Chinese (Used in Taiwan)
GB2312	16	Simplified Chinese (Used by mainland China and Singapore)
KOI6-R	8	An extended Russian set

Appendix C

Language Identifiers

Language	Code	Language	Code
Abkhazian	ab	Afan Oromo	om
Afar	aa	Afrikaans	af
Albanian	sq	Amharic	am
Arabic	ar	Armenian	hy
Assamese	as	Aymara	ay
Azerbaijani	az	Bashkir	ba
Basque	eu	Bengali; Bangla	bn
Bhutani	dz	Bihari	bh
Bislama	bi	Breton	br
Bulgarian	bg	Burmese	my
Byelorussian	be	Cambodian	km
Catalan	ca	Chinese	zh
Corsican	co	Croatian	hr
Czech	cs	Danish	da
Dutch	nl	English	en
Esperanto	eo	Estonian	et
Faeroese	fo	Fijian	fj
Finnish	fi	French	fr
Frisian	fy	Galician	gl
Georgian	ka	German	de
Greenlandic	kl	Greek	el

Continued

Language	Code	Language	Code
Guarani	gn	Gujarati	gu
Hausa	ha	Hebrew	he
Hindi	hi	Hungarian	hu
Icelandic	is	Indonesian	id
Interlingua	ia	Inuktitut (Eskimo)	iu
Irish	ga	Italian	it
Japanese	ja	Javanese	jw
Kannada	kn	Kashmiri	ks
Kazakh	kk	Kinya, Rwanda	rw
Kirghiz	ky	Kirundi	rn
Knupiak	ik	Korean	ko
Kurdish	ku	Laotian	lo\
Latin	la	Latvian, Lettish	lv
Lingala	ln	Lithuanian	lt
Lnterlingue	ie	Macedonian	mk
Malagasy	mg	Malay	ms
Malayalam	ml	Maltese	mt
Maori	mi	Marathi	mr
Moldavian	mo	Mongolian	mn
Nauru	na	Nepali	ne
Norwegian	no	Occitan	oc
Oriya	or	Pashto, Pushto	ps
Persian	fa	Polish	pl
Portuguese	pt	Punjabi	pa
Quechua	qu	Rhaeto-Romance	rm
Romanian	ro	Russian	ru
Samoan	sm	Sangro	sg
Sanskrit	sa	Scottish Gaelic	gd

Language	Code	Language	Code
Serbian	sr	Serbo-Croatian	sh
Sesotho	st	Setswana	tn
Shona	sn	Sindhi	sd
Sinhalese	si	Siswati	ss
Slovak	sk	Slovenian	sl
Somali	so	Spanish	es
Sundanese	su	Swahili	sw
Swedish	sv	Tagalog	tl
Tajik, Tajiki	tg	Tamil	ta
Tatar	tt	Tegulu	te
Thai	th	Tibetan	bo
Tigrinya	ti	Tonga	to
Tsonga	ts	Turkish	tr
Turkmen	tk	Twi	tw
Uighur, Uigur	ug	Ukrainian	uk
Urdu	ur	Uzbek	uz
Vietnamese	vi	Welsh	cy
Wolof	wo	Xhosa	xh
Yiddish	yi	Yoruba	yo
Zhuang	za	Zulu	zu

Appendix D

Country Codes

Country	Code	Country	Code
Afghanistan	AF	Albania	AL
Algeria	DZ	American Samoa	AS
Andorra	AD	Angola	AO
Anguilla	AI	Antarctica	AQ
Antigua and Barbuda	AG	Argentina	AR
Armenia	AM	Aruba	AW
Australia	AU	Austria	AT
Azerbaijan	AZ	Bahamas	BS
Bahrain	BH	Bangladesh	BD
Barbados	BB	Belarus	BY
Belgium	BE	Belize	BZ
Benin	BJ	Bermuda	BM
Bhutan	BT	Bolivia	BO
Bosnia and Herzegovina	BA	Botswana	BW
Bouvet Island	BV	Brazil	BR
British Indian Ocean Territory	IO	Brunei Darussalam	BN
Bulgaria	BG	Burkina Faso	BF
Burma, see *Myanmar*		Burundi	BI
Cambodia	KH	Cameroon	CM
Canada	CA	Cape Verde	CV
Cayman Islands	KY	Central African Republic	CF

Continued

Country	Code	Country	Code
Chad	TD	Chile	CL
China	CN	Christmas Island	CX
Cocos (Keeling) Islands	CC	Colombia	CO
Comoro Islands	KM	Congo	CG
Congo, Democratic Republic of the	CD	Cook Islands	CK
Costa Rica	CR	Côte d'Ivoire	CI
Croatia	HR	Cuba	CU
Cyprus	CY	Czech Republic	CZ
Denmark	DK	Djibouti	DJ
Dominica	DM	Dominican Republic	DO
East Timor	TP	Ecuador	EC
Egypt	EG	El Salvador	SV
Equatorial Guinea	GQ	Eritrea	ER
Estonia	EE	Ethiopia	ET
Falkland Islands (Islas Malvinas)	FK	Faeroe Islands	FO
Fiji	FJ	Finland	FI
France	FR	French Guiana	GF
French Polynesia	PF	French Southern Territories	TF
Gabon	GA	Gambia	GM
Georgian Republic	GE	Germany	DE
Ghana	GH	Gibraltar	GI
Greece	GR	Greenland	GL
Grenada	GD	Guadeloupe	GP
Guam	GU	Guatemala	GT
Guinea	GN	Guinea–Bissau	GW
Guyana	GY	Haiti	HT

Country	Code	Country	Code
Heard Island and McDonald Islands	HM	Holy See (Vatican City State)	VA
Honduras	HN	Hong Kong	HK
Hungary	HU	Iceland	IS
India	IN	Indonesia	ID
Iran, Islamic Republic of	IR	Iraq	IQ
Ireland	IE	Israel	IL
Italy	IT	Ivory Coast, see *Côte d'Ivoire*	
Jamaica	JM	Japan	JP
Jordan	JO	Kazakhstan	KZ
Kenya	KE	Kiribati	KI
Korea, Democratic People's Republic of	KP	Korea, Republic of	KR
Kuwait	KW	Kyrgyzstan	KG
Lao People's Democratic Republic	LA	Latvia	LV
Lebanon	LB	Lesotho	LS
Liberia	LR	Libyan Arab Jamahiriya	LY
Liechtenstein	LI	Lithuania	LT
Luxembourg	LU	Macau	MO
Macedonia, The Former Yugoslav Republic of	MK	Madagascar	MG
Malawi	MW	Malaysia	MY
Maldives	MV	Mali	ML
Malta	MT	Marshall Islands	MH
Martinique	MQ	Mauritania	MR
Mauritius	MU	Mayotte	YT

Continued

Country	Code	Country	Code
Mexico	MX	Micronesia, Federated States of	FM
Moldova, Republic of	MD	Monaco	MC
Mongolia	MN	Montserrat	MS
Morocco	MA	Mozambique	MZ
Myanmar	MM	Namibia	NA
Nauru	NR	Nepal	NP
Netherlands	NL	Netherlands Antilles	AN
New Caledonia	NC	New Zealand	NZ
Nicaragua	NI	Niger	NE
Nigeria	NG	Niue	NU
Norfolk Island	NF	Northern Mariana Islands	MP
Norway	NO	Oman	OM
Pakistan	PK	Palau	PW
Palestinian Territory, Occupied	PS	Panama	PA
Papua New Guinea	PG	Paraguay	PY
Peru	PE	Philippines	PH
Pitcairn	PN	Poland	PL
Portugal	PT	Puerto Rico	PR
Qatar	QA	Réunion	RE
Romania	RO	Russian Federation	RU
Rwanda	RW	Saint Helena	SH
Saint Kitts and Nevis	KN	Saint Lucia	LC
Saint Pierre and Miquelon	PM	Saint Vincent and the Grenadines	VC
Samoa	WS	San Marino	SM
Sao Tome and Principe	ST	Saudi Arabia	SA
Senegal	SN	Seychelles	SC

Country	Code	Country	Code
Sierra Leone	SL	Singapore	SG
Slovakia	SK	Slovenia	SI
Solomon Islands	SB	Somalia	SO
South Africa	ZA	South Georgia and the South Sandwich Islands	GS
Spain	ES	Sri Lanka	LK
Sudan	SD	Suriname	SR
Svalbard and Jan Mayen	SJ	Swaziland	SZ
Sweden	SE	Switzerland	CH
Syrian Arab Republic	SY	Taiwan, Province of China	TW
Tajikistan	TJ	Tanzania, United Republic of	TZ
Thailand	TH	Togo	TG
Tokelau	TK	Tonga	TO
Trinidad and Tobago	TT	Tunisia	TN
Turkey	TR	Turkmenistan	TM
Turks and Caicos Islands	TC	Tuvalu	TV
Uganda	UG	Ukraine	UA
United Arab Emirates	AE	United Kingdom	GB
United States	US	United States Minor Outlying Islands	UM
Uruguay	UY	Uzbekistan	UZ
Vanuatu	VU	Vatican City, see *Holy See*	
Venezuela	VE	Vietnam	VN
Virgin Islands, British	VG	Virgin Islands, U.S.	VI
Wallis and Futuna Islands	WF	Western Sahara	EH
Yemen	YE	Yugoslavia	YU
Zambia	ZM	Zimbabwe	ZW

Index

Symbols

& (ampersand) character
  and entity references, 120
  replacement of, 40
&amp entity, 40, 45
  in strict HTML, 60–63
&gt entity, 45
< entity, 45
* (asterisk) character
  with CSS selectors, 139–141
  in element type declarations, 108
< > delimiters, 5
  JavaScript/HTML conflicts, 35–36
  parser conflicts
  preventing problems with, 53
<?, ?> characters, and processing instructions (PIs), 44
; (semicolon) character, and entity references, 120

A

a element (anchor), 131
  in WML documents, 314
<A tags, 20
absolute positioning, 161
abstract modules (XHTML 1.1), 256
  content structure symbols (table), 257–258
  Forms Module example, 259–263
  simple example, 258–259
  user-friendliness, 288
a.content entity, 131
Active Server Pages (ASP)
  DOM in, 228–229
  in XHTML generation code, 208–209
ActiveX components, integrating with HTML, 34–35
:after selector (CSS), 144
align attribute (transitional/frameset DTD), 131
alt attribute (WML), 318
Altheim, Murray, 278
Amaya 2.4/Windows NT browser
  handling of HTML, 30–31, 97
  strict HTML documents in, 98

strict XHTML documents in, 98–99
transitional XHTML documents in, 97
XHTML/MathML support, 7
ampersand (&) character, 40
anchor (a) element, 131
ANY content model, 105
appendChild() method (DOM-based XHTML), 231
applets element (transitional/frameset DTD), 132
archy module-building tool, 278
area element, 132
ASP engines, DOCTYPE declarations with, 239
"Assigning Property Values, Cascading and Inheritance" (CSS2), 163
asterisk (*) character
  with CSS selectors, 139–141
  in element type declarations, 108
.attlist parameter entity suffix (XML-DTD), 266–268
[attName] selectors (CSS), 142
.attrib parameter entity suffix (XML-DTD), 265–266
attribute list declarations, in DTDs, 108–115, 126–127
attribute values (XHTML)
  case sensitivity, 37–38
  in CSS selector syntax, 139–140
  quotes around, 39–40
attributes (HTML)
  abbreviated attributes, 32–33
  case insensitivity, 28
  compact, for list items, 33
  omitting quotes from values, 33
  prefixes with, 47
attributes (XHTML)
  attribute types, 109–113
  default values, 113–115
  lower case for, 37–38
  modularization-related issues, 252–253
  namespace declarations, 45–46
attrs attribute, 128
attrs entity, 131
automation, XHTML for, 370–371

B

background-attachment property (CSS), 146
background-color property (CSS), 146
background-image property (CSS), 146
background property (CSS), 146
background-repeat property (CSS), 146
basefont element (transitional/frameset DTD),
    131
batch conversion, 200
BBTidy, 200
:before selector (CSS), 144
best-effort presentations, 27
bgcolor element (transitional/frameset DTD),
    132
block element (strict DTD), 130
Block entities (DTD), components, 128
block-level elements, in DTDs, 128
block.mix entity, struct.model entity
    comparison, 292
blockquote element, 131
body element, 130
    browser-related problems, 168
bookmarks (Nokia WAP Toolkit), 308–310
border attribute, dropping of in strict DTD,
    132
border-bottom-color property (CSS), 146
border-bottom-style property (CSS), 146
border-bottom-width property (CSS), 147
border-color property (CSS), 147
border-left-color property (CSS), 147
border-left-style property (CSS), 147
border-left-width property (CSS), 147
border property (CSS), 146
border-right-color property (CSS), 147
border-right-style property (CSS), 147
border-right-width property (CSS), 147
border-style property, 148
border-top-color property (CSS), 148
border-top-style property (CSS), 148
border-top-width property (CSS), 148
br element
    in XHTML conversions, 205
    in strict DTD, limitations, 132
browser developers, respect for standards, 170
browsers
    CSS with, 137–138
    development priorities, politics in, 248
    DOM-based XHTML forms in, 237

DOM-based XHTML templates in, 241
HTML for, disadvantages, 246–247
identifying using User-Agent field, 250
interoperability issues, 102
Mozquito support, 327
namespace support, 248–249, 300
XHTML 1.0 support, 168, 289
XHTML-FML forms in, 326–327, 355
XML data islands and, 293–296
XSLT converted XHTML in, 225
Building XHTML Modules, 255
    abstract module definition, 256
    DTD modules, building rules, 263

C

card element (WML), 310–311
cards, in WML documents, 310
cascades, in Cascading Style Sheets (CSS),
    163
Cascading Style Sheets (CSS), 17–18. *See also*
    CSS2 specification
    advantages of using, 135–136, 170
    annotative formatting, 137
    browser support issues, 138, 163–164
    cascades, 163
    id attributes, 41
    level 1/level 2 selectors (table), 140–144
    properties (table), 146–155
    replacement of FONT element with, 53
    selectors and properties, 138
    in strict XHTML, 60–63, 156–162
    syntax, 138
    in XHTML, 135
    in XHTML-FML, 342–344
    XSL comparison, 137, 216
case insensitivity, in HTML, 28
case sensitivity
    and DOCTYPE declarations, 180
    in HTML to XHTML code conversions, 203
    in XML/XHTML markup, 37, 175–176
CC/PP project. *See* Composite
    Capabilities/Preference Profiles
CDATA attribute type, 110–111
CDATA sections, 42
    containing < characters using, 54–55
    eliminating, 58–59
    in XML/XHTML documents, 44–45

cell phones
    CC/PP tools for, 251–253
    HTML for, disadvantages, 246
    Web pages for, 6
center element, 131
CGI.pm, XHTML-compliant modules, 210
Chameleon (Mozquito.com), 327
Character entity, defining, 126–127
character mnemonic entities, HTML-
    supported, 125
child elements, in XML, 5
Chinese encoding, in XHTML, 172
Chinese XML Now! (Academica Sinica), 172
class attribute (XHTML), 22–23, 127
    with CSS, 136
    in DOM-based applications, 236
class information, using with CSS selectors,
    140
.class parameter entity suffix (XML-DTD),
    268–270
.className selector (CSS), 142
clear property (CSS), 148
client/server relationships
    typical HTML-based applications, 13–14
    XML-based applications, 14
client-side image maps, in DTDs, 132
clients, supporting XHTML-DTD module
    integration, 288–290. *See also* users
cloneNode() method (DOM-based XHTML),
    236
Color entity, defining, 127
color property (CSS), 148
comments
    for HTML/JavaScript conflicts, 35–36
    user-readable, in XML, 296–298
    for XHTML-DTD module documentation,
    288
    XML/XHTML rules for, 42
compact attributes, 33
compiling,WML document code, 311
Composite Capabilities/Preference Profiles
    (CC/PP), 211, 251–252
conditional sections, avoiding, 278
container elements, XHTML-Biography
    module (table), 279–280
containment relationships
    CSS selector syntax for, 139
    XHTML within XML documents, 298–299
    XML and, 5

content
    content negotiation approaches, 250–251
    labeling in XML/XHTML, 22–23
    protecting, in XML/XHTML, 44–45
    separating from formatting, CSS approach,
    135–137
content models
    anchor (a) element, 131
    for XHTML abstract modules, 253–254,
    257–258
    for XHTML element type declarations,
    104–108
.content parameter entity suffix (XML-DTD),
    268
content property (CSS), 148
content type values, Mozquito Factory,
    predefined (table), 330–331
context
    identifying browsers, 250
    namespace-related problems, 249
CORBA, DOM specification for, 228
coreattr entity
    attributes in, 127
    in attrs attribute, 128
Cowan, John, 292
createElement() method (DOM-based XHTML),
    230, 231
createTextNode() method (DOM-based
    XHTML), 231
CSS. *See* Cascading Style Sheets (CSS)
CSS-aware browsers, 157–159
CSS2 specification, 16–17
    unofficial style sheet, 137
css:active selector, 143
customizing XML-DTDs, 120

D

data stores (XML), hierarchical structure,
    21–22
data type definitions (DTDs), 126–127
databases, storing XML documents in, 21–22
.datatype parameter entity suffix, 264–265
deck of cards structure (WML), 310
defaults, XHTML attribute values, 113–115
del element, 131
deprecated elements/attributes
    CDATA sections, 58–59
    FONT element, 53

Continued

deprecated elements/attributes *(continued)*
    hspace attribute, 132
    NAME attribute, 40
    param element, 132
    target attribute, 131–132
    vspace attribute, 132
detail elements, XHTML-Biography Module,
    280
developers, transitioning to XML/XHTML
    process requirements, 172
    training requirements, 168
dir attribute (XHTML), 127
    declaring, 117
direction property (CSS), 149
display property (CSS), 149
div element, 130
do element (WML), 312, 316
DOCTYPE declarations
    adding to documents, 54
    for ASP engines/XML parsers, 239
    in DOM-based XHTML, 230
    in HTML documents, 36
    in HTML to XHTML conversions, 169, 202
    internal subsets, avoiding using, 125
    in strict DTD, 124
    in strict HTML, 60–63
    in strict XHTML, 64–69
    in transitional XHTML, 179
    in XHTML-FML, 324
    in XML/XHTML, 42
    in XSLT conversions, 218
doctype-public attribute (XSLT conversion),
    218
doctype-system attribute (XSLT conversion),
    218
document body section (DTD), 130
document containers, in XML,, 298–299
Document Definition Markup Language
    (DDML), 292
document handling, HTML versus XML,
    15–16
Document Object Model (DOM)
    advantages, 242–243
    DOM API specification, 228–229
    form information, collecting and passing,
        233–242
    id attributes, 41
    implementing, variability in, 228–229
    levels, portions, 229

simple XHTML document using, 229–232
text document comparison, 227–228
with XHTML template documents,
    239–242
document repositories (XML), with XHTML,
    9–10
Document Style Semantics and Specification
    Language (DSSSL), in XSL, 215–216
document type definitions (DTD), 4–5. *See
    also* DTD modules
    choosing, 169
    instance karma for, 278
    document body, 130
    element type declarations, 104–108
    in XHTML documents, 41–42, 53–59
    XML Schemas standard, 103
document type definitions (DTD), XHTML 1.0,
    123–124
    anchor element section, 131
    applets section, 132
    attribute list declarations, 108–115
    block-level elements, 128
    entity set references, 125
    exclusions, 129
    forms section, 132
    frame section, 130
    general entity declarations, 119–120
    generic attributes, 127–128
    head section, 129–130
    html element, 129
    images section, 132
    in-line elements section, 131–132
    list section, 131
    objects section, 132
    other elements section, 131
    overall structure, 129
    paragraph and headings sections, 131
    parameter entity declarations, 115–119,
        126–127
    preliminary sections, 125
    tables section, 132
    text elements, 128
documentation
    abstract modules for, 277
    for XHTML-DTD modules, 288
documents, referencing, 20
double quotes, using in XHTML, 39
drivers, for XHTML-Biography Module, 283

DSSSL. *See* Document Style Semantics and
    Specification Language
DTD modules (XML), 263. *See also* document
    type definitions (DTD)
    adding/modifying driver files for, 283–286
    building new, 277–283
    converting to XHTML, 277–283
    creating custom, 120
    namespace/validation issues, 286–287
    parameter entity suffixes, 264–271
dynamic HTML (DHMTL)
    FML conversion to, 321
    ID attributes, 33

E

e-commerce order form (XHTML-FML)
    contact information form, 329
    editable lists/pull-down menus, 338–341
    formatting enhancements, 342–344
    input validation, 330–334
    integrating with shopping cart form,
        360–366
    mandatory field requirements, 334–338
    standard template, 328
    submitting forms to server, 333–334
element content structures (XHTML 1.1),
    symbols table, 257–258
"Element Prohibitions", 133
element structure, clarity of, in XHTML,
    38–39
element type declarations (DTD), 131–132
elementName selectors (CSS), 140–141
elements (FML), HTML 4.01 comparison, 367
elements (HTML), case insensitivity, 28
elements (XHTML)
    empty elements, 39, 205
    locating properly, 177–178
    lower case for, 37–38
    type declarations, 104–108
    XHTML-Biography Module (tables),
        279–280
    XHTML, eliminating overlapping, 178
elements (XML), tags for, 5
EMPTY content model, 105
encoding declarations, in XHTML documents,
    43
end tags (HTML), omission of, 28–31,
    204–205

end tags (XML/XHTML), 5, 65–66
    necessity for, 38–39, 176–177
entities, built-in, replacing HTML characters
    using, 45
entities, character mnemonic, referencing,
    125–126
entity declarations (XHMTL DTD), , 125–126
entity replacement (strict HTML), 60–63
entity set location URLs, 126
enumerated attribute types, 110, 112–113
Ericsson R380 WAP emulator, 306
error checking for XHTML-FML, 324–326
error messages, WML compilation errors, 311
events entity (XHTML DTD), 128
exclusions, content models for, 129
Extensible Markup Language (XML). *See also*
    XML data islands; XML parsers
    case sensitivity, 37
    child elements, 5
    Chinese character encodings, 172
    comment line rules, 42
    converting to XHTML, 216
    documents, as interim products, 18–19
    flexibility, 14–15
    freedom from document-oriented
        formatting, 14
    HTML comparisons, 5, 17–23
    HTML integration with, 292–293
    language identification, 47–49
    links in, 20
    namespaces, 45–47, 248–249
    PCDATA data type support, 108
    processing instructions (PIs), 44
    processing tools for, 173–174
    repositories/databases for, 9–10, 20–22
    root elements, 5
    Schemas, 272
    searching/indexing, 22–23
    scripts with, 19
    strict adherence to document types, 42
    style sheets with, 17–18
    tree structure, 227–228
    validation issues, 47
    vocabulary, 5, 278, 291
    XHTML integration with, 7, 291–293
    XHTML modules with, 300–301
    XSL with, 5, 164

Extensible Stylesheet Language
    Transformations (XSLT), 19, 209
    CSS comparison, 216
    local transformations, 216
    uses for, 226
    XML to XHTML conversion, 216–217
Extensible Stylesheet Language (XSL), 17–18,
    19, 215–217
    with XML/XHTML, 164
extensions
    for HTML browsers, 34–35
    for XHTML-DTD module documentation,
        288–290
external parameter entities, declaring in
    XHTML, 118
.extra parameter entity suffix (XML-DTD),
    268–270

F

:first-child selector (CSS), 143
:first-letter selector (CSS), 144
:first-line selector (CSS), 144
#FIXED attribute default, 114
float property (CSS), 149
Flow entities, components, 128
FML. *See* Forms Markup Language (FML)
focus entity, 128
:focus selector (CSS), 143
font element
    relationship to h element, 178
    in transitional/frameset DTDs, 131
FONT element (HTML), replacement of with
    CSS, 53
font-family property (CSS), 150
font property (CSS), 149
font-size property (CSS), 150
font-style property (CSS), 150
font-variant property (CSS), 150
font-weight property (CSS), 150
fontstyle entities (strict DTD), 128
form element, 132
Formal Public Identifiers (FPI), in XHTML 1.1
    files, 273–274
formatting
    annotative versus transformative, 137
    CSS for, 135–155
    in DOM-based XHTML, 236–237
    in HTML, "understood", 137

processing instructions (PIs), 44
    in HTML, 60–63
    in strict DTD, 130
    in transitional/frameset DTD, 131
forms
    DOM-based XHTML example, 233–242
    e-commerce order form (XHTML-FML),
        327–344
    FML for, 321–322
    text-based WML user-input form, 315–318
    XML data islands for, 293–296
Forms Markup Language (FML), 321–322
    comparison with HTML 4.01, 367
    creating, 323–324
    displaying, 326–327
    e-commerce order form example, 327–344
FPI. *See* Formal Public Identifiers (FPI)
fragmentation. *See* modularization
frames
    in HTML generated code conversions, 203
    segregating, 129
    and strict DTD, 170
    in XHTML modularization, 253
frames element (transitional/frameset DTD),
    130
frames section, in DTDs, 130
frameset DTD (XHTML 1.0), 123–125
    align attribute, 131
    center element, 131
    formatting elements, 131
    frames element components, 130
    list section, 131
    in transition to strict DTD, 170
frameset element, 129
frameset XHTML, style sheets with, 162
frameworks, for XHTML module, 278

G

Gelon.Net, Wapalizer WAP emulator, 306
general entities, declaring in XHTML,
    119–120
generation code (HTML), converting to
    XHTML
    case changes, 203
    complexity and issues, 201–202
    DOCTYPE declarations, 202

handling coding
inconsistencies/idiosyncrasies,
204–205
testing for XHTML conformance, 207
validating, 205–206
generation code (XHTML)
managing templates, 208–210
managing text, 208
modularization, 210–211
go element, 312
with text-based WML form, 316

H

h1–h6 elements
in CSS selector syntax, 139
in-line elements in, 131
hand-held devices, Web-enabling technology
for, 305
Handheld Device Markup Language (HDML),
305
head element, 129–130
building in DOM-based XHTML, 231
declaring in XHTML, 130
in html element, 129
in strict XHTML documents, 64
head section, in DTDs, 129–130
heading blocks, 128
heading elements (XHTML), mixing with text
elements, 118
headings section, in DTDs, 131
height attribute (WML), 318
height element (transitional/frameset DTD),
132
height property (CSS), 151
Hello World program, as XML document,
310–311
helper applications, in HTML browsers, 34–35
Holman, Ken, XSL training, 215
horizontal rule (hr) element, 131
:hover selector (CSS), 143
hr attribute, 131
hspace attribute, in strict DTD, 132
HTML. *See* Hypertext markup language
(HTML)
HTML-compatible browsers
automatic end tag closing, 31–32
extensions for, 34–35
handling of unrecognized tags, 33–34

overlapping tag support, 32
testing XHTML in, 168–169
variability in document appearance, 28–31
HTML documents, basic
in Amaya 2.4/Windows NT browser, 97
comment lines, 35–36
DOCTYPE declarations, 36
as end products, 18
example document, code for, 51–53
in Internet Explorer 3.01/MacOS 8.1
browser, 85
in Internet Explorer 4.0/MacOS 8.1
browser, 87
in Internet Explorer 4.01/Windows 95
browser, 89
in Internet Explorer 5.01/Windows NT 4.0
browser, 92
in Lynx 2.8.2/Windows 95 browser, 99
in Netscape Communicator 4.7/Windows
NT 4.0 browser, 79
in Netscape Navigator 1.22/Windows NT
4.0 browser, 70
in Netscape Navigator 2.02/Windows NT
4.0 browser, 73
in Netscape Navigator 3.0/Windows NT
4.0 browser, 76
in Netscape Navigator 6 Preview
Release/Windows NT 4.0 browser, 82
in Opera 3.62/Windows NT browser, 94
storing, 20–22
variability in appearance of, 27
XML data islands in, 34, 293–300
HTML documents, strict
in Amaya 2.4/Windows NT browser, 98
creating using strict DTD and entity
replacement, 60–63
in Internet Explorer 3.01/MacOS 8.1
browser, 86
in Internet Explorer 4.0/MacOS 8.1
browser, 88
in Internet Explorer 4.01/Windows 95
browser, 90
in Internet Explorer 5.01/Windows NT 4.0
browser, 93
in Lynx 2.8.2/Windows 95 browser, 101
in Netscape Communicator 4.7/Windows
4.0 browser, 81

Continued

HTML documents, strict *(continued)*
  in Netscape Navigator 1.22/Windows NT
    4.0 browser, 72
  in Netscape Navigator 2.02/Windows NT
    4.0 browser, 75, 75–76
  in Netscape Navigator 3.0/Windows NT
    4.0 browser, 78, 78–79
  in Netscape Navigator 6 Preview
    Release/Windows NT 4.0 browser, 83
  in Opera 3.62/Windows NT browser, 95
html element
  adding language information, 203
  adding XHTML namespace, 203
  adding xmlns attribute to, 178
  building in DOM-based XHTML, 230–231
  components, 129
HTML-Kit, 199
HTML Tidy conversion tool (Raggett),
    180–199
HTML to XHTML conversions, 53–59
  BBTidy for, 200
  case changes, 203
  choosing DTD type, 169
  code generators, 9
  complexity and issues, 201–202
  DOCTYPE declarations, 202
  handling coding
    inconsistencies/idiosyncrasies,
    204–205
  HTML-Kit for, 199
  HTML Tidy for, 180–199
  Java Tidy for, 199
  reasons for, 173–174
  static documents, conversion process,
    175–180
  syntactical requirements, 169
  testing for XHTML conformance, 207
  tools for, 180–199
  validating, 205–206
  XML parser compatibility, 171
HTTP 1.0 protocol, CC/PP with, 253
HTTP Extension Framework, 253
hypertext linking (HTML)
  identifiers and, 41
  multiple names, 33
Hypertext Markup Language (HTML). *See also*
    HTML documents
  anchor tags, 20
  case insensitivity, 28

  CSS with, 17
  coding inconsistencies/idiosyncrasies, 5–6,
    32, 204–205
  development/control of by W3C, 247–248
  document type definitions (DTD), 4
  early history, 4–5
  end tag omissions, 28–31
  HTML 4.0 specification, 123–124
  HTML 4.01, FML 1.0 comparison, 367
  identifying in XML documents, 294
  identifying using MIME, 250
  information leaks, 371–372
  limitations, 27, 245–246
  multiple names, 33
  parsers for, 15–16
  "understood" formatting conventions, 137
  W3C revisions, 3
  XHTML comparisons, 3, 5
  XML comparisons, 5, 17–23

I

i18n entity. *See also* internationalization
  attributes in, 127
  in attrs attribute, 128
  declaring in XHTML, 117
IANA. *See* Internet Assigned Numbers
    Authority
ID attribute type (HTML), 33, 110–111
id attribute (XHTML), 127
  in CSS selector syntax, 140
  replacing NAME attribute, 40–41, 169
  with name attribute, 65
  with WML card element, 310
identifiers, creating in XHTML, 40–41
IDRED, IDREFS attribute types, 111–112
IDREF, IDREFS attribute types, 110
#IDvalue selector (CSS), 142
iframe element, in transitional DTD, 130
images
  adding to WML documents, 318
  adding to XHTML-FML forms, 358–360
  in WBMP format, creating, 319
  XML data islands for, 293–296
images sections, in DTDs, 132
img element, 132
  in XHTML conversions, 205
img element type (XML), 294–296
ImgAlign entity, defining, 127
#IMPLIED attribute default, 113

!important mechanism (CSS), 163
in-line elements section, in DTDs, 131–132
indent attribute, in XSLT conversions, 218
indexing XML documents, 22–23
inheritance, in CSS2 specification, 163
Inline entity, 128
    defining in-line element content, 131
inline markup, 300
INPUT elements, ban on nesting of, 15
ins element (insert), 131
inserts, with XHTML-FML forms, 355–358
instance karma module-building tool, 278
interfaces, user, handling variability in, 10–11
internal parameter entities, declaring in
        XHTML, 115–117
internationalization
    attributes for, 127
    parameter entity declarations, 117–118
    XML/XHTML language identification,
        47–49
Internet Assigned Numbers Authority (IANA),
        language identifiers, 48
Internet Engineering Task Force (IETF),
        content negotiation approaches, 250
Internet Explorer 3.01/MacOS 8.1 browser
    HTML documents in, 85
    strict HTML documents in, 86
    strict XHTML documents in, 86
    transitional XHTML documents in, 85
Internet Explorer 4.0/MacOS 8.1 browser
    HTML documents in, 87
    strict HTML documents in, 88
    strict XHTML documents in, 88–89
    transitional XHTML documents in, 87–88
Internet Explorer 4.01/Windows 95 browser
    HTML documents in, 89
    strict HTML documents in, 90
    strict XHTML documents in, 91
    transitional XHTML documents in, 90
Internet Explorer 5.01/Windows NT 4.0
        browser
    HTML documents in, 92
    strict HTML documents in, 93
    strict XHTML documents in, 93–94
    transitional XHTML documents in, 92–93
Internet Explorer 5.5 browser, 295
isindex element (strict DTD), 130
Itsy Bitsy Teeny Weeny Simple Hypertext
        DTD, 292

J
Japanese encoding, with XHTML, 172
Java-based applications
    on HTML browsers, 34–35
    UTF-8/UTF-16 encoding support, 171
Java programming language, DOM
        specification for, 228
Java Runtime Environment (JRE), with
        Mozquito Factory, 323
Java Server Pages (JSP), in XHTML
        generation code, managing, 208
Java Servlet Library, XHTML-compliant
        modules, 210
Java Tidy, 199
JavaScript
    DOM specification for, 228
    XHTML-FML form compatibility, 366–367
    with XML, 19

L
label element, x:label comparison, 336
lang attribute, 47–49, 127
    in DOM-based XHTML, 230
    supplementing with xml:lang, 169
:lang (language) selector (CSS), 143–144
language identification
    adding to html element, 203
    IANA, 48
    overriding identifiers, 49
Latin-1 character set, referencing, 120,
        125–126
layering information
    CSS selectors and, 138
    in XHTML, 370
    in XHTML-FML, 357–358
left property (CSS), 151
letter-spacing property (CSS), 151
line-height property (CSS), 151
:link selector (CSS), 143
linking, in XML/XHTML, 20
list items
    blocks for, 128
    compact attributes for (HTML), 33
    HTML code structure, handling in XHTML
        conversions, 204–205
list section, in DTDs, 131
list-style-image property (CSS), 151
list-style-position property (CSS), 152
list-style-type property (CSS), 152

lists
    editable, in XHTML-FML, 338–340
    with strict HTML, 60–63
Lynx 2.8.2/Windows 95 browser
    HTML document in, 99
    strict HTML document in, 101
    strict XHTML document in, 101
    transitional XHTML documents in, 100

M

machine-to-human communications, 369–370
machine-to-machine communications, 11
Macintosh platforms
    Mozquito Factory on, 323
    XHTML conversion tools, 200
MacOS Runtime for Java (MRJ), with
        Mozquito Factory, 323
mandatory attribute, 335
map element, 132
margin-bottom property (CSS), 152
margin-left property (CSS), 152
margin property (CSS), 152
margin-right property (CSS), 152
margin-top property (CSS), 152
MathML module, 6–7, 173
Megginson, David, 136
menus, pull-down, in XHTML-FML, 338–341
metadata, in DTDs, 129–130
Microsoft data islands. *See* XML data islands
MIME content type identifier, 250
    with strict HTML, 60–63
mime.types files, modifying for WAP-related
        documents, 308
misc entity, 128
.mix parameter entity suffix, 270
mixed content models, XHTML in XML,
        107–108, 300
Mobile Access activity (W3C), CC/PP project,
        251
.mod parameter entity suffix (XML-DTD), 270
modularization
    CC/PP and, 252
    content/context issues, 250–254
    module-building tools, 278
    XHTML 1.1 Forms Module example,
        259–263
    XHTML 1.1 module implementation,
        272–283
    XHTML 1.1 specification, 125, 370–371

XHTML generation code, 210–211
    XML Schema modules, 272
Modularization of XHTML, 255
.module parameter entity suffix (XML-DTD),
        271
Mozilla browser, XHTML/MathML support, 7
Mozquito Factory (Mozquito.com), 320
    browser support, 327
    components, 322
    downloading/installing, 323
    when to use, 323
multiple names, in HTML documents, 33
myDoc object (DOM-based XHTML), 231–232
MyML tool, 173

N

NAME attribute
    changing into id attribute, 65, 169
    deprecation of, 40
    in HTML, 33
name separator nodes (DOM-based XHTML),
        236
namespaces, 45–47
    in custom XHTML-DTD modules, 286–287
    identifying HTML using, 293–296
    multiple, handling, 249
    in XHTML-FML documents, 324
    in XML documents, 47, 248–249
navigating WML user-input form, 316–317
navigation buttons, adding to WML
        documents, 312–313
negotiating frameworks, XHTML for, 370–371
Netscape browsers
    HTML document in, 52
    script element problems, 168
Netscape Communicator 4.7/Windows NT 4.0
        browser
    HTML document in, 79
    strict HTML documents in, 81
    strict XHTML documents in, 81
    transitional XHTML documents in, 80
Netscape Navigator 1.22/Windows NT 4.0
    HTML document in, 70
    transitional XHTML in, 71
Netscape Navigator 2.02/Windows NT 4.0
    HTML document in, 73
    strict HTML document in, 75, 78
    strict XHTML document in, 75–76, 78–79
    transitional XHTML document in, 74

Netscape Navigator 3.0/Windows NT 4.0
    browser
    HTML documents in, 76
    transitional XHTML document in, 77
Netscape Navigator 6 Preview
        Release/Windows NT 4.0 browser
    HTML documents in, 82, 295
    strict HTML documents in, 83
    strict XHTML documents in, 84
    transitional XHTML documents in, 82–83
NMTOKEN attribute type, 110, 112
noframes element
    in html element, 129
    in transitional DTD, 130
Nokia WAP Emulator, 307
Nokia WAP Toolkit, 307–310
NOSCRIPT element, in Mozquito-produced
        HTML, 367
notes, user-readable, adding to XML
        documents, 296–298
Number entity, defining, 127

O

object element, in strict DTDs, 132
object models, XHTML with, 226
object trees, versus text streams, 227–228
objects element (DTD), 132
Office 2000, converting to XHTML, 7
ol element (order list), CSS selector syntax
        for, 139
omit-xml-declaration attribute, in XSLT
        conversions, 218
onload event attribute, 130
onunload event attribute, 130
open source XML tools, 23
Opera 3.62/Windows NT browser
    HTML document in, 94
    strict HTML documents in, 95
    strict XHTML documents in, 96
    transitional XHTML documents in, 95
Opera 4 browser, displaying HTML in XML
        documents, 295
order list (ol) element, CSS selector syntax
        for, 139
other elements section, in DTDs, 131
overflow property (CSS), 152
overlapping elements, eliminating in XHTML,
        38, 178

P

p element (paragraph)
    coding inconsistencies/idiosyncrasies,
        204–205
    in-line elements in, 131
padding-bottom property (CSS), 153
padding-left property (CSS), 153
padding property (CSS), 152
padding-right property (CSS), 153
padding-top property (CSS), 153
page-break-after property (CSS), 153
page-break-before property (CSS), 153
page-break-inside property (CSS), 154
page property (CSS), 153
paragraph section, in DTDs, 131
param element, dropping of in strict DTD, 132
parameter entity declarations (XHTML-DTD),
        126–127
    avoiding, 278
    external parameters, 119
    internal parameters, 115–119
parameter entity suffixes (XHTML-DTD)
    .attlist, 266–268
    .class/.extra, 268–270
    .content, 268
    .datatype, 264–265
    .mix, 270
    .mod, 270
    .module, 271
parameterization, 263
parsing (document handling), HTML versus
        XML, 15–16
PCDATA data type, 108
personal digital assistants (PDAs), 6
    HTML for, disadvantages, 246
PHP scripting, in XHTML files, 209
PIs. *See* processing instructions
plug-ins, integrating with HTML browsers,
        34–35
pointers, in XML documents, 20
pop-up dialog boxes, 27
postfield element, 317
prefixes
    and custom XHTML-DTD modules,
        286–287
    namespace declarations using, 46–47
    with XHTML attributes, 47

prev /element, with text-based WML form, 316–317

processing instructions (PIs), in XHTML documents, 44

prolog (WML documents), 310

properties, CSS, listing of (table), 146–155

props, with XHTML-FML forms, 355–358

proxy servers, CC/PP and, 252

pull-down menus, in XHTML-FML forms, 338–341

Q

quotes
  around XHTML attribute values, 176
  around XHTML attribute values, 39
  omitting, in HTML, 33

R

radio buttons, adding to XHTML-FML, 339–340

Raggett, Dave, 180

registration, namespace-related issues, 249

relative positioning, absolute positioning comparison, 161

repositories, for XML documents, 22

#REQUIRED attribute default, 113–114

Resource Description Framework (RDF), 132

reusability
  Cascading Style Sheets (CSS) and, 135
  XHMTL and, 174

root elements (XML), 5

rounding, in shopping cart form, 349

S

s element (transitional/frameset DTD), 131

Scalable Vector Graphics (SVG), 19, 173
  with XSLT, 226

Schemas, XML, with XHTML modules, 272

script element
  Netscape browser problems, 168
  in strict XHTML, 64–65

scripts
  storing in external files, 58–59, 68–69, 102, 168
  with XHTML documents, 42, 67–69
  with XML, 19, 293–296

search engines, parsing rules, 15

searching, XML documents, 22–23

security issues
  HTML and XHTML, 371–372
  style sheets, 136

selectors (CSS), 138
  listing of (table), 140–144
  syntax for, 139–140

semicolon (;) character, and entity references, 120

server-side includes, handling in XHTML conversions, 205

servers
  in HTML-based applications, 13–14
  modifying for WAP-related documents, 308
  in XML-based applications, 13–15

setAttribute() method (DOM-based XHTML), 230

SGML Open Catalog entries, 273

SGML (Standard Generalized Markup Language), 4

Shape entity, defining, 127

shopping cart form (XHTML-FML), 342–344
  adding additional products/prices, 349–355
  adding first product/price, 345–347
  adding images, 358–360
  adding layers to, 357–358
  integrating with e-commerce form, 360–366
  running totals, 355–356
  totaling orders, 347–348

single quotes, for XHTML attribute values, 39

size attribute (XHTML-FML), 330

SMIL multimedia tool, 173

span element (DOM-based XHTML), 236

Special character set, referencing, 125

special entities (strict DTD), 128

src attribute, 111

Standard Generalized Markup Language. *See* SGML

start tags (XML), 5

storage, HTML versus XML, 20–22

strict DTDs (XHTML 1.0), 123–124
  block-element restrictions, 128
  body/div element limitations, 130
  content model limitations, 128
  deprecated elements, 130
  formatting properties, elimination of, 130
  lists section limitations, 131

reasons for choosing, 170
target attribute limitations, 131
W3C's emphasis on, 169
strict HTML documents
in Amaya 2.4/Windows NT browser, 98
in Internet Explorer 3.01/MacOS 8.1
browser, 86
in Internet Explorer 4.0/MacOS 8.1
browser, 88
in Internet Explorer 4.01/Windows 95
browser, 90
in Internet Explorer 5.01/Windows NT 4.0
browser, 93
in Lynx 2.8.2/Windows 95 browser, 101
in Netscape Communicator 4.7/Windows
4.0 browser, 81
in Netscape Navigator 2.02/Windows NT
4.0 browser, 75
in Netscape Navigator 3.0/Windows NT
4.0 browser, 78
in Netscape Navigator 6 Preview
Release/Windows NT 4.0 browser, 83
in Opera 3.62/Windows NT browser, 95
strict XHTML documents, 249
in Amaya 2.4/Windows NT browser,
98–99
applying CSS to, 156–162
in Internet Explorer 3.01/MacOS 8.1
browser, 86
in Internet Explorer 4.0/MacOS 8.1
browser, 88–89
in Internet Explorer 4.01/Windows 95
browser, 91
in Internet Explorer 5.01/Windows NT 4.0
browser, 93–94
in Lynx 2.8.2/Windows 95 browser, 101
in Netscape Communicator 4.7/Windows
4.0 browser, 81
in Netscape Navigator 2.02/Windows NT
4.0 browser, 75–76
in Netscape Navigator 3.0/Windows NT
4.0 browser, 78–79
in Netscape Navigator 6 Preview
Release/Windows NT 4.0 browser, 84
in Opera 3.62/Windows NT browser, 96
style sheets with, advantages, 162
strike element (transitional/frameset DTD),
131
struct.model entity (DDML), Block.mix entity
comparison, 292

structured content model, 105–107
style attribute, 127
with CSS, 136
style sheets in, 163
style element
in strict XHTML documents, 65
style sheets in, 163
style sheet information, adding to strict
XHTML, 67–69
style sheets. See also Cascading Style Sheets
(CSS)
advantages of using, 162
customizing, 136
multiple, referencing in CSS, 163
rules for applying, 163
security concerns, 136
storing in external files, 168
with XHTML documents, 42
Symbols character set, referencing, 125
Synchronized Multimedia Integration
Language (SMIL, with XSLT, 226
syntax
attribute list declarations (XHTML), 109
Cascading Style Sheets (CSS), 138
CDATA sections, 44–45
CSS selectors, 139–140
DOCTYPE declarations and DTD types,
124–125
element type declarations (XHTML), 104
element type definition content models,
105, 107–108
external parameter entity declarations, 119
general entity declarations, 119–120
HTML Tidy conversion command, 180
internal parameter entity declarations,
115–119
parameter entity declarations, 264–271
XHTML abstract modules, 256
XHTML default attribute values, 114–115
system identifiers, in XHTML 1.1 files, 274

T

table element, 132
tags (HTML), 5
abbreviated attributes, 32–33
case insensitivity, 28
end tag omissions, 28–31
overlapping tag support, 32
unrecognized, browser handling of, 33–34

target attribute, deprecating of, 131–132

target element (strict DTD), 130

technical support, for XHTML-DTD module integration, 288–290

templates

    for DOM-based XHTM, 238–242

    for XHTML-FML, 328, 349–350

    in XHTML generation code, managing, 208–210

testing, HTML code conversions, 207. *See also* validating

text

    content labeling, 22–23

    storing, HTML versus XML, 20–22

    in tables element, prohibitions on, 132

    in XHTML generation code, managing, 208

text-align property (CSS), 154

text-based documents, object (DOM) comparison, 227–228

text-based user-input form (WML), 315–317

    sending to server, 317–318

text-decoration property (CSS), 154

text elements

    in DTDs, 128

    in XHTML, 118

text/html identifier, 250

text-indent property (CSS), 154

text-transform property (CSS), 154

TextAlign entity

    in strict DTDs, 130

    in transition, frameset DTDs, 128

timer-based automation, in WML documents, 313–315

timer element, 314

title attribute, 127

    with WML card element, 310

title element, building in DOM-based XHTML, 231

title element (DOM-based XHTML), 235

top property (CSS), 154

training/retraining, for XHTML 1.0 adoption, 168

transitional DTDs (XHTML 1.0), 123–124

    align attribute with, 131

    center element with, 131

    creating an XHTML document using, 53–59

    DOCTYPE declarations, 54

    formatting elements, 131

    frames element components, 130

    list section, 131

transitional XHTML documents

    in Amaya 2.4/Windows NT browser, 97

    in Internet Explorer 3.01/MacOS 8.1 browser, 85

    in Internet Explorer 4.0/MacOS 8.1 browser, 87–88

    in Internet Explorer 4.01/Windows 95 browser, 90

    in Internet Explorer 5.01/Windows NT 4.0 browser, 92–93

    in Lynx 2.8.2/Windows 95 browser, 100

    in Netscape Communicator 4.7/Windows 4.0 browser, 80

    in Netscape Navigator 2.02/Windows NT 4.0 browser, 74

    Netscape Navigator 3.0/Windows NT 4.0 browser, 77

    in Netscape Navigator 6 Preview Release/Windows NT 4.0 browser, 82–83

    in Opera 3.62/Windows NT browser, 95

    style sheets with, advantages, 162

tree structures (tree model), 227–228

type attribute, 131

U

u element (underscore) (transitional/frameset DTD), 131

ul element, in CSS selector syntax, 139

Unicode encoding

    viewing characters in, 120

    XML support for, 47, 171

Uniform Resource Identifiers (URIs), with XHTML, 45

unordered list (el) element, CSS selector syntax for, 139

URIs. *See* Uniform Resource Identifiers

URLs

    entity set locations, 126

    as system identifiers, 274

User Agent Conformance, 23

User-Agent field (HTTP), identifying browsers using, 250

user input

    mandatory field requirements (XHTML-FML), 334–338

text-based WML forms, 315–318
user formatting, CSS for, 136–137
user-friendly modules for, 288
variable interfaces for, handling, 10
users
    ESLT transformations on local machines,
        216–217
    supporting XHTML-DTD module
        integration, 288–289
user's guides, adding to custom modules, 288
UTF-8/UTF-16 encoding
    in HTML generated code conversions, 202
    limiting documents to, 102
    support for, 171

V

validating/validation, 53–59. *See also* W3C
        HTML Validation Service
    custom XHTML-DTD modules, 286–287
    HTML code conversions, 205–206
    HTML documents, 36
    namespace-related problems, 47
    tool-converted XHTML, 200
    XHTML 1.0 requirements for, 41–42
    XHTML-FML form input, 330–332
validation attribute, 331
values (HTML), omitting quotes from, 33
values (XHTML), case sensitivity, 37–38
VBScript, with XML, 19
version declarations, in XHTML documents,
        43
version tracking, in XML, 21–22
vertical-align property (CSS), 155
visibility property (CSS), 155
:visited selector (CSS), 143
vocabularies, XML/XHTML
    extensions for, 49
    freedom from document-oriented
        formatting, 14
    for XHTML-DTD modules, 278, 288
vspace attribute, deprecating, 132

W

W3C HTML Validation Service, 41
    interbrowser compatibility, 102
    for strict HTML, 60–63
    for strict XHTML, 67, 69
    for transitional XHTML, 58, 59

WAP. *See* Wireless Application Protocol
WAP Bitmap format (WBMP), 318–319
WAP emulators, 305–307
Wapalizer WAP emulator (Gelon.Net), 306
WBMP. *See* WAP Bitmap format
WDG HTML Validator (Web Design Group),
        207
Web agents, XHTML for, 372
Web browsers
    HTML appearance, variability in, 27
    HTML for, disadvantages, 246–247
    HTML-compatible, 13–14
Web Design Group, WDG HTML Validator,
        207
Web sites
    archy/instance karma module-building
        tools, 278
    BBTidy, 200
    Chinese XML Now!, 172
    CSS2 specification, 17
    CSS2 specification, cascading rules, 163
    CSS2 specification unofficial style sheet,
        137
    Document Definition Markup Language
        (DDML), 292
    Ericsson R380 WAP emulator, 306
    Gelon.Net, 306
    HTML 4.0 specification, 123
    HTML-Kit, 199
    HTML Tidy, 180
    Itsy Bitsy Teeny Weeny Simple Hypertext
        DTD, 292
    Java Tidy, 199
    Mozquito Factory (Mozquito.com), 323
    Nokia WAP Toolkit, 307
    SGML Open Catalog entries, 273
    W3C CC/PP project, 251–253
    W3C element prohibitions, 133
    W3C HTML conformance checking, 36
    W3C Jigsaw server, 253
    W3C XHTML development strategies, 245
    W3C XHTML support information, 300
    WDG HTML Validator, 207
    "When XML Gets Ugly", 136
    WML/XHTML integration, 320
    World Wide Web Consortium (W3C), RFCs,
        127
    World Wide Web Consortium (W3C),
        specification details, 127

Continued

Web sites *(continued)*
    www-style mailing list archives, 164
    XHTML 1.1 specification, 255
    XHTML 1.1/XHTML 1.0 comparison, 272
    XHTML Basic, 170, 273
    XHTML discussion groups
    XML-Apache project, 210
    XML development tools, 23
    XPath specification, 215
    XSL-FO specification, 216
    XSL specification, 215
    XSL training/technical support, 215
    XSLT-related, 217
Web-TV, HTML for, disadvantages, 246
"When XML Gets Ugly" (Megginson), 136
white-space property (CSS), 155
width attribute, with WML images, 318
width element (transitional/frameset DTD),
    132
width property (CSS), 155
Wireless Application Protocol (WAP),
    300–301
    content negotiation approaches, 250
Wireless Markup Language (WML), 211, 305
    converting XHTML to, 174
    integrating with XHTML, 320
WML. *See* Wireless Markup Language
WML documents
    adding images, 318
    adding navigation buttons to, 312–313
    card element, 310–311
    deck of cards structure, 310
    prolog, 310
    submitting forms to server, 317–318
    text-based user-input form, 315–317
    timer-based automation, 313–315
    wml element, 310
wml element (WML), 310
word-spacing property (CSS), 155
World Wide Web Consortium (W3C). *See also*
    W3C HTML Validation Service
    Composite Capabilities/Preference Profiles
        (CC/PP) tools, 251
    DOM API specifications, 228
    "Element Prohibitions", 133
    emphasis on strict DTDs, 169
    Extensible Stylesheet Language (XSL),
        17–18
    HTML conformance checking, 36
    HTML development/control by, 247–248
    HTML revisions, 3, 4–5
    MathML, 6
    promotion of style sheet approach, 128
    Resource Description Framework (RDF),
        132
    Scalable Vector Graphics (SVG), 19
    XForms, 321
    XHTML development strategies, 245
    XML namespaces, 248
    XML Schemas standard, 103
www-style mailing list, 164

X
x:button element, 333
x:calc element, 347–349, 355
x:checkbox element, 339
x:form element, 329, 333
XForms, FML compliance with, 321–322
XHTML 1.0, 5–6. *See also* Forms Markup
        Language (FML)
    adopting, issues around, 167–168,
        173–174
    attribute defaults, 113–115
    attribute list declarations, 108–115
    attribute types, 109–113
    attribute values, formatting requirements,
        39–40
    browser variability, 27
    building new modules for, 277–283
    HTML browser variability, 27
    CSS with, 135–137
    case sensitivity, 37–38
    development of, 23, 373–375
    document type definitions (DTD), 123–124
    dynamic applications, 7–9
    element type declarations, 104–108
    extensibility/flexibility, 371–372
    FML iteration, 321–323
    future applications for, 369–375
    general entity declarations, 119–120
    generation code for, 208–211
    HTML comparison, 23–24
    identifiers, 40–41
    integrating WML with, 174
    integrating with XLink, 131
    as interim product, 18–19
    language identification, 47–49

links/pointers in, 20
machine-to-human communications, 369–370
MathML with, 6–7
namespaces, 45–47
PHP scripting with, 209
reusability, 174
security advantages, 371–372
static applications, 7–8
strict XHTML documents, 42, 249
transition from HTML, XML parser compatibility, 171
translating HTML to, syntactical requirements, 169
tree structure, 227–228
User Agent Conformance, 23
validation requirements, 41–42
version 1.1, 5–6
vocabulary extensions, 49
W3C development strategies for, 245
WML with, 320
in XML environments, 42–43, 173–174, 291–300
XHTML 1.0 DTDs
    attribute list declarations, 108–115
    element type declarations, 104–108
    parameter entity declarations, 115–119
XHTML 1.1 specification, 259–263
    abstract modules, 256–263
    adding/modifying driver files, 283–286
    DTD modules, 263
    Forms Module example, 259–263
    framework, 256
    implementation, 256, 272–275
    modularization in, 125, 249
    parameter entity suffixes, 264–271
    syntax framework, 255–256
    XML Schemas with, 272
XHTML 1.1 - Module-based XHTML, 255
XHTML 2.0, 211
XHTML Basic, 170, 273
XHTML-Biography Module
    adding driver for, 283–286
    building DTD module, 278–283
    namespace prefixes, 286–287
    validation issues, 286–287
XHTML conversions, from HTML generation code
    case changes, 203

complexity of, 201–202
    DOCTYPE declarations, 202
    handling HTML coding idiosyncrasies, 204–205
    testing for XHTML conformance, 207
    tools for, 180–200
    validating output, 200, 205–206
XHTML conversions, from static HTML
    attribute value formatting, 176
    end tags, verifying, 176–177
    locating elements properly, 177–178
    lowercase element names, 175–176
    XHTML definitions/declarations, adding, 178–179
XHTML conversions, XML to XHTML, 216–226
XHTML documents, DOM-based
    form information, collecting and passing, 233–242
    "Hello World: document, creating, 229–232
XHTML documents, strict
    in Amaya 2.4/Windows NT browser, 98–99
    converting to from strict HTML, 64–69
    in Internet Explorer 3.01/MacOS 8.1 browser, 86
    in Internet Explorer 4.0/MacOS 8.1 browser, 88–89
    in Internet Explorer 4.01/Windows 95 browser, 91
    in Internet Explorer 5.01/Windows NT 4.0 browser, 93–94
    in Lynx 2.8.2/Windows 95 browser, 101
    in Netscape Communicator 4.7/Windows 4.0 browser, 81
    in Netscape Navigator 1.22/Windows NT 4.0 browser, 72–73
    in Netscape Navigator 6 Preview Release/Windows NT 4.0 browser, 84
    in Opera 3.62/Windows NT browser, 96
XHTML documents, transitional, 85
    in Amaya 2.4/Windows NT browser, 97
    converting to strict HTML, 60–63
    creating, 53–59
    in Internet Explorer 4.0/MacOS 8.1 browser, 87–88
    in Internet Explorer 4.01/Windows 95 browser, 90

in Internet Explorer 5.01/Windows NT 4.0
    browser, 92–93
in Lynx 2.8.2/Windows 95 browser, 100
in Netscape Communicator 4.7/Windows
    4.0 browser, 80
in Netscape Navigator 1.22/Windows NT
    4.0, 71
in Netscape Navigator 6 Preview
    Release/Windows NT 4.0 browser,
    82–83
in Opera 3.62/Windows NT browser, 95
with XSL (Extensible Style Sheet
    Language), 164
XHTML-FML documents/forms
    adding images, 358–360
    contact information form, 327–344
    creating, 323–324
    displaying, 326–327
    editable lists/pull-down menus, 338–340,
        340–341
    error checking, 324–326
    formatting enhancements, 342–344
    input validation, 330–334
    JavaScript compatibility, 366–367
    layering, 357–358
    mandatory field requirements, 334–338
    multiple forms, 360–366
    reducing code in, 349–352
    shopping cart form, 345–356
    submitting forms to server, 333–334
XHTML-DTD modules
    adding user guides, 288
    CC/PP and, 252–253
    content model issues, 253–254
    integrating, 288–290
    namespace/validation issues, 286–287
    XHTML-Biography example, 278–283
    in XML documents, 300–301
XHTML user agents, 23–24
x:img element, 359
x:insert element, 355–356
x:item element, 339
x:label, HTML <label> comparison, 336
XLink standard
    integrating with XHTML, 131
    and XHTML modularization, 253
XML: A Primer (St. Laurent), 278
XML-Apache project, XML Server Pages
    (XSL), 210

XML Bible (Harold), 278
XML data islands (Microsoft), 7, 34, 370–371
    for contained documents, 298–299
    for images, scripts, forms, 293–296
    for inline/mixed up markup, 300
    for user-readable notes, 296–298
    in XML documents, 293–300
XML declarations
    adding to XHTML documents, 179
    browser-related problems, 169
    in HTML code conversions, 202
    and interbrowser compatibility, 102
    in XHTML documents, 42–43
XML developers
    tools for, 23
    using XHTML, 291
    Web browser applications, 293–294
XML DTD modules. *See* DTD modules
xml element, addition of to HTML, 248
XML Elements of Style (St. Laurent), 278
XML. *See* Extensible Markup Language
    (XML), 3
xml method, in DOM-based XHTML, 231–232
XML parsers, 16
    DOCTYPE declarations with, 239
    DOM-based XHTML files in, 241
    requirements of, 171
    validating HTML code conversions using,
        207
XML Schemas standard, 103
    and namespaces, 287
XML Server Pages (XSL), 210
xml:lang attribute, 47–49, 127
    declaring in XHTML, 117
    in DOM-based XHTML, 230
    in strict XHTML documents, 64
    supplementing lang attribute with, 169
xmlns attribute, 45–46
    adding to documents, 178
x:option element, 338–339
    with shopping cart form, 345–347
XPath specification, 215
x:prop element, 352
    adding images using, 359
x:pulldown element
    with e-commerce form, 338–339
    with shopping cart form, 345–347
x:radio element, 339

XSL. *See* Extensible Stylesheet Language
       (XSL)
  CSS comparison, 137
  transformative formatting approach, 137
XSL Formatting Objects (XSL-FOs), 216
XSL specification, 215
xsl:output element, 218
xsl:stylesheet element, 217
XSLT conversions
  output from, 218–226
  required elements/attributes, 217–218
  style sheets, 217
xsl:transform element, 217

x:template element, 349–350
x:text input element
  with shopping cart form, 345–347
  submitting forms to server, 333
x:textarea element, 339
x:textinput, 330–331
x:textoutput element, 347–349
x:toggle element, 340–341

Z

z-index property (CSS)

my2cents.idgbooks.com